The Good Years

Photograph given to the author by MacArthur with inscription reading: "To 'Rogers' of GHQ with cordial regards and best wishes. Douglas MacArthur."

The Good Years

MacArthur and Sutherland

Paul P. Rogers

PRAEGER

New York
Westport, Connecticut
London

Library of Congress Cataloging-in-Publication Data

Rogers, Paul P.
  The good years: MacArthur and Sutherland / Paul P. Rogers.
      p.   cm.
  Includes bibliographical references (p.   ).
  ISBN 0-275-92918-3 (alk. paper)
  1. World War, 1939–1945—Campaigns—Philippines. 2. MacArthur,
Douglas, 1880–1964. 3. Sutherland, Richard K. 4. Rogers, Paul P.
5. World War, 1939–1945—Personal narratives, American. 6. United
States. Army—Biography. 7. Soldiers—United States—Biography.
I. Title.
D767.4.R63   1990
940.54′8173—dc20   89-27560

Library of Congress Catalog Card Number: 89-27560
ISBN: 0-275-92918-3

First published in 1990

Praeger Publishers, One Madison Avenue, New York, NY 10010
An imprint of Greenwood Publishing Group, Inc.

Printed in the United States of America

The paper used in this book complies with the
Permanent Paper Standard issued by the National
Information Standards Organization (Z39.48-1984).

10 9 8 7 6 5 4 3 2 1

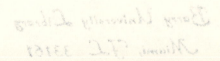

To

Arlene

Friend, Lover, Helpmeet

Her insistence impelled me to undertake the task. Her encouragement held me to my course. Her understanding overcame the great emotional stress created by the task. Her serene acceptance of long labor converted my impossible handwriting into legible typed copy through three drafts. We shared this task as we have shared all other aspects of our marriage.

Contents

Photographs follow page 194.

Maps

Acknowledgments

It is not possible to identify and to acknowledge separately the numerous people who contributed directly or indirectly to this book. Arlene, my wife, takes first place. Roger Egeberg, LeGrande Diller, Weldon Rhoades, and Howard Christy all read the manuscript and furnished detailed information and careful and objective criticism. They provided a continuum of effort on my behalf, and the book thereby has been enhanced. Other contributions have been identified and acknowledged by notes in the appropriate places.

Natalie Carney, Sutherland's daughter, shared with me the memories of Sutherland as husband and father before and after the war. She permitted me to cite her letters. The story is broader, deeper, and far more human than it would have been without her help.

Colonel Lyman Hammond, Mr. E. E. Boone, and Mr. Roger T. Crew of the MacArthur Memorial were unusually kind and helpful to me. Mr. Boone gave patient attention even to the most trivial and sometimes obviously foolish difficulties. Mr. Eulogio Leaño of the National Historical Institute of the Philippines must be thanked. There were many others.

Introduction

This book traces the relationship between MacArthur and his chief of staff in their joint exercise of the command function in MacArthur's headquarters during World War II. It is a sympathetic study written by an eyewitness observer of the events, and is corroborated by contemporary documents. By necessity it is the walking of an old trail. The story of MacArthur in World War II is now a familiar one, and the trail markers are obvious. This is a different journey, however. The book is not intended to shock but, rather, to illuminate and to establish perspective. It grew out of my determination to understand. It is the story of reasonable men performing rational duties in an activity that seemed to obliterate rationality.

This book is based upon my experience as stenographer and chief clerk in the office of Douglas MacArthur and his chief of staff, Richard K. Sutherland. I was the only member of the office staff who served continuously for the full term of the war, and the only enlisted man taken from Corregidor by MacArthur at the time of the evacuation. As part of my duties I organized and supervised the office files, and managed a force of six men. Over the course of the war I was promoted from private to master sergeant to warrant officer. MacArthur himself commissioned me at Lingayen in January 1945.

I am a professor and a scholar who has published widely in a very specialized area. In the writing of this book I have observed the established rules of my profession. I have used the official files of MacArthur's own office, many of which I typed and all of which I organized. I remember many of the circumstances that shaped the documents, and I doubt that anyone else will interpret those documents as accurately as I have. The books written by men who served as close to MacArthur, as I did, have been examined; I knew those men and am able to evaluate their records. I have gone to great lengths to confirm my recollections for use as a primary source, and have found a high level of reliability. I did not remember all of it, but what I remembered, I remembered accurately.

The time span of the entire story covers the period of the war, 1941 through 1945. *The Good Years* deals with the period July 1941 through December 1945. A later book will cover the years 1943 through 1945. In this volume, a section of introductory material establishes a sense of historical continuity and presents the major characters and events. My personal observation of events begins six weeks prior to the outbreak of the war and ends with the surrender.

The book deals with the problems of command. One set of questions involves MacArthur's control of his theater of operations: To what extent did he influence strategy? How did he exert influence? How did he translate strategic concept into tactical execution? Another set deals with the organization and control of MacArthur's staff: To what extent did he exercise personal control? How did he organize his staff? How did he manage the flow of documents and reports that were an important aspect of the daily work load? Finally, the book goes to the very heart of the command function: What principles governed the division of work between MacArthur and his chief of staff? To what extent were the two men able to subordinate their personalities to the joint exercise of command? What impact did the joint effort have upon their private personalities?

The cast of characters has been kept to an essential minimum. It reflects the hierarchy of relative importance that existed at the time. I have ignored those who made a transient appearance in the command. A 30-minute visit with MacArthur did not lay the foundation for deep judgment.

I have identified three separate entities. MacArthur the man and Sutherland the man are individuals with different backgrounds and psychological orientations, each moving with his own destiny. The third entity is MacArthur/Sutherland, a product of the dual efforts of both men acting jointly in the common command function. The problem of the book is to identify the precise nature of that common function, to examine the impact of the conflicting personalities of the two individuals on the joint activity, and to describe the impact of the exercise of the joint command on the personalities. Sutherland is the more interesting element in this problem. His involvement literally destroyed him.

This book presumes the ultimate rationality of the men and of their decisions. Men were selected because of their demonstrated, predictable rational behavior. They were constrained by procedures that ensured rational discussion and rational solution of problems. It is doubtful that any one was more egotistical or ambitious than any other. All had learned to behave rationally.

This book deals with a MacArthur who is gentle, sensitive, and sympathetic. His behavior falls within the accepted variations allowed any reasonable man in the circumstances of that time and place. He was angry when other reasonable men would have been angry. The expression of his anger fell within the accepted modes of civil discourse. His anger dissipated quickly and was soon forgotten, never intruding into the decision-making process. His will and his intellect were the masters of his emotion. All of this is equally true of Sutherland, with one major failure to understand the impact of pride. That matter is what makes this book unique.

MacArthur emerges as a disciplined man. His public image was consciously tailored to reflect his concept of the essential quality of military leadership, the appearance of complete self-assurance and self-control. He dominated men not only by assertion of strong personality but also by example. He displayed a strong sense of fairness and justice. He could be conspicuously emotional, but reason always overruled arbitrary passion. His first impulse in anger always gave way to disciplined reason.

MacArthur was an anomaly in the command structure in World War II. He was a former chief of staff who had no equals in the army. All the rest knew he could outsmart and outthink them. They were afraid of him but could not set him aside. He had enough appeal with the public to challenge even Roosevelt on certain issues if he was forced to do so. I am convinced that MacArthur was recalled to active duty only so there would be a Republican general in charge of affairs when the campaign collapsed in the Philippines, thereby deflecting the criticism that otherwise could have overwhelmed the party in power. I have marked out instances when MacArthur coached George Marshall in what a chief of staff should and should not do. Marshall must have bit his tongue with displeasure.

Most of MacArthur's contribution to the war was intellectual—it was what he thought that counted. Most of his physical activity involved the working out of ideas, communicating them, and motivating others to implement them. It was the ideas themselves that gave shape to the war and that constitute his contribution to the war.

I have traced back to MacArthur's appointment in July 1941 the development of certain basic themes that thread through the entire war. MacArthur's position on these themes did not change much although he himself did change.

The instrument through which MacArthur worked was his chief of staff, Richard K. Sutherland, the most important man on his staff. Sutherland occupied a unique, commanding position with respect to MacArthur. No one else had comparable influence in the formulation or implementation of policy. The relationship between the two men began in 1938 and endured until the end of the war in 1945.

The most interesting part of the story is the development of the "war within a war" between MacArthur and Sutherland. It was far more complex than I realized. MacArthur and Sutherland played their own games of strategy with each other. There were many elements in the game, but basically it was a test of skill and determination. That story occupies a great deal of the last third of the book.

In the winter of 1944, after six years of harmonious mutual respect, MacArthur and his chief of staff fell out. No one has attempted to explore the sources of the difficulty and to trace out the consequences of the explosion it produced, but there has been a general tendency to vilify Sutherland. I have delved deeply into the matter because I was involved in the explosion and shattered by it. This book is my attempt to reconstruct and to understand a tragedy in Sutherland's career that presented MacArthur with his greatest test of command authority.

The career curves of the two men in this period are paradoxical. The joint effort elevated MacArthur in a long, continuous, accelerating curve from the dark days of defeat to a final apotheosis at the end of the war. Sutherland's career followed the path of Greek tragedy. An initial elevation with MacArthur reached an apogee of pride with a fracturing of personal relations and a final disintegration of his potential. The problem is to understand why.

I have traced out the basic controversies that occupied MacArthur's attention during the war, following their development from origins in prewar Manila to the last days of the war, when they were still being debated. I have described the decision-making process in MacArthur's headquarters and in the higher echelons of authority, with emphasis on the essential rationality of the process and of the results.

I have not attempted to accumulate every trivial anecdote about MacArthur and Sutherland but have selected those matters which give an uncluttered view. MacArthur comes out of it as an exceptionally rational person, complex but nevertheless rational. He had a rare ability to identify the essential facts and relationships of a situation, to anticipate possible outcomes, and to impose disciplined reason on very strong emotional reactions.

The context in which the story is contained is the ebb and flow of the war that drew all of us together, carried us along on its roaring current over turbulent rapids, and finally dropped us like flotsam and jetsam as it slowed quietly over the last sandbar.

Every tidbit in the book is there for a reason. Seemingly trivial items are there because I think they help portray MacArthur's or Sutherland's character. I have tried to give the book immediacy, to draw readers into the very heart of MacArthur's office, where they can watch MacArthur and Sutherland at work, read their ideas as they were worked out together, and experience a sense of participation in their efforts. I have tried to make the details precise and exact, and to show how MacArthur used the men who came to him, generally by chance, and impelled them to work for him to the very limit of their powers, frequently beyond any frontier they had ever crossed before.

There is more to this book than meets the eye at first glance. On the surface it is a study of MacArthur as commander in chief of a theater of operations. It is also a fugue on George Kenney's remark that it was fun to work for MacArthur. Kenney was right, but he also was wrong, as the reader will learn. But this is the superficial side of the matter.

In its most profound aspects the book is a theological inquiry. It is a literary expression of the idea that is embodied in Picasso's *Guernica* or in the comparable paintings of Goya. It portrays the savage, random, senseless brutality of war. Careful readers will find clues to the theology, but unless there is a pause to think they will most likely be set aside. A young man, as I was, who ignores an absolutely inviolable deferment to enlist for service in the Philippines on September 1, 1941, against the good advice of the recruiting sergeant, has made a deep, conscious moral choice. To explain this assertion would result in more sermonizing than a typical reader can suffer.

The book is also an epic. The obvious hero is Douglas MacArthur, who evokes images of Cid Campeador, and El Gran Capitan, and, more recently, "Marse Robert" and "Old Jack." The real epic hero, however, may be Corporal Mays of the 31st Infantry Regiment, whose story is told in this book in a transcript of his own words. Mays is the infantry soldier who drove back the Persians at Marathon and the French at Waterloo, who took Grant to Richmond and Sherman to the sea. He is the best contemporary example I can find of MacArthur's enlisted counterpart, the epitome of what an infantry soldier should be.

Behind this book is the great vision of Apocalypse and the troubled doubt of Job. Over it all is the majestic image of MacArthur, like Mays at Davao, climbing the long ridge to Malaybalay, kicking his stubborn donkey, filled with the joy of battle, hot as fire and cold as ice, eager for the next encounter, untroubled by doubt or scruple, firm in his holy vocation, certain that some undefined deity has marked him for glory. MacArthur is unique. He is the last great warrior. Modern war will never tolerate another of his kind. All that remains is universal, dehumanized massacre done at long range by impersonal machines. There will be no glory.

I

To Action, September–
October 1941

Rogers enlists for foreign service; the voyage to Manila;
assignment to MacArthur's office; first days in Manila

1

Tasker H. Bliss

Dutifully I registered for the draft on my twenty-first birthday, April 18, 1941. I filed papers requesting special classification as a ministerial student. On August 26 I received my draft card with a IV-D classification. I had debated the issue all summer long, and by the time I received the deferment, I had decided not to use it. I marched down to the recruiting office in Des Moines, Iowa, and answered the call of duty.

The recruiting sergeant asked what he could do for me. I replied that I wanted to enlist for the Philippines. He leaned back, pulled a form out of the desk drawer, leaned forward again to write. He asked my name and other pertinent facts.

"Where was it you wanted to go?"

"To the Philippines, sir."

He paused a minute. "The only opening for the Philippines is in the medical corps. You really wouldn't want that."

I persisted. "I'll take any assignment in the Philippines."

He continued his gentle discouragement with a better offer. "We have an opening in the medical corps over at Camp Grant, Illinois. Don't you think you'd like that?"

"I want to go to the Philippines."

He looked at me for a few moments and finally said, "Son, I admire your courage."

The date was September 1, 1941.

I was told to report to Fort Des Moines, on the edge of town. There I was taken to a barracks with two or three other new recruits. We were shown how to make our bunks and told to clean the latrines. My first army assignment was to scrub the urinals and toilets. I did it well, without complaint, accepting the duty with a certain irony. At supper three soldiers served food into metal trays as we walked past. The last item to be served was jello. The server, in great distress, plopped it on the tray with a bare hand, apologizing that the mess sergeant had told him to do it that way.

On September 7 I was sworn into the service, then given a train ticket and $10 to make the trip to San Francisco. No uniforms were issued. I was told to go home until the train left on September 10. Two MPs were on hand to see that I had reported to the depot as scheduled and that I did get on the train. I reached San Francisco on September 12 and was then taken by truck to a ferry that carried me to Fort McDowell on Angel Island. I was issued two uniforms and assigned to a barracks under the care of a corporal. I cleaned the barracks, sweeping up dirt and paper. One sheet on the floor displayed a full-page photograph of a General MacArthur who had been named commanding general in the Philippines. I looked at it curiously and then threw it in the trash barrel. The corporal who was in charge of the barracks had some significance for me. A general was beyond my comprehension.

I spent three weeks at Fort McDowell. Half a dozen times I was assigned to the rock crusher detail, where I swung a hammer and shoveled rock, and was called for KP duty twice. In my free time I made three trips to San Francisco, where I visited the Museums of Natural History and Fine Arts, the Aquarium, and Chinatown. I had very little money to spend but did not care very much. While I was swinging a hammer at the rock crusher during the third week of September, the Japanese were rehearsing a very special naval exercise.

Finally, after much waiting, we were told that our transport was in the bay and that we would leave the next day for Manila. Precisely at 12:30 on the afternoon of Saturday, October 4, *El Aquario*, an army ferry, pulled away from Angel Island. We lolled on deck, leaning on the rails as the barracks of Fort McDowell were lost to view behind us, talking and laughing, relieved that the days of waiting were now over, eagerly anticipating adventures we were sure the future held for us. We slipped by Alcatraz and rocked gently across the last channel into the army dock on the San Francisco side of the bay, where U.S. Army Transport *Tasker H. Bliss* (formerly the *President Cleveland*, chartered for this duty) awaited us.

Soldiers stood in small, orderly groups along the dock, talking and joking, whiling away the time as soldiers learn to do, waiting being the greater share of a soldier's duty. Some units were in summer uniforms because we were bound for the tropics. Others were in winter uniforms because it was quite cool in San Francisco. According to a plan that had been prepared in advance, each unit picked up barracks bags and filed up the gangplank, answering "Here" as names were called, and filed down to assigned positions in the hold, finding bunks as each could. That done, everyone climbed back up the ladders to the deck to watch the departure.

Engines began to growl. Anchors were raised. Tugboats strained and grumbled, pushing us out into the channel. Our voyage had begun. The *Bliss* and another transport, the *Holbrook*, rolled gently under the Golden Gate Bridge and out into the open sea, where the wind was pushing up waves sufficiently high to transform the gentle rolls into violent rocking and pitching. Heads and stomachs, unable to find stable equilibrium, did queer things and almost all of us began to suffer, in varying degrees, the agonies of seasickness.

The evening menu seemed at the time to be a devilishly contrived attempt to intensify our discomfort. I can still recall the combined odor of fuel oil, sauerkraut, wieners, and beans. I did not eat my allotted ration, sucking on two oranges instead. I was fortunate; only once in my career, three years later, would I suffer the ultimate indignity of retching and vomiting. I fasted for 24 hours, eating my first meal at Sunday supper.

As the evening wore on, oil and vomit combined in a nauseating stench, and those who were seasick stumbled to the rail, into the wind and spray, frequently transferring the foul mess from internal organs to exterior clothing, a small improvement if any. I remember watching one poor lieutenant who tried to wipe his face with this hand, succeeding only in smearing himself completely. I lived in a world of enlisted men and relished the sight of an officer in a humiliation I did not share. At that time I had not had any direct contact with officers.

My bunk was in hold number 4. Officers and the three higher grades of noncommissioned officers occupied first- and second-class quarters. The rest of us, some 1,600 soldiers, went into holds 3 and 4. There was no ventilation. Beds consisted of canvas bunks stretched between metal frames, in four tiers, with just enough room to lie flat on our backs or stomachs. When we turned over, we hit the men above and below us. We did not have blankets for three days (the only days we needed them), and I used my rolled raincoat for a pillow.

Stale air and the stench drove me out of the hold the first night. I simply stretched out on the deck, shivering in the damp sea wind, dozing and turning, trying to find a more comfortable position.

I spent the second night below. Lights were turned off at 10:30 and the hold became a dank, dense, stifling prison. I went to sleep only to be wakened by the screams of some poor soldier who was having a nightmare. The place seemed alive with terror and I, too, wanted to scream. I calmed myself by climbing out of my bunk and bracing my back against the steel frame. I slept below for three more nights and was awakened in the same way. Finally we approached Honolulu, five days after our departure from San Francisco.

It had been raining, and a rainbow arched over the tropical splendor of the island, dropping down into the ocean on either side. As we watched, another bow formed above the first. As the band played "Aloha," we gazed in openmouthed wonder at the beauty of the scene. It was a royal welcome. But we got no more than that. Shore passes had been issued but were revoked, and we spent the night on deck, free of rolling and pitching, warm in the tropical night, watching scudding clouds break into patches of clear sky and brilliant stars.

It is easier to let soldiers off a ship than to herd them back on. Ten hours is barely sufficient time to find the customary ingredients of shore leave: whiskey and women, or women and whiskey, depending on the individual's priorities. Many of us, of course, wanted nothing more than sightseeing, or if we wanted more than that, were unable or afraid to take advantage of opportunity. There was some muttering of complaint but not very much. We were reasonable men.

We pulled away at four in the morning on Friday, escorted by a cruiser that covered us for the remainder of the journey. Several patrol bombers gave us air cover for a short while and then droned off into the distance.

Officers and the privileges of rank became an increasingly conspicuous part of my reality during the voyage. At Fort Des Moines and Fort McDowell I seldom saw and rarely thought of officers. On board ship they were difficult to ignore. Officers had beds, private freshwater showers, ice water, library and recreation facilities, and a good mess. Troops slept in the hold, washed in seawater in crowded latrines, and ate in inadequate mess facilities. There was one latrine fore and one aft. These facilities provided one toilet for every 45 men and one saltwater shower for every 73 men. There were two water fountains, one fore and one aft. There were no laundry facilities. The mess seated 156 men at a time. Feeding and cleaning required a continuous operation. The 400 officers had 60 percent of the deck space; the 1,600 troops crowded into the remaining 40 percent.

Colonel Clyde Selleck, commanding officer of troops, had 12 doctors and 12 nurses on board to deal with medical problems, especially on the night of October 19, when food poisoning had men vomiting all over the blacked-out ship, sprawling in agony in bunks in the dark holds below deck. Hundreds were sick, and 106 severe cases were hospitalized in a makeshift facility that was improvised by nurses on the promenade deck.

The lack of shower and laundry facilities posed a personal problem for which there was no solution. I found a bar of GI soap, learned that it would lather even in seawater, and used it for washing my face and shaving. My clothing stank, but nothing could be done about that. All in all, it was better than an African slaver—but not much!

Selleck wrote to friends: "I'm going to do my best to inform official Washington of the conditions aboard, hoping that it won't be necessary to continuously subject our citizen soldiers to the conditions of '98." He later commanded the 71st Division at Lingayen beaches and in Wainwright's sector of the Bataan defenses where conditions were even worse and where he experienced great misfortune.

I volunteered for duty as a typist on the staff of *The Bliss Bugle* after we left Hawaii. There is an entry in my diary concerning this assignment that is notable for its irony, in view of what lay ahead: "Although I dislike typing, it's better than KP."

The assignment led me into a chore that was both enlightening and distasteful. Somewhere between Honolulu and Manila I was told that I would act as court reporter at a hearing. I protested that I was not a court reporter and did not believe I could handle the assignment. I was told by the noncom in charge that I was the only stenographer available and I would have to do it. So, reluctantly,

Map 1
The Philippines

LUZON

Lingayen

MANILA

Corregidor

MINDORO

San Bernardino

VISAYAS

SAMAR

PANAY

LEYTE

PALAWAN

NEGROS

CEBU

Surigao

0 — 100
(MILES)

Del Monte

MINDANAO

Davao

PHILIPPINES

I appeared as the official reporter at my first and, thankfully, last hearing. I was not prepared stenographically or psychologically for what followed.

It happened that as troops slept on deck, homosexual advances had been made by one soldier and accepted by a number of others, several of whom were acquaintances of mine. One of the men, filled with remorse, had reported the matter, not realizing that he was incriminating himself.

The hearing began, and I dutifully wrote down in Gregg shorthand intimate details of events that astounded and shocked me. The hearing went on for two days of unrelenting discomfort. Shaking my head, not certain that I could deliver a transcript, I sat down to work at the typewriter. I held to the task for a day. Finally, whether in despair of stenographic ineptitude or in moral shock, I simply walked away from the desk, leaving notebook, typewriter, and incomplete transcript. I told the sergeant that I had exhausted my skill and could do no more.

The accused party escaped trial because of my failure to provide an accurate transcript of the hearing. Six months later he was taken prisoner when Corregidor fell and died in prison camp, or so I was told later.

The last few days of the voyage I was called to the office of Colonel Selleck, who needed a stenographer. I reported with fine military style, saluting at attention, stating as ritual required, "Private Rogers reporting as the colonel ordered." He looked at me with surprise, asked me to sit down, and proceeded to dictate several messages that I transcribed without difficulty. When I delivered the final copies, he asked me to look him up after I arrived in Manila, saying that he needed a good man on his staff.

Events were already moving in another direction. On October 20, four days before we reached Manila, I was reassigned to the Detached Enlisted Men's List, Headquarters Philippine Department. I did not understand what it meant.

The voyage finally came to an end. During the night of October 23 we entered San Bernardino Strait and sailed up through the Sibuyan Sea. About nine the next morning, as we lolled on the deck, watching the beautiful islands around us, we had a taste of what we might expect in the future, although none of us realized it at the time. There was a sudden "swoosh" and a roar as two P–36 fighters dived over the ship from bow to stern, rolled up in a steep climb, then returned to cross midship, shaking the ship under us, the wind from their props blowing off our caps. They repeated their runs in a splendid show of airmanship and ended it by flying alongside the ship, one plane on each side, so close and so low that it seemed we could have touched their wing tips.

In the early afternoon the ship slipped past the mass of Corregidor Island. I looked up at the gun emplacements set in the hills with an eerie feeling, impressed by the sense of their great power. It was my first sight of the fortress. There would be other visits.

We docked about eight, and as the band played, we debarked, marching down the gangplank, glad to be off the ship with the hope of beds, freshwater showers, and good food.

2

One Calle Victoria

The sergeant shouted, "Rogers."

I answered, "Here."

"Step over here. You're going up to MacArthur's headquarters."

Four of us stood aside while the others loaded into trucks and were driven away. We climbed into the back of the remaining truck and rattled down from the port area to Fort Santiago.

Fort Santiago was on a triangle where the old wall of Intramuros runs down to the Pasig River as it empties into the east side of Manila Bay. It was occupied by Headquarters Philippine Department, the command for the U.S. Army in the Philippines. Its barracks, built in the open tropical style with wide arcaded verandas, tall ceilings, and walls open to the mild air, were a far cry from those at Fort Des Moines or Angel Island. Service in the Philippine Department was luxurious, although the old hands complained continuously and bitterly about the deprivations they endured.

I was assigned a bed and slept through the first night of what I thought would be a three-year hitch in the Philippines. Next morning I sat down for my first breakfast at a table set with linen, good china, and flatware. Filipino mess boys served breakfast: platters of papayas, bananas, and oranges; biscuits, rolls, and toast; eggs, fried and scrambled; ham, sausage, and bacon; and milk, coffee, and juice. As they ate, the soldiers complained of the poor quality and poor service. I do not recall anyone complaining that he had insufficient quantity. I learned that in spite of rough language and brutish behavior, certain rules of etiquette prevailed and were enforced by threats of violence when they were breached. I intercepted a biscuit on the platter as it passed down the table to someone who had asked for it. "You bastard, short stop me again and I'll break your God-damned arm." I was startled, but I got the message loud and clear. So it was at lunch and dinner: relative elegance, great abundance, and constant complaints.

I was taken to Headquarters Philippine Department for a series of IQ and aptitude tests, which occupied the morning, and returned to the barracks for lunch, which matched the plentiful opulence of breakfast.

After lunch I returned to headquarters and was summoned to an office with three others where the roll was called. My name was read. I snapped to attention, answering "Here, sir." The lieutenant looked surprised and said, "No wonder they want you in MacArthur's office." A few minutes later I was in a truck bouncing through Intramuros to Headquarters USAFFE (U.S. Army Forces in the Far East). I was taken first to a stenographer's office occupied by Master Sergeant Turner, a sleepy 20-year veteran. An empty desk in the office had been used by my predecessor, who had returned to the States. I learned that he had left Manila at the same time I had left San Francisco and that our paths had crossed somewhere in mid-Pacific. His departure had left a vacancy for which there was no local replacement. At the time of my arrival, I was the only unattached stenographer between Manila and San Francisco. On the basis of the work I had done for him, Colonel Selleck had recommended me for the empty slot at USAFFE.

I was interviewed by Colonel Carl Seals, a kindly, fatherly gentleman who was MacArthur's adjutant. He commented that although I had not had basic training, my high school ROTC would take care of that deficiency. It was far from true, in light of events already in motion. He dictated a letter that I transcribed. He was satisfied with the result, being assured, among other things, that I could spell.

Seals took me to the office of Richard Sutherland, MacArthur's chief of staff. Sutherland interviewed me in some depth. The first matter of discussion was the fact that I had volunteered for service in the medical corps. I told Sutherland that before I enlisted, I had made up my mind to serve in the Philippines in any capacity. The only opening for the Philippines had been in the medical corps, and so I accepted that opening, not having any other preference.

Sutherland knew from the records that I had a IV-D draft classification and asked why I had enlisted. I replied that I had decided that I could not use the draft exemption in good conscience because I did not feel I could let someone else do my fighting for me. Having made up my mind not to take advantage of the exemption, I had decided to enlist rather than submit to the draft. I added, with a simplicity bordering on arrogance, that I had felt it was God's will that I should come to the Philippines. Sutherland looked at me sharply and sat silently for a moment.

Sutherland said gravely that I would be working for "one of the biggest men in the United States Army," and he described the confidential nature of the work and the responsibilities involved in it. I told him that I had worked for the treasurer at William Jewell College, was aware of the demands of such a position, and could be depended upon to fulfill the obligations imposed upon me. Sutherland smiled and told me I would have a good rating if I could do the work and could keep my feet on the ground.

He dictated a long dispatch that I transcribed to his satisfaction. He apparently had subjected me to what he considered a rigorous test of dictation, and he said that no one else in the headquarters could have taken the dictation as well as I had. Thereafter I regularly took dictation from Sutherland until the last days of the war.

That evening in the barracks a sergeant advised me that certain precautions must be taken. I must always sleep under a sheet and keep a shoe close at hand at the head of my bunk, to discourage any unwanted attention during the night. I confided my hopes that I would have a quiet tour of duty, aspiring "to make sergeant" before it was over. Already I had gone off the deep end. No one ever was promoted in his first hitch, even to private first class. I was advised to keep my dreams to myself, to keep my mouth shut, and to be careful.

Headquarters USAFFE was located at Number One Calle Victoria in a rambling wooden building on top of the Old Wall on the west side of Intramuros; south of Santa Lucia Gate, which opened onto Bonifacio Street; and opposite San Augustin Church, above a bastion that stood out from the wall in a grassy area which formerly had been the moat. A mysterious person arrived daily long after I reached my office and always seemed to leave just before Master Sergeant Turner folded up his small traveling clock and covered his typewriter, signaling the end of a working day. One afternoon during a stroll, as I was walking out Santa Lucia Gate, I encountered a black limosine that carried a red flag with the three stars of a lieutenant general. I stopped to salute, and the figure slouched inside raised his hand in a loose response. I did not know who he was.

I reported to my office every morning at 7:30. I adopted the pattern Turner had mastered and followed to everyone's satisfaction. After lunch I returned briefly to the office and, on Turner's signal, left for an hour or two, to wander around the streets of Intramuros. Our regular work hours were 7:30 to 5:00, though I frequently was required to stay later than 5:00 when work had to be finished. On most days we had no more than three hours of work. In time I learned that my basic commitment was availability. I was expected to be on hand whenever I was needed, at any time during the 13-hour day. So I was available.

I was reliable and dependable. I was sober, always, and therefore always on duty. I never let a personal whim or desire stand between me and duty. I was willing to serve without complaint or excuse. Since I did not drink, smoke, gamble, or chase women, I did not have any compelling distractions to tempt me away from the demands of my job. It was a matter of much waiting, punctuated by periods of intense, interesting activity, which, I suppose, is the nature of most soldierly work.

We alternated duty on Sundays, and Turner let me have my first Sunday in Manila as a day off. I wandered in the company of another recruit, enjoying the delights of the exotic paradise that had been the object of my enlistment, down the crowded streets, past busy shops, to General Luna Street, past the Cuartel de España, which housed the 31st Infantry Regiment. I walked through the

Cuartel expecting to find giants, I think. I visited several old cathedrals, cautiously, as befitted a young Protestant who was uncertain whether they might not house the devil.

Passing the shop of Sing Lee, a tailor in Intramuros, I made my first intentional move to share in the wonderful glories of imperial power: I gave Sing Lee a chit (IOU) for 50 pesos, against my next three paychecks, for five uniforms. I needed the uniforms; my original issue of four did not meet the requirements of a climate that made a daily change imperative, especially for anyone who had to take dictation from a general. Or so it seemed to me at the time.

Sing Lee, not being a fool, took the chit to the "highest authority" in the world of enlisted troops—the first sergeant, who exercised his right of parental supervision over new recruits, or anyone else, for that matter. He cut the order to two uniforms, and that is what Sing Lee delivered in less than a week. I am sure he received his first payment for he was waiting beside me at the pay table on November 10 when I received my first pay. Sing Lee received the first installment on the debt but no more. Not even the first sergeant could control the events that lay just ahead.

I had learned the wonderful power of "jawbone" (credit) authenticated by the signing of a "chit," my first lesson in deficit financing, which was particularly workable when the doubtful credit of an unknown soldier could be supported by the unquestioned majesty of a stern first sergeant. I might walk in the company of generals, but in my proper world, and in Sing Lee's, first sergeants had precedence.

I understood very well the importance of my assignment and wrote home:

They put me right to work as private secretary to General Sutherland, chief of staff, and General MacArthur, Commanding General of USAFFE and one of the biggest men in the U.S. Army. I really feel important. . . . It's the best job I could possibly have pulled down.

Boy! I really feel good taking dictation from a general. He's a fine fellow—Sutherland, I mean. I haven't done any work for General MacArthur yet. They're breaking me in gradually. This army correspondence is difficult to learn—it's all so different. Their forms aren't at all like regular business correspondence. And everything has to be just so.

When I got here they sent me to work for General MacArthur, Commanding General, and his chief of staff, General Sutherland. The work is interesting as we receive reports and letters that give us an "inside" picture of the Far Eastern situation.

These big officers are really swell to work for. They're O.K.

I had been in the army for more than three months before I was paid. We had a small advance at the time of embarkation but nothing more. I do not recall that I felt particularly limited. The army fed and clothed me. My contribution to the fund to pay bunkboys and messboys was three dollars per month, on a payroll deduction basis. I did not engage in any expensive activities.

On October 29, 5 days after my arrival, I had only 60 centavos (30 cents) cash on hand. That was all that remained of the ten dollar advance I had received at Fort McDowell. A letter written two days later indicates a certain sense of restriction.

I haven't been able to get anything to read for the past week and I'm too broke to go to the show—I don't feel like it anyway. . . . We'll be paid on November 10, so I'll be all right then . . . and I should have about 50 pesos coming. . . .

If these guys keep their word, I should get some kind of rating right soon—a second-class specialist rating, anyway, which would mean about $50 to $60. . . . Of course, it all takes time. [At that time my pay was $21 a month.]

After I get straightened out, I'm going to start sending money home for you to put away for me. I can live on $15 a month here, and the more I get saved, the easier it will be when I get out.

On November 10, a G–2 technical sergeant came by to say that the "eagle was flying" and put me in a truck to take me over to Philippine Department. We stood in line and eventually I reached my turn at the table. I gave my name. The first sergeant stopped shuffling papers and money, looked at me, and said, "So *you're* Rogers. Where the hell have you been shacked up? We've been looking for you for three weeks. Where have you been?"

I replied that I had been working. He commented that was a likely story, but before he could proceed, my G–2 companion interrupted him. "He's telling the truth. He works for MacArthur." The first sergeant knew he had met more than his rank. I might be a private, but I worked for the ranking officer in the command. It was enough. He asked me no more questions, and I was paid. I heard someone remark with wonder, "Three months without getting paid! My God!" Ten days later I had to apologize to my mother for being too broke to send her a birthday present.

The same G–2 sergeant took me to a local night club that evening. I turned down liquor, cigarettes, and a woman in that order. That was the last social invitation I had. Later, in the mess line, I heard a G–3 staff sergeant say, "We'll get some whiskey in that son of a bitch if we have to put it in with a syringe." No one ever did until after I was 50 years old, and then precious little.

I wrote home that "I would like to have that set of books over here where I could use them." I referred to the set of Harvard Classics I had bought the year before, paying for them in installments of $5 a month. In those days, when the minimum wage was 40 cents an hour and a weekly paycheck was $16, the $5 represented a heavy investment in intellectual stimulation. It was worth it. I still have the books. By the time I left home, I had read all the historical and literary items, and a considerable portion of the philosophical ones. But it was not the education I needed. Like Henry Adams, I would later confess that an education suited to the needs of a nineteenth-century gentleman did not correspond to the realities of the twentieth century, which were running in a different direction. I have lived to see mere numbers replace both revelation and reason, or some combination of the two, as the proper criterion for truth. I think, perhaps, I have lived too long in that respect.

Thanksgiving arrived unexpectedly. The weather did not give its usual warning of cool, crisp, frosty mornings, or even snow, and there was no sparkle of autumn leaves falling into huge piles along sidewalks. Moreover, there was no interruption in office routine. I went to work that day as usual and remained there until afternoon, when MacArthur and Sutherland left, MacArthur to have the afternoon with his family and Sutherland to play golf. I returned to barracks for Thanksgiving dinner.

It was a fine holiday spread—oyster stew, roast turkey, sage dressing, giblet gravy, baked Virginia ham, cranberry sauce, creamed corn, candied sweet potatoes, ice cream, fruit cake, jelly roll, layer cake, mince pie, pumpkin pie, coffee, cigars, cigarettes—all served by Filipino mess boys who carried heavily laden platters up and down tables to satisfy the impatient demands of the soldiers.

A feeble attempt was made to sing the Doxology and to recite the Lord's Prayer, to which I gave an enthusiastic support not shared by all. Nevertheless, the ritual had an impact and the mess boys received fewer profane complaints about the performance of their duties. I am sure that they, if not the Lord, were awed by the power of religious piety.

Three days later many of us were moved from Fort Santiago to a barracks at One Calle Victoria. It was a step down for two reasons. First, I was forced to perform manual work that hitherto had been left to Filipinos; second, the new barracks was inferior to the former one.

During the luncheon period we dismantled bunks, hauled mattresses, footlockers, and headlockers downstairs and up, loaded and unloaded trucks, perspiring in the humid heat. We finally heaped everything in the center of the new barracks floor, washed up, and rushed back to work.

I returned at the end of the day to find that a miracle had been wrought by the Filipino bunk boys. All was arranged, bunks in neat rows with blankets taut over mattresses, corners squared, footlockers at the foot of each bunk, and headlockers along the wall behind each.

For $3 per month, deducted from my monthly pay, my bed was cared for, my shoes were shined, my clothing was laundered and arranged in the proper locker, my dishes were washed, and my food was cooked. Like a young lord and master I could devote the remaining $18 of my pay and energy to the pursuit of the finer things in life.

The new barracks was on the second floor of a building that formed the outer wall of the courtyard in front of our staff headquarters. Below us was a row of storage rooms and adjacent to them, the kitchen. It was an old, old structure, built by the Spaniards in centuries past, and must have known moments of glory when Spanish bugles summoned Spanish and Filipino infantry to man the walls in defense of Manila.

A mess was set up. At the Philippine Department enlisted mess, a rough decorum had ruled. The first day at Headquarters USAFFE mess was a different experience. The mess hall was small, dingy, and crowded. The table service consisted of field equipment. I had no sooner sat down to eat than the mess sergeant appeared from the kitchen. His eyes were red and his face was bloated. In one hand he held a cleaver and in the other he clutched a butcher knife. He prowled up and down between the tables like a wolf, intoning, "I know what you bastards think about my food. By God, you'd better eat it or I'll cut out your God damned tongues." There was a great hush and a great gulping of food.

One day I strolled down to the University of the Philippines to inquire if I could study some language. I could use Spanish for reading, writing, or speaking within limits, but I had never been in a situation where it was used every day by many people. My knowledge was limited to literary vocabulary without any conversational or technical competence. I was directed to the classroom of a young woman who taught Italian, which I thought I might learn as a literary language. I was reluctant to enter the classroom, which was occupied by five young Filipino girls and a female professor. I was received graciously by the professor, who interrupted the class to talk to me. She had studied at the University of Wisconsin, a stranger away from home, and understood the loneliness of my situation. The young ladies had learned that soldiers were beneath their social level and were obviously concerned and afraid. I promised to become a member of the class, but other events intervened. After the war broke out, one of the correspondents attached to Headquarters USAFFE sought me out to say that the professor had asked him to inquire what had happened to me. He suggested that I send her a note, which I did, on the General's note paper.

After I had been in USAFFE a month, I was sitting in my office one sleepy afternoon. Sergeant Domingo Adversario, one of MacArthur's two orderlies, put his head through the door. "Rogers, the General wants you. Bring your pad." Notebook in hand, I walked down the hall to MacArthur's office for my first meeting with the General.

As I entered the long room, MacArthur was pacing back and forth. He motioned to a chair beside his desk and said, "Rogers, sit down and take this message." He began to dictate immediately, while I was still in the process of opening my book, with "My dear Marshall." I was two sentences behind him. He rapidly dictated a long, single-spaced letter to George Marshall, striding up and down as he talked. Without notes, MacArthur's thoughts rolled out with the precise, consistent, logical order that one expects of highly trained troops on review, ranks arrayed in long straight lines, marching at quick step, without pause or hesitation, relentlessly to a predetermined goal.

I transcribed the letter and returned it to him. He soon called me to the office. As he sat at his desk, he signaled me to look over his shoulder, indicating where he had found an error. He asked me to check my notes, but very obviously a typographical mistake had been made. I said, "I am sorry, sir. I read it with Sergeant Turner, but we missed it." He asked me to make the correction.

As I looked over his shoulder, I noticed the black hair combed carefully over the thin spot on top of his head. His right hand trembled as he pointed to the letter. His voice was husky with a slight guttural rasping; pleasant but decisive.

Handsome, poised, in perfect command of himself, yet gentle and benevolent in speech and manner, he had tested me. He knew I was not afraid of him and not likely to be flustered under pressure in the exercise of my professional skills. It remained to be seen what I might do in other circumstances.

II

Beginnings, 1900–1941

Filipinos liberated; insurrection; struggle for independence;
Quezon; Commonwealth; MacArthur arrives; Military Mission;
Sutherland arrives; We Will Defend

3

Insurrection

Forty years before I placed my order with Sing Lee, another U.S. soldier had wandered through Intramuros, much as I had done. The young private walked through the open gateway at One Calle Victoria, sauntered across the courtyard, and looked up at the building above him. More than 200 years old, it sprawled along the top of the wall that faced Manila Bay. Down in the moat was a bastion that protected a sally port which opened through the wall at this point. The campaign was over, and the Spanish flag had been lowered by the Spanish garrison. Americans now occupied the city. It had been a good fight. There had not been too many casualties. The "dagos" had used a great deal of ammunition, but their marksmanship had not been very good.[1]

General Arthur MacArthur had led his brigade from the southern suburbs of Santa Ana and Paco, and occupied the city. His duty had been to keep the "niggers" out of Manila. The young private did not care much for either the "dagos" (the Spanish, who were presumed to have started the war in the first place) or the "niggers" (the Filipinos, who seemed determined to complicate the situation).

The private had been away from home for three months. He had enlisted in May for this campaign and had been in the Philippines since the last of June. He had spent two months down around Cavite. Finally, on August 1, the order had been issued for the advance on Manila, and in two weeks the Spanish had surrendered. Now, at the end of August, he was learning to enjoy the old city of Manila, which was firmly under the control of the United States. He was not sure what would happen next, but for the present it was far different from life back in Iowa. The private and MacArthur were there because Admiral Dewey had arrived earlier. Dewey had come because the Spanish had arrived some 400 years earlier.

The Spanish soldiers came in the sixteenth century. They had run out of wars at home. Seeking their fortunes, they had moved across thousands of miles of ocean, carrying the royal banner of King Philip II, with Spanish priests who carried the cross as the ensign of their mission. They came and they conquered. They were the best soldiers in Europe, and they had the world's most magnificent navy, which controlled the seas of the world.

They came to the Philippine Islands, as they called the new territory in honor of King Philip; put down the opposition of the people they found there; and became their masters. Soldiers and priests divided the land between them, forced the Filipinos to work it, converted them to the Catholic faith, and prospered. They were isolated from the storms of two centuries that shook the Spanish empire until they were virtually its last survivors.

The Spanish masters bred sons and daughters who frequently were only part Spanish, the other half being Tagalog or some other indigenous tribe, and the class of mestizos multiplied. The social structure of Spanish society was modified to find a place for the mestizos halfway between the Spanish and the Tagalogs, who occupied the lower stratum. The Chinese came at about the same time and also intermarried. The racial mixture became exotic and complicated. Social rank was based on skin color. Wealth, power, and education followed the same pattern.

From the beginning the Filipinos struggled to regain control of their own destinies. They concentrated their increasing hatred against the friars, who held a great share of the land and were merciless masters. There were uprisings against the priests by the Filipinos, who insisted that they were obedient servants of the king and devoted sons of the Catholic church. They demanded only an end of injustice.

By the end of the nineteenth century, young mestizos, educated in Europe, came home with the ideas of the French Revolution and began to organize the Filipino people, for whom they acted as leaders and organizers, in a struggle against the few thousand Spaniards who held the power of society.

There were four elements in the struggle: the Spaniards who had been born in Spain (the *peninsulares*), the Spaniards who had been born in the islands (the *insulares*); the mestizos; and the Tagalogs. The young mestizos forged a revolution led by themselves and reform-minded *insulares*, and manned by the Tagalogs. As time would reveal, they did not have the same objectives, but for the moment they were united in a common endeavor to rid themselves of Spanish administrators and Spanish friars. Dr. José Rizal was the first leader. A mild man, he sought reform through education, persuasion, and economic development. For advocating such extreme views, he was shot and hundreds of other Filipino leaders were executed and tortured.

By 1896 the Filipinos had an army of some 20,000 irregular troops in Cavite Province, south of Manila. The Spanish opposed them with 10,000 regulars. The Spanish had a naval squadron in Manila Bay, but it was not destined for a glorious end. The revolutionary army was commanded by 29-year-old Emilio Aguinaldo, who was preparing to drive the Spanish out of Manila.

Meanwhile, thousands of miles away, the Cubans had risen in rebellion. A storm was raised in the United States, where there had always been a great interest—not always altruistic—in that island. In February 1898, the U.S. warship *Maine* was blown up in Havana harbor and popular opinion, properly or improperly informed by jingoistic journalists, demanded war against Spain. Although no one had evidence, who else but the Spanish would have done such a thing?

In the same month the secretary of the navy was away from his office one afternoon. He left the assistant secretary, Theodore Roosevelt, in charge. In the secretary's absence Roosevelt ordered the construction of new naval vessels and naval guns. In addition, he ordered Commodore George Dewey to Hong Kong, to be in a favorable position to strike the Spanish fleet in Manila Bay if war was declared on Spain.

War was declared on April 21. Dewey steamed to Manila Bay to find the Spanish squadron. On May 1 his squadron slipped quietly past the hulk of Corregidor Island, which was silent, and steamed into the bay toward Manila, where he expected to find the Spanish ships lined up under the protection of the guns mounted on the wall of Intramuros.

Fortunately for Dewey, merchants in Manila preferred not to be caught in the fire of Dewey's guns and refused to permit the Spanish squadron to take refuge under the wall. The squadron had steamed back to Cavite, where Dewey found and proceeded to sink it. Dewey was thereby master of Manila Bay but not of Manila. The guns on the wall could very well destroy his small squadron if he attempted a direct attack. He had no troops to mount a land attack. He cabled Washington, ''I have not sufficient men to hold.''

His problem had been anticipated. Even before they knew of his predicament, leaders in Washington had decided to send an army to the Philippines, and a call was raised for volunteers. And that is how our young private happened to be at the sally port that would serve as my refuge four decades later.

Dewey held Manila Bay, the Spaniards held Manila, and Aguinaldo held Cavite Province and controlled most of the Filipinos, who regarded him as leader of an independent Filipino republic. Our young private arrived two months later and a fourth element entered the game—the U.S. Army. Other players shared Manila Bay with Dewey: five German warships, three British, one French, and one Japanese. None were large, but they were large enough to make a difference.

Aguinaldo and the Filipinos wanted an independent, sovereign republic controlled by and for Filipinos, and all the others should leave. The Germans wanted the islands for Wilhelm II, who craved any addition he could get for his growing empire. If the Germans could not have the islands, they certainly did not want the British to have them. The British did not particularly want the Philippines but were very sure that the Germans should not have them. The French were there simply to watch and see, and to pick up anything they could without any expectations at all. The Japanese were not counted for much, although they had defeated China just three years earlier. They did not demand anything but agreeably offered to buy if anyone would sell. The Spanish in Manila certainly did not want Aguinaldo in Manila but did not see how they could keep him out, and looked only for a graceful way out of a sticky situation, preferably with honor. The British, French, and Germans preferred to leave the Spanish in control, since that would eliminate the necessity for a division of the spoils, but they did not know what to do with Aguinaldo. The United States had no official position on its ultimate aims but, having come, found it impossible to leave.

A compromise solution was worked out in Manila with all parties except Aguinaldo present. Dewey would make a naval attack on Manila, doing as little harm as possible. The army would march from Cavite and attack by land, doing as little harm as possible. The fight would be hot enough to satisfy Spanish honor. If that condition was met, the Spanish would surrender. Everyone present understood that the basic mission of the U.S. Army was not to shoot Spaniards (except by accident) but to be sure that Aguinaldo did not enter Manila.

The game was played out. Dewey sailed into position to fire on Manila. The Germans steamed between Dewey and the Spanish guns. The British and Japanese steamed in to support Dewey. The French steamed to the side of the Germans. Dewey proceeded to bombard Manila without interference. The army moved up from the south. The Spanish surrendered. Arthur MacArthur's brigade, coming in behind the brigade that led the attack, was able to keep the Filipinos out of the city. For the moment the puzzle had been solved.

Our young private was stationed with his unit near Pandacan opposite a long line of trenches, 14 miles of them, that surrounded the city on the north, south, and east. The trenches were filled with Filipino soldiers. The Filipinos wandered into town in their blue uniforms and met U.S. soldiers in brown. Insults led to fights. Fights led to insults. Aguinaldo demanded recognition of the rights of Filipinos to govern themselves. He was ordered to keep his troops out of Manila.

A correspondent on the scene wrote on September 12, 1898: "They cannot see our position and we cannot reach theirs. We know that our honor and faith will not be broken with them. It all means that sometime we shall fight."[2]

Five months later, on February 4, 1899, our private was patrolling his post in the dark near Santa Mesa, at the edge of Manila. Four Filipinos in uniform came down the road. Our private ordered them to halt, but they continued to approach. The private fired and killed a Filipino lieutenant, and a comrade killed two other Filipinos.[3] The Philippine Insurrection had begun.

There followed two years of bloody, bitter struggle. In reality it was never finished, and isolated outbreaks occurred as late as the 1930s. Eventually 100,000 U.S. soldiers were in the battle with as many as 70,000 Filipinos. In this conflict 2,000 U.S. soldiers died, 14,000 Filipinos were killed, and 6,000 were wounded. Hundreds of thousands of the Filipinos were held in concentration camps where abuse and torture were common. The Filipinos fought bitterly in attack, they fought in retreat, they fought as guerrillas, and, cornered in the mountains, they still fought. It was the first show of strength by Asian peoples against the white masters, a foretaste of the hell of Vietnam that would demonstrate the short memory of U.S. leaders who continued to believe for 50 years longer that Asians could not and would not stand in battle against white soldiers.

Aguinaldo was taken at last by ruse. An ambitious major, whose hopes for a general's star in the regular course of routine promotion seemed a dim and forlorn hope, decided to stake his career and his life on raw courage and good luck. It was the age of Kipling and of empire and of sheer gut bravado, damning all consequences save one, when prudence could still be set aside with a hope of winning. Frederick Funston put together a plot. He would assemble a small group of faithful Filipinos and march with them, his hands and arms bound, into the very heart of Aguinaldo's last refuge. The Filipinos would present themselves as guerrilla *insurrectos* with Funston as their prisoner, and thereby gain admittance to the presence of Aguinaldo. By ruse or force they would carry him off.

Funston went to General MacArthur with the scheme. MacArthur shook his head in disbelief and warned that there seemed to be no chance at all of success; yet, under the circumstances, he was required to give reluctant approval. If the caper failed, he would lose one major. If the caper succeeded, a long, costly war would end. No one else had a better stratagem. Funston marched away as he had planned, an apparent prisoner, and disappeared into the countryside. Then, in the fullness of time, he marched out with Aguinaldo, who at last had found an escape from his own hopeless battle.

Aguinaldo was brought to MacArthur, who persuaded him, by an offer of amnesty, to take the oath of allegiance. Aguinaldo was weary, and he took the oath. A few months later one of his young lieutenants was persuaded by friends to visit Manila under safe conduct; there he learned from Aguinaldo himself of the oath he had taken. The young lieutenant was stunned, but emotion yielded to reason. He also took the oath of allegiance and returned to his friends in the hills. He persuaded them to follow his example. His name was Manuel Quezon.

Aguinaldo's independence movement in the form of armed rebellion collapsed. The movement would now be reshaped under the leadership of young Filipinos like Manuel Quezon, Sergio Osmeña, and later Manuel Roxas, who tied their hopes to an enlightened United States that might prepare the Philippines for nationhood at some unspecified future date.

One enlightened American, a witness of the events, observed:

For four long years, slaughter and destruction have ravaged one of the fairest lands on earth, converting what might be a paradise into a pandemonium.

What evils have these poor Tagals not suffered in that time? Arbitrary imprisonment, torture, confiscation of property, banishment to unhealthy places, military executions, bombardments, the storming and burning of towns, and the bubonic plague.[4]

These facts would leave a mark for half a century, and even longer.

4

Tutelage

The United States had an empire and, like it or not, must govern it. A civilian commissioner was sent to Manila to transfer power from General Arthur MacArthur, commanding general of the VIII Corps, to Judge William Howard Taft, new governor of the Philippines. MacArthur was not gracious, but Taft, moving with a dignity and authority that matched his physical size, ignored the slight and proceeded to work out a doctrine of "Philippines for the Filipinos." MacArthur departed to observe the Japanese destruction of Russian power. Thereafter military commanders in the Philippines accepted without obvious dissatisfaction the primacy of the civilian government.[1]

A government was established. The U.S. governor was appointed by the president. A commission was appointed by the governor, in the first decades always with a U.S. majority. After 1907 an assembly was elected by the Filipino people. The single issue in the politics of the Philippines was independence. All parties were pledged to attain it, the only difference being timing and method. It overwhelmed all other matters, detracting attention even from serious economic problems. The political process was dominated by lawyers who accepted the separation of church and state and moderate constitutionalism as their basic principles. The emotional involvement of the population with the idea of independence provided grist for the political mills of the three lawyers who guided affairs. Quezon, Osmeña, and Roxas dominated the Nacionalista Party for almost four decades. I met all of them, in separate situations in which I was a very minor and passive party to the exchange. Quezon was always the dominant member of this triumvirate. Although the others challenged him, individually and jointly, Quezon always gravitated to the top. He chortled on one occasion in 1931: "You see those two fellows do not dare try to oust the old man yet, sick as he is . . . if they break with me, they will be on the losing side."[2] The same boast would have applied in 1941 as well.

The problem posed by the Philippines did not concern a great many U.S. civilians after 1901, but the thorny question of Philippine independence was permanently welded into the platforms of the two U.S. parties. Republicans were determined that independence was not a matter of even remote possibility. The Democrats were opposed to the idea of permanent control, although the implementation of independence might be deferred to some vague future date when foreign powers should agree to neutralize the islands.

There was some talk, early in the century, about the possibility of statehood for the Philippines. There was some support among Filipinos, but the support quickly died when an American announced: " . . . statehood for Filipinos would add another serious race problem to the one we have already. The Negroes are a cancer in our body politic, a source of constant difficulty, and we wish to avoid developing another."[3] The statehood issue thus died in infancy. At this period some Filipinos began to look to the Japanese, who, as fellow Asians, would accept them without any hint of racial arrogance.

In 1912, with the victory of the Democrats, the matter of independence came up in Congress. The Jones Act of 1916 gave the first official promise of ultimate independence. It set up a new governmental structure that provided for more autonomy. A bicameral legislature was provided. The lower house was elected by Filipinos and the senate was filled by appointees of the governor-general. Under Democratic governors-generals there was considerable transfer of power from the governor-general to the various administrative departments, which were managed by Filipinos. With the return of the Republicans to power in 1920, the structure of the Jones Act remained but the philosophy that had inspired it was set aside. The new governor-general began to draw back into his own hands the power that had been relinquished by his Democratic predecessors.

In the 1930s there was a short discussion of dominion status, an idea that would be revived during World War II. The matter was discussed in 1929 with Osmeña and Quezon. Quezon took the idea to Manila and presented it to his followers. He found very little support for a permanent attachment of the Philippines to the United States.[4]

The Democrats returned to power in 1932 with President Franklin Roosevelt. Roosevelt was bound by the traditional party position that eventually independence would be granted to the Philippines. He looked with some favor on an early solution of the problem. Two major elements of his support, the farm and labor blocs, also took this view. To these were added others who were concerned about the impact of the colonial status of the Philippines on "racial purity." Moreover, it was commonly accepted by military and naval advisers that the Philippines could not be defended except at great cost. All facts considered, a grant of independence might produce more benefits than costs.

The Tydings-McDuffie Bill passed Congress in 1934. Quezon worked tirelessly to get a bill that would be tolerable to the Filipinos and would permit him to return to Manila as the father of Filipino independence. What came out of his maneuvering was temporary dominion status with a promise of independence in ten years. A constitutional convention was called to work out the structure of the new government of the Commonwealth of the Philippines. There would be a president, a unicameral legislature, and a supreme court. The transition period would be monitored by a U.S. high commissioner. The president's powers were very great, and serious minds were not sure that any limits had been imposed upon his authority. Nevertheless, the constitution was approved and elections were held. It is hardly necessary to say that Quezon was called upon to serve as president with Osmeña as vice-president. Roxas was relegated to a minor role but remained the third power in Philippine politics.

Quezon, if fortune was kind, might survive ten years more to become first president of the Republic of the Philippines. In the meantime he must prove to the United States and to his own people that Filipinos could govern themselves. He was faced with immense problems. There were many who doubted that if the Filipinos were left to themselves, they could develop a truly democratic political process. The distribution of political power in the Philippines was notoriously skewed. The wealthy dominated the process with the professional politicians following these leaders. There did not seem to be any popular discontent among the general population. One party dominated the governmental process, and a privileged few dominated the party. The remainder of the nation gave approval. The opposition consisted of fringe parties that represented a nostalgic remnant of Aguinaldo's populist revolt. Opposition based on a modern, radical search for social and economic justice for the masses had a very small voice and was ignored. The hints of a corrupt electorate persisted until after World War II. A visitor to MacArthur in Tokyo predicted that the election scheduled for 1946 might not be honest. MacArthur replied, with pragmatic realism, "Paul, you're absolutely right, but the Filipinos will hold as honest an election as you ever had in the state of Indiana."[5]

Quezon approached matters with characteristic disregard of those who fretted that democracy required more than one party. He found the idea of "partyless democracy" an attractive idea, especially since he had become a master at manipulating that kind of a system. In one way or another, he could usually hammer out a consensus in his favor.

Even less manageable than political democracy was the problem of financial viability of the Commonwealth. It was not a matter of fairness; it was a matter of making ends meet in monetary terms. The government must find revenue to provide state services. The new law would shut an independent Philippines out of U.S. markets. The Philippines would not be permitted to levy tariffs on imported U.S. goods. The result would be economic recession in the Philippines, falling state revenues with rising state expenditures. No attempt was made either in the United States or in the Philippines to develop a gradual readjustment process.

With commonwealth status came the need for a military program of self-defense. By 1935 all U.S. leaders of both services were convinced that the Philippines could not, and therefore would not, be defended. The only contrary voice was that of General Douglas MacArthur, and Quezon turned to him for aid. The two men formed an alliance that lasted beyond Quezon's death. It was predicated on the principles that the Filipinos should, and must, be free and that they must be prepared to defend their national independence.

In the United States the vision of Aguinaldo's insurrection still weighed heavily on the minds of those who were old enough to have memories of the events, especially in the War Department. Added to their conviction that the Philippines could not be defended was the smoldering fear that an armed Filipino citizenry constituted a greater threat to U.S. interests than did Japan's bold adventure. Filipino officers and noncommissioned officers sent to the United States for training were not permitted to learn the mysteries of the .50 caliber machine gun or the new Garand rifle, on the grounds that knowledge and possession of such weapons constituted a direct threat to national security. Many felt that arms and munitions sent to the Philippines for defense might well be turned against the donor.

The Philippine Insurrection of 1899 left moral scars that never quite healed. Like the Vietnam experience, it evoked memories of a bitter, bloody struggle, seen by some as a moral mission gone wrong and by others as an imperialist dream also gone wrong. Independence had been promised, but the prospect did not satisfy anyone. There were many who felt that the Commonwealth would fail and the old state of affairs would be resumed. Quezon was not seen as a genuine head of state. The U.S. government refused to grant honors any higher than those given to the governor of a U.S. state. During a world tour in 1939, Quezon received honors due the head of state in all countries save the United States.

General Douglas MacArthur's career had been a rather rapid and sustained rise to the pinnacle of success normally accessible to the U.S. professional soldier. Events moved quickly and predictably for this young officer who graduated from West Point just as the Philippine Insurrection came to an uneasy end. He served one tour in the Philippines in 1903 and was introduced to Manuel Quezon and Sergio Osmeña. In 1905 MacArthur was assigned as aide to his father, who was in Japan observing the final stage of the Russo-Japanese War. He was promoted to captain in 1911 and served a tour with Pershing in the Mexican campaign. After the declaration of war in 1917, MacArthur was promoted to colonel and transferred from engineers to infantry. He went to France with the 42nd Rainbow Division. By 1918 MacArthur was a brigadier general in command of the division. His first postwar assignment was superintendent of the U.S. Military Academy, where he served until 1922.

Then MacArthur, age 42, was swept into a sudden marriage. He was posted again to the Philippines, his second tour. The MacArthurs made a home in the old structure at One Calle Victoria. It was turned over to them by the Philippine Constabulary, which had used it as a headquarters. There they could watch the beautiful sunsets slide down behind the distant bulk of Bataan, which could be seen across the bay on a clear day.

MacArthur cultivated Quezon and other Filipinos, made an obvious display of affection for Filipino troops, and refused to recognize a color line in social activities. During this tour the first draft of "War Plan Orange" for the defense of the Philippines was laid out. In January 1925 MacArthur became the youngest major general in the army. He was reassigned to the United States during the Coolidge era and was divorced in 1929.

MacArthur was posted to the Philippines again in 1929 for the two-year tour. He discussed with Quezon the growing threat of the Japanese presence in the Far East and its implications for the Philippines. MacArthur was disturbed by the growing Japanese colony on Mindanao. Quezon, on the other hand, was delighted with the injection of Japanese capital and entrepreneurship, which fostered economic growth. They were both correct. "War Plan Orange" was updated during this tour.

MacArthur was appointed chief of staff of the U.S. Army in 1930. The five years during which he served in this position did not provide any opportunity for spectacular innovations in the nation's defense posture. The world economy had collapsed in 1929 and U.S. leaders, grasping at the only wisdom they had learned and unwilling to listen to new prophets, proceeded to intensify their problem by reducing expenditures to balance budgets. Others sought to restore prosperity by reducing military spending. An insignificant defense structure was diminished almost to destruction.

The National Defense Act of 1920 had projected a 280,000-man army. Such an army was considered capable of providing a fail-safe defense against any future need. Even in the apparently prosperous years under President Coolidge the goal was never reached. After the great collapse in 1929, the size of the army fell steadily. In 1930 the total strength was 138,000. Two years later it had fallen to 134,000.[6]

As chief of staff MacArthur was an instrument of the secretary of war, who represented President Hoover. He served as adviser to these men and to various congressional committees. Where budgets were concerned, he was bound by law never to seek in Congress funds that had not been requested by the president. One chief of staff had bluntly stated: "There is a proviso prohibiting any official of the Government coming before a Committee of Congress and arguing for more money than is permitted under the Budget."[7] Within this constraint MacArthur was perhaps as aggressive as anyone else had been, but there is no evidence of audacity. On the contrary, in retrospect one might feel he had not been audacious enough.

MacArthur shared the ideology that motivated Hoover. He was a conservative in the sense that most Americans were conservative at the time. It was a passive conservatism that merely accepted values that had dominated society for half a decade. It mixed political, religious, social, and economic ideology as a homogenous mass, one element inextricably bound to another. MacArthur was also a pragmatist. He was a member of an administration that had his loyalty.

MacArthur performed his duties conscientiously, without any particular controversy. His goal was to preserve the structure of the existing army, inadequate as it was, which seemed to be the best he could hope to achieve under the circumstances. MacArthur *did* fight within that framework of administration policy to preserve a well-balanced structure, refusing to accede to those who were willing to grant more to air and mechanized forces at the expense of the infantry. MacArthur would have none of it.

As the Great Depression worsened, unemployed veterans marched to Washington to petition for a bonus. They camped in the city and demonstrated. The Communist Party took up the cause, which had enough support to cause uneasiness. Anxious for the maintenance of public order, Hoover ordered MacArthur to use troops to clear the city. MacArthur must have felt distaste for the assignment, insofar as it was directed against veterans and former soldiers. He felt less distaste in the matter of putting down communism. In full uniform he supervised but did not directly control the operation. The uniform was intended to indicate a sense of honor for the nation's veterans, and his presence was a token of concern for their welfare. Others saw it differently. As in many other cases, MacArthur would have found it difficult to understand why. Nevertheless, he emerged from the Hoover years as a symbol of militarism, booted and spurred, an enemy of the struggling masses, opposed to aviation in general and to military aviation in particular, and greedy for money that could be better spent on more humanitarian goals.

Franklin Roosevelt became president in 1932. Whatever Roosevelt did later, in 1932 he pledged budgetary reductions of 25 percent. Like MacArthur, Roosevelt held sound economic policy to be an immutable dogma. Unlike MacArthur, he soon would learn better. MacArthur continued to play a cautious hand as chief of staff under Roosevelt. There is no record that he ever went to battle with Hoover. He was less gentle when Roosevelt threatened a cut in 1935.

MacArthur recorded the encounter thus:

I felt it my duty to take up the cudgels. The country's safety was at stake, and I said so bluntly. The President turned the full vials of his sarcasm upon me. He was a scorcher when aroused. The tension began to boil over. For the third and last time in my life that paralyzing nausea began to creep over me. In my emotional exhaustion I spoke recklessly and said something to the general effect that when we lost the next war, and an American boy, lying in the mud with an enemy bayonet through his belly and an enemy foot on his dying throat, spat out his last curse, I wanted the name not to be MacArthur, but Roosevelt. The President grew livid. "You must not talk that way to the President!" he roared. He was, of course, right, and I knew it almost before the words left my mouth. I said that I was sorry and apologized. But I felt my Army career was at an end. I told him he had my resignation as Chief of Staff. As I reached the door his voice came with that cool detachment which so reflected his extraordinary self-control, "Don't be foolish, Douglas; you and the budget must get together on this."[8]

Roosevelt's New Dealers, whatever they thought of military spending, found one acceptable use for the military in implementing the Civilian Conservation

Corps that gave the country an exercise in mobilization. The army was given the task of organizing the induction and supervision of 271,000 unemployed young men. The corps was inducted, supplied, organized, and put to productive work in less than 60 days. In World War I it had taken 90 days to mobilize and process 181,000 men. Whatever the success had been, MacArthur preferred to have the army out of the program, and many of MacArthur's opponents sided with him on this point. In 1935 MacArthur proposed to add two months of military training to the existing CCC program and enroll CCC graduates into a military reserve. There was great opposition.

MacArthur was an anomaly in the New Deal administration. Secretary of the Interior, Harold Ickes, once said:

I had asked Chief of Staff MacArthur to come in on some Army projects. He had presented a very large list running into the hundreds of millions. . . . MacArthur is the type of man who thinks that when he gets to Heaven, God will step down from the great white throne and bow him into His vacated seat, and it gave me a great kick to have him in and break the news to him. While he was here, though, two or three of the members foolishly asked him some questions which gave him a chance to deliver a lecture on the subject of the necessity for the little old peanut Army posts that we have scattered around the country.[9]

MacArthur was held for one year beyond the normal term, probably to assist in the passage of the appropriations bill through Congress in 1935. On September 18, 1935, he retired as chief of staff. He had already found another assignment. He went off to Manila, where he could employ his professional knowledge. Quezon, the president of the Philippines, found a military adviser.

5

Military Mission

MacArthur arrived in Manila in 1935 with a rich experience of political and fiscal realities. He had learned to cope with both under Hoover and Roosevelt. He could expect no greater financial resources in the Commonwealth of the Philippines. It would be no mean challenge to develop a defense structure, constrained by the commonly accepted ideology, in a political economy that struggled to come to grips with a world wallowing in economic stagnation. It presented a fine intellectual puzzle for which MacArthur was eminently qualified. Since Washington had forged the framework of a new republic, no U.S. general had such an opportunity. MacArthur, if he could not be the father of the Republic of the Philippines, might well become its godfather.[1]

The position of the U.S. government was defined ambiguously. Japanese intentions, on the other hand, had become unmistakable in the last years of MacArthur's tenure as chief of staff. Manchuria was invaded. The League of Nations protested and ordered an investigation. Japan withdrew from the League, then openly renounced the limitations that had been imposed by the Naval Limitation Treaties of 1922. The actions constituted open defiance of the great Western powers. Such defiance was common in those days. Italy and Germany learned to follow the pattern. The United States should have taken some action but did not; under the conditions of the economy and the state of public opinion it could not. Or so it seemed.

In retrospect, massive rearming of Guam and the Philippines would have been the historically accepted response to such a challenge. Instead, the Philippine Independence Act had declared to the world that at the end of a ten-year probationary period the Philippines would be cut loose to fend for itself. Such an action might seem to imply that the United States would withdraw its military forces as well as its political machinery. But that option was rejected also. Between 1935 and 1941 the United States refused to accept either alternative and tried to find a middle position that would maintain military bases that no one believed could be defended, on the one hand, and avoid any obligation to pay the financial and real costs of providing full-scale defense, on the other.

MacArthur spent five and a half years as military adviser to the Commonwealth of the Philippines. When all is said and done, it was not a harmonious tour of duty, and one wonders why he endured it. The fact that he did so is evidence of an inner commitment and some sense of obligation. One might add that while alternative employments available to MacArthur might have been more satisfactory, they would not have provided a path to glory. A realist in 1935 would not have seen much evidence of any glory to be had in his situation. Only events can establish whether the dreamer of dreams is a Joseph or a Don Quixote. MacArthur had sat long enough in the halls of power to understand the vagaries of fortune that had to be ground out in the mill of intense political competition. He also understood that glory does not come to one who is not willing to face the competition and to master it, or to suffer the pangs of disappointment if things do not work out. He also had great faith in his own capacity for matching ploy with counterploy in the chess of politics.

MacArthur's appointment as military adviser was shrouded in political maneuvering. It was part of a political process in which a great many fingers were dabbling. MacArthur acted on his own behalf. He did not sit idly to await the call of duty. He had private reasons for making such a move, and he did everything he could to enhance the status of his position and to give the greatest possible scope to his ambitions. Various centers of power were involved in the decision. Quezon, the secretary of war, and Roosevelt, all for their own reasons, supported MacArthur's appointment. Apparently the only serious question was whether he should be named high commissioner or military adviser.

Quezon felt that his position of authority inevitably would be enhanced by the presence at his side of a leading U.S. military officer. The secretary of war saw an opportunity to free himself of the perplexing responsibility for the defense of the Philippines. Roosevelt, among other things, saw an opportunity to move MacArthur beyond the reach of a major party that was looking eagerly for a candidate to take his place in the White House. On the other side of the issue was Secretary of the Interior Ickes, basically an antimilitarist and suspicious of MacArthur, who feared that MacArthur would undercut the authority of the high commissioner and of the Interior Department.

MacArthur set off with his staff on the long sea voyage to Manila. During that voyage he met Jean Marie Faircloth, who became his companion and friend and, two years later, his wife. MacArthur moved his staff and headquarters into the familiar One Calle Victoria.

During the first year he had triumphs. His National Defense Act for the Philippine Commonwealth was passed. He was appointed field marshal general in the Philippine Army. The National Defense Act created opposition, and the marshal's baton created jealousy. A hurried coalition developed between the high commissioner and the U.S. Army as represented by the Philippine Department to ensure that neither Quezon's high office nor MacArthur's high rank would deprive them of priority in honors or precedence. The U.S. establishment in Manila decreed that the high commissioner would take precedence over Quezon where protocol was involved. It was further decreed that rank in the Philippine Army would not entitle a U.S. Army officer to corresponding honors or salutes from U.S. Army units.

The exalted rank of field marshal general and the baton that was its outward symbol must have resulted in some ridicule in certain circles. A precedent had been set by the U.S. Navy, providing rank as an inexpensive substitute for the reality of power. The commander in chief of the Asiatic Fleet, which patrolled the South China Sea and paraded the U.S. flag in and out of Asian ports of call, wore the four stars of full admiral. This contingent was smaller by several magnitudes than other commands, which comprised more ships and were led by men with fewer stars. It was all a matter of symbol and ritual. The added stars— or, in MacArthur's case, the field marshal's baton—gave him precedence over, or at least equal status with, representatives of other imperial powers. These, it might be added, were embarrassed by the disparity between their ranks and their resources. It is quite likely that MacArthur was more concerned that he outrank Admiral Thomas Hart, who was closer at hand than British, Dutch, or French counterparts. It certainly gave him social precedence over other generals who happened to be stationed in the Philippines.

MacArthur understood the very palpable impact of a display of symbols even when they were devoid of content. In this situation it was the only reality the Philippines could afford. Future increments of real power might well follow the otherwise hollow display. Eventually 100,000 Filipino troops, covered by their own air forces, might pass in review before their field marshal. Perhaps there was one elemental satisfaction under all the reality. A marshal's baton is a marshal's baton, and no other U.S. officer had carried one.

MacArthur's proposal for the defense of the Philippines was built on the principle of a citizen army. There would be a small regular army of some 20,000 or so soldiers supported by an air force of 250 light bombers and 50 to 100 motor torpedo boats. The entire population would stand as a ready reserve to be called into action when needed. Every year a new class of trainees would be inducted for military training. At the end of their training they would pass into the reserve units and would have an annual call for additional training and service. Filipinos would be subject to some form of military service between the ages of 10 and 50. At any given time 100,000 troops could be mobilized for duty. MacArthur estimated that the cost for the first decade would be $80 million: $30 million to maintain the regular army, $35 million to train reserves, $5 million for the motor torpedo boats, and $10 million for the bombers.[2] In retrospect one smiles at the objections that were raised on the grounds of cost. By current standards it was a minuscule amount. At that time it was considered to be an unbelievable drain on a small economy.

MacArthur brought to Manila a personal staff of four officers: an aide, a physician, and two assistants. The aide was a captain; the others were majors.

One of them, Major Dwight Eisenhower, would rise later to high command in World War II in another theater. All of them had left the Military Mission by the end of 1939. Sidney Huff, a retired naval officer, joined the mission as a civilian naval adviser in 1936 and remained with MacArthur for many years.

The group of personal advisers was drawn from officers assigned to the Philippine Department but detached for specific tasks in connection with MacArthur's training program. As many as 30 officers and 100 enlisted men served in this capacity at any given time during the five years of the Military Mission. No single individual served the entire period. Officers were reassigned to other tasks, or they came to the end of their tour of duty and returned to the United States. Some of the officers who served the Military Mission would later return as members of the Headquarters USAFFE staff. A very few of this group would go to Australia when MacArthur left Corregidor.

In any event, the actual details of the mission program were left to the staff. They prepared the plans and supervised their implementation. The actual work was carried out by other officers drawn from the Philippine Department. MacArthur energized and permeated the entire process. He was the symbol of authority and command that set the purpose for a great many individuals whose work without him would have led nowhere.

In the second year of MacArthur's tenure, opposition grew on all sides. The high commissioner, the commanding general of the Philippine Department, and various forces in the Philippine political structure united to oppose MacArthur's defense plan. Pressures in Washington resulted in a notice to him from the War Department that he would be recalled at the end of the year for reassignment to duty in the United States. MacArthur chose resignation. After 1937 he no longer represented the U.S. government. Quezon issued an executive order announcing that MacArthur would continue to perform his duties as a retired civilian.

There is no record of any precise conflict between MacArthur and his military and civilian superiors in the United States. One might believe, on the basis of attitudes that uniformly and universally dominate bureaucratic hierarchies of any nature, that in his new situation MacArthur had outgrown the army structure. The small group of major generals who stood at the peak of military authority, solidly entrenched in jealously defended privilege, could not be comfortable with a field marshal general in their midst.

MacArthur technically was only one of the group in terms of his appointment within the U.S. Army. His status in the Philippine Army was another matter. It could be ignored officially, but it was too colorful to be ignored by the public. MacArthur was given a choice that in reality was no choice at all. To remain in the U.S. Army he would have to accept assignment to some humdrum command in the United States that probably would have been just one more step on the road to retirement. An assignment could easily be found to make retirement even more desirable. Given all the perquisites of his status in the Philippines, any arrangement that would perpetuate it would seem preferable.

The affair caused MacArthur far more anguish than he displayed at the time.

During the dark days of early 1942, in a period of great stress, he relived the decision in trying to find a solution to a particularly hard choice.

The National Assembly of the Commonwealth began to fret about the cost of defense. The Filipinos began to question the effectiveness of MacArthur's program. The number of participants in the program began to decrease, and those who did enroll did not seem to develop into qualified soldiers. There was friction with the commanding general of the Philippine Department over jurisdictional matters. Finally Quezon himself, under intense political pressure, began to pull away from MacArthur's program and to avoid any action that might antagonize the Japanese and invite retaliation. By the end of 1939 it must have seemed that in spite of MacArthur's resolve, his program soon must collapse.

Why did he stay? For one thing, he had nothing more challenging to do. In Manila he had a title and a command. In retirement he might find greater serenity but little to challenge his intellect and his vigor. Moreover, he had a good salary. With the salary he had the glitter and pomp of command and of all the rituals it entailed. But most of all, he had a very good life that neatly matched his needs. In 1937 he and Jean Faircloth returned to the United States, where they were married. At long last MacArthur had the feeling of a happy marriage. He wrote later:

On the morning of April 30, 1937, I married Jean Marie Faircloth in the Municipal Building in New York. It was perhaps the smartest thing I have ever done. She has been my constant friend, sweetheart, and devoted supporter ever since. How she has managed to put up with my eccentricities and crotchets all these years is quite beyond my comprehension. . . . Our son, Arthur, was born on February 21, 1938, and with my little family I would be lonely no more.[3]

The family whiled away their days in the penthouse of the Manila Hotel, sauntering in the terrace garden, looking out over the bay or down into Intramuros. The problems imposed by his duties were not as difficult as the ones he had encountered in Washington, and did not intrude into his family life. It was a simple, abstemious existence. One small cocktail a day, a movie almost every evening, the intimate affection of an adoring wife and an adored son, good books, and quiet meditation filled his hours and his days.

Laced through it all was MacArthur's conviction that he was a man of destiny. He was a Joseph in Potiphar's house who had never seen a pit. Unlike the biblical Joseph, MacArthur's career had marched relentlessly in a sustained progression up the ranks to the pinnacle of command. He still wore the multicolored robe that was evidence of favor. Events in the world were unrolling on a path that must lead inevitably to his feet. Then he would be needed. In the meantime he could afford to wait. As I wrote earlier, a soldier's life consists of much waiting punctuated by infrequent intervals of intense activity. The Military Mission was a period of waiting.

6

Sutherland Arrives

Howard Sutherland was born in St. Louis (1865) and grew up there. He studied at Westminster College in Fulton, Missouri, from which he graduated in 1889. During the four years at Westminster he courted a local girl, Effie Harris. Sutherland stayed in Fulton for the following year as editor of the Fulton *Republican*. He and Effie were married, and the young couple went off to Washington to the Department of the Census. Howard did course work in law at George Washington (then Columbian) University.[1]

In 1893 Sutherland decided to move to Elkins, West Virginia, with his pregnant wife and two young daughters. On November 27, as the train neared the junction at Hancock, Maryland, Effie's time came, and the trip was interrupted. Their first and only son, Richard, was born. When Effie was able to travel, the hectic journey was resumed.

Howard set up on his own in coal, timber, and railroads, and prospered. His family grew with the addition of three more daughters. Richard was buried in feminine competition and domination.

Howard took his turn in local politics, and in 1908 went off to the West Virginia Senate at Charleston for a four-year stint. Richard trudged up the hill to Davis and Elkins College (then a preparatory school). In the fall of 1910 he went off to Phillips Academy at Andover, Massachusetts, where he studied French, German, Latin, and mathematics. Twenty years later a professor wrote to remind him of their short association.

In the fall of 1911, State Senator Sutherland was confronted by a determined eighteen-year-old Richard. The son wanted a military career but the father refused to discuss the possibility. The son wanted West Point, and it was in the power of his father to secure the appointment. The senator balked. Perhaps he considered military life unworthy of his son, an inferior calling, and on that ground held fast. Young Sutherland was told he could go to any university he chose, but never to a military school. Sutherland went to Yale, entered the ROTC cadet corps, and in 1916 joined the Connecticut National Guard as a private.

The old senator had lost the game. He had deprived his son of a very valuable rung up on the ladder of his chosen career. Thereafter the son would face an ill-concealed disparagement: "Sutherland is not a West Point graduate, he's a *Yale* graduate." This fact may have contributed materially to the seeming arrogant superiority he assumed as he rose to power over men who were West Point graduates but were nevertheless subject to the authority of a Yale graduate.

Sutherland's first year at Yale was a calamity of health problems—pneumonia and appendicitis with postoperative difficulties—that played havoc with his academic performance and set him back one year. Succeeding years were more fortunate and quite successful. Sutherland majored in history and languages and played football. He was determined to find military glory in spite of his father.

The Mexican fracas came in 1916, and General John J. Pershing rode off to the border with a clutch of future generals, Captain Douglas MacArthur and Lieutenant George Patton included, to put down Pancho Villa and to restore order. The Connecticut National Guard was called up, and with the contingent went Private Richard Kerens Sutherland. The senator might keep him out of West Point, but he could not keep him out of the army. In 60 days Private Sutherland had a commission in the field artillery, and 60 days after that he transferred to the infantry. Six months later he was in France, now a captain, commanding a front-line unit in combat. By this time the father had completed two terms as U.S. Congressman and had moved up to the U.S. Senate where he served one term.

Captain Richard Sutherland attended a British tank school, then he came home to peacetime service in the regular army. He married Josephine Whiteside of Chattanooga. Their only child, Natalie, was born in 1920. Sometime during this period Sutherland served as instructor at Shattuck Military Academy. In 1923 he was posted to the Infantry School for a tour.

In 1928 Sutherland did his stint at the Command and General Staff School at Fort Leavenworth, Kansas. This was "horsemanship time" for the Sutherlands. Sutherland was a member of the riding team, and Natalie started riding there. She developed a passion for horses that endured until young womanhood brought other passions.

Almost immediately after completing the course, Sutherland was sent to France, to the Ecole Supérieure de Guerre. He spoke French fluently and attended lectures in French, but he did not particularly like the French people. The family spent two years there. Sutherland was in Washington in 1932–1933 for a tour at the War College. After graduation he was assigned to the General Staff Corps.

The situation of the 15th Infantry Regiment in Tientsin was precarious in the spring and summer of 1937. The Japanese had decided to occupy China, and a new war was on the way. The 15th Infantry and the 4th Marines in Shanghai were the most far-flung representatives of U.S. military power, two isolated outposts swallowed up in the landmass of China, surrounded by millions of hostile Chinese. These two regiments were supported by the Philippine Division, headquartered on Luzon with the 31st Infantry Regiment and the Philippine Scouts. Assignment to either Tientsin or Manila was a routine component of an officer's cycle of duty.

In 1937 Captain Richard Sutherland, who had been assigned to General Staff Corps duties for several years, was posted as battalion executive officer in Tientsin. He arrived with his wife and his daughter, who was sixteen. In March 1938 Sutherland was promoted to major. In July he received orders to proceed to Manila to serve on the staff of Douglas MacArthur. He packed up his family and boarded a ship for the trip to Manila via Japan and Shanghai. Predictably, Josephine and Natalie were seasick, a condition Sutherland could not understand and would not accept with tranquility. It was just one more bother on a bothersome trip. He growled, "Put them to bed," and tried to find ease for their discomfort.

Natalie recalls:

The ship was filled with Japanese officers and troops returning to Japan. The only other [non-Asian] passengers were a young student and a German woman.

Our room was next to two Japanese girls. Every night the Japanese officers got drunk. One night three of them rampaged up and down the hall, beating on [the] locked doors of the poor girls. We could hear them sobbing. Daddy didn't dare interfere for fear of a ghastly incident. The ship's officers eventually quieted the officers down.

We spent two weeks in Japan on vacation. We sailed to Manila aboard the *Empress of Japan*. We stopped in Shanghai. A Chinese man shot a Japanese soldier while we were ashore. The Japs closed all the bridges and we couldn't get back to the ship, which was sailing around midnight. We were somewhat desperate until we met a Scotsman who had a small cabin cruiser. He volunteered to take us to our ship. He turned off all his lights and sneaked out [to] the *Empress*.

The Sutherlands moved into a nipa cottage on the bay west of Nichols Field. Sutherland had easy access to his office in Intramuros, to his plane at Nichols Field, and to the golf course at Fort William McKinley. Josephine became close friends with Jean MacArthur and Aurora Quezon, the wife of the president. Josephine was from Chattanooga, Tennessee, and Jean MacArthur from Murfreesboro, Tennessee.

It is my judgment that Sutherland truly loved his wife and his daughter, and was a thoughtful husband and parent. Sutherland and MacArthur were not much alike as parents. It is only in retrospect, after the children are grown, that any reasonable man dares take credit for his philosophy or his performance on that score. Natalie learned that when "Daddy" said "no," he meant precisely and exactly that, and neither tears, coaxing, flattery, nor flirtation would change the verdict. So it was with Josephine. Sutherland was tender and affectionate with his family, but as firm as a young infantry officer must be. Natalie remembers a warm, loving father whose firmness was matched by affection and support. He helped her, instructed her, and supported her.

Sutherland took in his stride all the constraints of marriage. He once remarked to me in a burst of candor:

Rogers, you will learn what it means to be married. I am a carpenter, a good one, one of the best. I can make joints which will match those of a master craftsman. I used to want tools to make the job easier, but there was always a new dress or new shoes or doctor bills. You will learn!

Over in the PX while I was in China there was a Leica camera. I wanted it so badly I could taste it. But we just didn't have the money. Some enlisted man got it instead.

I know now, of course, just what he meant.

For three years Dwight D. Eisenhower and James Ord had served as MacArthur's principal advisers. No official line was drawn between the two men but since MacArthur had chosen Eisenhower and Eisenhower had chosen Ord, there was an unofficial line of command. The men apparently worked in relative harmony with MacArthur but without any appreciable evidence of deep understanding and rapport. No one sensed any particular desire on MacArthur's part to replace either of them.[2]

Ord was killed in an airplane accident in 1938. Sutherland was ordered down from Tientsin to fill the vacancy thus created. He was promoted to lieutenant colonel and served as Eisenhower's junior partner. Both men carried the "local rank" of colonel; that is, in dealing with the army structure in the Philippines, their actual rank was ignored. With respect to their local activities they were one grade higher in the pecking order. This practice enhanced their authority in dealing with Headquarters Philippine Department.

During the spring of 1938 Eisenhower decided to ask for a leave so that he could make a personal tour of the Far East. It was not an unusual request, and it raised only one problem: Who would fill Eisenhower's shoes during his absence? MacArthur insisted that he must have a chief of staff. Eisenhower turned willingly to the obvious solution. Sutherland had been in China and Japan, and perhaps his experience attracted Eisenhower's attention. Sutherland was to move up in the unofficial pecking order to the higher position. Eisenhower would have a memorable lesson in the proper calculation and evaluation of unknown outcomes.

The precise events are not known, but Sutherland bragged in 1945 that he had outwitted Eisenhower. The same conclusion was repeated by others. MacArthur was attracted to Sutherland, who proved to be a remarkable match for MacArthur's intellectual orientation. It was a rare meeting of sympathetic minds and talents, the details of which can be inferred from the subsequent joint exercise of command. MacArthur was determined that this temporary replacement for the absent Eisenhower should become permanent. He and Sutherland worked out a command agreement that would survive seven years of hard experience. It appears that Sutherland would be charged with details of operations and planning, and Eisenhower would have logistics and supply. Sutherland settled in and awaited the return of his associate chief of staff.

Eisenhower returned to Manila to find himself harnessed with a partner who seemed as likely to lead as to follow in any contest of push or pull. Sutherland dominated those areas which would lead to glory and honor. Quartermasters are praised but seldom lead triumphs. Eisenhower protested to MacArthur that he could not accede to an arrangement that others must see as a reduction in prestige. MacArthur replied coolly, with complete detachment, that Eisenhower was free to seek other assignments if he chose; but Sutherland would control planning and operations. Eisenhower preferred to take his leave, and did so. The night before his departure he lamented to LeGrande Diller that his career had been ruined, another failure to calculate and evaluate future outcomes.

Eisenhower had trapped himself. His tour of the Far East gave MacArthur an opportunity to reorganize his staff and to use a new talent that pure chance had brought to him. MacArthur never regretted the choice he had made. Sutherland finally did regret it. He never had the choice of finding other employment but, long after he found it to be intolerable, was held firmly to the task he assumed so willingly in 1938.

Major Richard J. Marshall, a quartermaster expert, arrived to replace Eisenhower, and the basic elements of MacArthur's top command structure were in place. At their first meeting Sutherland told Marshall that someone in the place had to be a first-class son of a bitch. It was obvious that the Old Man would not be the one. Marshall could not fill the bill. Sutherland was the only one of the three who had the capacity, and he intended to use it.

The precise operational execution of the new arrangement developed over the years. Sutherland's and Marshall's statures increased as their specific duties were adapted to the expanding needs of successive commands. The basic division of responsibility and authority, however, remained firm.

7

We Will Defend

Between 1935 and 1941 MacArthur's plans for defense of the Philippines were defined and implemented in Manila independently from the military policymakers in Washington, for whom he had been the chief spokesman for the preceding four years. The Commonwealth of the Philippines was a province of the Department of the Interior, personified by the old curmudgeon Harold Ickes, a New Deal liberal. Ickes resented the military for two reasons: He was opposed to militarism, and he was opposed to the funds the military drained away from nonmilitary needs. Moreover, he had inherited the attitude of his department, which traced back to the rivalry between Arthur MacArthur, the chief military authority during the insurrection, and William Howard Taft, the first civilian governor, who replaced him. Douglas MacArthur would later protest that Ickes saw the Philippines as just one more of the national parks, which also were administered by the Department of the Interior. Perhaps MacArthur was correct.[1]

The U.S. Navy had its bases and a gaggle of vessels in the Philippines. The bases, which had been the object of U.S. involvement in the first place, were considered indefensible. The assortment of vessels was called the Asiatic Fleet, a title more substantial than the force it represented, and MacArthur on at least one occasion commented acidly on the discrepancy between the claim and the reality. At any rate, the Asiatic Fleet was highly mobile, and if it could not defend its base, it could move elsewhere until the odds changed in its favor. Dewey had demonstrated the danger of being cornered inside Manila Bay.

The U.S. Army, now controlled by George C. Marshall, was in charge of the U.S. military contingent in the Philippines. It included one regiment of infantry, the 31st, billeted in the Cuartel de España in Intramuros; the harbor defense system, centered on Corregidor; the garrison at Fort Stotsenburg, which stood by the side of Clark Field with its bomber air base; and several fighter bases near Manila and throughout Luzon. In all, 30,000 men, including some 12,000 Filipinos, served as an integral part of the U.S. Army.

Policy and planning for the army and navy were controlled in Washington, the two services operating more nearly as competitors than as forces in a common cause. The navy's plans for war in the Far East anticipated a withdrawal of the Asiatic Fleet in the face of a superior force. Later the entire Pacific Fleet would return to destroy the enemy. "Later" was generally believed to be, although it was never specifically spelled out, a matter of perhaps two years. Insofar as the army was concerned, its program for war was set out in "War Plan Orange," which assumed that army forces in the Philippines would withdraw to defenses on Bataan. They would stand under the cover of the great coastal defense guns on Corregidor until they could be relieved. It was commonly believed that the defense could not be maintained for more than two or three months. Since the War Department and the Navy Department planners worked in splendid isolation and mutual distrust, no one ever bothered to confront and to reconcile the serious gap between the two time periods. In those days no one took the air force very seriously, and no plans at all were made for it. There were not very many planes in any case.

Two years before MacArthur had moved to Manila, while he was still chief of staff, his War Department planners had warned:

The Philippine Islands have become a military liability of a constantly increasing gravity. To carry out the present Orange Plan—with its provisions for the early dispatch of our fleet to Philippine waters—would be literally an act of madness. . . . No milder term can be employed if facts are squarely to be faced. In the event of an Orange War the best that could be hoped for would be that wise counsels would prevail, that our people would acquiesce in the temporary loss of the Philippines, and that the dispatch of our battle fleet to the Far East would be delayed for two or three years needed for its augmentation.[2]

MacArthur noted the report and ignored it. No funds were available to correct the problem.

During the years of MacArthur's tenure as military adviser, no funds were available for the military, and little serious attention was given to the containment of Japan's obvious expansion. Policy was motivated by the grim realization that nothing must be done to provoke the Japanese into open war. After 1938, with events in Europe moving the United States closer and closer to involvement, the specter of a two-ocean war raised apprehension.

In 1938 the question of priority in such a contingency was raised, apparently for the first time. The problem was posed: "Are the Philippines and Guam essential to U.S. interests?" The reply was negative. They must not be essential, or they would have been fortified four years earlier, when Japan notified the world that it intended to have naval superiority in the Pacific. The only wild card in the argument was the matter of public opinion. If Japan moved against the Philippines, the American public might insist that American pride be defended, regardless of whether the Philippines was essential.

In September 1939, when Germany moved into Poland, the matter of a two-ocean war again was discussed. It was decided that the Atlantic and the Caribbean represented the vital interest. Only a defensive posture would be possible in the Far East. Ignored was the possibility of a refusal of public opinion to accept these priorities. It had been acknowledged that Guam would be lost. There probably would be an attempt to attack and blockade the Pacific Fleet at Pearl Harbor.

At the same time U.S. and British planners divided the world into two sectors. The United States would be responsible for defense of the Pacific, and the British would be responsible for the Atlantic. The planners set to work to plan a two-ocean war.

Three possible courses of action were presented to George C. Marshall. The Philippines could be reinforced and fortified. Or ''War Plan Orange'' could be implemented, in which case defeat would be ensured. Or the United States could withdraw from the Philippines. Marshall ''noted'' the proposal and sent it to file without any attempt to resolve the dilemma spelled out in it.

By 1940 it was generally agreed that there was great need for fortification of the Philippines, but scarce resources could not be used for that purpose. In the summer of that year, the commanding general of the Philippine Department began to press the War Department for a resolution of the dilemma. All during the summer and fall of 1940 he repeated his recommendations for the dispatch of a composite air wing, a regular army division, an antiaircraft regiment, and reinforcements for harbor defense troops. War Plans Division, considering this request in the light of events in Europe, recommended instead withdrawal of U.S. forces to Hawaii, leaving the western Pacific to Japan.

By January 1941 a change of course was in the making. It was decided to provide funds for reinforcement of the Philippines. However, George C. Marshall warned the commanding general of the Philippine Department that nothing new was in the offing.[3] ''We are doing everything we can for you, and I am sure you understand our limitations.'' During the next four years Marshall would find many different wordings for this message. The purpose of the new policy was ''to impress Japan with the fact that we mean business.'' The Japanese were not impressed.

MacArthur, who for many years had been isolated from the War Department, reestablished his relationship by writing directly to Marshall in February 1941. He spelled out his own plan for the defense of the Philippines and asked for revision of ''Orange'' to provide for the defense of the entire archipelago. MacArthur's request was supported in principle by the commanding general of the Philippine Department, although he did not consider it an urgent matter. His own plan for Philippine defense was under consideration, and he did not care to see MacArthur steal the forces before he received them. MacArthur got 15 coastal defense guns. Marshall felt that MacArthur's Filipino force should not be reinforced at the expense of the U.S. contingent.

In July 1941 Marshall notified his staff of a change in policy.[4] He stated that it had become ''the policy of the United States to defend the Philippines.'' He made an important qualification, however; efforts in the Atlantic must not be jeopardized. It was commonly understood both in Manila and in Washington that the determination of the United States to show the Japanese "that we mean business" had come belatedly, if not too late.[5] The oil embargo that had made fortification of the Philippines seem essential must surely force the hand of Japan. The men who commanded the government of Japan could hardly be expected to turn aside from present successes in the face of a bluff. They seemed to be sure of at least a fair chance of winning, and there was little to cause any fear.

One has the uncomfortable feeling that Roosevelt had decided to resolve the uncertainty of the situation by forcing Japan either to move into a Pacific war or to move out, as a withdrawal from China would signal. Either action would make it easier to deal with the matter of global strategy. Perhaps he relied on the British belief that even if the Philippines collapsed, Singapore would remain as the ultimate bastion of opposition. The British had advocated such a view and had suggested that U.S. naval forces be made available for a joint defense of Singapore. At any rate, provocation of Japan would reduce the gap of uncertainty. The decision in Washington gave the Japanese eight months at most. Failure of Japan to act in the winter of 1941–1942 would bar any move at all. U.S. planes, tanks, guns, and men were being loaded for Manila. Air bases were being surveyed in the Pacific, in Australia, and in the Netherlands East Indies. Filipino boys were being trained.

It was predicted that a Japanese attack most likely would come in the winter months, after the rice had been harvested and before the monsoons. There would be no declaration of war. The invasion force would comprise 100,000 troops. The landing in force would be made in Lingayen Gulf and would move south through the Central Plain to Manila. There would be massive air attacks against airfields and other defense installations. There was no particular originality in the estimate, which had been the basis of U.S. planning for at least half a dozen years. Now it was overlaid with a high degree of urgency and immediacy.

The only question remaining was whether, under the new conditions, the Philippines could in reality be defended. It has often been said in this connection that MacArthur was optimistic. No one knows whether he was or not. The only record consists of public statements in which a display of optimism is required as a means of discouraging the enemy. Whatever reservations MacArthur may have had, in public he displayed assurance and confidence. It must be said that he was magnificently consistent, there being no record of any evidence of doubt.

MacArthur affirmed repeatedly, in circumstances that demanded he be taken seriously, that the Japanese would not move until April 1942.[6] One is tempted to write off his opinion as fanciful optimism although he was not given to such fancy and he had reason to choose that date as preferable to the one customarily advanced in prewar plans.

General Lewis Brereton, MacArthur's air force commander in 1941, wrote in his diary: "In the fall of 1941 our best military and political opinion considered an attack by Japan unlikely before 1 April 1942. The program for the defense of the Philippines contemplated that by this date all the planned defense forces would be in place.'' Anyone who advocated a date earlier than April 1942 would, in effect, presume inevitable defeat in the Philippines. Since official War Department policy was built on the premise that the Philippines *could* be defended, any date earlier than April 1942 would have made all the preparations seem a little foolish. The purpose of it all, both the actual building of the defenses and the oratory, was to bluff the Japanese into inactivity. If war came before April, ''Orange'' would be the only resource.

MacArthur was a rational man. He knew as well as anyone the capabilities of any army. In any rational game he could move with reasonable assurance that his judgment was as good as anyone else's. He also could expect his fair share of good fortune. He knew as well as the Japanese that whatever short-run success might be expected, there could be no hope of ultimate victory except through a series of developments that ranged beyond any reasonable hope of fulfillment. A move by Japan against the United States would represent a very great long-run gamble that might produce suicidal results for Japan if the odds ran in the wrong direction. If Japan had uncertainties, as indeed it did, little could be served by public displays of doubt on MacArthur's part. The public posture of the commanding general is part of the arsenal of defense. Whether MacArthur, sitting on the edge of his bed at night, speaking privately to his wife, was equally confident, no one knows.

MacArthur later wrote: ''Any place could be defended if sufficient men, munitions, and money were available, and above all sufficient time to train the men, to provide the munitions, and to raise the money.''[7]

These facts seem so obvious and so reasonable that a commanding general is hardly expected to use them as a prelude to every statement he makes. The crux of the matter was time. If the time slot had been cut too fine, the cutting had been done by Roosevelt and Churchill, who also had good reason for their actions and for obscuring their basic convictions in the matter. They, too, were caught in a dilemma, particularly Roosevelt, who was required publicly to proclaim peaceful intentions while equally publicly taking belligerent actions. Some would claim that they had been deceived, but a wise man, when confronted with deeds that do not coincide with words, knows how to read the message.

III

Command, July–November 1941

MacArthur recalled to command USAFFE; headquarters organized; Filipino troops called up; air force organized; MacArthur sets limits to Navy influence; dominance over High Commissioner and Quezon; declines to be military governor

8

USAFFE

The storm broke with fury as clouds swirled in over the bay, scudding and rolling out of the South China Sea, over Mount Natib and Mount Bataan. The wall of rain cut down from the northwest, sliding along the slope of the Zambales Mountains, deluging the port area, Fort Santiago, and the Walled City, before it finally reached the Manila Hotel, which stood posted like a sentinel over the Luneta and the port area.

Field Marshal General Douglas MacArthur peered through the open doors of his penthouse apartment, the presidential suite of the Manila Hotel, watching the palms whip in the wind, beaten by driven bullets of water cascading from the roof to the ground in a window of wetness. He stood in his underwear, draped in a nondescript dressing gown that flowed over him with the imperial carelessness that comes from long, familiar use. The field marshal looked down at his diminutive wife, to whom he was "Gin'ral" in public and "Sir Boss" in private. The December–June marriage was filled with genuine affection that he needed deeply. She had come to him late in a lonely life to fill a need that no one else had been able to measure or to satisfy. Tiny and self-effacing, she had become the rock of support to her husband's massive ego. The formality of her address hid the tenderness they felt for each other. "Gin'ral" and "Sir Boss" had become terms of affection and endearment. They were used habitually, to the bewilderment and confusion of outsiders, who puzzled at the apparently complete domination by the field marshal general of his wife, none really understanding that within a few short years she had become a great source of encouragement and comfort.

A wail from the nursery interrupted the intimate conversation that flowed silently between the two, spoken words hardly being necessary to express the love that both felt. Field Marshal General MacArthur had been unprepared for the new role imposed upon him by the inexorable vicissitudes of marriage and cohabitation. He never mastered it, perhaps because he never understood its demands. He was a grandfatherly father who had forgotten the behavior required of a mature young lion in dealing with cubs. Or, remembering, he was unwilling to exercise it. This grand figure of authority and dominion, power and destiny, before whom other men of power stood in hesitant temerity, could find for his infant son only endearing, yielding surrender. There were no rebukes, no cuffs, no impatient rejection: but perhaps a giant neglect of one overwhelming obligation: to understand and to perform the duties of a father. He paced with the infant, protecting him from the random raindrops that blew in from the terrace.

The phone rang and his wife called to him, her voice filled with eager excitement, that the long-awaited letter had finally arrived. The field marshal general began to turn, but paused to watch as the clouds broke over the bay, layered into multicolored bands of brilliant light, opening to the golden glory of a sun that increasingly filled the sky. He finally felt the impact of the message. "Sir Boss" must set aside his marshal's baton to become Major General Douglas MacArthur, U.S. Army, commanding general of the U.S. Army forces in the Far East (USAFFE). Events had opened a door to him, beckoning with a vision and a promise of glory. MacArthur almost absently handed the infant to the nurse who stood close by to receive him, turned aside with obvious impatience, and shouted into the hated telephone, "Dick, I told you so. Destiny is with me. Stay with me and rise to glory."[1]

It was not a surprise. Several months earlier MacArthur had offered his services to Roosevelt in any capacity, military or civilian—which, of course, was a polite reminder that he wanted to be either commanding general or high commissioner in the Philippines. This was old business and had been discussed many times over the years. His faithful service, his experience, and his unique rapport with Filipinos qualified him for either position. Roosevelt replied graciously through his aides, held his peace, and let the matter bubble in the cauldrons of administrative procedure, knowing very well that the pot finally would be peppered to his taste, however many cooks put their ladles into it during the simmering.[2]

The greatest reluctance might well come from the army itself. This huge mass of administrative seething had gotten rid of MacArthur with some effort. Ordinary generals could be oozed out of the turmoil in the usual process of ingestion, assimilation, and elimination, without difficulty and without pain. MacArthur had passed through the long process, leaving discomfort along the way, and somehow could never be eliminated. Promoted early, he was constantly out of place with men who held similar rank but were somehow never quite his peers. Retired early, because no comfortable place could be found for him, he dominated in retirement.

But perhaps the choice of a commanding general seems inevitable only in retrospect. By 1941 all of the obvious leaders of the military establishment were being replaced by younger men who were relatively unknown but presumably more flexible intellectually and more robust physically. More important from the viewpoint of Washington, the younger men had been elevated by the current administration and presumably would be less independent and more amenable to control.

MacArthur had been retired some five years. His political sympathies were closer to the philosophies of Coolidge and Hoover than to the views of New Deal liberals who now dominated Washington. MacArthur was 61 years old, and a question might be raised as to whether his physical constitution would provide enough stamina to endure the great strains that active wartime command certainly must impose. Moreover, he was considered an egotist, capable of unpredictable assertion of independence, with an intense sense of personal honor that did not always sit comfortably in the give and take of political compromise.

On the other side of the coin, MacArthur had given faithful service to Republicans and Democrats alike. In spite of his own convictions concerning military preparedness, he supported Hoover's defense budgets. In the Bonus Crisis he had carried out the directive of his government to maintain peace and security by force. Moreover, he presented himself in uniform to supervise the process, by that action taking full responsibility for whatever might happen and drawing at least some of the fire away from those who had made the decision he carried out. He had confronted Roosevelt openly and bitterly in support of increased defense expenditures at a time when Roosevelt was being pushed to keep them at diminished levels. Events were changing rapidly, and even in 1933 and 1934 Roosevelt must have seen that MacArthur was likely to be correct in his judgment. All in all, MacArthur's record was not one of rebellion, however independent he might be.

MacArthur had one overriding asset that no one else could provide and no one else could attain. He had been identified with the Philippines through the period of the struggle for independence, the formative years of tutelage, and in the transition period of the Commonwealth. He would be more capable than anyone else of galvanizing the Filipinos to determined action in the coming struggle.

MacArthur certainly exerted pressure in his own behalf, but as matters sometimes work out, the decision may have been made by Roosevelt and confided to MacArthur long before the official announcement was made. No other officer on the scene could reasonably feel offended by his appointment. To Roosevelt, who had worked with MacArthur before and probably felt reasonably sure that he could outwit and outperform him in any public controversy, the appointment of a Republican general might build a bridge to the opposition at a time when such support was essential. And, not least, if the new Far East policy ran into disaster, it would be politic to have a Republican general in charge of the debacle.

MacArthur's appointment was defined by Washington in terms of the Philippines Defense Project of 1940, and the new command perhaps was seen as a simple expansion of the Philippine Department.[3] MacArthur saw the matter differently. The old form could not be stretched to fit the great increases of men and equipment that already were flowing into the new command. Within three weeks he announced to George Marshall:

It is expected that before the end of the year the new camps will be completed, the remaining men will be called, and ten complete divisions will be in training. If war develops we will immediately complete the mobilization, utilizing public buildings and other civilian resources which will become available. The Philippine Army will have its camps vacated by January 1 and will then call its regular quota of trainees and continue its normal development, utilizing its own funds. I shall organize a Theatre of Operations, utilizing other partially trained manpower to provide essential units and installations.

The strategic plan contemplates the use of seven Philippine Army divisions and the U.S. Army division on Luzon, organized into a North Luzon Force, a South Luzon Force and a General Reserve. Three divisions will be employed in the southern islands, two in the Visayans and one in Mindanao, under a single command designated the Visayan-Mindanao Force. This is deemed necessary to defend against marauding raids and to prevent seizure of landing fields for operations against Luzon. The location of superior enemy air forces in these islands would render the situation in Luzon most acute. You will recall your recent approval of the coast defense installations was to protect and to deny to the enemy these rear areas of Luzon.[4]

MacArthur drove home this point during September 1941. He was offered a signal officer, whom he rejected with a lecture.

I believe you have misunderstood purpose and duties of officer requested. I am organizing a theatre of operations comprising troops and installations comparable to an army. The officer desired is to be chief signal officer of army on my staff charged with signal corps work pertaining to theatre of operations. It is essential that he be a graduate of highest service schools and familiar with problems from viewpoint of an army headquarters. Position comparable to CSO on staff of army commanders in the U.S. although the problem presented here is more complicated, of broader magnitude and requires more originality. Assignment calls for highest talent in your senior command.[5]

Ten days later, in connection with the appointment of a chief surgeon, he wrote:

I am organizing a theatre of operations comprising troops and installations comparable to an army. Officer designated should be graduate of highest service schools and must be familiar with problems from an army viewpoint. He will be charged with problems of organization and training of army units and coordination for military purposes of all medical installations of the Philippines.[6]

There has been a general tendency to find some relationship between the group of men who staffed the Military Mission, Headquarters USAFFE, and the ''Bataan Boys'' who traveled with MacArthur to Australia. The questionable validity of the idea builds on the obvious fact that MacArthur commanded all three groups. But only he and Sidney Huff covered the entire span of years from the opening of the Military Mission in Manila to the final collapse and surrender of Japan. Huff was never in a position of power, had no private ambitions, and was the only officer to cover the entire span of MacArthur's service in the Far East after 1936. Two original members of the Military Mission left in 1938.

Sutherland came to the mission in 1938, and Richard Marshall joined a year later.

The Military Mission drew on officers otherwise assigned to Headquarters Philippine Department, which was the official representative of the U.S. Army in the Philippines. Some of these officers later came into USAFFE and some were evacuated with MacArthur, but not all. Some officers were new additions drawn into USAFFE from the United States.

The first member of USAFFE was, of course, Major General Douglas MacArthur.[7] General Order No. 1 announced the formation of the new organization and MacArthur's acceptance of command. Before the month was out, MacArthur had the third star of lieutenant general. A day later General Order No. 2 announced the appointment of Colonel Carl Seals as adjutant general and Lieutenant Colonel Richard Sutherland as chief of staff.

LeGrande Diller was appointed aide-de-camp to MacArthur on August 1, 1941. Diller's appointment was a boundary marker in the unspecified barrier that separated MacArthur's sphere of authority from Sutherland's. The appointment fell in a gray area of uncertainty. Diller had been assigned to the staff of the Philippine Division under Jonathan Wainwright. One afternoon he happened to play a round of golf with Sutherland. Sutherland suddenly remarked that the Old Man needed an aide; Diller seemed to have the proper qualifications. Diller, a captain at the time, was agreeable. Sutherland took the papers to MacArthur, saying that he had just found a new aide for him. MacArthur grumbled that he usually chose his own personal aides. Nevertheless, MacArthur read Diller's file and agreed to the appointment. Diller is certain that Sutherland appointed Morhouse aide in 1941 and Egeberg in 1944. I accept Diller's judgment, although Egeberg does not.

Toward the end of August, General Order No. 8 announced full staff appointments. Sutherland, now a brigadier general, was assigned as chief of staff. The deputy chief of staff was Lieutenant Colonel Richard Marshall. Lieutenant Colonels William Marquat, Constant Irwin, and Lewis Beebe were assigned as G–1, G–3, and G–4 respectively. Lieutenant Colonel Hugh Casey joined as engineer officer, Colonel Spencer Akin as signal officer, Colonel Charles Stivers as G–1 (with the reassignment of Marquat as antiaircraft officer), and Lieutenant Colonels Joseph Sherr as Akin's assistant and Charles Willoughby as G–2. Sidney Huff was commissioned lieutenant colonel and appointed aide-de-camp in December. Lieutenant Colonel Francis Wilson was appointed aide to MacArthur in late November and was assigned as Sutherland's assistant. I arrived in Manila on October 24 and was assigned as stenographer to Sutherland and MacArthur.[8] By that time the Headquarters USAFFE staff had grown to 18 officers. Enlisted men were detached from Headquarters Philippine Department for staff duty and housekeeping functions at USAFFE. During December the enlisted men were attached to Headquarters USAFFE with more officers. By the end of the year Headquarters USAFFE comprised 180 officers and men.[9]

The two signal officers did not seem to have any prior connection with the others except in that general sense in which officers in those days of scarcity could very well know and be relatively familiar with all of their colleagues. There were not very many of them in active service. Akin apparently was not known by either MacArthur or Sutherland prior to his arrival in Manila, nor was Sherr. The Signal Corps constituted a specialized branch of the service from which it was difficult to move into the mainstream of command and staff assignments. Akin was aware of this limitation but was never able to overcome it.[10]

Of the entire group Carl Seals was the apparent senior, although his position in the pecking order of things did not indicate it. His appointment was contained in General Order No. 2 with that of Sutherland. Sutherland had a lower rank, but his assignment as chief of staff gave him priority in the ordering of the assignments. Seals was a relatively older man, although this judgment must be tempered by the fact that Sutherland was 48 and Marshall was even younger. My memory would have placed Seals as more nearly MacArthur's equal in age, but a very young man is a poor judge even of relative ages. (In this case my memory was correct and was confirmed by the facts.) Seals was portly, dignified, with a sober but not forbidding mien, almost gentle in discourse. He was the first officer I saw when I entered Headquarters USAFFE, seated at a small table at the top of the stairs as one came into the "casa" that housed MacArthur's staff. He seemed to have some special relationship with MacArthur, but I never learned what it was. There seemed to be no obvious sign of this relationship that I can recall, just an air of separation from those officers who were younger and who seemed to be involved in the activities of the command. He was rather more relaxed with MacArthur than the others. Seals seemed to float on the periphery, respected but not part of the activity. Yet his presence pervades the personal file that remains as MacArthur's record of the USAFFE period.

Seals took me to Sutherland (about whom a great deal will be said elsewhere). I met a man who was just entering his professional maturity. Poised and commanding, he dominated. He was not particularly severe or forbidding, but he exuded an air of complete self-control and self-discipline that quelled any tendency to relax into easy familiarity. I never stepped across the invisible line that Sutherland's demeanor drew around him, barring any access to the real man who lay behind it. I suspect that only a few of his colleagues knew him at all.

Richard Marshall was the next officer I met. He was the third man in MacArthur's hierarchy, falling easily into place behind Sutherland and the Old Man himself. Physically he was a smaller man than Sutherland, tending to stockiness and even bordering on rotundity. He had a handsome, boyish face that was round and plump, almost swarthy, with a heavy beard. Long before the end of the day he was no longer clean shaven. Marshall's eyes were sleepy, which gave him a languorous appearance. His voice frequently matched his appearance, losing the crisp, sharp edge of command and seeming to fall into conversational drowsiness. Unlike Sutherland he had an air of open affability and approachability. There was no affectation in his behavior and no mannerism.

Marshall exuded simple common sense and was calm and unflappable in any situation. Nothing seemed to shatter his self-assurance. His mouth broke easily into a smile. He was quick to find humor and to express it.

Nevertheless, Marshall had a will of iron that matched Sutherland's. He was independent even in acquiescence. When he yielded to the judgment or command of another, he did so without losing his air of self-determination and autonomy. He had come into his maturity as a quartermaster, a service he had mastered. He was an outstanding staff officer and exercised command easily and effectively. Unlike Sutherland, Marshall could be liked. He was not openly ambitious. He moved in and up the hierarchical structure, rising to authority when his turn came but apparently not grasping for it. He was a sea anchor in troubled waters, stabilizing a situation even when he did not command it.

Of all the others at One Calle Victoria, the one I remember best is "Billy" Marquat. Unlike the others, he was unmilitary, uninhibited, not given to self-discipline or even self-control. I have no idea what his background had been prior to his involvement with the MacArthur command. He was a unique element in that milieu. All seemed to respect him. Like Marshall, Marquat was shorter than Sutherland, mature of build but certainly not stocky. He enjoyed fine food but was never as rotund as Marshall. He wore a trim, dark mustache but it tended to be slightly irregular. Marquat's uniform never fell as neatly into place as Sutherland's. His bearing seemed to bend toward a slouch. He never exuded an air of command. Only the insignia of rank and assignment gave evidence of his stature. Without them he would have fit quite well into any sergeants' drinking party. He was loud, irreverent, and profane, and wandered like the bull in the china shop through the otherwise sober, disciplined round of headquarters life. He served MacArthur punctually, effectively, and predictably in many assignments through the war and the occupation of Japan.

Francis Wilson came to the headquarters very close to the outbreak of hostilities. He had a subordinate role, serving as Sutherland's assistant, more than a chief clerk but never with a command of his own until relatively late in the war. He was a thin man with an elegantly trimmed mustache. He was quiet in demeanor, seeming to endeavor to avoid conflict but not stooping to ingratiation. His assignment required more "yes, sirs" than "no, sirs," and he had very little opportunity to assert himself. When he found the opportunity, he did not hesitate to take advantage of it, dressing down others with ferocity. He was essentially a gentle man in a violent calling. I respected him and looked upon him as a father figure.

I spent 60 days at One Calle Victoria. The center of my existence was Sutherland. Occasionally I did some work for Marshall. I did not talk with Seals very often. Marquat I remember because he was a unique personality in that milieu. I occasionally encountered Huff and Diller. I had half a dozen meetings with MacArthur during this period, some of which have been described elsewhere. I saw Master Sergeant Turner every day, but we were not friends for the obvious reason of age. All of the others were shadows. I did not understand the structure of the headquarters, nor did I know the function of any staff section save Marquat's, and that only because I knew his clerk. I barely understood the gradations of rank and what they implied.

One thing I understood very well. I had been assigned to ''one of the biggest men in the U.S. Army'' and to his chief of staff. I had fallen into a very fortunate assignment, and Sutherland had set a match to smoldering ambition. I had come to the Philippines to find glory, and I began to realize that most likely I would find it. Like MacArthur, but not like Sutherland, I felt a comfortable relationship with a power greater than MacArthur to whom I had innocently entrusted my destiny. Like the young recruits of Cromwell's regiment, I had a Puritan's arrogant disregard for the vanities of life and an arrogant disdain of death and destruction. At the time it stood me in good stead.

9

Land Forces

It was obvious from the beginning that an invasion of the Philippines could not be repulsed by the U.S. contingent garrisoned in the Philippines. When I arrived in October 1941, this garrison consisted of some 31,000 army troops. This small force included 2,500 U.S. officers and some 30,000 enlisted personnel. Fewer than 2,000 of the enlisted troops were American. The remainder were Filipinos. Even as late as October 1941 the War Department felt that it had stretched reality to the limit by offering to send one U.S. division to the Philippines. The relief convoy that left Hawaii at the outbreak of war included only two divisions. These two would be the only U.S. infantry divisions available to MacArthur after his arrival in Australia and, plead as he might, he could get no more for a year. A far greater force than this would be needed to carry out even the objective of "Orange," which assigned only a limited temporary holding action around the harbor defenses of Manila Bay.

The only source of manpower was the Filipinos themselves; specifically those Filipino young men who had come up through Philippine Army training camps organized by MacArthur's Military Mission in the past four years. Whether the Military Mission had been successful or not, it had set in place the groundwork for a rapid, massive mobilization of Filipino manpower.

A directive issued by Roosevelt on July 26, 1941, called the armed forces of the Commonwealth of the Philippines to active duty. The War Department authorized $10 million to initiate a training program. Two days later MacArthur received a radio message from the War Department that set realistic boundaries to his enthusiasm. He must stay within the limits prescribed by the Philippine Defense Project of 1940. Only the equipment authorized by that project would be made available to him. He would be given 400 reserve officers for training purposes. MacArthur asked two days later that the reserve officers be selected from men who could meet the unique conditions required in the training of

Map 2
Disposition of USAFFE, December 8, 1941

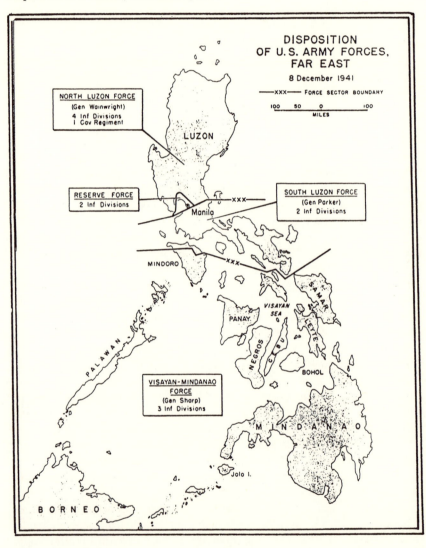

Source: U.S. Army.

Filipino soldiers. They should have had actual duty with regular army combat troops and should be able to operate with complete self-assurance.[1]

Press Release No. 1 of USAFFE spelled out the general plan for mobilization of the Philippine Army. Unless war came, the normal training activities of the Philippine Army would not be interfered with. Only the reserve divisions would be called into active service. Training camps would be constructed to house the reserves. Philippine Army units would retain their own uniforms, pay scale, promotion list, rations, and code of military law. The training would be under the direct supervision of U.S. Army officers.[2]

President Quezon was notified which units were to be mobilized by September 1. Initially one regiment would be called up in each of the ten military districts.[3] These cadres would provide the basis for a later call-up of the entire division. An order was issued to the Philippine Department to prepare for training. U.S. officers and enlisted men were to be made available. Training would proceed according to current War Department instructions. Insofar as possible, Filipino officers would command Filipino units, although in initial stages U.S. officers would be assigned where Filipino officers were not available. It was also announced that eventually three commands would be established: North Luzon Force, South Luzon Force, and Visayan-Mindanao Force.[4]

Nine boards were set up by a separate order to select training camp sites throughout the Philippines. It was anticipated that by January 1, 1942, sufficient housing would be available to accommodate the 75,000 men of the ten divisions that would be called up before that date. Administrative, supply, and financial arrangements were set out. The call-up order was issued on August 19, and on September 1 the first Filipino elements of the USAFFE ground forces arrived at the training camps.[5]

On the last day of August, MacArthur wrote a personal letter to George Marshall to inform him of the status of affairs in the USAFFE training program. He also pointed out certain problems with respect to the only regular U.S. division in the Philippines.

I was disappointed in my inspections of the Philippine Division. Its training is adequate up to the battalion echelon, but little has been accomplished beyond that point. This is not due to any fault or lack of efficiency in the personnel which is of the finest. It is the logical result of its task training for the execution of a specialized mission in which it, acting alone, had to cover an enormous front. The 31st Infantry, for instance, with completely inadequate training facilities in Manila, has never operated as a unified whole for combat training; infantry and artillery are in separate garrisons and have not trained together; training for cooperative missions between air and ground troops has been very limited; a division Command Post Exercise last week, said to be the first one in several years, showed the most glaring deficiencies. This division must be the only one in the Army that is not up to strength and its training cannot possibly compare with any of the Regular divisions in the United States. I consider it at present incapable of acceptable offensive operation as a division. Its smaller components, however, are satisfactory, and it will respond very rapidly to a modern training program. I shall transmit very soon my plans and recommendations for its reorganization and regrouping for efficient training with a view to developing it into an effective unit of the General Reserve, prepared for offensive combat.[6]

A letter of September 7 to the commander of the Philippine Department pointed out specific problems and gave MacArthur's views on the general principles to be observed in training.

The efficient execution of the training program requires preliminary planning and long hours of preparation after the schedule of the day's active work is completed; it requires preparation as thorough as that of a student studying his lessons for the morrow. Every officer and every non-commissioned officer should know before he beds down for the night the exact program for the next day and be prepared to execute it.

An essential feature of this training program is the preparation of Philippine officers and non-commissioned officers to assume authoritative roles. They must be trained in their duties, instructed in leadership and be taught how to train their men. To the maximum extent possible American officers should instruct through Filipino leaders, operating in such a way that they not only teach the leaders, but also increase their self-assurance and build up the confidence of the soldiers in their own officers and non-commissioned officers. No instructions should be given directly by the United States Army personnel when Philippine Army officers or non-commissioned officers are competent to do it. The objective is to produce effective fighting units, officered by Filipinos.

In my inspections to date I have found large groups of trainees and their officers standing and sitting around doing nothing. In at least one large group of hundreds of officers and men there was a complete lack of decisiveness in instructional procedure. Some American officers were practically ignorant of what was going on, and a pall of inactivity was evident. U.S. Army officers must so organize their instruction that they teach, by example, correct procedure and methods.

Above all, a policy of suppression and repression must be avoided. These men must be instructed from the beginning in the broader aspects of attack and defense. Lectures should be given on an attack by a battalion or larger unit, for example, explaining the various phases and showing how the component elements cooperate to drive the attack home—lectures given not only once but many times, until the doctrine begins to sink into their minds. Only in this way will they understand the reasons for the individual duties which they are required to learn and perform. Modern warfare requires the individual soldier to have a complete comprehension of the mechanism of the modern battle. I repeat, do not suppress or repress; the broader the perspective, the more rapid will be the absorption of detailed instruction.[7]

A general service school was established to provide a six-week course of instruction for the officers who would soon arrive from the United States to direct the training of the Filipino units. There would be 10 division commanders, 100 divisional staff officers, 40 regimental commanders, and 120 battalion commanders. As officers arrived from the States, they were assigned to the school as participants and directors. Colonel Clyde Selleck, for whom I had worked on the *Tasker Bliss*, was one of these officers.

MacArthur had high hopes for this burgeoning Filipino Army, which in the course of time would be commanded entirely by Filipinos. He remembered the ferocity of Aguinaldo's insurrection army, and hoped that young men of the 1940s could be inspired to emulate the enthusiasm of their grandfathers.

Emilio Aguinaldo, who was just a few years older than MacArthur and who was still alive, watched with unrestrained irony. While Quezon, Osmeña, and the others tied their fortunes to the United States, this wily survivor stood in the shadows, keeping alive in near solitude the spark of rebellion and the desire for independence. As long as he did not become involved in outright rebellion, he could not be touched. Even in the years that followed, he was held by the Americans to lie beyond the reach of retribution for whatever he might do. No one was really sure how much influence this patriot still had with his countrymen, and it is a mark of Aguinaldo's unusual power for survival that no one cared to find out. He simply sat in the shadows, occasionally asserting that the Americans should go home and let the Filipinos rule themselves. He was a powerfully powerless man who did not share MacArthur's dream. Aguinaldo was a realist. He could read the true temper of the times and could measure the willingness of the generation of the 1940s to shoulder the burden carried by the generation of 1898. He must have smiled bitterly as he watched the young recruits march away to their training camps.[8]

The U.S. officers who arrived regularly on army transports to take command of these Filipino boys may have brought an equally bitter smile. They were reserve officers of an age at which men have acquired sufficient substance to know that they have something to lose. Perhaps some, probably none, had volunteered for the assignment. Some certainly must have looked with regret at comparable assignments with U.S. troops in the United States. Certainly none shared MacArthur's infatuation with this exotic world for which they had no proper acculturation. On the trip across the Pacific, Selleck could count the troops down in the holds as "his boys." It is not likely that he had the same feeling for the Filipino recruits who were forced into his command. It was a strange milieu in which officers and men were equally unwilling companions in an adventure not of their liking.

There are conflicting reports of the Filipino soldier. MacArthur's were predictably favorable; others were not. MacArthur looked at the matter from a high vantage point. The others had to face the day-to-day grind of converting raw, unwilling recruits into soldiers and were subject to the irritating frictions that were an inevitable part of their day's work. The others did not identify with the cause of Filipino self-realization. They were outsiders. Yet there are reports that register a positive reaction to a difficult situation. The only evaluations available were made after the war, by officers who had suffered in prisoner of war camps, hating MacArthur and usually his Filipino troops with almost equal passion. They could not accept the fact that they had been abandoned long before the Japanese came ashore.[9]

The Filipino reserves were not the equivalent of Aguinaldo's insurrection force. In Aguinaldo's force emotional commitment to the cause of social justice had fired the Filipino peasants who provided the manpower and united them with the mestizos who led a common endeavor. By 1940 a different social environment existed. There was no commonly perceived cause, no voluntary commitment, no compelling vision of social justice. All of this had been replaced by a draft of young men who would be led by U.S. officers against their fellow Asians.

There were many difficulties. Reservists declined to accept active duty assignments. Trainees organized strikes and demonstrations against officers, as well as terrorist activities in the provinces. Individual soldiers ran amok while in uniform. There were difficulties of language. Company-grade officers were Filipinos, but they frequently could not speak directly with their troops because of differences of dialect. The problem was even more serious for field-grade officers and general officers, who spoke only English. Moreover, inadequate supplies of weapons, munitions, and facilities prevented proper training. Many of the recruits and reservists called up for active duty did not fire a rifle in training. There was no transport nor communications equipment.

There were more positive reports that Filipino recruits were eager to learn and that discipline problems were nonexistent. In this case, as in others, different officers saw the fact differently, and it is difficult to know to what extent the reports reflected reality and to what extent they reflected the subjective orientation of the man who wrote. The record of subsequent events is complicated by such conflicts.

The Filipinos certainly were not the equivalent of the Japanese who would later meet them in battle. Neither were the U.S. officers and troops. No one was prepared psychologically to match the brutal ferocity of the Japanese, which was inculcated and unrelentingly displayed and enforced by the officers. Japanese generals were not given to agonizing over the inequities forced upon them by unkind fate. They were merciless with subordinates, and the death penalty for infraction of minor rules or insubordination was inflicted frequently enough to serve as a constant reminder that duty, however painful, was preferable to the consequences of unwillingness to obey. As for the officers, suicide was accepted as the only atonement for even insignificant errors of behavior or judgment, or for simple bad luck for which they could not reasonably be held at fault.

Under "Orange" only two infantry regiments would have been available for combat, or perhaps three if the marine regiment at Shanghai had been transferred back to Manila. Such a force could not have defended even Bataan. The major stand would have been made on Corregidor.

MacArthur's adaptation of "Orange" took into account the 100,000 Filipino soldiers who were scattered throughout Luzon. They were in good position to cover the only beaches that were suitable for the landing of hostile forces. There were only three of these on Luzon. Concentration of these forces on Bataan would require a series of marches from peripheral camps. The only significant change made by MacArthur was the decision to attempt to hold the beaches. This was not a radical concept. Even in December it might have been successful.

MacArthur's plan anticipated that only Luzon and the Visayas would be held. Mindanao was thought to be untenable. Coast artillery was emplaced to block the major entrances to the central islands. Lewis Brereton was ordered to build airfields in the Visayas. As it turned out, engineering considerations and pressure of time required that the bases be built on Mindanao, and to that extent MacArthur's plan was distorted to conform to practical reality.

At any rate, in November 1941 MacArthur had ordered construction of air bases outside the range of Japanese land-based bombers and that heavy bombers be moved away from Clark Field. During that month the infantry divisions on Luzon were dispersed to cover the beaches but with access to lines of withdrawal that would take them into Bataan. If they could not hold at the beaches, a modified version of "Orange" could be utilized with a greatly expanded defensive operation based on Bataan. If this option was needed, Corregidor, not Bataan, still would be the more important defensive bastion. It was believed, correctly, that the Bataan defenses could hold no longer than two or three months. Corregidor would hold perhaps a month or two longer.

10

My Air Force

The development of "MacArthur's Air Force" involved three separate but interrelated phases. The central focus, of course, was the expansion of the air force in the Philippines as both a defensive and an offensive weapon against Japan. This involved the reorganization of the Philippine Department Air Force as an integral element of USAFFE, integration of the Philippine Army Air Corps into USAFFE, and the development of new airfields to accommodate new planes that were projected for allocation in the very immediate future. A second aspect of the process was the preparation of a line of bases that could be used in ferrying heavy bombers from the United States to the forward bases in the Philippines and fighters from Australia to the Philippines. The third aspect was the synchronization of air forces of the four major allied powers in the Southwest Pacific—Australia, Britain, the Netherlands, and the United States—which would move within a common network of air bases to meet the Japanese wherever they might attack.

The integration of the Philippine Army Air Corps into USAFFE, in itself, did not contribute very much quantitatively to the force, the bulk of which would necessarily be American, in marked contrast with the land forces, where the relative proportions of Filipino and U.S. forces would be reversed. Nevertheless, MacArthur considered the integration of the two forces to be imperative.

Some days after MacArthur assumed command of USAFFE, he announced the formation of Air Force, U.S. Army Forces in the Far East, with Brigadier General Henry Clagett as commanding general. President Quezon had been notified by letter on August 1 that the Philippine Army Air Corps would be called into USAFFE, and the order was issued several days later. Available to Clagett's new command were 31 bombers and 100 fighters plus an assortment of noncombat planes. Except for 31 P–40s the planes were obsolete and unfit for combat. They were only the present reality, however. There was the promise of future additions that would make MacArthur's new air force one of the most powerful in the Far East. Nine B–17 heavy bombers were promised for immediate delivery, and by the end of the month the flight had arrived in the Philippines. This was merely the first installment.[1]

Clagett forwarded to MacArthur a study on air force requirements.[2] Although there is no record of a response by MacArthur, his eyes must have sparkled with excitement and approbation. The numbers were grand enough to match his greatest hopes. At the same time the report spelled out problems involved in providing an adequate air defense for the Philippines that should have caused serious minds no little concern. Clagett's report estimated that the Japanese had 1,000 bombers and 1,000 fighters (both land- and carrier-based), and 37 fields from which they could operate. The report identified 61 land target areas in Japan and 800 Japanese vessels as potential objectives for USAFFE bombers and fighters. It projected the possibility that Japan would strike either in a simultaneous attack or in successive waves at USAFFE fields with carrier-based fighter support.

Clagett estimated that he would need 270 heavy bombers, 162 light bombers, and 486 fighters to destroy all Japanese targets. These numbers reflected planes actually operational. In 1942, at any given time about one-fourth of the planes available in the area were operational. To put the specified planes in the air simultaneously and to keep them there, on the basis of experience of the sub-sequent years of action, USAFFE would have required at least three times the numbers stated: almost 1,000 heavy bombers, 500 light bombers, and 1,500 fighters. Clagett did not address this particular problem. He probably felt that he would be fortunate to see a small fraction of that figure.

Planes were only part of the package. Trained crews would have to be pro-vided. Also needed were 56 airfields, 14 million gallons of gasoline, 7,000 tons of bombs, and 1 billion rounds of machine-gun ammunition. Clagett noted, parenthetically, that antiaircraft artillery, searchlights, and balloons had not been considered in his estimate. In addition there must be weather squadrons, air warning service units, and, most of all, air base groups with maintenance and supply squadrons. He must have 50,000 officers and men. To get the project started, he would need $83 million for airfield construction. There is no record of the disposition of this report.

Clagett's report has been cited in detail to clarify and to dramatize the great discrepancy between what was needed and what eventually would be made available. The final reduction of Japan required far more than Clagett could visualize, and certainly more than he would have dared propose. An air force requires more than planes and their crews. It requires a vast array of ground-based installations and support facilities. Without them, planes are wasted in operations and on the ground between missions.

When the air force made its final assault on Japan during the spring of 1945, it had three conventional air forces—the Fifth, Seventh, and Thirteenth—each of which was larger than the one requested by Clagett plus two strategic bomber (B–29) air forces—the Twentieth and the Twenty-first. In addition, the navy had thousands of carrier aircraft. It is not certain that these alone could have ended the war even in 1945.

Two days before Clagett submitted his recommendation, George Marshall had radioed MacArthur that the War Department proposed to supply more planes as soon as airfields became available.[3] He added that $2.2 million had been allocated for airfield construction. Marshall promised that planes would be provided to give MacArthur one heavy bomber group, one light bomber group, and one fighter group, all of which was about 10 percent of what Clagett asked for. The gap between what was needed and asked for and what could be expected was obvious.

A radiogram from Washington in late September itemized the aircraft re-inforcements that could be expected by USAFFE in the coming 12 months: 26 B–17s would depart from the United States in October, and 35 more in January 1942; 52 light bombers and 50 P–40s would move in November and December; 35 B–24 heavy bombers would be sent in January 1942. More would be provided as soon as available; 170 heavy bombers, 86 light bombers, and 195 fighters would move forward between April and October 1942.[4]

During the next 30 days two heavy bomber squadrons flew from the United States to the Philippines, and the development of the USAFFE air force began. Heavy bombers were easy to move. They could fly 2,000 miles on a one-way trip without refueling, and although the Pacific was broad, its expanse was punctuated conveniently with small knobs or slivers of coral beach that could be converted into serviceable landing fields, some with very little space to spare. From Hawaii there were two general approaches to Clark Field. The northern route ran directly west: more than 2,000 miles to Wake, 1,500 miles to Guam, and 1,600 miles more to Clark Field. All of these bases were in the possession and control of the United States, which eliminated any necessity for international agreement. Moreover, it was the most direct and shortest route. However, it was vulnerable to Japanese interference. Guam was especially close to Japanese naval and air bases in the Marianas.

An alternate route ran southwest to Fiji or New Caledonia and then back northwest through New Guinea to Clark Field. An even more circuitous one ran from New Caledonia across northern Australia to the Philippines. For the next three months the routes were surveyed and developed.

Almost casually the Pacific was divided into two major areas of responsibility. It was necessary to define the line at which command of ferried aircraft would pass from the air force commander in Hawaii to MacArthur. At first the transfer point was designated as Darwin, Australia. Later, Rabaul was named as the terminal point of a line that ran northwest through the Solomons. There is no evidence of friction or dispute, all parties concurring in a decision that seemed obvious and necessary. Although it was not seen as such, the eastern and north-eastern boundaries of MacArthur's future authority had been defined.

The bombers that flew the Pacific ferry route from Hawaii through Fiji and New Caledonia to Australia, and then north to Del Monte Field in Mindanao and Clark Field in Luzon, were destined to move back along that route to Australia, then through the Netherland East Indies to Singapore. A network of air bases fanned out through Australia. To the northeast of Australia the network spread to Port Moresby, Lae, and Rabaul in New Guinea. To the northwest the fields traced a line across the Netherland East Indies to Singapore and the airfields in Malaya. Fields were built or expanded to meet the needs of the B–17s that were beginning to move across the Pacific. A second line of support was developed through Africa and India to Singapore.

A civilian engineer surveyed the Southwest Pacific to locate appropriate areas for airfields and organized their construction. Oil, bombs, and ammunition were moved to the key points in the vast network. The British, Australian, and Dutch governments readily gave their assent to the project, which had been designed for mutual defense against the Japanese threat.

By the time I received my first promotion in December 1941, I had typed most of the place-names that would occupy our attention for the remainder of the war. They were mere labels to me. I had no understanding of spatial significance or strategic importance. Nor did I have any understanding of the events that had made all the typing necessary. I had absolutely no thought of what the future might hold.

All planners were committed to the premise that the Japanese had unmistakable superiority in naval forces but were vulnerable with respect to air forces. It was felt that if the United States and Britain could mass greatly superior air forces in the Singapore area, they could drive the Japanese out of the skies by sheer attrition and then proceed to the destruction of the Japanese fleet. The U.S. Pacific Fleet and the British Far Eastern Fleet would unite under the cover of land-based planes and drive back any Japanese attack. Roosevelt and Churchill were both "naval persons." The Pacific was a naval theater of operations in which ground forces would have only a peripheral role. U.S. infantry would hold Manila Bay, and the British infantry would hold Singapore. The naval forces would fight the significant battles.[5]

In September it was decided in Washington that the USAFFE air force required a new commander. As usual in such situations, MacArthur was advised of the proposed change and was given a list of names from which he could choose. He selected Major General Lewis Brereton, and the arrangements were made for his assumption of command in the Philippines.

Brereton arrived in Manila on November 4. He was met by Clagett and his staff. He telephoned MacArthur and was told to come immediately to the Manila Hotel. He was given a cordial welcome. He was a newcomer and was not well known to MacArthur. MacArthur was wrapped in his perennial dressing gown. Brereton passed it off casually: "I apparently had fished him out of his bath inasmuch as he came out in his dressing gown."[6] MacArthur was enthusiastic. He slapped Brereton on the back, threw an arm over his shoulder, and walked him to a chair. "Well, Lewis, I have been waiting for you. I knew you were coming and I am damned glad to see you. You have been the subject of considerable conversation between myself, George Marshall and Hap Arnold. What have you brought for me?''

Brereton had brought secret messages from Marshall as well as a personal notice that reinforcements were on their way to the Philippines. It is noteworthy that the sealed briefcase that contained Marshall's letter went directly to Sutherland at One Calle Victoria.

Brereton was told to report to Calle Victoria the next morning. MacArthur met Brereton and Sutherland in his office. He read the message from Marshall and exploded with enthusiasm.

He acted like a small boy who has been told that he is going to get a holiday from school. He jumped up from his desk and threw his arms around me and said, "Lewis, you are just as welcome as the flowers in May." He then turned to his Chief of Staff and said, "Dick, they are going to give us everything we have asked for." After discussing with Sutherland the contents of the letters, he then gave me the most concise and clear-cut estimate of the situation that I had yet received. In his opinion, which was the same as that of most informed men, it seemed likely that nothing would happen before 1 April 1942.

...MacArthur is an extremely sensitive man, and if he weren't so coldly logical I would think that he was intuitive.

I noticed again one of General MacArthur's traits: he cannot talk sitting down. It seems to me that the more clearly he enunciates his ideas, the more vigorous his walking becomes. He is one of the most beautiful talkers I have ever heard and, while his manner might be considered a bit on the theatrical side, it is just part of his personality and an expression of his character. There is never any doubt as to what he means and what he wants.

Another impressive characteristic is General MacArthur's immaculate appearance. He is one of the best-dressed soldiers in the world. Even in the hot tropical climate of Manila, where he wore cotton shirts and trousers which for most people became wet and wilted in an hour, I have never seen him looking otherwise than as if he had just put on a fresh uniform.[7]

What MacArthur had asked for was a complete revision of the war plans for the Philippines. "Orange" did not reflect current conditions. It had anticipated a limited temporary defense of the harbor and Manila Bay. It presumed very limited forces, no air force or navy, and a very small contingent of ground forces. The organization of USAFFE, the call-up of the Philippine Army units, and the arrival of the B–17s and P–40s created a new situation and a need for revision of plans.

"Orange Three" was the third revision of the army plan for the defense of the Philippines against an attack by Japan. The first edition was prepared in the early 1920s. In those days a second Filipino insurrection seemed to be a more likely occurrence than an attack by the Japanese. Corregidor was conceived of as a final refuge for the high commissioner. Bataan would be held by army forces as a defensive screen. Corregidor would be held by the harbor defenses that were essentially coast artillery units. It was not an unrealistic concept. The artillery on Corregidor could easily hold off the greatest naval forces in the world. In those days air power was not a significant factor.

By the mid 1930s, when the second edition of "Orange" was approved, affairs had changed radically. The fear of a Filipino insurrection still persisted, but Japan was now a major threat with an obvious intention to dominate the South China Sea and the western Pacific. Its navy was the greatest force in the Pacific, and it had a modern air force. Japan had moved into Manchuria and would soon move into China.

Under the new circumstances, comparing costs and benefits, reasonable minds even in the military began to feel that there was little in the Philippines to justify a relatively great expenditure on defense. The debate of the late 1930s hinged on the behavior of a rational attacker. MacArthur, as military adviser, held that he could organize a defensive apparatus that would cause a rational aggressor to turn aside. By this time air power was a critical element in the game, even more critical than traditional sea power. MacArthur, of course, implied that the force must be in place—a trained, equipped, coordinated force. The cost of such a deterrent, while apparently great in current terms, would be far less than the alternative cost of fighting a long war to recover what had been lost by default. The answer was to leave the Philippines before a test could be made. But the same public opinion that would not permit spending for defense would not tolerate any idea of abandonment. This ambiguity defined the structure of the Pacific war.

By July 1941, when U.S. inaction had induced the Japanese to commit themselves more and more deeply in Asia, the idea of a rational aggressor was no longer realistic. The Japanese had made a commitment from which they could not easily withdraw. Highly charged emotional factors now outweighed rational factors of benefit and cost. Yet, at this time, half a decade too late, Roosevelt decided to draw a line. It was not a deterrent but a challenge that could not be ignored.

The new policy implied that the Japanese could be bluffed out of the game by a threat of reinforcement of the Philippines. The official position taken in Washington in July, that "the Japanese will not move before April 1942," made the bluff seem realistic. But that date ran contrary to all reason. It rested on the assumption that a fully equipped enemy that had been involved in combat for a decade would wait until the next opponent had established a firm defense. Nevertheless, the policy was determined and must be implemented. MacArthur proceeded with enthusiasm and energy to overcome the time disadvantage. He set aside the concept of a static defense of Bataan and Corregidor. He requested that a new plan be developed for the defense of the entire archipelago. It should anticipate an aggressive defense to drive back a Japanese assault force, preferably before it could consolidate a position on the beach. Forces currently scheduled for the Philippines should be sufficient.[8]

Time would be critical. The various elements of the defense could not be in place before April 1942. All plans were to be based on the assumption that the

Japanese would not move before that date. MacArthur must have prayed to his Gods that they would not. If the Japanese did move before April, all bets were off and their assistance would be needed urgently.

Brereton came with a promise of two groups of heavy bombers, two groups of fighters, one group of light bombers, and related support aircraft. Construction of airfields began immediately, especially in the southern islands, to house the new planes. MacArthur wanted fields in the Visayan Islands, but terrain prevented rapid development there. A complex was rushed to completion at Del Monte in Northern Mindanao, where full-service runways could be built in two weeks with hand labor.[9]

Brereton later wrote:

I told General MacArthur that I wanted a week to inspect the installations and, as various conditions come to light that need attention, I would like to make recommendations and get construction under way immediately. It was agreed that I would get together with General MacArthur's Chief of Staff, G–4, Quartermaster, and Engineer, and work out a continuing construction program.

"Okay, you and Dick [General Sutherland] go to work, and let me know if there are any difficulties," General MacArthur said.[10]

Brereton flew off to Australia to reconnoiter the ferry routes and to establish contacts with the Dutch, British, and Australians. "I had unlimited authority from General MacArthur to obligate funds and initiate action."[11]

MacArthur reported to George Marshall:

Brereton has taken hold in an excellent manner. He has just returned from Australia where I sent him to make the necessary contacts with the R.A.A.F. and other authorities in order to complete plans and expedite action on the ferry route. I am sending him immediately on a similar mission to the N.E.I.[12]

11

MacArthur's Navy

Admiral Thomas G. Hart was not comfortable with MacArthur though they were acquaintances of long standing. Hart had been a close friend of MacArthur's older brother and had known MacArthur long enough to be at perfect ease. But MacArthur was not easy to be with. He was always "apart," never one of any group, even as a young officer. While others congregated in a pride of young lions, MacArthur prowled alone on the edge of the pack, pacing nervously or lounging in detached isolation. He could never join the free and easy banter of leisure. Others joked and laughed, not intending to be taken too seriously, and therefore unafraid to play the fool. MacArthur simply could not join in such conversation. His personal dreams of glory suffocated any small tendency to frivolity.

Out of his blazing ego poured a steady torrent of self-centered oratory: elegant, polished, and sculpted. His voice crackled and shuddered with taut emotion, lightning flashed from his eyes as he paced nervously, leaving his visitors to listen with apprehensive dismay and discomfort. Hart had been through this and had learned that MacArthur could not change. He had tried once, ineffectually, to dampen the fire: "Douglas, can't we just relax and talk?" He had learned to sit, observe, and listen—and to avoid MacArthur as much as possible. Ordinary men are uncomfortable in the presence of the Olympian gods.[1]

Hart arrived at Manila Hotel for the necessary but not necessarily welcome visit. The Filipino orderly ushered him into the waiting room with the announcement that MacArthur would soon present himself. Hart sat looking at the floor with some impatience, felt a flurry, and looked up to see MacArthur stride through the door, still in underwear and socks, as if he were on full parade, arm and hand outstretched in greeting his old friend. To Hart's great surprise, MacArthur was wrapped in an ancient dressing gown that may have been pink or violet or dusty rose, or faded yellow, or salmon. He was dressing for dinner with High Commissioner Francis Sayre.

Hart's nervousness was increased by the fact that he was facing the former chief of staff of the U.S. Army, and he felt the inadequacy of his rank in such splendid company. He outranked MacArthur by one star, had his own fleet, had no need to hesitate, but he was cowed. How did one deal with a former chief of staff? With this former chief of staff he had no options. MacArthur would deal with him, as he had always done, leaving an officer of superior rank feeling that he had been tested, although he could not understand why. He was afraid of MacArthur, knew that MacArthur was his superior in intellect and experience, and understood very well that present rank was not the true measure of the men's relative expectations. Perhaps he felt with some discomfort that the man in the "pink gown" had placed the proper values on their respective futures.

The initial skirmish between the new commanding general, USAFFE, and the commander in chief, Asiatic Fleet, opened with an instruction issued by Admiral Hart to the commander of the Yangtze River Patrol at Shanghai. It directed that the navy shore patrol at Shanghai assume responsibility for policing the conduct of U.S. servicemen in Chinese ports, including army personnel ashore as members of leave parties. The instruction seemed reasonable enough under the circumstances of time and place. Leave parties were isolated groups of soldiers outside the territory of any army installation, beyond the careful eyes of the military police and therefore beyond the control of anyone. In the highly charged environment of Japanese-occupied China, with Japanese-U.S. relations running at high temperature, the exuberance of U.S. soldiers ashore in an exotic port was a matter for more than ordinary diplomatic concern.[2]

Reasonable or not, the instructions violated a principle that ran through the army from bottom to top and down again. The army would never be subject to navy control. Even the lowest private ashore, drunk on the streets of Shanghai, relied on this commonly accepted principle in defying the navy shore patrol, whom he detested even more bitterly than the military police (whom he hated also but only as a member of the family). An army commander who set aside the principle would have been held guilty of treasonable abandonment of his troops to outsiders.

MacArthur personally called Hart, a fact that indicates the state of agitation. MacArthur despised telephones, was never comfortable with them, and used them only when he felt that he had to—and then infrequently. There is a memorandum of the call that merits quotation in full.

Upon receipt of the Mailgram, 110730, the Commanding General, United States Army Forces in the Far East, telephoned to the Commander-in-Chief, Asiatic Fleet;

He protested the issuance of such an order without prior conference;

He protested the assumption of command by Naval authorities over officers and enlisted men of the Army;

He requested information as to the authority under which the Commander-in-Chief issued such an order;

He protested the transmission to him of any order which included him as one of the agencies to take action in pursuance thereto;

He requested a conference with the Commander-in-Chief.[3]

The memorandum passed from mouth to ear among the enlisted men at One Calle Victoria with great glee. In their behalf the Old Man had taken on the commander in chief, Asiatic Fleet, in person and had called him to account. In those days MacArthur still walked around his headquarters, sitting on the edge of the desks of his clerks, making small talk about their personal affairs and their families at home. In Shanghai, of course, the shore patrol would continue to do as it pleased with army personnel, but there was some comfort in the belief that the peaks of Olympus would roll with the thunder of protest at their unjust and illegal treatment.

MacArthur saw the matter in a much grander context. The directive, however reasonable it seemed and however trivial the impact might be, was just one more item of evidence of the intention of the navy to dominate the army in the Pacific. The commanding general, U.S. Army Forces in the Far East, wrote directly to Admiral Harold Stark, commander in chief of the U.S. Navy, an old colleague and friend, acknowledging the obvious need for cooperation between the services, asserting that such cooperation did exist, but protesting the illegal nature of the directive.[4]

Four days after MacArthur signed the letter to Stark and sent it off via Pan American Clipper, he received a long letter from the Asiatic Fleet in which Hart spelled out certain arrangements that had been agreed to upon prior to MacArthur's assumption of command of USAFFE. The arrangements provided for army assistance and support of naval operations by army reconnaissance planes and bombers. Hart suggested that the matter of cooperation should be given a formal command structure so that all efforts would be properly coordinated to achieve greatest effect. He offered to place under the control of MacArthur any navy planes that were assigned to land objectives and closed with a recommendation that any army air forces assigned to overwater missions be subject to navy control.[5]

MacArthur replied with disdain that the principles of cooperation had already been defined in 1935 when he was chief of staff by joint army-navy agreements that would certainly be observed by him when the need arose. The present disparity between air and naval forces seemed to preclude any reasonable requirement that army forces should operate under navy control.

MacArthur wrote on November 7: " . . . air force of this Command which is rapidly being built up to an initial strength of 170 bombers and 86 light bombers, with pursuit in proportion . . . a powerful army air striking force. . . . " He then pointed out the relative weakness of naval forces available:

The term "Fleet" cannot be applied to the two cruisers and the division of destroyers that comprise the combat elements of the naval command. This is especially striking when judged in comparison either with the potential enemy naval forces in the Western Pacific or with the Air Force of this command.[6]

MacArthur concluded that it would not be reasonable to assign his air forces to such a weak partner. Copies of the correspondence went to George Marshall with the warning that Hart's letter "would indicate that the navy may be seeking strategic control in this area."[7]

This must have stung Hart. He replied, expressing a desire to settle the issue directly with MacArthur, without "adding to the load which Washington is carrying." He pointed out with some sharpness that conditions had changed since the joint agreement had been reached in 1935, adding pointedly that the "date is 1941."

Hart went on to correct MacArthur's estimate of the naval forces in the Far East. "You have been informed wherein lies the main power of this command; it is not confined to 'two cruisers and a division of destroyers.' "[8]

Hart had good reason for sharp rebuttal. Long before MacArthur's new command was authorized, the navy had been involved in discussions with the British and the Dutch in an attempt to reach an agreement concerning a joint international response to any attack by Japan on any of the Western powers in Asia. It was presumed that the British Eastern Fleet and the U.S. Pacific Fleet would join in a common effort against Japan. In addition to ships, the United States would provide bombers and fighters. The British would contribute Australian and Indian ground forces. The general outlines seemed inevitable; only the details of the command arrangements required sharp definition.

Hart insisted that his letter had not contained any hidden meaning. There was no intention on the part of the navy to limit the freedom of action of army air force operations.

MacArthur's reply was written two days later. He agreed wholeheartedly that there must be cooperation and coordination, and stated that the army air force commander had been instructed

to perfect the machinery that will make possible complete and instant coordination with naval air forces. I am completely confident all necessary details can be arranged to facilitate every possible form of mutual support that will insure the successful accomplishment of our several missions.[9]

However, he held firm on the basic principle: "We are entirely in accord with one exception—the exercise of actual command over my Air Force." And there the matter stood. "My" air force will not be commanded by the navy.

By this time George Marshall had digested the letters he and Stark had received from MacArthur. He wrote to MacArthur expressing some satisfaction that "intimate liaison and cooperation and cordial relations" existed between the two services. He instructed MacArthur to support naval operations in "action not directly concerned with immediate threats against the Philippines."[10]

MacArthur's reply was adamant. He promised full cooperation for navy operations but did not yield on the broader issue:

This point has never been at issue here. The subject of discussion that was initiated by Admiral Hart was the assumption of command by the Navy over Army air units. . . . The most effective results can normally be obtained here by a coordination of mission rather than by unity of command under the Navy. As far as air units are concerned the Air Force commander is insistent in this regard.[11]

A letter from George Marshall dated December 5 acknowledged MacArthur's radiograms and informed him that coordination through cooperation rather than unity of command would be applied in joint operations in the Far East in a "very complicated command system." However, MacArthur was warned that it might be necessary to assign air force units under navy control to Singapore. In this case they would have to operate under unity of command exercised by the Asiatic Fleet. Five days later the debate had become an exercise in futility. Air force units eventually did fly to the aid of Singapore but never under navy control.[12]

Too much can be made of the record. There is no evidence of personal antagonism between the men. They knew how to read between the lines. The letters are for the record of history and do not always reveal that both parties understood and accepted certain facts that lay behind the written words. Nevertheless, the issue of command was a real one for MacArthur, and letters written in 1945 were as adamant on the subject as those written in 1941, or in 1935, for that matter.

The inability of MacArthur and Hart to work closely together did not stem from personal rivalry or even from interservice rivalry. It resulted from the fact that the two men were working under the authority of directives that moved them inevitably away from each other on increasingly divergent paths that could never meet. Out of Washington came orders to MacArthur to defend the Philippines. Out of Washington came orders to Hart to move somewhere to the south to fight with some combination of allied naval forces. The navy and the army planned for two entirely different Pacific wars, both probably convinced that either war would result in defeat. "Orange" would destroy MacArthur's army on Corregidor. The navy plan would destroy Hart in Malaya or the Netherland East Indies. Washington ordered MacArthur to stand and fight, and ordered Hart to withdraw to the south. George Marshall was prepared to order MacArthur's air force south to fly under Hart's command at precisely the same time he was assuring MacArthur and Quezon that "we will defend the Philippines."

Hart concluded on the evening before the war began that Washington was using him without keeping him fully informed. He believed that "In ordinary times such treatment as that would force me to ask for my immediate relief."[13]

MacArthur and Hart needled each other mercilessly. This was accepted style in the military in those days. They both enjoyed the dueling, especially when they won a point. All that aside, Hart believed firmly that the personal feud did not affect preparation for war. Both men were professional soldiers and would not permit themselves to be distracted from their duty by personal pique.

The sharpness of tone that characterized MacArthur's dealing with Hart is not present in dealings with the commandant of the 16th Naval District. This officer, unlike Hart, had a very close community of interest with MacArthur and the Philippine garrison, since he and his command were an integral and permanent part of it. He commanded all the fixed land installations in the environs of Manila Bay that were essential to the support and servicing of a fleet—dry docks, repair and supply installations, oil storage, medical facilities, and all the other paraphernalia of a permanent naval base. This was navy, but a dry-land navy, with no means of escape by water, bound to the land forces by contiguity of time and space. Service rivalry separated them from their army neighbors, but the rivalry was softened at least partially by the knowledge that when the chips were down, the cruisers, destroyers, and submarines would sail off, leaving the permanent shore parties to their fate.

MacArthur was inclined to consider the 16th Naval District as part of his domain and therefore treated its commandant gently and with affection, noting in his correspondence with Hart the harmony and goodwill shared by these two commands. Hart was not particularly happy at the neat seduction and abduction of his shore installation but let the matter rest, reflecting, perhaps, on the wisdom of a sailor's not being too inquisitive about the behavior of those who will inevitably be left behind. The commandant realized that unless he had more good fortune than anyone had a right to expect, he would have to hunker down in the bowels of Corregidor to die or surrender with MacArthur. He certainly was not "MacArthur's Navy," but he shared with MacArthur a deep community of interest.

MacArthur did have a navy, however, a minute sliver of a navy, in which he took great pride and which would bear him to glory. In the early days of the Military Mission he had been authorized to develop, as part of his defense structure for the Philippines, a patrol of torpedo boats that, in conjunction with the force of medium bombers, would intercept any attacking naval force. Sid Huff had been instructed to arrange for the construction of this small fleet. Although he had never seen or heard of such a craft and had never been involved in negotiations of such a magnitude, Huff set to work, inspired by MacArthur's open, unlimited expression of confidence. An order was placed with a British firm for ten small ships. Only one was completed, the needs of the British taking precedence over the needs of the Philippines. An agreement was finally reached to rescind the contract. The British made available to the Philippine government ten engines and a complete set of plans and specifications, and gave permission to build the craft locally. By that time the navy had been persuaded of the usefulness of such craft and had initiated their production in the United States. Six were sent to Manila and six others were scheduled for future delivery.

12

Civil Affairs

Six days out of Manila, *Tasker Bliss* wallowed along between the Mariana and Caroline Island groups, territory fortified heavily with Japanese naval and air bases. Manuel Quezon, president of the Commonwealth of the Philippines, was writing a letter to Franklin Roosevelt, president of the United States, still the protector and master of a not-yet-independent Filipino state. Quezon nervously looked at the map of the Pacific and realized that directly between the Philippines and its powerful protector lay a Japanese barrier. He may have guessed that the Japanese were already preparing to close the barrier tight, cutting the most direct route between U.S. reinforcements and supplies to the Philippine garrison. He may also have known that U.S. bombers no longer used this route to fly into the Philippines from Hawaii but instead were swinging in a broad arc to the south, west, and then north into Clark Field to avoid the Japanese barrier. The implication of this state of affairs was not lost upon him.

His letter moved directly to the point, without those embellishments of rhetoric and flourishes of style that Quezon could weave so skillfully:

Today's press reports seem to point strongly to the possibility of actual involvement of the United States in the war . . . the course of recent events in Japan is far from encouraging to those who would hope that there may not be armed conflict between the United States and Japan. Should this unfortunate situation arise, it is but natural to expect that the Philippines will be the scene of such a conflict.[1]

Quezon pledged his cooperation and the support of the Filipino people:

Our government and people are absolutely and wholeheartedly for you and your policies, and . . . we are casting our lot with America no matter what sacrifices such determination may entail.

Mr. President, since at a time such as this it is of the utmost importance that the Government of the Philippines should have complete understanding and cooperation with the military and naval authorities of the United States, I believe you will be pleased to know that General MacArthur and I are in perfect accord, and that the government and people of the Philippines are placing at his disposal everything that he needs to accomplish the great task of defending the Philippines. I could almost say as much regarding my relations with Admiral Hart, although, owing to the nature of the Navy's work, our connections are not so close and our contacts so frequent as those I have with General MacArthur.

Mr. President, it is, of course, a dreadful thing to contemplate the horrors of war, but there is this consideration in which I almost find cause for rejoicing that such an awful situation should arise before the severance of the political ties now existing between the United States and the Philippines; and that is, because the Filipino people are thereby afforded the opportunity to prove in supreme efforts and sacrifices not only our deep appreciation of the great things which America has contributed in the upbuilding of this new nation of ours, but also the fact that the democratic ideals of the United States have become our sacred heritage, and that to preserve such a precious gift we are willing to pay the price in blood and treasure.[2]

Quezon mentioned cooperation with Hart and MacArthur, but did not refer to High Commissioner Francis B. Sayre, the civilian representative of U.S. control. His immediate superior was Secretary of the Interior Harold Ickes, and, one step removed, the president of the United States. Sayre was the successor of William Howard Taft, first civil commissioner and the watchdog over U.S. interests in the not-quite-autonomous Philippines. He had been charged with the observation of events in the islands and was required to report to his superiors any developments and problems that would affect U.S. interests. He was the civilian counterpart of the highest military authority in the islands.

Before July 26, 1941, Sayre had worked without too much difficulty[3] with the commanding general, Philippine Department, a man of respectable but not outstanding credentials. He was a soldier who had risen to his highest potential and would soon retire after a successful career. He had no aspirations to greater glory and most likely was glad to be so close to the freedom and the leisure of his pension. He and Sayre had worked out a council to deal with the matter of civil affairs in the event of war.

Sayre wrote later that Roosevelt's appointment of MacArthur to his new command "fell like a bombshell on Manila. From that time on President Quezon gave to General MacArthur loyal cooperation and support. . . . From then on he had immense power. . . . With his new responsibilities General MacArthur became exceedingly busy."[4]

MacArthur preempted the Philippine Department command when he assumed command of USAFFE in July. Sayre was thereby confronted with the dilemma that had baffled Hart: How does one deal with a former chief of staff? Sayre, like Hart, had snubbed MacArthur when he was military adviser, a capacity that had no official status within the U.S. government. Like Hart, Sayre had simply stared past the glitter of the field marshal general's title and baton, and had tried to ignore his obviously privileged position with Quezon. Sayre, however, had more to fret about than Hart. MacArthur had been considered for the post of high commissioner in 1935. The same proposal had come up in early 1941 when the threat of imminent war had tilted the decision to the military side and MacArthur had been appointed commanding general instead.

Thus Sayre was dealing with a potential competitor for office who had close connections with the two heads of state with whom Sayre must work, Roosevelt and Quezon. Like Hart, Sayre must find a way to dominate MacArthur or he would be dominated. Like Hart he could not muster the force to carry it off and gave ground to a more dynamic personality who occupied a more advantageous bargaining position. Under existing arrangements, if war came, MacArthur would automatically become military governor of the Philippines, replacing both Sayre and Quezon as the legitimate source of authority. It was not much of a poker game.

Sayre, reading the portents, saw red clouds to the north. He had already taken action. At the end of September he wrote to MacArthur concerning the organization of civil defense in the Philippines. He sent with his letter a report of his military liaison officer that pointed out what he considered to be complete lack of concern and preparation, compared with similar activities in the Netherland East Indies and Singapore. Sayre suggested conferences involving representatives of Quezon, MacArthur, and himself to remedy the problem.[5]

MacArthur, as he had done with Hart, moved to action. He disposed of the charge of "indifference and inertia" with a simple rebuttal: "I see neither one or the other, only commendable poise and self-control."[6] He then moved to the heart of the matter and wrote a lecture about the source of power in the Philippines. The executive power in the Philippines was vested in the Commonwealth government by the Tydings-McDuffie Act. That government had enacted laws giving the chief executive of the Commonwealth authority to control civil affairs in time of emergency. Sayre and the ranking U.S. Army officer in the Philippines had acquiesced in the arrangement. MacArthur was not a party to the conversations, but as military adviser to Quezon he had provided a "comprehensive procedure in case of war after the Philippines becomes independent."

Since his appointment as commanding general, USAFFE, MacArthur had revised the plan. It could be implemented at any time. With the outbreak of war "responsibility would tend to pass from civil to military authority," the precise arrangement to be decided by the president of the United States. MacArthur explained to Sayre that he and Quezon were in constant contact, and " . . . there is the most complete coordination between the present civil effort and future military control. . . . President Quezon has not only been cooperative but has shown every effort to adopt and accomplish any suggestion that I have made."[7] MacArthur concluded:

. . . the closest coordination already exists between the two Executive departments concerned—the Commonwealth Administration and the Military Authority. These two groups as to advice and cooperation are now completely integrated and I cannot see how the present cordial relationship could be improved. I would suggest therefore that if you have proposals for changes or acceleration or further development, you might well submit them to the authority now executing the program. I am sure President Quezon is eager to improve further the defensive potentialities within the natural limitations of the situation. For myself I am always glad to discuss this or any other pertinent matter.[8]

On October 18 MacArthur sent to the War Department a memorandum concerning a proclamation to be issued in the event of hostilities. The proclamation had been outdated by MacArthur's appointment and required revision "to designate the new Commanding General USAFFE as Military Governor" in the document.[9]

MacArthur went on to urge that the proclamation, which would establish a military governor, be issued "only in case of the actual disintegration or recalcitrance of the Government of the Philippines," and then certainly not without MacArthur's recommendation. He referred to the "strong and completely effective" cooperation that existed between himself and Quezon. Control could be exercised most effectively through Quezon's acting in cooperation with MacArthur. If Quezon refused to cooperate, the proclamation would then be issued. But until the situation deteriorated, and only at the "decisive moment" (to be determined by MacArthur), the proclamation should be used as leverage to remind Quezon that it could, if necessary, be implemented. MacArthur advised that if events required, he would not hesitate to establish himself as military governor, but he preferred to work with Quezon through voluntary cooperation.

Douglas MacArthur, then and three years later, was unwilling to assume the unwelcome duty of imposing even a temporary military dictatorship upon the Filipino people unless conditions made it an essential ingredient of holding together the military situation. He preferred to work with Quezon, with whom he had adequate influence, although not necessarily absolute control. Events had woven the careers of the two men so tightly together that they had a common self-interest which made coercion unnecessary. MacArthur perhaps remembered the experience of his father as military governor and preferred not to repeat it. He did not want to rekindle into flames the spark that Aguinaldo still carried deep in his heart, a spark shared by many Filipinos. Washington feared Japan. Quezon, and perhaps MacArthur also, feared internal explosions within the Philippines.

MacArthur the younger drew from the experience of MacArthur the elder. Arthur MacArthur had been involved as military governor in a conflict with a civilian commissioner. It is common to trace the difficulties to personalities, but it is doubtful that any personalities which could rise to high position could have bridged the structural weaknesses of a divided administration in an active military theater. Such arrangements have always resulted in friction and disarray. When the structural differences extend from the bottom to the top of the hierarchy, as they did in 1901 and 40 years later, the friction is even more acrimonious. The two parties feel called upon to uphold department loyalties and to exaggerate the smallest and most trivial matters into matters of high principle. The friction between MacArthur and Admiral Hart reflected just such a problem. The gulf between the War Department and the Interior Department was even more difficult to bridge than the gulf between the War Department and the Navy.

MacArthur pointed out this more likely source of friction:

In the unlikely event that the establishment of a Military Governorship becomes necessary, my plan of action would envisage the imposition of adequate control, but execution would be secured through the President and the established hierarchy of government.

It is deemed pertinent to point out one danger. The High Commissioner has expressed an opinion that a suitable form of control would be by an expansion of his office and the placement of members of his staff in every department of the Commonwealth Government, and at one time worked out a plan to that effect which he explained to me in detail. Such a conception would alienate the Filipinos and completely deteriorate their defense effort. It is possible that some steps are being taken with a view to action along this line. I am confident that the decision of the War Department is correct that control should rest in properly constituted civil authority while it continues to function, and in the military in the event of the failure of civil government; that the only danger lies in mixed control and hazy definition of authority.[10]

Sayre entered the fray two weeks later. He informed MacArthur that he, too, had responsibilities in the matter of civil affairs, by instruction of President Roosevelt. Sayre acknowledged that he had no other "jurisdiction or powers to assume responsibility," but he felt that he should be kept informed so that he could fulfill his duties.[11]

MacArthur replied two days later. He explained to Sayre that civil affairs

are being carried out under the executive direction of the Commonwealth Government. The liaison as to basic policies in so far as they affect the military is accomplished by conferences between the President of the Commonwealth and myself.[12]

He went on to say that

the President [of the United States] acting through the War Department is in direct control of such military affairs and functions here through the Commanding General as his executive agency. There is no intermediate link in the military chain of command.[13]

Or, simply stated, in military matters "I represent the President of the United States in the Commonwealth of the Philippines." MacArthur concluded: "I repeat again what I have so often said that within the spheres of our respective authority I am only too glad to function in the most complete accord and co-operation."

The same sentiments were expressed in another letter sent to Sayre two weeks later. The debate would lie in abeyance for two years, to be revived as MacArthur was preparing his return to liberate the Philippines.

MacArthur met Sayre and Hart at a conference at the end of November. Sayre and Hart sat while MacArthur paced back and forth, smoking a black cigar, asserting that the Japanese would not move before April. Hart felt otherwise, but only time would tell. Sayre has left his impression of MacArthur:

Tall, spare, with a thin face, receding dark hair, piercing eyes, and low, resonant voice, he gave the impression of drama in his bearing, his action, and his words. Sharp and observant through his glance, he seemed always indrawn and playing his part as a great actor. Although never seeming to lose himself in an emotional outburst, he was a skillful orator, conscious always of the effect upon his listeners. With his keen trenchant mind and his far-reaching knowledge of history and of military strategy as part of history, he could hold listeners spellbound . . . a man of strong positive character . . . he held himself aloof from the crowd—he gave the effect of being inscrutable and enigmatic. His personality lacked the open, democratic American approach.[14]

In the manner of all animal kind, MacArthur had asserted his dominance and had marked the boundaries of his territory. He had outbravadoed Hart by sheer bullying and bluff. He had read Sayre a lecture on constitutional law. He had tucked up his sleeve a trump card that would ensure his dominance over Quezon. Hart and Sayre were outsiders and fair game, and MacArthur had old scores to settle with them both. He and Quezon were friends, but Quezon had been fickle before and might be just as fickle again. MacArthur would meet cooperation with deferential courtesy. He would match rebellion with military dictatorship if circumstances demanded it. Quezon was not an outsider, but he might become one. The others were easy game. MacArthur's dressing gown and his affability were simply marks of assurance and self-confidence that reinforced his formal authority. Brereton did not resent the informality but was rather flattered by it.

The familiarity and informality were only apparent. Behind the display of informal civility, hidden from the eyes, one could sense steel armor. Familiarity in other men might breed contempt, but never in MacArthur. One knew that it was simply a whim that ran in one direction only, and that he would never tolerate a response in kind. Like George Washington, he used the trait as a firm shield against all who attempted to intrude into his privacy. Even in his underwear, draped in a dressing gown that would make anyone else ridiculous, MacArthur appeared to be cool, detached, and master of the situation. The key was his uncanny display of self-control and mastery of his own impulses. He controlled himself and thereby controlled others.

MacArthur had his theater of operations: his infantry, his air force, his share of the navy; he also was the power behind the throne of civil authority in the Philippines. Speaking to the U.S. Senate after the end of the war, MacArthur expressed his own view of the authority of a commanding general of a theater of operations:

A theater commander is not merely limited to the handling of his troops; he commands the whole area, politically, economically and militarily. At that stage of the game when politics fails and the military takes over, you must trust the military. . . . I do unquestionably state that when men become locked in battle, there should be no artifice under the name of politics which should handicap your own men, decrease their chances of winning, and increase their losses.[15]

The recall to active duty and the organization of USAFFE had thrust MacArthur the former chief of staff into a new role that was not clearly defined but that opened visions of a great potential in the future. Over and over again MacArthur had reminded Washington that he was now commanding general of a theater of operations. Everything he had done between July and December 1941 served to mark out the boundaries of his new authority and to claim the respect and precedence his new role justified and demanded.

The configuration of his situation was defined more by traditional precedent and usage than by statute and regulation. MacArthur certainly considered himself more highly placed than army commanders in the United States, although his rank and his command were not appreciably greater. Unlike the continental commanders, MacArthur was poised for combat in a place where battle was a very great possibility if not a certainty.

Moreover, unlike the continental commanders, MacArthur commanded an international contingent, and his position was determined by more than the customary army regulations and bureaucracy. He had a very special relationship with a potential, if not an actual, head of state. Directives from Washington must be couched in terms of a broader diplomatic reality. Quezon, of course, was not head of a sovereign state. He was in the process of becoming the head of a state, in transition from dependency to sovereignty. It was an unclear situation where potential was more significant than present fact.

During the interval between July and December, MacArthur floated on the clouds of hope and imagination, where future possibility crystallized momentarily into precise form without any present substance. Events would change all present actuality, and anything could happen as a result. It was the last moment before Divine creation had transformed chaos into form. MacArthur could not have said as much in these terms, but he could understand that he was on the verge of a transformation that could lead either to a great glory or to a great abyss. Only time would reveal the final outcome. For the present he was the commander of a theater of operations, and he would claim every last grudging drop of the respect and deference to which he was entitled.

There is a cliché in the literature that MacArthur was optimistic. During this period he was neither optimistic nor pessimistic. He realized quite coldly that all outcomes were equally possible. There could be glorious victory, and there could be crushing defeat. MacArthur proclaimed the official stupidity sent down from Washington that no attack would come until April 1942. At the same time he sent Sid Huff to find two bullets for his pocket derringer and growled that he would never be taken alive. Lesser souls bought supplies of toothpaste and soap to carry them through a hard campaign or through prison camp, hoping just to survive, with or without glory.

MacArthur knew that the Philippines had already been relegated to a minor role. The debate with Hart over command of army air left veiled the fact that when the Japanese struck Malaya, the entire air force would be ordered to the south, to fight under any commander chosen to lead the Allied defenses, whatever his nationality or his service. If that commander was successful, MacArthur might well slip back into limbo as the lost leader of a lost cause. He knew this, although one would search in vain to find evidence of that fact in anything MacArthur said or wrote at the time. A British officer would be called first to command by the very nature of things. MacArthur could only await the outcome of events over which he had no control. If the British commander failed to hold Singapore, then MacArthur's turn would come if he could hold the Philippines. But all of this was hidden by uncertainty and doubt.

Thus it is not enough to assert simply that MacArthur was optimistic unless one is willing to explore the depth of the meaning of that ambiguous term. In this case it implied only hope that the uncertain future would turn in his favor and a determination to play his own secondary role to the limit of his power, trusting to a poorly trained Filipino infantry to bring him to glory. MacArthur knew it *could* be done. He knew also that it *might not* be done. This is an uneasy optimism.

IV

"Orange Three," December 1941

Japan emerges as military threat; game of bluff; Japan decides to fight; early warnings; Japan strikes; bomber force destroyed; days of waiting; Mays at Davao; landing in Luzon; withdrawal to Bataan

13

Strike South

The Japanese could insist with good cause that the Americans had started it all by pushing them out of their self-imposed isolation into the sweeping current of world affairs. Insofar as precise beginnings can be found for historical movements, they would be correct. For centuries the Japanese had been isolated by geography and by intent from the impact of the European contacts that had drifted up the western fringe of the Pacific basin. They desired isolation and were prepared to defend it by force of arms. The United States was determined that Japan should not be isolated and that its markets should be open to the growing output of the rapidly expanding industrial machinery of the United States and other Western powers.

In 1853 four U.S. ships forced their way into Tokyo Bay. The commander of the expedition came ashore with 300 marines. The Japanese watched the procession with hate and disdain. Three decades were required for the transition, but by 1888 Japan had a written constitution and was committed to modernization. Six years later, following the pattern set by the European powers, Japan invaded China, won the war, and took Korea, Taiwan, and Kwangtung as the prize of victory. The world was startled. Ten years later the world was impressed when Japan defeated the Russians on land and sea. Japan's future path had been set.

In 1922 the young Hirohito became regent for his father, and in 1926 became emperor. He was determined that Japan should be the peer of the United States and England. He set out to modernize the army, to expand the navy, and to develop Japanese industry. The army and the navy were needed to guarantee access to resources and markets. The resources, iron and oil in particular, and the markets could be had in Malaya, the Netherland East Indies, and China.

Japan vacillated for years between two strategic plans, Strike North and Strike South. Strike North looked to Siberia and Mongolia; Strike South looked more realistically to the South China Sea for resources and markets. Hirohito picked the Strike South plan in 1930 and pushed it to destruction. The expansion began in 1931 with the occupation of Manchuria. Japan's navy was the equal of any in the world, although the world either did not know it or did not care to know. The League of Nations voted to condemn the act of aggression the moment that Japanese troops were invading northern China. Japan withdrew from the League in a gesture of defiance. Japan was far away; Washington and London were confronted with a more pressing menace in Hitler, who by 1933 controlled Germany and was becoming a disruptive influence in Europe.

In July 1937 Hirohito ordered the invasion and occupation of China. Japanese troops crossed the Marco Polo Bridge outside Peking, and several months later they landed at Shanghai and occupied Nanking. The Japanese conquest of China was under way. Sutherland had arrived in time to witness all of this firsthand.

Germany occupied Austria and the Rhineland. Czechoslovakia passed without opposition into German hands. The German invasion of Poland finally brought reaction, and World War II was under way. By June 1940 German troops were pushing east toward Russia and England was being bombed.

The Japanese might well have entered the war in 1940 after France and the Netherlands had fallen and England stood isolated in Europe. Various factors made them hesitate. The situation in China could not be stabilized. The Japanese navy was reluctant to become involved in a major war with the United States. It was not certain that there would be even a short-run advantage, and there was overwhelming agreement that the long-run prospects could all be negative. Moreover, the Russians posed a threat on the northern frontier. A move to the south would require withdrawal of forces from Manchuria, and Stalin might decide to fill the vacuum.

There seemed to be certain advantages that could be had immediately with only the threat of war. A simple threat had forced the British to close the Burma Road, the major supply route to the Chinese. The Americans would not agree to a British proposal for joint action in the Pacific unless Japan made an overt move. Japan easily obtained control over French territories in Indochina. As a result of these concessions from the major powers, Japan had temporarily weakened the position of China and had moved one step closer to control of rubber, tin, and oil supplies.

Roosevelt was not prepared to make a military attack, but he had formidable weapons: an embargo on the sale of U.S. steel to Japan and the threat of an oil embargo. The great game of bluff that began with Strike South and the invasion of China now exerted devastating pressure on Japan. In not many months there would be no oil for either industry or military needs. By February 1941 Japan had reached a decision that the stalemate must be broken, by war if necessary. A neutrality pact with Russia removed pressure on the Manchurian flank. The Japanese were now free to move south. The navy was given the task of attempting to negotiate a peaceable solution. An admiral was sent to Washington to achieve by diplomacy what the army was prepared to obtain by force if negotiations failed.

Roosevelt was not prepared to give in, probably having decided that war must come. The Japanese must make the first overt move. The only demand he made was that Japan should agree to withdraw from China. Except for pride, little would be lost by such action and much would be gained.

During the fall and winter of 1940-1941 Japanese Admiral Yamamoto had begun to plan for war. He was not particularly optimistic. He felt sure that he could run wild for six months, but if the war were to last longer than that, there would be little hope for success. He stated that Japan must challenge the world and be prepared to die in the attempt.

During the summer of 1940 Yamamoto had worked out a plan for the attack on Pearl Harbor as a prelude to action. In November the draft plan was sent to Hirohito, who gave conditional approval. In January 1941 a special command was set up to prepare army plans for war. During the spring intelligence was gathered. In July a full-dress palace conference was held to authorize preparations for war. Orders were issued to call up reserves. A special command for Strike South was created. Forces were alerted to prepare for new uniforms, rations, and amphibious manuals.

The United States, joined by Britain and the Netherlands, announced an oil embargo against Japan. MacArthur was called back to active duty and USAFFE was organized. During the second week of September, while I was serving my first week of duty scrubbing floors, spittoons, and urinals at Fort Des Moines, Strike South was being rehearsed in Tokyo. The Japanese navy complained, "We are growing weaker while the enemy is growing stronger." A deadline of October 10 was set for a final decision. Had the deadline been adhered to, I would not have reached Manila and this book would not have been written.

The diplomatic efforts collapsed. The Japanese insisted that they must keep China and must have oil by diplomacy or war. The United States, England, and the Netherlands insisted that Japan would have oil only if it agreed to leave China. Both sides prepared for war, which was taken as inevitable. The question was no longer "what" but "when."

On September 6 a conference was held in Hirohito's presence for a final decision on war. The position papers had been read beforehand, and all that remained was the reading of speeches to fix responsibility for the action being taken. It was decided that if diplomacy failed, Japan would go to war.

I was breaking rocks at Fort McDowell when Yamamoto rehearsed his plan for the Pearl Harbor strike. The Japanese were convinced that diplomacy had failed already. Tojo was granted dictatorial war powers. Just after *Tasker H. Bliss* left Guam, Yamamoto's strike was approved.

About the time I made my first payment to Sing Lee, Hirohito approved the final draft of the war order, which was then sent to the printer. It was agreed that November 30 would be the final cutoff date. War must begin if nothing had been achieved by that time. December 8 was scheduled as the target date.

On November 4 the Supreme War Council met to evaluate the situation. It was agreed that a short war could result only if the U.S. Pacific Fleet was destroyed, if there was a consequent loss of will to fight in the United States,

Map 3
Japanese Plan and Disposition of the Armies, November 1941

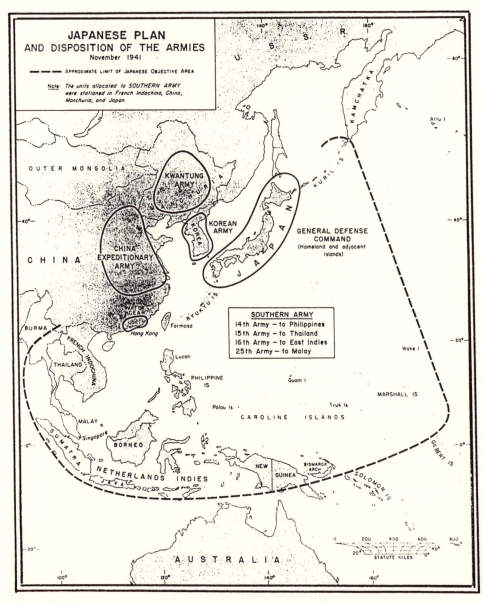

Source: U.S. Army.

if Germany succeeded in an invasion of England, and if resources needed by the United States could be cut off. It was recommended that the war order be approved. A day later the cabinet supported the recommendation and the emperor gave approval.

By this time neither side could withdraw. The Japanese representative in Washington sent a warning: "The United States is not bluffing. If Japan invades again, the United States will fight with Japan. Psychologically the American people are ready. The navy is prepared and ready for action."[1]

14

Attack

Five days after my arrival in Manila, I wrote to my parents, "By the time you get an answer back to me the chances are that we may be at war. Roosevelt is becoming more and more belligerent. But, let it come. I have a nice job in an office and I won't sleep in the mud, I hope."[1] I am grateful for the caution or prescience that impelled me to add the qualifying phrase.

Three weeks later, on November 22, I noted:

We had a practice blackout all over Manila last night. Another fellow and I walked around town a while and then went to bed at 7:30. It really seemed funny. . . . We got a kick out of the headlines in one of the Manila papers. Two big headlines announced that Manuel Quezon had pledged the Commonwealth government to aid and support the United States, and that Britain promised to do the same. Neither one of them could continue military operations if we stepped out.[2]

As a matter of fact there were two practice blackouts, the second one on Friday, November 23. In my letter of the 22nd, when I said "funny," I did not mean "comical" but "strange." I was young and naive, but not a fool. I was devoted to Roosevelt, but my devotion was strained during the 1,500 days that lay ahead.

There were two early warnings from Washington. The first, on November 24, was sent to all navy commanders in the Pacific, and Admiral Hart passed it to MacArthur. The second was sent directly to MacArthur in Manila and to the commander in Hawaii on November 27. I saw this message. There is no entry in my diary, but my recollection of the contents is sharp and clear, with almost verbatim accuracy. The dispatch read:

Negotiations with Japan appear to be terminated to all practical purposes with only the barest possibility that the Japanese Government might come back and offer to continue.

Japanese future action unpredictable but hostile action possible at any moment. If hostilities cannot, repeat cannot, be avoided the United States desires that Japan commit the first overt act. This policy should not, repeat not, be construed as restricting you to a course of action that might jeopardize the successful defense of the Philippines. Prior to hostile Japanese action you are directed to undertake such reconnaissance and other measures as you deem necessary. Report measures taken. Should hostilities occur you will carry out the tasks assigned in revised Rainbow 5.[3]

A similar message went to all navy commanders. Sutherland issued orders directing all troop commands to field positions on November 28. No other specifics were given to subordinate commanders.[4]

The official history states that men went about their work as usual, and so they did. I did not record any official matters in my diary until after December 8. There are no entries between November 23 and December 5. On Friday, December 5, I attended a Mozart anniversary concert performed by the Manila Symphony Orchestra.

On Saturday, December 6, the promotion list that had been on my mind ever since my first interview with Sutherland was published. My highest aspiration had been specialist second class, but I was promoted to private first class specialist first class, the highest specialist rating, which gave me the pay but not the authority of a technical sergeant. I hasten to add that I was not singled out above others. The orders carried 29 names, 7 of whom received specialist first class ratings: Farr, Gardner, James, Oldwater, Robinson, Rogers, and Woodhouse. I cannot recall the men who bore the names. I remember discussing with someone the insignia that the rank conferred, one chevron above with six rockers below. I have seen photographs but have never actually seen or worn them. At the time they seemed to me about one-fifth of the distance between ''buck-ass'' private and full general.

On Sunday, December 7, Sutherland attended a party given in honor of General Lewis Brereton.[5] Brereton recorded in his diary that at that party he learned for the first time of the imminence of the war when he was told by Sutherland that it was a matter of days or even hours.[6] I was in bed, resting for the next day of work. Sutherland was back in his quarters before three in the morning of December 8. It was about seven in the morning Hawaii time.

Sutherland sat on the edge of his steel cot with a deep sigh of fatigue. It had been a good party. He smiled when he recalled the disbelief in the eyes of Brereton when he had told him that war was probably on the way—a matter of hours. The smile faded with the realization that those hours were ticking away, that it would soon be sunrise of another day of routine. Sutherland felt some regret for the relaxed life of the Military Mission, when a few hours a day was enough time to handle the flow of work. Then another smile with the thought that it had not been so long ago when he had arrived in Manila, not sure how he would get on with the Old Man.

Sutherland had been warned of MacArthur's peculiarities, his ego, his dramatic style, his sense of destiny.[7] He had also visualized the experience to be gained under such tutelage. MacArthur's chief of staff, if he kept his feet on the ground, would not be lost in the struggle for advancement. The Old Man needed a sober, practical judgment to keep his oratory, as well as his decisions, within the realm of ordinary reason, which for most men is the measure of rational behavior.

Sutherland admired George Marshall and respected this quiet, determined architect of a new army. His stint with MacArthur had not altered this opinion very much. To Sutherland success meant performance of one's duties and the promotions and assignments that came with it. He had no metaphysical yearning for destiny or historical greatness.

Nevertheless, Sutherland had served MacArthur well, had hidden his deeper doubts under a veil of official attention to duty and respect, falling quickly into step one pace to the rear and to the left of the Old Man, walking carefully to avoid friction, and learning as he walked. He had been told often enough that he was being groomed for the highest office in the army.

But now, at three in the morning, December 8, 1941, the radio blared out a call to duty and Sutherland's life changed. He was MacArthur's chief of staff, and from the moment he picked up the phone to call the Old Man to announce the beginning of the war until exactly four years later, he had no rest from his obligation. On his shoulders fell the detailed drudgery of the war. MacArthur would have the glory and the honor; Sutherland would have the labor. He would be tested to the limit. MacArthur's final judgment would be one of respect and approbation. Sutherland would leave with bitter despair and resentment.

Diller called Sutherland first. Diller had been called by a correspondent who had picked up the news on commercial radio. Spencer Akin arrived almost at the same time with the official message that the Japanese had attacked Pearl Harbor. Then Akin awakened Pat Casey and told him. Diller called the other staff officers and delivered Sutherland's order that they report to headquarters.

Sutherland's first call, at 3:30 A.M., was to MacArthur. He called Brereton immediately afterward. He then dressed and drove to his office. Brereton came in at 5 A.M. and talked with Sutherland. Brereton was a fighter, and his first reaction was to retaliate for Pearl Harbor with a strike on Formosa.[8]

The air force consisted of 35 B–17s, 107 P–40's, and other obsolete aircraft. Half of the B–17s had been moved to Del Monte, out of range of Japanese bombers, at the insistence of MacArthur. During the first week of December, Sutherland had repeatedly ordered Brereton to move the remaining planes south. Far East Air Force had failed to make the move because they expected another 35 B–17s to arrive soon in Mindanao and felt there was not enough space there for the entire fleet of 70 bombers. The fighters, of course, remained on Luzon, where they could intercept attacking Japanese aircraft.

The most serious shortage that day was radio and telephone communications, especially at the command level. MacArthur had good connections with Washington, as did Admiral Hart and Brereton. Internal communications were in a shambles. Akin had been in the Philippines for less than 30 days and had not had time even to plan for an effective system, much less set it in place. Communications between high command and field headquarters were unreliable. An army field telephone radio network connected MacArthur with Brereton, but it was not reliable.

Sutherland gave tentative approval for the Formosa strike but wanted to confirm the order with MacArthur before action was taken. Brereton left to alert the bombers at Clark Field to prepare for local missions and those at Del Monte to prepare for a strike on Formosa.

By this time Sutherland felt the need for assistance and called First Sergeant David Clawson "to get Rogers over here right now." Clawson walked to my bunk in the barracks, shook me gently, and quietly said that I should go to the office. The general was there and needed me. I dressed hurriedly and ran down the stairs, across the courtyard, and up to my office, where I uncovered my typewriter and waited drowsily for action.

My diary for that date is uninspired: "Honolulu bombed. Called to work at 5:30. New officer personnel. Japanese bomb Tarlac, Baguio, Clark and Nichols Field."[9]

Sutherland's day was far along by the time Wilson arrived to begin the daily record of activities. At 8:50 Sutherland called Brereton and told him to "hold off bombing of Formosa for the present." Brereton could not specify any particular targets, and Sutherland did not believe that an attack on Formosa in general would yield productive results. At 9:03 the first report of Japanese planes over Luzon came in, and Sutherland called Washington to report the fact. By this time he was immersed in a multitude of problems.[10]

Brereton had received the information that had been passed to Sutherland. He issued orders by radio to send the B–17s at Clark Field aloft without bombs, to escape the incoming Japanese. This message was intercepted on Formosa by the Japanese, who interpreted it to be an order to strike Formosa. To meet this supposed threat they sent a second force of 108 bombers and 84 fighters to strike Clark and Iba. The planes took off at 10:15.

The first Japanese strike did not attack Clark Field and Manila but turned east over Lingayen Gulf and struck Tuguegarao and Baguio, then turned north toward home base. As they withdrew at 10:30, an all-clear was sounded at Clark Field.

The B–17s were called back to base, and the P–40s and P–35s that had failed to intercept the first Japanese strike also came down to refuel at Clark. At 11:30 all bombers and fighters were on the ground. For the next half hour or so the bombers were being loaded with bombs and lined up for takeoff for the attack on Formosa. The fighters were refueling on the runways.

At 11:30, at Nielsen Field, just outside Manila, the air warning service began to receive reports of the incoming second Japanese strike and interpreted it correctly as moving toward Clark Field. At 11:45 a warning was sent from Nielsen to Clark by teletype and by radio, but neither message was received. By 12:15 the last fighter had been refueled and the squadron was in formation for the takeoff.[11]

The modern reader will ask what happened to radar. There was none in those days. Air warning depended on visual sightings and telephone communication.

At 11:50 MacArthur called Sutherland and directed him to check with Brereton about Japanese air operations during the previous two hours. Brereton reported to Sutherland that two groups of Japanese bombers were operating over Luzon. He told Sutherland that a mission would be sent out "this afternoon."

Japanese accounts indicate that Zeros arrived over Clark Field about 12:30 and circled at 22,000 feet for 10 minutes. They watched one flight of P–40s take off to return to their base at Iba. They watched the orderly array of bombers and fighters on the field below.[12] At 12:45 Japanese bombers came over the target area, entered their bombing runs, and destroyed planes, hangars, and installations. A second wave added to the destruction. Finally the Zeros came down for a series of strafing runs, completing the ruin of Far East Air Force. By the end of the attack, 17 B–17s and 53 P–40s had been lost. The Japanese lost 7 Zeros.[13]

At 1:12 P.M. Brereton called to report that Formosa would be bombed "tonight."[14] The decision to order the Formosa strike sealed the fate of the B–17s. They were safe in the air and could have flown in great circles all day or could have found shelter at Del Monte. Honor seemed to require some retaliation for Japanese aggression, but Sutherland's first, commonsense reaction had been the correct one.

Brereton had lost the B–17s stationed at Clark Field, but he still had the squadrons stationed on Mindanao that were out of range of Japanese attack. One order was sent to Del Monte ordering an attack on Formosa for the morning of December 9. The bombers were to top off at Clark Field at daybreak. The group commander at Del Monte suspected that the message had been sent by fifth columnists and refused to move. The order was transmitted again in code, but was not decoded and delivered until after midnight. At 7:30 of December 9 one mission of six B–17s finally left Del Monte. They landed at Clark Field to refuel and took off immediately. It was too late to strike Formosa, so they flew until dark, then returned to base. A second flight of B–17s left Del Monte at 2:30 P.M. that day but did not land at Clark Field until after dark. The crews slept in their planes on the field.

On December 10 one plane left Clark Field at 5:30 A.M. to reconnoiter targets in Formosa but ran into fighters just after takeoff. It circled until dark and landed at Clark Field.

In the first 48 hours of action, Far East Air Force had lost half its bombers and fighters without being able to retaliate in any manner.[15]

General Henry (Hap) Arnold, the highest air force commander in Washington, radioed MacArthur on December 9 (Manila time) to urge that steps be taken to ensure that U.S. planes would not be destroyed on the ground. MacArthur, who had been chief of staff while Arnold was still a field-grade officer, replied the next day that all was under control.[16]

Finally, on December 10, Far East Air Force made its first and last serious

Map 4
Luzon

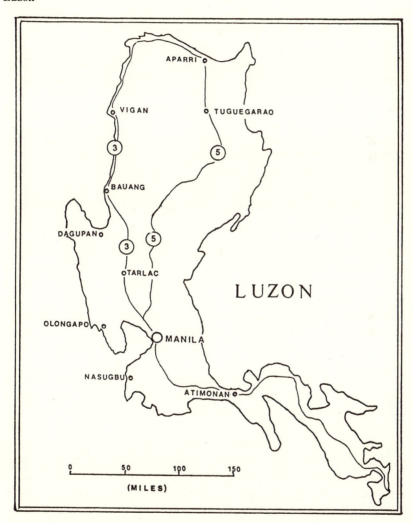

offensive strike. The Japanese landed at Vigan and Aparri that morning. Eight B–17s supported by fighters reached the target area and inflicted some damage. Later in the day the Japanese roared over Luzon, hit all airfields, and destroyed all the operational planes left in the area. Fortunately, they could not reach Del Monte.[17]

Arnold decided to get directly to the heart of the matter. He was feeling the heat of criticism and needed facts to defend himself. On December 11 he called for an explanation, shouting, "What the hell is going on there?" Brereton asked that Arnold withhold judgment until a report could be submitted. Brereton went to MacArthur with the problem. "He [MacArthur] was furious; it is the only time in my life I have ever seen him mad. He told me to go back and fight the war and not to worry." There is no record in the MacArthur or Sutherland diaries of this incident, but it has a ring of truth.[18]

One cannot infer from Brereton's words exactly what behavior was associated with the emotional labels "furious" and "mad." Nor does it give a clue to the reason for the anger. It is quite likely that what Brereton perceived was a sudden rise in the volume of MacArthur's speech, a quickening of delivery, the usual facial expressions of exasperation and discontent, and a sweeping gesture of the arms.

The cause of the exasperation is not difficult to infer. Arnold had received assurances from MacArthur that the events of the first two days could not be traced to error of judgment or behavior by the air forces. Not satisfied, Arnold had broken across the channels of command to question MacArthur's official report. No details had been given because no one had the time or the means to acquire and interpret them. In battle, today's operations and problems are more important than yesterday's misfortunes.

Though there were many problems to be faced on those two days in Head-quarters USAFFE, this event seems to overshadow all the others. Yet, at the time, the air force was only one element in the game over which Sutherland had no direct control. He could, and did, cajole Brereton's staff to take precautionary action. MacArthur himself could not move the planes; the order had to be given by Brereton. MacArthur could fire Brereton, but he could not issue a direct order to the squadron commanders. It seems apparent that squadron commanders on those days did not always obey orders from Brereton.

The Japanese had not waited until April 1942. The planes sent so willingly to the Philippines were not yet a combat air force and would not be for months. They were simply a gaggle of planes and crews, without adequate communication, not yet coordinated as a team, and therefore uncertain and awkward in action. The Japanese air units had been fighting for a decade, and had closed most of the gaps in their structure, and had learned how to improvise to fill the gaps that remained. Perhaps this was the source of the extraordinary luck of the Japanese. Their tactic was quite simple: wait until the Americans fly half a dozen or so planes into unprepared airfields, send in random strikes until they are caught on the ground, and destroy them.

Brereton described the hide-and-seek operations that characterized air force operations for six months longer. A diary entry of December 15 records:

We had been dodging back and forth between Del Monte and Clark Field, trying to keep up maintenance and to carry out operations. Some days it was necessary to keep the bombers in the air all day during the daylight hours in order to avoid their destruction on the ground by the Japs. It was a game of hide-and-seek that wore out men as well as planes. No one who was not present can realize the difficulty in completing the repair work. It must be remembered that there was not a single spare part, engine, or propeller in the Philippines. The only tools available for such work were those in the possession of the crew and the officers.[19]

Brereton went to Sutherland with a request that the remaining planes be withdrawn to Australia. Sutherland concurred, and the men went to MacArthur, who also concurred immediately.

During the war a great many planes, probably most, were destroyed while on the ground. As late as November 1944, when the navy was undisputed master of the central Pacific and after the cream of the Japanese pilot corps had been decimated, Japanese bombers sneaked over B–29 bases at Saipan, inflicting great damage, not just once but repeatedly over a period of two months. All of this at a time when radar was highly developed. Radar and counterstrikes against Japanese bases had little effect. Planes are most vulnerable when on the ground, and therefore great efforts are made to strike them there. The problem was endemic in that war.[20]

Richard Marshall, who was a steady soul in times of adversity, remarked to Sutherland, "Well, Dick, it doesn't make much difference. If we hadn't lost them on the ground at Clark today, we would have lost them later, in the air or on the ground, and it wouldn't have made any difference at all."[21] I am afraid he was right.

I can recall only one result of my contribution to the war effort on December 8. Sutherland dictated a message that, among other things, directed that enemy aliens be interned. I typed it and took it to his office, which was empty. A short while later Richard Marshall came by my desk to ask me to correct an error. I had typed "interred" for "interned." Marshall said grimly, "Rogers, you have the right idea, but unfortunately we can't do it that way."

During the afternoon Francis Wilson came by my office with a dispatch just received from Washington describing the action at Pearl Harbor. As he handed the dispatch to me, he said with some bitterness, "Rogers, you'd better read this. We're all finished over here." I did not believe him.

Without diplomatic or other declaration 60 Japanese carrier borne dive bombers attacked airfields and Pearl Harbor, Oahu, at 8:00 A.M. damaging hangars and planes on ground. 3 US battleships reported sunk and 3 others seriously damaged. Second air raid at 11:00 A.M. Six transports were reported in Japanese forces. Reports of attacks on Wake and Guam. All air attacks made with bombs, torpedoes and machine guns. First objectives seem to be air and naval installations and shops. Times are Hawaiian time. Reports received that Singapore attacked by air. Fighting at Kottbaru and landings at Kemes Sina. Bulk of British air has been committed. Limit this information to essential officers. Inform Hart.[22]

On December 10 what was left of Hart's Asiatic Fleet moved south. The main force had pulled back to join the British and Dutch before the war began.

On December 18 President Roosevelt sent President Quezon a check for $10 million for Filipino war relief. I was impressed with both the amount and the signature of the drawee. I learned later how worthless even $10 million could be under wartime circumstances.

A number of promotions for general officers came on December 20: 12 brigadier generals, 4 major generals and 1 full general. MacArthur received his fourth star; Sutherland became a major general; Akin, Marshall, and Casey became brigadier generals. My diary notes with some pride: "I work for three of them" (MacArthur, Sutherland, Marshall.)

During the evening there was a meeting in the anteroom as they pinned on stars in the traditional ritual, with some merriment. Marquat, whose name was not on the list, walked through, commenting loudly and grimly, "Son of a Bitch! Everybody got a star but Billy Marquat."

I wrote several letters home during this period, but they were never delivered. The Pan American Clipper had not made scheduled flights since the beginning of the war, and there was no further mail service.

By December 23 the air force has been reduced to 22 P–40 and 5 P 26 fighters and 7 B–17 bombers. The bombers were ordered south to Australia. The fighters were used thereafter only for reconnaissance.

15

Invasion

For two weeks Sutherland filled long, long days, absorbed in the details of a war that began in disaster and that gave little hope of foreseeable improvement. The navy was gone. The air force was obliterated. Land forces were in the field, positioned to meet the enemy whenever and wherever he might come ashore. Sutherland's desk was the control center of the war effort. Calls came from Quezon, Wainwright, Sharp, Hart, Brereton, King, and many, many others; and two or three times a day, MacArthur. Clark Field was bombed, Iba was bombed, Davao was shelled, transports at Vigan and Olongapo were bombed; road blocks on highways and field artillery had to be emplaced; saboteurs, Red Cross, Sakdalistas, and B–17s had to be moved south; the 4th Marines had to be in place; canteens had to be set up for troops; there had to be promotions for officers, bomb shelters for the Manila Hotel, a new location for USAFFE, the use of ROTC cadets, and of airfields in Del Monte, convoys for blockade runners, Wainwright's relocation, plans to move currency, ad infinitum. Daily operations reports, press releases, strategic radio messages had to be dictated, read, and approved.[1]

No one doubted that MacArthur was the ultimate authority. The entries in Sutherland's diary and his behavior give evidence of his own deference, both in appearance and in reality, to MacArthur's preeminence. Nevertheless, insofar as operations were concerned, MacArthur gave general direction to Sutherland and left details of execution to him. I do not recall, nor do I find any evidence of, misplay or misunderstanding. Affairs moved smoothly and evenly, which reflected the unusual consensus that had been achieved by the two men.

The first landing came at Davao, one of the major cities on Mindanao and a center of Japanese settlement. The city was defended by a detachment of the 101st Philippine Division. This unit, like all the others, consisted of Filipino soldiers commanded by U.S. officers and cadres of U.S. regulars detached from the 31st Infantry Regiment for this duty. One squadron of Japanese cruisers and another of destroyers covered a landing of two infantry battalions, tanks, and assorted service troops. The official history describes the landing as follows: "The only opposition offered to the landing force came from a machine gun squad which inflicted numerous casualties on the enemy before it was knocked out by a direct hit from a Japanese shell."[2]

In March, when we were at Del Monte waiting for B–17s to evacuate us to Australia, Sutherland called me to his desk and gave me a report, saying, "Rogers, you had better read this." It was a report made by the U.S corporal who had been in command of that machine gun squad. Sutherland carried the report with him to Australia, where it was dutifully filed in a folder marked "Davao Force Records." The report, an interrogation of Corporal Mays, deserves a verbatim recording because it is a primary document of considerable interest. Moreover, it is a fitting prelude to the action two days later on Luzon.

Corporal Mays and Sergeant Macner sat drinking beer in Last Blue Cabaret in the Santa Ana barrio of Davao. They were the advanced outpost of the Davao Force defensive position that was strung out along the perimeter of the beach. It was a tense night. No one could sleep. The Japanese would land at dawn. The tension had come like a fog, hung over the city, creeping into every nook and cranny of every building, leaving everyone drawn with anticipation. It was a rumor, but a rumor filled with a spine-tingling sense of reality.

Macner and Mays had been detached from the U.S. 31st Infantry Regiment to provide a cadre for the 101st Philippine Army division now assigned to the Visayan-Mindanao Force. This force had the mission of covering the new airfields that were being completed at the Del Monte pineapple plantation on the northern slope of the Bukidnon Plateau. The Davao Force, a regiment of the 101st Division, had been sent to Davao to provide a "forlorn hope" defense against the Japanese who must surely land.

Macner and Mays had a detachment of Filipino soldiers who were green and unsteady. The two soldiers had never seen live combat, but they were long-time service professionals who knew the tools and the skills of their trade. Both exuded the air of complete self-assurance that MacArthur had specified as essential in his division commanders. Neither man was well educated. Neither was particularly endowed with great intellectual powers. Both had raw courage, guts, self-confidence, and an ebullient set of convictions. The language of the report obviously had been laundered before it was passed up to division headquarters.

Like all the others, Mays was filled with a premonition of impending action.

"Major, a lot of funny things happened. I often laugh at some of the things that took place. I knew that something funny was going to happen the night before, but I did not know what. All the civilians were quiet and many had suspicious looks on their faces. We had three civilian politicos on our Staff who were, though I cannot prove it, Jap Agents and who helped the Japanese in landing at Davao. In addition to these, there were so many fifth columnists in the City that it was hard to tell who was on what side.[3]

Just before dawn a Filipino civilian ran into Last Blue shouting that a Japanese ship had entered the harbor and was unloading troops into small boats. Macner gathered up his Filipino gun crew, ran to a machine-gun post on the pier, and opened fire. The small boats withdrew to the mother ship and Macner, who got off the first fire in the battle, disappears from history. He had attracted attention. Several Japanese planes roared over the pier area, dropping flares to give the naval gunners a target.

In the meantime Mays ran back to the regimental command post, found a machine gun and a crew, loaded them on a truck, and raced back to the pier to reinforce Macner. As the truck rolled to a stop, a Japanese shell tore into it, knocked the engine to pieces, blew off Mays's helmet, and threw him to the ground. The concussion had frozen the gun's firing mechanism, and Mays could not get off even one burst.

Undaunted, Mays went back to his command post, found a second truck, machine gun, and crew, and roared into action again:

By this time, everything around me was burning. I could see those damn Japs in big life boats coming. They were packed like sardines poured in to [sic] a can. . . . Well, all my gun crew were about to run away from me at the Pier. It was hot, everything around us was burning, a hotel was on fire and a Chinaman was inside on the top floor screaming and crying. He was about to burn up and bullets were flying and I had no time to try to save his life. He was about to cause my men to run, so I took my M–1 rifle and squeezed one off. The last shot got him. I then turned around and said to my men, now if any of you run, I'll do the same thing to you. I'll even give you a 200-yard start before I let go. Now you stay here and fight. You should have seen them; they were plenty scared. I had one man holding the ammunition box while another one pulled the belt through. They didn't run, as badly as they wanted to. I could shoot better than the Japanese and they decided to take a chance on the Japs hitting them.

Whether Mays had learned the basic rules of tactics or whether inborn aggressive wariness filled the need, he held fire.

I decided to wait and let the suckers come in close. When the leading boat got 200 yards away, I opened up on the rear boat. I had them then. They tried to turn around but they could not get back. I "levelled off" all four of them. Then I saw some more coming, one man waving a flag. He was just waving it back and forth, so, I gave him a burst. That finished him. His boat turned back toward the transports but "I gave it to them." I shot plenty of those rascals but some had landed some place else and I had to pull out because they were closing in on me. I then pulled back and went up the road to the . . . junction which I had been told to fall back to.

I doubt that any 31st Infantry corporal ever referred to anyone as "rascal." Their customary epithets were far more colorful. The major who recorded this was just too squeamish.

Orders came down to destroy all supplies in Santa Ana and then to withdraw.

A young officer, Lieutenant Sharp, led the detail, taking Mays and his Filipino troops with him in an ancient Oldsmobile sedan. By this time the Japanese were ashore in force. Mays drove into an intersection, pulled to the right, and saw before him the muzzle of a cannon and behind it the turret of a Japanese tank.

Well, I must have "paid the Priest off" the night before. They opened up on us with two .30 caliber machine guns and a .50 caliber gun. You should have heard Lieut. Sharp. He said, "Oh, Lord, they got us." I looked at him and sweat bumps were on his face as big as gum drops. I don't know how I looked, but I tell you the truth, I was scared.

Mays then commended his superior.

Sir, Lieut. Sharp ought to get credit for something. He came down to the dock and all along the line to transmit orders, for us to get out. He was under machine gun fire, 6" Naval firing, bombs and machines guns from dive bombers, 'most all the time. He is responsible for the supplies being destroyed. He's the reason why those Japs down there now are hungry. They are even eating rotten eggs now.

As for himself, Mays was modest and self-effacing. He had been commissioned for a display of command competence under fire and had been recommended for a decoration. This is the only section of the official report that correctly transcribes the diction of the man.

I've heard about all this medal business. They have made me a Lieutenant shucks, Major, you know I'm a corporal. Dey can take dat Lieutenant rating away from me, but there is one thing dey can't take away from me. I saw plenty during those few minutes I was on the dock at Santa Ana pier. I heard a lot too. I experienced things which not many people ever experience. The first few seconds I was under fire I got cold as ice, den I got hot just like a crap shooter shooting dice. Den I stayed hot. Dat's one thing dey can't take away from me. Dat's all I think I should have.

Mays was asked about casualties.

Sir, that's hard to say. So many ran . . . that we haven't seen since. Out of 1900 men in the Regiment when we were at Davao there were only about 200 left when we reorganized at the upper end of the Togato road. . . . Not many out of one platoon I believe 25 were killed. In the whole Regiment, I don't believe over 200 were killed.

Mays and his small detachment, separated from the regiment, plodded up the long trail from Davao to Malaybalay, where the headquarters was in position. The withdrawal occupied two weeks.

It took us 11 days to get back across the mountain to Malaybalay, our Division CP. We ate camotes, and some chickens and eggs. Some of us ate monkey but I didn't. I just as soon eat my baby sister. One of the funniest things happened on the way back: I had an automatic rifle and it got a little heavy, so I got me a little native pony to carry it.

Corporal Collins also had an automatic rifle. We tied both automatics on the pony. Well, the damn pony was about to give out. I was leading and Corporal Collins was behind him. We started down an embankment and the pony stopped. I said to Collins, give him a kick in the . . . So Collins let one go, and that damn pony jumped on top of me, broke my nose and almost my leg. Collins and I almost had a duel over that. We began to think that after all that fighting at Davao we should get killed by a damn Filipino pony. That would be *something*. You know I never told you when you were my Company Commander back in 31st, that I could cook 'cause you didn't ask me, but I did the cooking on the trip back from Davao to Malaybalay. And, Sir, they liked it too. You know if a man gets hungry enough he likes anything to eat.

Neither the battle nor the withdrawal cooled Mays's ardor or dampened his enthusiasm. He was asked to compare the fighting qualities of the Filipino and Japanese soldiers.

Well, Sir, they are just alike. You could line up one platoon of Japanese and one platoon of Filipinos against each other and I'll bet my bottom dollar that none would be killed on either side. They would all run like hell. . . . There are about 10,000 Japs down there and if you'd take two American regiments down there and some one [sic] should just tell them that the Americans were coming, they would jump into the sea or else take off for Japan. Their leadership is terribly poor.

MacArthur and Sutherland were infantrymen, and Mays was one of their kind. He was a natural soldier. He had met the criteria MacArthur had set for his field officers when he enjoined them to display "that demeanor of confidence, self-reliance and assurance which is the birthright of all cultured gentlemen and the special trademark of the Army officer."

On December 20 at 8:00 A.M., while Corporal Mays was at Santa Ana pier in Davao, firing at the barges of Japanese infantry chugging ashore, Sutherland was in his office preparing for another day of headquarters activity. He talked for 30 minutes with the tank commander who was preparing to move north to support the forces dug in around Lingayen Gulf. Then Sutherland called MacArthur to discuss a promotion for Pat Casey. At 8:50 he talked by telephone with the air force concerning reconnaissance reports. Five minutes later he was talking with Casey about four new airfields to be constructed in Mindanao.

Corporal Mays by this time had pulled away from Santa Ana pier and had begun his long retreat up the mountain roads to rejoin his command on Northern Mindanao, where those fields were to be built. Sutherland and Marshall called in other staff officers to discuss the possibility of organizing Moro units to be used against the Japanese. At 9:15 Stivers came in to talk about moving Head-quarters USAFFE to a new location. At 9:30 MacArthur came to the headquarters and sat in Sutherland's office, discussing the situation in general. The morning wore on with no spectacular events.[4]

About noon Sutherland called me into his office to dictate a short report to Washington concerning the events of the morning: "Enemy attacking Davao with land forces from four transports. Engaged by advance elements of 101st Division. If more than predatory effort I plan to launch guerrilla warfare throughout Mindanao with Mohammedan population."[5]

The day wore on, and then another. On December 21 at 10:15 P.M., Sutherland sent an operations radio message to Washington reporting the obvious fact that "fighting continues in Davao region." He also reported significant new developments on Luzon:

Sharp engagement developed this afternoon along shore north of Lingayen Gulf involving elements of Eleventh Division. Navy reports fifteen vessels, transports escorted by destroyers ninety miles off Lingayen headed thereto. . . . Estimated time possible arrival three AM local time.[6]

Then he went to bed. He would need his rest, because the next three days would be very long ones.

Everyone knew where the major landing should come. There was only one beach on Luzon that could handle a large assault force. On the wide, shallow beach that rolled south like a ribbon of sand from San Fernando to San Fabian, then west to the Bolinao Peninsula, five major highways led from the beach to Manila, only 100 miles to the south.

The Japanese decided to make their assault on the 20-mile stretch below San Fernando. The coastal plain is only three miles wide in this area and rises sharply to a mountain barrier to the east. Highway 3, the major north-south highway in Luzon, runs along the beach, stringing together half a dozen small villages at three- or four-mile intervals. The most important are Bauang, Aringay, Agoo, and Damortis.[7] At Damortis the highway bends east for three miles or so to Rosario, then pulls south to Manila. Just east of Rosario a highway runs over the mountains to Baguio and circles west again to Bauang.

Late on the night of December 21, 85 transports steamed into anchorage fronting the shoreline several miles offshore.[8] They were nursed along by a naval task force of two battleships, half a dozen cruisers, more than two dozen destroyers, assorted torpedo boats, seaplane carriers, other service vessels, 150 landing craft, and 50 powered sampans. Fifteen of the landing craft carried tanks. As the transports settled at anchor, the major part of the covering force, including the battleships and most of the cruisers and destroyers, pulled away to find safety in the open sea.

On board the transports were 3 infantry regiments and 2 tank regiments with almost 100 tanks. The troops were edgy and irritable. The infantry was trained and well equipped but had never seen action. All officer ranks were nervous. Great secrecy had been maintained until the very last moment. They felt that critical information was being withheld, and they were suspicious.

Their commander, Lieutenant General Masaharu Homma, sat nervously drinking tea, then paced anxiously. He confessed later that this had been an extremely

Map 5
Lingayen Gulf Landings, December 22–24, 1941

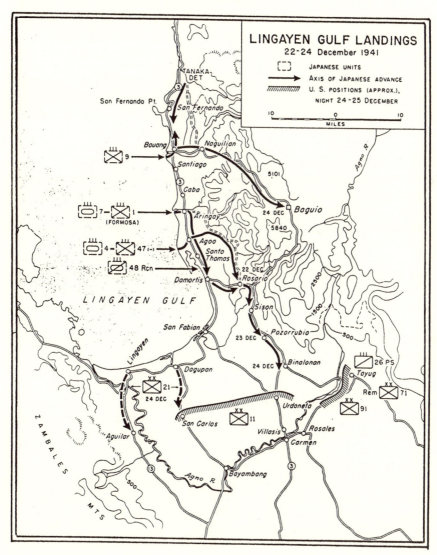

Source: U.S. Army.

anxious moment. He thought that the forces on Luzon outnumbered him. In spite of the fact that the latter had neither air nor naval support, he could not ignore the possibility of some unforeseen disaster. The events of early morning did nothing to dispel his doubts.

It was a cold, rainy day. The wind had risen, and the water in the gulf heaved and rolled in heavy waves, rocking the transports. The soldiers huddled on deck and below, wet and disgruntled, apprehensive of the duty that lay ahead of them. They were afraid of their sergeants and officers, but knew better than to make an obvious show of fear or displeasure. Their officers had a reputation for not tolerating weakness or foolishness.

Many of the soldiers, who had been farm boys, were seasick and moved clumsily to their places, waiting for the order to climb down the nets into the barges for the trip to the beach. It was not an easy task, because the waves tossed the barges up against the transports and pulled them away, rising and falling rapidly and irregularly. More than one soldier feared, with justification, that he might well drown before he saw action.

The order was given while it was dark, and troops began to scramble down. The barges, filled to capacity with 150 men, were cast away for the run to the beaches. The landing craft pitched and heaved, rocked and rolled. Some were capsized, leaving their cargo of soldiers to struggle in the water, sinking to their death. The attack was in progress, and there was no time to rescue the unlucky.

The naval escort fired above them at the beaches; and the roar of guns to the rear, with the shriek of the shells overhead, and the thunder of the explosions on the beaches, combined with wind and sea to make the beaches, even if they were lined with enemy forces, seem a haven of rest. Salvo after salvo belched from the guns of cruisers and destroyers. The men in the barges began to notice with surprise that there did not seem to be any answering fire from the beach, which gave hope that perhaps it would not be too bad after all.

One transport suddenly exploded under the impact of a torpedo launched by submarine, and those who remained on board the convoy waited for the next explosion that inevitably must follow. It never came.

Then four B–17 heavy bombers flew over the convoy, strafing cruisers and destroyers. The transports waited for the bombs that must follow, but none came. The bombs had been dropped at Davao in Mindanao, far to the south. The planes pulled up and roared away.

Several of the transports weighed anchor to find quieter and smoother water on the south side of the beach area. They had come into range of artillery at San Fabian and Dagupan. The transports came under fire, but to their surprise no hits were registered and no damage was done.

The runs to the beach required half an hour. The first barges filled with infantry and artillery were thrown by the heavy sea onto the beaches at Agoo at 5:17 A.M. Fifteen minutes later the first infantry and artillery troops were ashore at Aringay. Two or three hours later troops began to land at Bauang.

Radios had been put out of commission by salt water, and there was no communication between the beachhead and the convoy. The landing barges were tossed about so roughly that heavy equipment could not be unloaded. Some of the craft, after being unloaded, were swept up on the beach, where they were overturned and left stranded. It was not a propitious beginning.

USAFFE forces had been in the field for three weeks. Behind the beaches stood four USAFFE divisions—the 21st, the 71st, the 11th, and the 91st—and the 26th Cavalry Regiment of the Philippine Scouts, backed by very little artillery and a provisional tank group. The 21st Division with the bulk of the artillery was south of Lingayen, Dagupan, and San Fabian. The other three divisions were stationed southeast of the area, prepared to move forward to meet the developing battle.

Like the Japanese infantry the Filipino troops had not seen action. Unlike the Japanese they were not well trained or well equipped. Worse yet, many did not fear their officers and few had learned the discipline that would lead them to accept leadership. They were boys forced into a military role.

Before the month was over, many would run away, leaving behind true soldiers who, equally frightened and apprehensive, would show what they could do. And on the first day the Philippine Scouts would show that Filipinos, properly trained and equipped, could fight with the best of them.

At 5:00 A.M. one battalion of infantry was ordered to move forward to Agoo to meet the Japanese who were landing on the beaches, and drive them into the sea. The battalion reached the beach, moving slowly and nervously through the thickets. For the first time they heard and felt artillery fire and saw tanks lumbering toward them, rattling and roaring, turrets swiveling, seeking targets, their black muzzles spouting fire.

Seeing their comrades fall screaming and bleeding in the sand, the line of Filipino soldiers disintegrated and melted back into the brush, first running, then walking in silence to the seeming safety of the shadows and solid trunks of trees. They fled south, and no one could stop them. By 10:30 the Japanese had secured control of the narrow beachhead, had moved out to the highway, and were on their way south toward Damortis.

The Japanese who came ashore at Aringay met no opposition at all. The tanks and artillery landed, consolidated the beachhead in the area, and moved out to the highway toward Agoo and Damortis.

At Bauang the 71st Infantry Regiment was waiting to meet the Japanese landing. It had a twofold task. One wave of Japanese was coming to the beach from the line of transports out in the gulf. A second Japanese column was marching south down Highway 3 north of San Fernando. They had landed at Vigan and Aparri earlier in December, had secured the airfields there, and now moved south to support the main landing at Lingayen. The 71st was ordered to intercept them before they reached Bauang.

One battalion went to Bauang to cover the beach. It reached the area before the Japanese came ashore. The main force formed a defensive line in the brush and thickets behind the beach and hurriedly set up three machine guns to be used against the Japanese who were now approaching the beach. As the first barges lurched into range through the heavy seas, the guns opened fire. After a few spurts of fire, one of the machine guns jammed. As the Filipino sergeant struggled to free the firing mechanism, the gun crew looked around nervously. Having nothing to keep them busy, they began to feel the precariousness of their situation, especially since they were without a weapon. Then the second machine gun fell silent, and that crew also was deprived of useful activity in the face of the Japanese barges. Suddenly one man broke and ran to the rear. The two sergeants in charge of the crews looked up from the guns to see their crews fading into the thickets. The remaining gun continued to fire until the Japanese were on the beach returning the fire. The crew, finding themselves alone, left the gun in the sand and ran to the rear. The entire battalion joined the fleeing gunners. The defensive position collapsed as Filipino troops ran back to Highway 3 and began to move south, without any semblance of order, many without weapons, toward Damortis.

The other battalion that had been sent to intercept the Japanese column marching down from the north moved too slowly, and the Japanese reached the landing force at Bauang without meeting any opposition. The 71st Infantry battalion withdrew along a back road to Baguio.

By 10:30 the Japanese held the beaches securely and were moving south at will.

The 26th Cavalry of the Philippine Scouts stood in reserve at Pozorrubio at 5:00 A.M. Ordered forward to establish a holding line, they clattered north, a platoon in jeeps and scout cars in the lead. The advance patrol reached Damortis at 7:00, in time to meet the growing rush of retreating soldiers. At 7:30, a few miles north of Damortis, they met advance elements of a Japanese tank regiment. Contact had been made and the advance patrol withdrew to Damortis, where they established a defensive line and waited for the arrival of the main body. By 11:00 they were joined by the 26th Cavalry. With two companies of the 71st Infantry Division they threw up a major roadblock. They had just completed their task at 1:00 P.M. when Japanese tanks came in to attack. The 26th Cavalry called for help. Wainwright asked for tank support. The tank commander sent forward one platoon of five tanks.

The tanks moved north through Damortis to the roadblock, where they joined the battle. The command tank maneuvered off the road, and while turning was hit and destroyed by antitank fire. The other four tanks were hit and withdrew from the action. This would not be the last time that tanks would arrive to save a tight situation, only to be destroyed or disabled, leaving the infantry to fight the hard way. There is no easy way to win a battle.

Wainwright called to order Clyde Selleck to move his 71st Division forward to the Damortis roadblock. Preceding his troops, Selleck hurried to Damortis and arrived at the roadblock about 4:30 P.M. He found that he was facing two Japanese columns, one marching down the back road from Aringay and the other down Highway 3. Selleck felt that the Philippine Scouts had fought to exhaustion. They had held back the Japanese infantry, artillery, and tanks for four hours. Selleck decided to try to maintain the roadblock with two companies of his infantry and ordered the cavalry to fall back east of Damortis to set up another defensive line. He expected that the remainder of his division would arrive soon to reinforce them. It did not arrive until the next day. As the Scouts withdrew, the infantry began to collapse and finally retreated, leaving Damortis to the Japanese.

Selleck did not believe he could hold, and withdrew the entire force south to gain room for maneuver. What was left of the 71st Infantry, the tanks, and the 26th Cavalry pulled south of Rosario, where they dug in. The Japanese moved forward and stopped west of Rosario for the night.

By midnight the Japanese who had come ashore nervous and apprehensive had achieved almost instant victory at a very low cost. They held the beachhead securely; they were moving up the Aringay Valley toward Baguio; they had occupied Damortis; and they controlled Rosario.

The battle for Luzon had left the beaches and had rolled south down Highway 3 toward Manila when Sutherland came to the office at 8:00 A.M. on Monday, December 22. The war was two weeks old. Sutherland went into conference with Charles Willoughby, and the two men analyzed the reports that had come in during the night. Forty minutes later air force reconnaissance reports came in. MacArthur was called immediately. Wainwright was called and informed of the facts that had been received from the air force.

At 9:30 Sutherland called me in to dictate a report to Washington: "Seventy to eighty transports protected by naval vessels now sending troops ashore in the vicinity of Agoo twenty kilometers north of Damortis in Lingayen Gulf. Employing barges carrying about one hundred fifty men."[9]

By that time Sutherland had begun to notify various commanders of the situation and instruct them as to plans for their subsequent operations. The various staff chiefs were called into the office for individual instructions. Sutherland called President Quezon to describe the events of the morning and to inform him of publicity that would be released concerning it. About 1:00 P.M. MacArthur was informed of a radio message to be sent to Washington and of the publicity that was being prepared.

During the afternoon Casey reported on plans for the demolition of installations and bridges in the north. Akin was called in concerning the problem of moving signal corps facilities. At 3:20 a call was made to Corregidor to prepare for the movement of the command post of Headquarters USAFFE. Wainwright was called at 3:30 to report on the situation at Lingayen. He and Sutherland discussed the operation, and Sutherland told him of the plans being set in motion.

At 3:50 Sutherland called me in to dictate a second report to Washington and a press release declaring Manila an open city. The two documents were typed and taken by Sutherland to MacArthur, who made small changes. They were then retyped.

Initial concentration of seventy to eighty transports in Lingayen Gulf on the front Aringay-Agoo-San Fabian indicate[s] major enemy effort in strength estimated at eighty thousand to one hundred thousand men of four to six divisions. I have available on Luzon about forty thousand men in units partially equipped. I anticipate that this enormous tactical discrepancy will compel me to operate in delaying action on successive lines through Central Luzon Plain to final defensive position on Bataan to cover Corregidor. When forced to do so I shall release Manila and the metropolitan area by suitable proclamation in order to save civilian population. I will evacuate the High Commissioner and the Government to Corregidor. I intend to hold Corregidor.[10]

This radiogram was held 24 hours before dispatch. A second operations report was sent to Washington at 5:30 to summarize the day's action.

Sharp action developed along the coast south of Agoo. Enemy destroyers approached coast near Damortis and were driven off by fire of our one five fives. No landing was made there. We threw forward elements including echelon of tanks and Twenty-sixth Cavalry dismounted to develop enemy positions between Damortis and Agoo. Encountered and dispersed hostile infantry. Gained contact with heavy tanks south of Agoo. Our troops have behaved well and our block of the defiles is holding.[11]

Just before Sutherland left the office for dinner, he conferred with Akin and Marquat concerning a move to Corregidor. He returned to the office at 8:20 and remained there until almost 4:00 A.M. to monitor the events in Lingayen and Mindanao.

The gravity of the situation had become obvious, and the activity of the day reflected careful thought. It was not a helter-skelter reaction of panic but the implementation of decisions that had already been worked out. Nonmilitary details had been provided for. During the day all government securities, money, and checks owned by individuals were collected and shipped to Corregidor for safekeeping. It was the first step of a full-scale evacuation. During the afternoon MacArthur called the High Commissioner Sayre and President Quezon to notify them of the impending move.[12]

Even soldiers in battle must sleep, and there was not much action during the night of December 22. At daylight on the morning of December 23 the battle was renewed. The main elements of the 71st Division pushed ahead during the night, and by 6:00 A.M. of December 23 they were near Sison, some four miles below Rosario, where they prepared a defense line. One infantry regiment and an engineer regiment formed the main line and were supported by the division field artillery in the rear. The 26th Cavalry had taken heavy casualties in the first day of fighting and was ordered to move back through the new defense line some ten miles south to Pozorrubio, where they would reorganize.

In the meantime the 91st Division, which had been held in reserve at Cabanatuan, was ordered to move its combat team north to join the 71st on the line at Sison. It was scheduled to arrive at noon.

About 9:00 A.M. two battalions of Japanese infantry probing south from Rosario struck the Sison line. The 71st Division artillery held them under fire. The Japanese, surprised at the resistance, were pinned down for three hours. Then reinforcements arrived. Tanks and planes were called in to support the Japanese attack.

The 71st Division troops had held the line for three hours, watching the enemy pinned down by their artillery, knowing that the 91st Combat Team should arrive shortly to support them. Then Japanese planes screamed along the line. The Filipinos grovelled in the dirt as bombs exploded in their midst and bodies were broken. Then the fighters came down, the chatter of their guns creating more panic than the bullets, which no one could see or hear. Already shaking with fear, the 71st line troops heard the roar and rattle of tanks that now joined the battle. It was too much for untrained minds and spirits. The line broke and ran to the rear, leaving the artillery uncovered and defenseless.

The 91st Combat Team did not appear. While moving north, they came to a downed bridge and had to make a detour. When the battle at Sison reached its peak, they were straggling along carabao paths far from the action. There is no reason to believe that their presence would have changed the result. They were no better prepared than the soldiers in Selleck's shattered division.

The 71st poured toward Pozorrubio. When they began to feel the fatigue of retreat, they stopped to reconsider. Their officers herded them in disorder into a new defensive line before Pozorrubio. By 7:00 P.M. the 91st Combat Team finally filed into the defensive position with the 71st. The 26th Cavalry was ordered again to move back three miles to Binalonan to set up a defensive position that probably was intended as much to stop the retreat of the 71st and the 91st as to stop the advance of the enemy.

After dark the Japanese moved against the 91st Combat Team sector and the green troops, faced by artillery, tanks, and screaming infantry, had their turn at rout, running in panic to the rear, out of Pozorrubio. Joined by the 71st Division troops, they moved back to the perimeter being prepared for them by the 26th Cavalry Scouts.

In two days of fighting the Japanese had moved out of the beachhead and down the shoulder of the mountains to the wide plain. They had broken three USAFFE divisions that opposed them. The 21st Division, along the Lingayen-Dagupan coast, was too far to the west to join the action. The Philippine Division, further south, was held in reserve. It was the only unbroken force between the Japanese and the approaches to Bataan. It could not be hazarded in the battle to the north.

The attempt to stop the Japanese at the beaches and to drive them back to the sea had failed. The only remaining option was to return to "Orange" and move back into Bataan and Corregidor for a long siege.

On December 23 Sutherland was back to work at 8:15 A.M. for an immediate conference with the staff chiefs concerning the move to Corregidor. It had become obvious that Wainwright's force at Lingayen would not hold, and orders were prepared for a withdrawal of the South Luzon Force into Bataan.[13]

Sutherland called Quezon 30 minutes later to inform him of events in the north and of the intended withdrawal of the South Luzon Force. More important,

Quezon was notified of the impending move of Headquarters USAFFE to Corregidor. The remainder of the day was spent in conference with various commanders and staff officers.

At 10:30 A.M. the daily operations report went to Washington:

Fighting continues in north with enemy exerting heavy pressure to debouch south from the defiles. He is making maximum use of his air in support of infantry and light tanks. Scattered enemy bombing yesterday throughout the archipelago, heavy at some points. Fighting continues in Mindanao. Nine of our B–17s coming in from Darwin bombed twelve transports at Davao. Results indeterminate, possibly negligible. Bombers now in air awaiting clearing of overcast to hit enemy at Lingayen area.[14]

16

Retreat

The defense of the beachhead had collapsed, and the troops had begun a long retreat into Bataan. A great deal of energy has been expended in an effort to rationalize the decision to make a beachhead defense. Only two options are available to any commander in a similar situation. He can meet the enemy at the beach or he can organize a defense in depth, meeting the enemy after they have established a beachhead. At Leyte and Lingayen in 1945 the Japanese chose the latter alternative. A rational case can be made for either option, and the choice must depend upon the particular facts that characterize a given situation. A decision to defend at the beach is not particularly evidence of optimism.

MacArthur wanted to see a Filipino army standing on the beaches, engaged in a fierce struggle with an armed invader, driving him back into the sea. It was not unreasonable to think that this might happen, and Homma was apprehensive that it would happen. Given a little more time, MacArthur could have fielded an army of more than 100,000 well-equipped troops, supported by air and naval forces and the full Pacific Fleet covering the sea approaches to the Philippines. By 2:00 P.M. of December 8, when the last shreds of hope for air cover were scattered over Clark Field and the Pacific Fleet was battered at Pearl Harbor, there could be no hope of air or naval support. Only one hope remained. A determined infantry still might make the landing so costly that it could not succeed. MacArthur knew that the two lines of action were not mutually exclusive. If the beach defense collapsed, the withdrawal to Bataan would still be a viable alternative.

Facts are not known until they are known. After the event the outcome generally seems inevitable enough, and one can easily trace out sufficient evidence to support that appearance of inevitability. Before the event the issue is always in doubt, even when the odds for success are quite short. In this case the odds did not seem to be excessively one-sided.

The Filipinos who had fought long and hard for independence deserved the privilege and the obligation of defending it in battle. It might have been better, perhaps, to have had four good U.S. infantry regiments on the line of the beaches instead of the untried, unprepared Filipino boys who stood there, but it *was* a Filipino beach and the independence of the Philippines was at stake.

Nevertheless, all this aside, "Revised Orange Five" had been approved as the plan for action. MacArthur was ordered on November 27 to implement it. Nothing could be changed by the disaster at Pearl Harbor and at Clark Field. The affair was in motion.

No one could ever say in shame or derision that the attempt had not been made. The officers who afterward recalled their opposition would have said just as bitterly, "We didn't win at the beaches because we weren't asked to do so. Had we been given the opportunity, we would have been victorious."

It is difficult to envision the advantage of an immediate withdrawal into Bataan and Corregidor, leaving the Japanese to occupy north Luzon without opposition. It would have filled the defensive positions on Bataan with raw recruits who had never fired a shot to meet an enemy who had not been depleted by hostilities. The Japanese had had to fight their way down the valley to Bataan, and they arrived footsore and weary. They had been worn out in the march. At the same time the Filipinos had been transformed into a fighting force.

MacArthur's real problem was one of timing. He had to disengage at precisely the right moment, not one hour too soon and not one hour too late. It had to be *after* every reasonable man could honestly assert that the attempt had been made and had failed, and *before* a retreat had become a rout that would put the Japanese at the Calumpit Bridges in time to intercept the South Luzon Force in their move into Bataan. This was the most difficult part of the matter, but it was a matter of tactics and maneuver that required only ordinary prudence and courage. One does not need to tell defeated men to retreat; one only needs to control the pace of the retreat, keeping it orderly and manageable.

Between Lingayen and the march into the defensive positions on Bataan, the Filipinos who had broken at the beachhead were transformed from green, nervous recruits into aggressive soldiers. The observer who reported them as running in disorder to the rear at Bauang and Agoo found them, a week later, to be aggressive and cocky. By the end of January, on Bataan, they brought Homma's 14th Army to a standstill and sapped it of the capacity and will to fight. By Homma's later testimony, at that time the Filipino forces could have driven him out of Bataan and out of Manila as well, and some were willing to make the attempt. By then it was too late. "Orange" must be played out to the bitter, ignominious end.

"Orange" required a simultaneous withdrawal of the North and South Luzon Forces into major defensive positions on Bataan. The key to the maneuver was control of the bridges over the Pampanga River on Highway 3 at Calumpit, about 30 miles north of Manila. The junction of Highway 3 with Highway 7, which led south to Bataan, was at San Fernando, perhaps ten miles north of Calumpit. Both North and South Luzon Forces had to move past this junction because it provided the only access to Bataan. If the Japanese could gain control of San Fernando and Calumpit before the South Luzon Force moved onto Highway 7, they could divide MacArthur's forces and achieve an early victory.

The North Luzon Force withdrew rapidly before the Japanese assault, never able to establish and hold a defensive line, but they did begin to give evidence of a willingness to fight. The Japanese did not always find it easy going. A major roadblock was thrown around the bridges; it held until January 1, when the South Luzon Force cleared the bridges. The bridges were then destroyed. The first mission of "Orange" had been completed successfully.

The withdrawal in general was an orderly one. The successive defensive lines held long enough to meet the tactical situation without the loss of any single major unit. There were troop losses, but on the other hand, troops that had run away at the beaches began to drift back to rejoin their units in the march to Bataan. The North Luzon Force, which left Lingayen with some 28,000 men, settled into the Bataan defenses with only 16,000. Some of the missing 12,000 had died, some had been wounded, and some had simply drifted away, a loss of almost 45 percent of troop strength. The South Luzon Force reported 15,000 men at the beginning of the withdrawal and could account for 14,000 on Bataan, a loss of only 1,000 men. The men who could not hold at the beaches would now show what they could do on Bataan.[1] Homma's forces had lost 627 killed, 1,282 wounded, and 7 missing.

The vulnerability of the headquarters at One Calle Victoria to air attack was so obvious that it is remarkable the Japanese did not demolish it early in the war. Squatting on the wall of Intramuros, it was an easy target for any dive bomber pilot who became bored with the tame and less important shipping in Manila Bay. During the first week of the war, an air raid shelter had been established in the sally port that ran through the wall under the headquarters. Regulations spelled out the need for proper behavior in the limited premises. There would be no sleeping. The rules of military courtesy would govern who relinquished the limited seats to those who entered late. I do not recall that any bombs fell in close proximity, but we could all watch and hear the bombs falling across the way in the harbor.

The idea that Headquarters USAFFE might eventually have to find safer quarters arose very early, long before the war, in a letter written by Hart to MacArthur. In August 1941 Hart suggested that "we look also to the occupancy and use of Corregidor as the ultimate command post. That is where the Navy first went underground, as you know, and we are pretty well set up there."[2]

Quezon wrote later:

I never imagined that I would ever have to take refuge on Corregidor. I had known for years that the fortress of Corregidor had been built as the last stronghold of the American forces in the Philippines and as a safe refuge for American Governors-General in case of grave danger.[3]

Quezon did not specify the source of the danger, but the original decision may have looked more directly at Filipino insurrection than at foreign invasion.

The idea of moving to Corregidor came up on December 17, when MacArthur sent Huff to tell Quezon that he should be prepared to leave Manila on four hours' notice. Sutherland and MacArthur had already discussed the matter, and arrangements had been made in Malinta Tunnel for high-ranking refugees.[4]

On December 13 and again on December 19 Sutherland's diary notes a discussion about a new location. On December 20 Sutherland talked about "alternate headquarters at LaSalle." Presumably "LaSalle" referred to LaSalle University, but more likely it was a code for Corregidor. By December 22, after the Japanese had landed at Lingayen, the matter was urgent. At 5:10 in the afternoon, just before he left for dinner, Sutherland had a conference with Akin and Marquat about a "command post move." The night of December 22/23 was filled with momentous events, and at 8:15 A.M. on the 23rd Sutherland called in the staff chiefs to notify them of the planned move. During the morning of December 24 the move got under way.[5]

On December 22 Sutherland had prepared a radio message to alert the War Department of the inevitable withdrawal to Bataan. Speaking for MacArthur, he concluded, "I will evacuate the High Commissioner and the Government to Corregidor. I intend to hold Corregidor." The dispatch was dictated and typed late on the afternoon of December 22 but was not transmitted until the following day.[6] On the afternoon of December 23 Sutherland remarked to Marshall with some bitterness, "Here goes Orange Three." the next day, Christmas Eve, the Japanese landed on south Luzon. There was some fighting at the beaches and the towns, but apparently no rout of the kind that had occurred at Lingayen. Nevertheless, by evening the Japanese had secured the beaches, had taken all the towns, and had moved inland some ten miles. It is not inconceivable that the South Luzon Force could have held up or even pushed back the Japanese, but conditions in the north made an immediate withdrawal imperative. The retreat was ordered, and elements began to move north toward Bataan, some 100 miles away.

Very early in the morning of December 24, at 5:40, notice went to Washington of the Japanese landing in south Luzon and of MacArthur's intention to evacuate Manila.[7] At 7:30 the open city proclamation that had been prepared two days earlier was issued to the press. Sutherland spent the next two hours in conferences with staff officers and commanders. Brereton was instructed to move his staff to Australia.[8] In the meantime MacArthur had called Sayre and Quezon, telling them that they would leave Manila at 2:30 P.M. on the *Mayon*.

At 11:00 A.M. of December 24, 1941, Headquarters USAFFE was assembled and notified that Manila had been declared an open city and would be evacuated. All general headquarters officers were promoted one grade and were allotted one suitcase and one bedroll. The enlisted men were told to bring a field pack and one barracks bag.

I walked out of my office, down the stairs, across the courtyard, and up to the second floor barracks where I had been billeted for the past few weeks. Most of the others had already completed their task, and only two or three soldiers were around to show me how to assemble my field pack. I finally got it together tightly enough to withstand several repeated drops to the floor. I did not have the slightest idea of what should be done with its contents.

I rummaged through the footlocker at the end of my bunk, taking out the clothing and toilet articles, absent-mindedly tossing into it an open box of soap flakes that I did not care to take with me but considered too valuable to throw in the trash can. I looked at the civilian suit I had worn to Angel Island, San Francisco, where I was issued my first uniform, a sweater, and the Bible that had been an inseparable part of my existence for years—read, underlined, thumbed through, and memorized. I pulled down the lid, fastened the lock, and walked back to the office. I would see it again, surprisingly enough.

In the courtyard papers were being burned and trucks were being loaded. No one, then or later, told me the details of any move; I never had any part in their execution except waiting for orders and following the generals for whom I worked. Turner left, and I do not recall ever seeing him again. I sat alone all day, typing dispatches. About time for supper (5:00 P.M.), which I did not get, a young private who had come into headquarters at the same time I had and who had been my companion in walks around Manila, put his head inside the door to say that he had been detailed to keep me company. So we sat gossiping about trivia. We both knew that it was a serious situation and were uncertain about the future, but we ignored it (as soldiers must) and made a joke of a bad situation (as soldiers will).

At dusk MacArthur walked out of his office and called, "Rogers." I jumped up and scrambled to the anteroom where he was waiting, looking around in a last farewell to the office that had been his home and headquarters. His glance moved around the walls that held mementos from former days. His attention focused on a flag tied to a staff in one corner of the room. A red pennant that carried four white stars, it had flown on his car when he was chief of staff. He was again a full general, promoted four days earlier.

MacArthur pointed to the flag and said, "Rogers, cut off that flag for me." I was nonplussed. I did not have a knife or even scissors, and did not know where to get either. He repeated, "Rogers, cut it off." In desperation I untied the thongs, rolled up the pennant, and handed it to him. He said, "Thank you," then, pushing it under his arm and turning away, he said, "Well, Dick, I guess it's time to go. There isn't anything left to do here."

MacArthur, followed by Sutherland and two privates, walked out the door and down the stairs to limousines that waited below. He and Sutherland stepped up through the door, which was held open for them by the driver of the first car. Behind MacArthur's car stood a second one. The driver pulled open the door, and the other private and I climbed into the luxurious Packard sedan, impressed with the pullout bar and the other accoutrements that occupied our attention as we followed MacArthur to the pier.

At the port area the *Don Esteban*, a small ship, stood waiting. The General and Sutherland walked up the gangplank to the ship; my friend and I followed. No one told us where to go, and we moved as far forward as we could from MacArthur and his immediate party, but not far enough to intrude on the officers who occupied the deck in front of us.

We slouched down on the damp steel deck, our backs against the side of the cabin, while the engine began to growl, stirring the water. The *Don Esteban* grumbled away from the dock, shuddering with the initial effort, grinding against the water, until it was under way.

Behind us Manila was burning, a spectacular display of sound and light. Fire and smoke illuminated our departure, and exploding munition dumps added to the sound. Ahead the sky was filled with stars.

Shortly after the ship left the dock, MacArthur's party began to sing Christmas carols and were joined by the officers and men. My friend and I were less timely in our choice. We softly sang a few naughty ditties that we had picked up. They were not that many nor were they all that naughty, but it was the best we could do. We were soldiers on the way to battle, and Christmas hymns did not seem quite appropriate—or so we thought.

Sometime around 8:30 P.M. the *Don Esteban* pulled up under the shadowy hulk of Corregidor at the North Dock. There was a scramble as we debarked, and a ride up to a huge, empty barracks on Topside. I took a cot, set it up, stretched myself out on the canvas in the warm night air, and fell asleep. It was already Christmas morning.

On January 1 Richard Marshall made a final withdrawal, and January 2 the Japanese entered and occupied Manila. Washington was advised: "For the present I am remaining in Manila establishing an advanced headquarters on Corregidor." The first-person pronoun was not intended to be taken as a personal reference. It was used as an impersonal reference to the rear echelon under Marshall that remained in Manila; MacArthur was its commanding general and, therefore, its personification. Had the question of meaning been raised with MacArthur, he would have looked puzzled that one could not understand such an obvious statement.

A dispatch on Christmas Day reported:

Forward echelon moved this date from Fort Mills to Bataan and is establishing CP. Administrative echelon remains Fort Mills. Remaining at Manila is base echelon. Will be impossible to report numerous minor administrative items because of congestion of communication facilities. I shall assume such authority to continue normal administration as is necessary unless advised to the contrary.[9]

Manila had been declared an open city—the Japanese were given public notice that the city would not be defended. They could enter when they chose, without meeting any opposition. There was no requirement that the city be clear of U.S. troops until the Japanese entered the city. The technicality required only that

U.S. troops leave before the Japanese made their entry and took possession. The fact that Marshall stayed behind to destroy supplies was no threat or hindrance to the Japanese, who could have entered Manila on Christmas Eve had they chosen to do so. Rear Echelon Headquarters USAFFE would have fled before them without a fight.

Bataan would hold until defeated. The last defense would be made on Corregidor, which was stocked with food. It was here that MacArthur would make the last stand, holding to a bitter end.

V

Citadel, January–March 1942

Advance GHQ to Topside; first air attack; under fire; down to Malinta Tunnel; Rogers prepares to die; Sutherland as deputy commander; MacArthur and his troops

17

Corregidor

Christmas Day of 1941 dawned with the glory of a tropical sunrise. Light streamed through the open arcades and filled the huge, empty room. I awoke with a start and walked out to the veranda. I faced south and looked down over the parade ground. A row of large officers' quarters lined the open field. A flag fluttered on the tall staff. There was a flutter of activity as the officers began to leave for the day's work. The troops were all in the artillery positions, where they now lived and served their guns. This Topside area had housed the headquarters of Fort Mills but now provided living space for MacArthur and his staff as well.

I walked to the opposite side of the barracks and looked north toward Bataan, three miles across the bay. I looked down the slope of Morrison Hill to the Middleside area, which squatted below Topside on a small plateau. A hospital, quartermaster warehouses, and machine shops were draped across the top of the plateau.

A row of gun batteries curved around Morrison Hill in an arc below Topside. Roads and railroad tracks spread like tentacles from the parade ground and Middleside to the gun emplacements. These great coast artillery batteries with 12-inch mortars and 14-inch rifles, impregnable against naval gunfire, protected Manila Bay from any intruder. Several ravines—James, Cheney, and Ramsay— cut down the hill to the beaches or cliffs below. A small road ran around the island on a shallow beach.

Off to the east, toward Manila, were Bottomside, Malinta Hill, and the low, tapering tail of the island. Bottomside filled the flat, narrow area between Morrison Hill and Malinta Hill. There were two docks on each side of the island here, various service facilities, and the tiny village of San Jose, which housed the small civilian population of Corregidor. The west entrance to Malinta Tunnel cut into the center of the hill.

Map 6
Corregidor Island (detail)

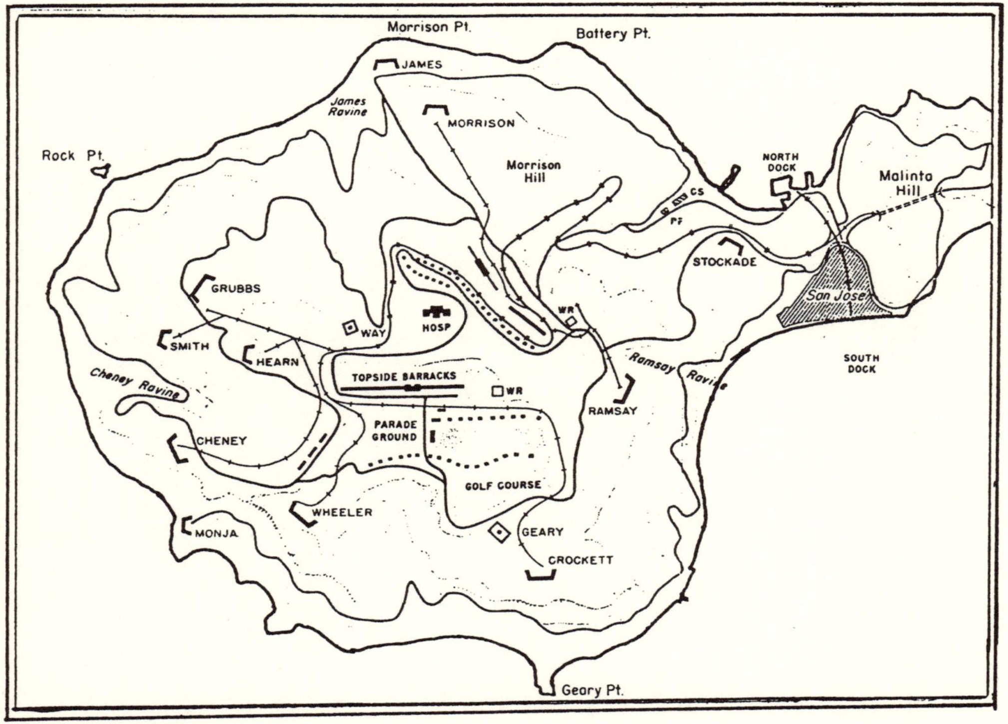

Source: U.S. Army.

Malinta Hill, laced with a system of tunnels, was designed for use as a warehouse and hospital facility in the event of attack, a safe storage area for munitions and supplies, and a haven for the wounded while crews in the emplacements fired the guns in open defiance of an enemy surely bent on self-destruction.

On the tail of the island was a small airstrip, an afterthought that certainly was not part of the island's defenses. It was symbolic of the shortsighted understanding that sees only today's needs, forgetting that yesterday's impregnable fortress may be tomorrow's tomb.

I walked off to find the latrine so I could wash and shave, then went downstairs to find the new office. Headquarters USAFFE was divided into three sections. One echelon was in Manila with Richard Marshall. A second was in one of the laterals in Malinta Tunnel. This group included the bulk of the headquarters staff. I cannot recall now precisely what lateral they occupied. I do not recall that I was ever in it. I suspect memory simply fails to recall the fact. The third advance echelon had moved to Topside with MacArthur and Sutherland. It included the four staff chiefs, their clerks, three of the aides, and a small group of enlisted personnel who provided housekeeping services.

The first few days on Corregidor were a relatively peaceful prelude to the brutal weeks that followed. We set up headquarters on the ground floor of the Topside artillery barracks. MacArthur, his family, and his staff moved into the residential quarters around the parade ground. The small headquarters detachment was billeted in the huge Topside barracks. Two of us found an empty room on the second floor above the offices. A canvas cot and a wooden box constituted the furnishings of my quarters. The mess sergeant managed to serve turkey for dinner that Christmas Day, but there were no trimmings; it was a far cry from the opulence of Thanksgiving. We would see much worse.

Two sergeants of the 4th Marine Regiment, who served as guards for MacArthur's office, took up quarters on the opposite side of the large room I had taken for my quarters. Between the two soldier clerks and the marines there was only one brief encounter. During the day one of them took my wooden box. That evening I reclaimed it. The marine came off duty later in the evening and attempted to take it back. I protested, although he towered over me. At the time I did not consider that a general's stenographer may have a certain vicarious stature that cannot be violated with impunity. The sergeant grinned, and I kept the box. For me, RHIP (rank has its privileges) extended only to generals.

Headquarters USAFFE was located in three rooms at the southeast corner of the barracks, sheltered by a veranda that ran along the southern side of the building, facing the parade ground. MacArthur had the corner office. Sutherland occupied the next one to the west. The third, slightly larger office housed Willoughby, Wilson, and others, Rogers, and another clerk or two. The offices were connected by open doorways. A wide arcade opened each room to the veranda.

I found a pinup of a shapely, scantily clad young woman, cut it out, and taped it to the pullout tray on my desk. She traveled many miles with me. I also came across a copy of a news magazine that dated back to September or October. It carried the vivid headline "Japan Does Not Dare Attack." Inside was a major story reciting the various weaknesses of the Japanese—nearsightedness, flimsy planes, capsizing battleships—and extolling the powers of the mighty U.S. Pacific Fleet and air force and the limited but courageous defenses in the Philippines. My faith in journalists died. Perhaps it had been a brave show intended to deter the Japanese.

Every day in the early afternoon there was an air raid. Waves of Japanese bombers in formation bore in toward Corregidor. Antiaircraft guns opened fire and, after a few rounds, the attackers pulled away to strike the harbor area of Manila and Cavite. We were emboldened by the effectiveness of our fire and assured ourselves with great conviction that Corregidor could not, and would not, be bombed.

On December 29, about noon, the air raid siren blared a warning, and a little later antiaircraft guns began to fire their usual show of bravado. I was standing at my desk. The firing was more sustained and seemed more urgent. Then machine guns began to chatter. There was a rush of falling bombs and explosions. Someone shouted that the marine sergeant, my opponent of several days before, had been killed by a bomb blast while standing guard at MacArthur's empty office.

In pure reflex all of us dropped to the floor. I curled up under my desk, and Wilson was in behind me. Others were under tables when one could be found. It was an instantaneous reaction, a thoughtless and automatic response like that of an animal suddenly startled. We got up and looked at each other sheepishly, saying nothing in excuse for ourselves or in ridicule of others. On the floor was a six-inch piece of metal, jagged and hot, a fragment of a bomb that had exploded just outside the building.

My buzzer sounded. I walked hurriedly to Sutherland's desk, notebook and pencils in hand, ready for dictation. He motioned for me to sit down and began to dictate. His voice was taut. He had finished a line of dictation when the second run began. The roar of the planes grew louder, the clatter of their machine guns seemed on top of us, there was the whoosh of falling bombs, and this time the explosions rocked the room. Sutherland sat at his desk and I sat beside it, waiting for the next phrase. Sutherland glanced up at the ceiling, then resumed dictation.

The third run started. The roar of the engines came closer and closer. Sutherland remarked that we should get to the corners of the room, where we would have some shelter. He took one corner, I took another, and Wilson found a third. It was not much protection, but it was better than sitting in the open, waiting for random bomb fragments. The third string of bombs exploded, and dust covered the room. I remarked, to relieve my tension, that I had always wanted my hair to stand on end. Sutherland snapped at me, "Damn it, Rogers, your hair isn't standing on end." Wilson looked at me sharply. I felt properly foolish at my temerity. I suppose that irony has its own proper place. I realized for the first time that Sutherland was at least as nervous as I was, and possibly more, for he seldom used profanity, even under stress. My diary records only one brief reaction. "God! What a sensation!"

MacArthur had sent Mrs. MacArthur and his son to an air raid shelter when the warning sounded. He stood on the parade ground to watch the show. As the Japanese planes screamed over, he and Domingo Adversario, his orderly, dropped into a shallow ditch, Adversario on top of MacArthur and shielding the General's head with his helmet. Adversario was wounded. MacArthur did not take cover even when the entire Topside area was disintegrating and burning around him. He was still standing erect in the shambles as the last planes droned away.

The waves of bombers continued through several additional passes, and dictation went on. When the bombs rushed down, we moved to the shelter of our respective corners. I refrained from any further attempts at familiar humor.

An officer came in to report to Sutherland on what was happening. The Topside area was a smoking ruin. There was a circle of craters around the headquarters end of the building, some within 25 yards. On the last run a large bomb had been dropped in the center of the long barracks, tearing a hole through all three floors. The roof had collapsed in that area.

Sutherland decided to evacuate. He ordered all officers into a bomb shelter at one of the gun batteries. The sergeant was directed to take the enlisted men to the shelter of Malinta Tunnel. We dutifully lined up in a column of twos and began the march. I was at the tail of the column with a friend whose name I cannot recall. The line moved past the barracks and across the first set of railroad tracks. We followed the second line of tracks that led down toward Grubb Battery. Somewhere north of Hearn Battery the two of us broke away from the rest, cutting down the hill until we reached the road. We turned right, walking downhill until we were hailed from Way Battery, just above us to the right. It was a pleasant, quiet stroll through the woods. We laughed and joked as we walked. We had wandered like two innocent fools out of one danger into another. The remainder of the column marched steadily away from us to safety. Seasoned soldiers stand together. They find comfort in company. We were not seasoned soldiers. While the others sat safely in the tunnel, we were exposed for two more hours.

Our stroll in the sunshine was interrupted by the second and third stages of the air attack. Twenty-two light bombers came in for an hour of fun. This group hit Middleside just as we reached their target.

Suddenly, above us on the hill, a voice shouted, "You stupid bastards, it isn't over yet. Take cover!" The guns began to fire. We had walked from Topside to the batteries covering the Middleside hospital and warehouse area. We fell into a ditch, listening to shells rise and bombs fall, exploding and throwing dirt over us. We were back in the middle of the action, and there we remained for another bombardment. My friend offered me a cigarette. I accepted it, thought a minute, then returned it, deciding that it was hardly sensible to pick up a habit that would be difficult to satisfy in the present conditions. That was the closest I ever came to smoking.

Time loses all meaning in such circumstances. We stood up once or twice to try to see what was happening, falling back to cover in the ditch when planes roared over us. We could see smoke and dust over the rise of the hill, but all of the buildings were out of sight around a bend in the road. A third and final wave came for the last run. Sixty bombers had the last hour of the air show. Sixty tons of bombs were dropped on the island during this raid. Finally there was silence. It was just three o'clock.

We left the ditch and wandered on down the road. We turned the bend and for the first time realized what had happened. The entire Middleside complex was a smoking ruin. Useless attempts were being made to put out fires. We did not know where to go or how to get there. Somewhere above Ramsay ravine, we were picked up by a truck that was going back up to Topside to move our headquarters down to the tunnel.

Equipment was loaded into trucks. I took the notebook and pinup from my desk, then my typewriter, boarded the truck, and rode down the hill to the tunnel. "This tunnel surely looks good," I wrote in my diary.

This series of air attacks slackened on December 30 but resumed on December 31 and continued until January 6. All surface structures on the island were destroyed either by bombs or by fire. Bomb craters were spread uniformly at 25-yard intervals over the entire surface of Corregidor. After January 6 air attacks were suspended until March 24, when there was another week of bombardment. The final series of attacks began on April 9 and continued until the surrender on May 6.

18

Malinta Tunnel

Malinta tunnel was a maze of underground passages cut in solid rock. It was laid out in a precise grid that conformed to the topography of Malinta Hill. The basic element of the tunnel was a roadway running east-west through the hill, about 20 feet wide and arched to the same height. A railroad track ran through it with raised sidewalks on either side. Railroad cars screeched, grunted, and rattled back and forth until the electric lines were so badly damaged that they could no longer be repaired.

Rows of lateral tunnels cut back from the main roadway, 150 feet long with a 10-foot arch, interlocked by connecting passages. Another grid lay to the north of the main complex. A north-south road served as a main thoroughfare with laterals branching out to both sides that were used for a hospital. A third grid was dug to the south and used as a navy supply depot.

MacArthur's headquarters were housed in lateral 3 which was my office and home for ten weeks or more. The bulk of Headquarters USAFFE was located in a different lateral for several days, then was moved to Bataan. I found my desk, put down my belongings, and wandered out to sleep on the bare sidewalk along the side of the main roadway.

The next morning I reported to work at 7:30. Sutherland came in. He motioned me to his desk for dictation and asked, ''Rogers, where did we stop?'' I read the last two sentences of dictation, and he resumed the line of thought. When I typed the first draft of the long message, I found that neither of us had missed a word. The events of the previous day had been a good performance on both sides. Sutherland got a silver star for his work and I recall a certain twinge of jealousy. I did not get my reward until March 11. March 30 was a day of change and therefore received more attention in my diary, events seeming more significant when they are new and changing.

The air attack of the day before had been the first of a series that would continue for five days. During the day the Japanese bombed the water storage tanks, and salt water was mixed with fresh drinking water. As a result we drank brackish water. I recorded, "It surely tastes awful. What I wouldn't give for a drink of good ice water!" Moreover, "I have missed dinner for the past three days and survived on two sandwiches per day."

In the late afternoon I left the tunnel to go back to Topside for a cot and anything else I could find. I found the cot. As I walked past the library, I took three books at random. They turned out to be Wilde's plays, Oliver Wendell Holmes, and Emerson's poems. I hitched a ride back down to the tunnel. Later I would find more books. My letters indicate that by the middle of February I had read the *Aeneid*, Tennyson's plays and longer poems, Bryce's *Holy Roman Empire*, and a number of novels.

That night, after Sutherland left the tunnel, I walked to the cold storage plant with several other fellows to get a drink of fresh water. It was really good. The nights before, I had slept just outside the entrance to Lateral 3 on the concrete sidewalk that ran along the road in the main tunnel. Now I set up my cot with a blanket for a pillow.

By January 5 bombs had demolished power transmission lines, and I was no longer disturbed by the grinding and growling of locomotives. Later in the month my cot disappeared, and I slept for two nights on the bare sidewalk. Then I found a blood-stained hospital stretcher that I used as a bed for a week. Later I found another cot, and I kept this one folded under my desk during the day.

I wonder now why I slept where I did, and where everyone else slept. If I knew then I cannot recall now. There is no indication in the diary that I was particularly afraid to leave the tunnel; I did so frequently. No one ever told me what I should do, and I suspect I simply did what was obviously reasonable. That is, I stayed close to my post of duty, where Sutherland could find me if he wanted me. One night Huff walked by, watched me sitting on the cot sprinkling foot powder on my feet, and remarked, "Taking care of your feet, Rogers? That's a good soldier."

By the time we reached Corregidor, my position was well established as a loner and as one who had extraordinarily compelling duties.[1] Sometime in February I was urged to get out of the "Goddamned tunnel" to spend a couple of days with a company of the 4th Marines who wanted to show me what it was like to be a marine. I had gone over to their camp with the two marine sergeants, Bundy and Thompson, who served in Lateral 3 as MacArthur's orderlies. One of them remarked, "You can believe him. He can't get away. MacArthur expects him to be there from morning to night. That's his duty, twenty-four hour service."

A field kitchen was set up on December 31 at the east entrance to the tunnel, and we reported twice a day for meals. We sat in the dirt with messkits. Rice was the basic ingredient of our meal, with fish or other bits of meat that must have included carabao. No one ever asked since we all knew that in the Philippines dog meat was considered a delicacy. "Rice and raisins" was considered a treat, and even "cream beef" was honored by being called that and not given the customary army label, "S.O.S." There were even wieners on occasion, and mule steak when five mules were killed by artillery fire.

A dog, Duke, made the rounds at each meal. He was a pampered animal, a reminder for lonesome soldiers of happier times and better days at home. He refused to eat wieners. I remember feeding him stew, sharing my food and my spoon with him. There was a momentary revulsion, but I suppressed it with the thought that we were comrades in a tight situation. I might eat him before it was over—and he might eat me! There were no longer complaints or swearing at mess boys. No one talked about the better days in Manila. Everyone knew what the future held, and each in his own way reconciled himself to it.

On my first night in the tunnel I slept by a stack of boxes that contained cans of tomato juice. I took one can but, I am glad to say, never another. It was not fear but a sense of moral obligation that restrained me from taking more.[2] The juice was reserved for hospital use. Barges that had been sunk close to the shore provided a scavenging ground for "sea treasure"—liquor, candy, cigarettes, and other goodies. The treasure trove was duly exploited, and I expect units stationed in the nooks and crannies of the craggy terrain of Corregidor had private caches of luxury that gave solace in otherwise difficult times.

I craved not whiskey but chocolate and had tiny pieces on two occasions. On January 5 a friend gave me a piece from a bar he had found on the barge. I waited a long time for another. My diary entry of January 19 reads, "Oh, for some chocolate candy!" On March 9 I traded my watch for an entire half-pound bar of hospital chocolate. I intended to eat it all by myself, but I broke the bar into inch-square bits and passed them around to my comrades, taking two small pieces for myself. Each person took a piece without a word—none was expected or needed.

On January 26 I wandered over to the remains of San Jose, formerly a thriving village in Bottomside. It had been obliterated, but in the midst of the rubble stood a chimney covering a baker's oven where the operator of the local *pan-adería* plied his trade. God knows where he got the ingredients or how he survived. He sold a loaf of bread for 25 cents, and a quarter of a loaf provided an excellent meal. The bread was fresh and tasted almost like cake. In addition, I bought a dozen doughnuts. These were the only gastronomical delights of the ten weeks I spent on Corregidor.

For the first week the latrine at the west end of the main tunnel provided an increasingly deteriorating facility. It obviously was overcrowded as men of all ranks tried to maintain normal hygiene, and it soon collapsed under the burden. I went three days without washing. Later we improvised, getting salt water where we could find it for washing and shaving. A note for January 8 records that an enlisted man complained to MacArthur that it was unfair that officers shaved in fresh water while enlisted men had to use brine. My diary records that MacArthur decreed that officers must also shave in salt water. The anecdote is recorded as a fact. I usually identified rumors as such.

I had no regrets concerning my fortunes. I was young with no responsibilities nor dependents. On January 1 I had given myself up to certain death. I would have made the same decision had I known the outcome when I enlisted in September. I hoped I would have the courage to die bravely, no matter how death came. I increased my GI insurance from $1,000 to $10,000 at a cost of $40. I felt that an advance payment of $40 in anticipation of $10,000 to be paid to my parents before the expiration of 90 days was a very good investment.

On January 7 a group of us walked down to the ocean southeast of Malinta Hill. It was a beautiful sandy beach, the sky was blue, the water was warm. It was my first swim in the ocean. It was more than a pleasant diversion—it was the only bath or shower I had had for two weeks. It was the last I had on Corregidor. Performance of basic physiological and hygienic functions is hidden in memory, part of a repetitive routine of life, like other bodily functions, that simply pass unnoticed. I remember eating just two or three times. I remember once squatting over an open trench latrine sharing my labors with a Filipino sergeant.

There were two areas for social gathering for Malinta Tunnel "Rats"—the east entrance and the hospital entrance to the north. I used the east entrance, not because of its attractiveness but because it was close to my post of duty in Lateral 3. In the period after lunch or just before sunset, a crowd would gather to gossip, joke, promenade, flirt when a partner could be found (which was not often), or just enjoy the pleasure of fresh air and sunshine that had become very precious to us.

The few civilians on Corregidor made up some of the party. Colonel Carl Seals escorted his wife to a chair, and they sat and talked quietly. The General and Mrs. MacArthur arrived to stroll around the area, visiting with officers and (less frequently) enlisted men. The General, with a cigar or cigarette in a long holder (rather than the pipe that he used later), swinging a cane rhythmically and decisively, not showing either anxiety or concern, smiled and laughed, a perfect specimen of confidence and optimism. No one could guess the great weight that rested on his shoulders in those troubled times.

Petite Mrs. MacArthur, sometimes with sunglasses and sometimes without, her hand under MacArthur's arm, talked constantly, either to the General or to others, with apparent lighthearted unconcern.

MacArthur had the use of a portion of one lateral in Malinta tunnel. Two small rooms, each seven by nine feet, had been partitioned off for his family in the third lateral on the south from the west entrance of the tunnel. They were dark and poorly lighted, with meager furnishings and no plumbing. As everywhere else in the tunnel, the air was dank, musty, and dusty. The quarters available to the MacArthurs were just slightly more private, but hardly more commodious or comfortable, than those available to anyone else. Headquarters enlisted men fended for themselves, using whatever shelter they could find. They had never had privacy in the best of barracks and did not expect any. MacArthur was relatively worse off than his troops. The MacArthurs found relief from their dreary tunnel apartment in a small cottage on the tail of the island near the airfield. For a while they had pleasant conditions there. Early in February Japanese artillery fire drove them back to safety.

At other times General and Mrs. MacArthur joined the more socially respectable group that used the north hospital entrance as a gathering place. President Quezon, his wife and family, and his entourage lived in the hospital lateral area. The tone of the gathering in that area was more sedate and more elegant. A Filipino major, Mrs. Quezon's aide and bodyguard, always kissed her hand when she rose and left the group. Quezon's daughters socialized with all present. I seldom went into that area, but one evening when I was passing down the crowded lateral, I found the Quezon girls talking and laughing with several soldiers. Maria was sewing a button on a soldier's shirt, and in a vain attempt at gallantry I suggested that I would tear off a button if she would sew it on. I was rewarded with a prim, "But that would be wasteful." She had logic and propriety on her side, and I retreated.

Another time I was at the north entrance, I passed Colonel (Senator) Manuel Roxas, who was sitting in the sun. With characteristic bitterness he asked, "Well, Rogers, do you still want to go to Bataan?" I replied, "I am not sure, sir." I wondered how he came to know that I had asked Sutherland to let me go with him to Bataan.

Malinta tunnel was both a refuge and a prison. When the bombs or shells from Japanese artillery fell, one could feel secure as they spent themselves on the rock above, the roar rumbling through the laterals and the ground shaking under the impact. At other times it was a dusty, musty, crowded, dark, damp hole in the ground, and one yearned for the sunshine and fresh air outside.

I slept inside, not because I was afraid but because it seemed a logical thing to do. No one ever bothered to tell me where "home" was supposed to be. Those who spent their lives in the tunnel did so because they were ordered to be there. Those who served outside did so because they were under orders. At one time or another the parties would have been glad to exchange situations. Of course, those outside could assume a certain air of courage, and they did. But each did his duty and tolerated the vicissitudes, pleasant or unpleasant, that filled up his time.

By early February the end for Corregidor was clearly in sight. The forces on Bataan were holding a tight perimeter, but irreplaceable supplies were giving out. No one doubted the fact of defeat; only the timing was in question. Machine guns were installed at each end of the tunnel. I had never been close to a machine gun before, and I wondered how I would behave when the time came to fire them.

The boy's short legs struggled to match the father's long stride. Towering far over his head, the gold braid of his father's cap glittered in the sun. His father's cane cut the air. The face that smiled in tender, affectionate baby play now wore the official mask of command that separated baby play from soldier play. Dark eyes wandered nervously up to the father's stern face, then sought comfort in the mother's face but found only anxiety. Soldier play faces stared curiously down from all sides. The boy sensed that somehow all those faces displayed toward him, in a softer way, the respect displayed to the father. He sensed that he had authority and occupied an exalted space in this chaos.

Strong arms grasped the boy in a rough embrace. The boy's eyes slid up along sergeant's stripes to a hard helmet, into stern eyes and a mouth that wanted to smile but did not. Out of the sun into the shadow. A shattering roar, smoke, shouts. The mother reached out a reassuring hand, murmured, "Arthur, it is all right, we are safe." Into a small, dark, dusty cubicle marked off by blankets strung from wire. Down on a canvas cot and the warmth of a mother's arms. Again a shattering roar, then another and another. Earth shaking, sudden darkness, muffled shouts. Mother's arms and nurse's hand. Dick's voice: "General, there are a dozen bombers up there. We got two of them." Daddy's voice: "Dick, did they get Manuel into the tunnel? I must go down and see him." The boy knew there would be no baby play, and he lay down to wait for sleep.

Outside, in the tunnel road, the casualties were lifted from trucks and carried hurriedly to the hospital lateral, blood dripping from the canvas stretchers. A bomb had come through the roof of an artillery dugout.

It was over in an hour. The boy slept in apparent peace. The mother sat quietly by him, hand ready to offer assurance. The father slumped on a cot. Gone was his soldier face. There was no "baby-play" face. There was just a wan, drawn face that no one outside ever saw. The father thought what he need not say. The four-year-old baby was a veteran, battle-hardened, who had stood under enemy fire, afraid but not bending to tears or fright. He and his mother had marched into battle to set an example for thousands of Filipino boys who stood in the lines on Bataan.

The father was reconciled to the fact that they all might die in battle. The mother accepted what the baby could not understand. They were symbols of a pledge that the Filipinos would not fight alone in vain. They were symbols of help to come. They were more dear to the father than the Filipinos, but the strange soldier-play face had led them into danger and would keep them there. He could not deny his son one ounce of affection. He could not bear to inflict one ounce of discipline or punishment. All that aside, to meet the demands of duty and a sense of honor, he exposed a sensitive child's soul to the hazard of a violent death. He had bestowed on his only son a strange and dangerous legacy that would carry him to very great glory or to very great despair.

Sandbag barriers were raised across the entrances to protect the inhabitants of the tunnel against blast. I do not recall any particular feeling of despair or any great show of bravado. On half rations we were wasting away. The first artillery attacks began on February 5 and continued with varying intensity until the surrender on May 6. Corregidor and the other islands in the harbor defense system came under daily attack that soon developed into a more or less uniform pattern. Japanese artillery opened fire early in the day. When their fire slackened, harbor defense guns responded for a short period, but were seldom successful. The Japanese then resumed action, firing at sporadic intervals during the remainder of the day. There was seldom serious damage, but the harassing fire made life outside the tunnel extremely hazardous for those who were not close to shelter.

The tunnel was quite safe. It was cut deep in the rock, but we frequently had to reassure ourselves of the fact. As artillery shells shattered on the rock above, a muffled roar reverberated through the laterals, dust fell from the roof, the dim yellow lights flickered or faded into black darkness. At times like this the stale, warm air became a stifling fog as we waited tensely for light to return, each sitting isolated in the darkness, alone with his own thoughts, not daring to break the silence with even a whisper. Death was in the air, living with us intimately and menacingly. We all knew it was there, although we never gave expression to our emotions.

Rumor on rumor passed swiftly from mouth to ear and on again, creeping into every crevice, natural or man-made, on the island. No one believed them except in the sense that they gave small relief in a tense situation.

One night the report circulated that the *Ranger* had slipped through the blockade and was anchored near Corregidor in Manila Bay. As the word flew from one man to another, enthusiasm grew and each one felt the momentary thrill that salvation had come, knowing all the while that hard logic gave little firm support to reason as opposed to enthusiasm. It could not be true, but who would not yield to the temporary (if forlorn) hope that an aircraft carrier had finally made its way to our lonesome frontier of action? *Ranger*, of course *had* come through the blockade and was anchored off Corregidor, but it was not the carrier, just a small tubgoat. The elation had been built on a slippery foundation of uncertainty. No one really believed it but it brought momentary hope.

Ten days later word passed that a Japanese submarine had shelled the west coast of the United States. It was added, although no one could verify the fact, that MacArthur had radioed the commanding general of the 9th Corps Area that help would be sent from Corregidor to assist in the defense of San Francisco if the troops there could manage to hold out just a little longer.

Word crept over the island that Homma had committed suicide in MacArthur's former Manila Hotel penthouse. With the rumor marched MacArthur's reported tart comment: "I hope he didn't mess up my bathroom." Whatever MacArthur said, or did not say—and no one who repeated the story could be sure—it briefly lifted the fog of despair. None of us realized that the rumor was built this time on the solid fact that Homma's failure to crack the Bataan defenses had left him in disgrace and despair. At that time the remnants of his battered army could not have defended Manila had MacArthur chosen to take it.

Everyone found someone, somewhere—not too far away—on whose shoulders he could cast in blame, reproach, or ridicule the burden of responsibility for the senseless idiocy of the situation. MacArthur, who would have worn the laurels of victory had there been any, was naturally enough chosen to bear the brunt of defeat. He was ridiculed and reviled as the closest and most accessible target by men whose psychological processes had to find a tangible, plausible reason for their discomfort and dismay.

MacArthur bore his burden with dignity and grace, never showing, at least in public, the terrible weight of a personal agony which matched that of any private soldier in the Philippines. Perhaps his was even a greater agony because of the sense of personal responsibility. He knew what the troops felt and said, and his sensibility reeled under that knowledge. Those who saw him in public would never have known. The foolish took his display of moral and physical courage as arrogant disregard of those who could afford to pretend not to have any of those qualities. Appearances to the contrary, there was moral and physical courage to spare on all sides.

Almost every day—sometimes several times a day—MacArthur strode into Lateral 3, head high, cheerful and smiling, careful not to catch his cane on a chair or someone's leg. Occasionally he greeted one or another of the senior officers on the way down the crowded aisle. Those sitting along the aisle often felt the cuff on his sleeve as he swung his arm. At least I did as I sat, like the others, facing the wall, either typing or reading. At the very end of the portion of the lateral that was allocated as office space he passed Sutherland's desk with a "Good morning, Dick." His own desk was immediately behind Sutherland's. MacArthur sat, sometimes bent over dispatches or reports, sometimes leaning back, foot propped against a desk drawer, talking to Sutherland, who, turned in his chair to face the general, had his back to the rest of us.

Behind the General's desk, in the rear portion of the lateral, bunks were stacked in double tiers as sleeping quarters for officer personnel. That area was always very dark. The forward office area was very poorly lighted. Occasionally the General, who had always paced in his office, paced back and forth down the long aisle between the bunks, Sutherland crowded slightly behind him, talking earnestly about some pressing bit of business.

Opposite MacArthur's desk, in an empty space along the wall, the two marine sergeants, Bundy and Thompson, stood guard. It was very informal guard duty and they lounged rather than stood at their post, gossiping when MacArthur was not at his desk, trying to look more official when he was.

His tasks performed, MacArthur picked up his cap, grasped his cane, assumed a look of affable, relaxed unconcern, and marched back down the aisle, chin high, out the lateral entrance and away to Mrs. MacArthur and his son.

Sutherland remained at his desk all day, engrossed in the details of the war that MacArthur left in his capable hands. Sutherland, as MacArthur's chief of staff, to a very great extent, ran the war.

In a letter written to Chynoweth one finds confirmation of Sutherland's command authority.

I have sent and will continue to send a number of officers to you on the ships that go to Panay. Some of them are excellent and some are no-good. I am operating under a policy that every non-productive man must leave this garrison.

I relieved you [from Sharp's command] in order that you would be able to function without the rigid restrictions that Sharp seems to place upon his subordinates. I have an idea that you have felt much freer ever since. I know that it will facilitate our business here.[3]

Sutherland's statement expressly assumes a personal responsibility for the change of command: "I relieved you. . . ." Later in the letter he states: "I am sending a finance officer." I think this is an accurate measure of the underlying reality.

It was Sutherland who called the commanders on Bataan to deliver commands, advice, or precautions. In important matters he consulted MacArthur, but in less critical affairs, speaking in MacArthur's name, he gave the order, confident with reason that MacArthur would support him. The two men had worked together for so long and had such confidence in each other that there were few situations in which Sutherland could not anticipate with certainty what MacArthur's reaction would be. For practical purposes MacArthur and Sutherland were one where official matters were concerned. Mutual respect, affection, and confidence had welded them into a single-minded understanding of the demands imposed upon them.

Life magazine for April 13, 1942, has a picture of Lateral 3 that was taken in late February. The picture looks back toward the rear of the lateral that was my post of duty. On the left side is an empty chair numbered 92F. There are three officers bent over their work. I am the fourth person, my head thrust forward, looking toward the camera. The two soldiers standing behind me are Bundy and Thompson. Standing in the center aisle is General Edward King. Far back on the right, behind a light, are the blurred faces of Sutherland and MacArthur.

Day after day these officers and men reported to their desks, worked as duty demanded, and, when there was no work, pored over maps and charts as if their effort could produce some result, yet knowing that there was only one final outcome. Two of the officers held their glasses on their heads with a chain of rubber bands because the earpieces were broken.

They were all professional soldiers doing their duty as conditions demanded, with all the competence they could muster, with great dignity and composure, without showing complaint or anger although they must certainly have felt it.

This is the hell of a "citadel" defense that MacArthur despised. There is no obvious glory in sitting like cornered rats waiting for the end. There is no display of courage or valor; just a silent death watch. But courage, valor, and glory there were, in truth, and I felt it then as I feel it now.

On February 28 I purchased a pen and pencil set for 35 pesos. Bundy and Thompson came to me with a gold pen and pencil set I could have for 50 pesos. I protested that I did not need it and certainly could not afford it; my cash balance had been reduced to 35 pesos. They told me that I certainly would need the pen in the future and agreed to take 35 pesos. Thereafter I was treated with unprecedented deference by them. Several days later they told me they had seen my name on a list in the general's desk. I accepted the information in silence, not wishing to be involved in knowledge obtained through devious channels.

On March 2 I walked up to Middleside with a friend, Roy Thulson. Two days later my diary reads, "I'm lonesome and hungry, Damn it!" It was a timid lapse into profanity. I became more proficient with later events of the war.

On March 5 I wrote in my diary, "God pity the hospitals when the rainy season begins." We had just received first reports of massive malaria in Bataan.

The last entry in the Corregidor diary, for March 9, is the notation that I had traded my watch for a piece of chocolate.

Lateral 3 would soon be far behind me.

19

Soldier's Duty

It is not accurate to say that those on Corregidor did not complain about their fate, and it surely was not true of the men on Bataan. Complain and curse they did about the fact that they were abandoned and betrayed. But, complain or not, they fought. I did not hear the army radio station, nor was I involved with the releases being written for transmission over that station. There were few radios in those days. When I talked to others, they probably did not reveal their feelings about MacArthur and the war. So I can honestly say that I did not hear any complaints about the man I worked for or about the state of our affairs in the Philippines.

I was deeply aware of the feelings of MacArthur and of Quezon about it. I was the one who typed their messages to Roosevelt and Marshall and who read the replies. I centered resentment where it properly belonged—on Roosevelt's broad shoulders and secondarily, but more bitterly, on the British, whom I pretended to believe were at the heart of the problem. This was the first in a series of conflicting loyalties that beset a man in changing conditions. I felt a great affinity with Roosevelt and a certain Democratic county judge up in Independence, Missouri, Harry Truman, past whose house I hauled trash to sell at a junkyard on the other side of town.

Even on the trip to the Philippines I was confronted with issues that touched the quick. There had been an argument all the way from San Francisco to Manila, generally one-sided, that a battalion of draftees had been sent overseas in violation of the law. I could not develop any passionate interest in the matter, but it made sufficient impact to be remembered 40 years later. I do not recall that we ever reached a judgment as to the truth of the matter and I have never bothered to research it since.

As it became apparent that the Philippines were to be sacrificed to the European theater, however reasonable it may have seemed in Washington and London, the matter was too close to my own interests to be ignored. MacArthur and

Quezon fretted to Roosevelt, and undoubtedly in the privacy of their personal conversations made remarks that could not be made to Roosevelt, or about Roosevelt in the presence of the troops. Knowing where the responsibility rested, regardless of the merits of the case, I growled about Roosevelt, and insofar as my scruples permitted, and with the limited vocabulary I allowed myself, vented my resentment on the British. On December 27 I commented in my diary about a Christmas message from Congress that "we are *behind* you." The next day I saw a précis of MacArthur's radio message to the War Department suggesting that the War Department, not MacArthur, should issue propaganda regarding the inactivity of U.S. naval forces.

On January 5 I commented critically about a press release I had just typed concerning Japanese bombing on Christmas, New Year's Day, and Sunday, and destruction of churches, which "was construed to show Japanese disrespect for Christian tenets. (Propaganda) Even we use it. Inability to spot particular objects at such height. Why would they hit a church when more valuable military objectives are present?"

On January 8 a radio from Roosevelt stated that losses in capital ships made it impossible to mount a naval effort in the Pacific and announcing the organization of ABDACOM (Australian-British-Dutch American Command). I noted bitterly in my diary:

The appointment of Brett as deputy C-in-C in the Far East has stripped MacArthur of anything but his stars. The center of action for the United States is Australia—the Philippines are a side issue. *America First*!

The President of the United States is sacrificing his own citizens to save the British. If we had only listened to the few who said so.

Some of the officers consider the whole thing already lost.

On January 13 I wrote, "Wavell appointed Supreme Commander, Brereton deputy SC and Hart Supreme Naval Commander of the ABDA area. Damn all politicians including Roosevelt."

Five days later I noted, "Roosevelt radio speech—'definite change in Phil. situation in seventy two hours.' What does that mean?" On that day came the first broadcast of the Voice of Freedom. On the same day I quoted from Carveth Wells, *North of Singapore*:

p. 119. "Hongkong will fall in two days. . . ."
p. 84 "I presume that govts like our own and the British have their reasons for supplying the munitions of war to a potential enemy, but I must admit that I cannot understand them."

On February 6 I wrote, "Reported landing of reinforcements false. Why do they put them out?"

After that I became too used to propaganda and deception to take any further notice. I had reached the depth of cynicism on that score. It must have been different for those on Corregidor and Bataan who did not see, as I did, that the source of policy was in Washington rather than in Lateral 3 on Corregidor. They traced all the deception to MacArthur and looked no farther. The men on Corregidor were affronted by the display of his gold-splattered cap, his cane, and his cigar. Those on Bataan, who did not see him, preferred to think that he skulked in fear in the depths of Malinta Hill, spewing out lies to deceive his troops.

I suspect that most of the troops, being reasonable men, understood the facts and acknowledged to themselves that they had been trapped by circumstances. Officers who had sufficient rank to know the history of "Orange Three" certainly knew what to expect, and such knowledge must have filtered down to lower ranks. But even reasonable men must have an emotional outlet in such circumstances, and MacArthur was as good a target for scorn and revulsion as anyone else. Those who had time and talent churned out a literature of hate that is preserved as a testimonial to the depth of despair and disenchantment.

MacArthur's single visit to Bataan on January 10 and his message left great bitterness among many who heard it. In a Japanese prisoner-of-war camp one of the officers who had been present wrote in anguish of despair and defeat:

Who had the right to say that 20,000 Americans should be sentenced without their own consent and for no fault of their own to an enterprise that would involve for them endless suffering, cruel handicap, death, or a hopeless future that could end only in a Japanese Prisoner of War Camp in the Philippines? Who took the responsibility for saying that some other possibility was in prospect? And whoever did, was he not an arch deceiver, traitor and criminal rather than a great soldier? Didn't he know that he was sentencing all his comrades to sure failure, defeat, death, or rotting in a Prison Camp?[1]

He may reasonably be excused. He had watched his troops suffer and he had suffered. Even assuming that he had been deceived—and this requires some credulity in itself—the deceit had little to do with his suffering. He was a soldier. He had been ordered to the Philippines and given command of a combat division. Thirty thousand other Americans also had been placed in jeopardy by an impersonal military process. Many had volunteered for the duty that now confronted them. Whatever MacArthur had said, or not said, their fate had been sealed by their orders. The decision to defend the Philippines had been made in Washington, not because Washington had been persuaded by MacArthur's insistence but because it seemed required by an international diplomatic game of bluff. Whatever MacArthur told his troops on January 10, 1942, they had only the choice of surrender or hopeless battle. Would they have chosen surrender? Had they surrendered, would they have received better treatment from the Japanese? Would their condition have been any better because MacArthur, whom they despised, was there to share their suffering?

There was no deception. When MacArthur spoke on January 10, he could still believe that there was hope of relief. The door had not yet closed, although the wind of events was inexorably moving it. MacArthur had documents that spelled out in detail the kind of relief which was enroute or scheduled for shipment in January and February 1942. He merely repeated to his officers in general terms information he had received from George Marshall.

It was not until January 30 that MacArthur was told indirectly by Roosevelt that there was no hope of relief in the foreseeable future. MacArthur did not visit the troops again, nor did he make promises to them again. He pleaded for a diversion of all Allied naval and air forces from the Atlantic for a crushing blow against Japan. He noted the great losses in Murmansk convoys and argued that the supplies being lost there to submarine attacks could be used to greater advantage in the Philippines. One last convoy, at sea when the war broke out, was diverted to Brisbane, and MacArthur repeatedly urged the movement of its cargo north to the Philippines. With his back to a bitter last wall of defense, he thought only in terms of attack.[2]

It was too late. The tide was running in another direction. In Washington, Dwight Eisenhower, now War Department operations officer for the Pacific, on January 22 wrote across a document: "We've got to go to Europe and fight." He had heard his own call of destiny.

MacArthur knew what he was doing to his men, but he was driven by duty. His orders required that he sustain the defense to the ultimate limit of endurance, then destroy what was left of the command in one final act of defiance. I did not doubt then, nor do I doubt now, that had he been ordered to remain on Corregidor, the surrender would have been made by others over his dead body.

The past 40 years have taught young men and women to belittle generals, and that is not all bad. But it does not do very much to prepare them for that inevitable day when they or their brothers or their sons will have to stand as we did, unwillingly, in fear and desperation, to fight in a war that all will acknowledge as necessary.

The duty of a soldier is to kill, not in blind, senseless rage but on command; to kill purposefully; and when the purpose has been achieved, to stop killing, also on command. Killing is not easy, nor has it ever been. The technique has to be learned and has to be reinforced by discipline. There are times when even highly trained professional soldiers must be driven to battle, but because they know how to exercise their skills, the killing is done more efficiently. The duty of officers, noncommissioned and commissioned, is to teach the skill of organized slaughter, to organize it, to lead soldiers to it, and (if necessary) to drive them to it. It is seldom pleasant in the doing.

At the very peak of the command structure stands the one man in whose hands lies the ultimate responsibility and authority for all the killing that the situation requires. He, too, is under orders from above. Roosevelt ordered that there should be no surrender:

I therefore give you this mission in full understanding of the desperate situation to which you may shortly be reduced. . . . I particularly request that you proceed rapidly to the organization of your forces and your defenses so as to make your resistance as effective as circumstances will permit and as prolonged as humanly possible.[3]

This was interpreted as a "no surrender" order not only by MacArthur but also by the War Department.[4]

MacArthur would have slaughtered his command and his own family in the execution of that order. Even those who prefer not to slaughter and be slaughtered must learn to stand prepared to fight in anticipation of the day when some great irrational force drives some madman to disrupt the orderly intercourse of nations and plunge the world into war. Each man and each nation must find its own answer. I had chosen the principle that I would not let another man do the killing and dying for me. I put the matter politely: "I will be man enough to shovel my share of the ordure of life if shovelling be necessary."

One of MacArthur's naval commanders wrote at the end of the war: "War is a savage business. To every decent individual must come the difficult task of accommodating one's principles of human conduct with the brutalizing one of killing and destruction."[5]

As I have written this book and have tried to trace out the chain of events that led MacArthur, Sutherland, and Rogers to this spot and this time, it seems to be a chain of stupidity forged by passionate, unthinking men who wanted glory without calculating the cost of the adventure. Or, wanting peace, they were forced to war because they could not find the resources and the will to forestall it. Perhaps the ancients had the proper answer. The Gods made them mad—and the Gods are not dead! A generation that believes God is in the machine, and that truth is measured as the standard deviation of an unequal flow, properly adjusted for uncertainty, to be arrived at by the recording of electrical impulses on magnetic tape—all in the interest of making people feel they are happy—has already gone mad.

As MacArthur sat in frustration on Corregidor, watching his army fight to destruction, he must have suffered demolishing pressures of self-doubt. He had been proven inadequate on premises he had imposed upon himself. Others argued that a successful defense of the Philippines could not be made. He had made the trial on the premise that a true leader could take his troops into battle and achieve a victory.

Not everyone would have held MacArthur to the stringent logic his own statements might have required. Between the commanding general and the troops stands a line of subordinates whose performance is critical to the execution of any plan. Performance of the troops is an essential element of a successful campaign. No commander can create victory by sheer exercise of will, no matter how forcefully that will is exerted, if the subordinate commanders and troops do not share the same sense of urgency or desire for victory.

In the case of the officers, the sense of urgency and the desire for victory must be sufficiently strong to impel them to drive themselves and their troops to destruction in the effort to achieve success. The pressure on these officers is greater because they are in direct contact with the men they are sending into battle. They see the suffering, and they must react to it in varying degrees, depending upon their individual capacities.

The commander in battle must exert continual pressure to sustain and to shore up the will of his officers as they feed their troops into the process of destruction. If their resolve slackens, he must strengthen it. If their resolve collapses, he must replace them with others whose will has not been shaken.

The commander at the top also is subject to a deterioration of will. He also is subject to a higher authority, farther away from the battle, who can watch it with even greater detachment and, as occasion demands, strengthen or replace the man who directs it.

MacArthur's will was sufficiently strong to sustain itself. Given the order to fight without surrender, he needed no further attention. His tenacious will drove itself. The order from above to fight merely confirmed his own desire to find victory in battle. He might need a restraining hand but never a spur to action.

MacArthur did not tolerate self-pity in himself, nor did he tolerate it in others. By mid-January reports received in Headquarters USAFFE began to reflect the sympathy of unit commanders for the suffering of their troops. MacArthur would have none of it. Under ordinary circumstances the facts merited sympathetic understanding, but these were not ordinary circumstances. The men involved were soldiers in battle.

MacArthur wrote a directive to all unit commanders. It was signed by Carl Seals ''By command of General MacArthur,'' but my judgment is that MacArthur wrote the draft himself:

1. The Commanding General is very much displeased at continuous reports stating that troops are tired and need relief. He wishes such reports to cease.

2. The fatigue of troops in campaign is universal. The enemy has to contend with exactly the same conditions as our troops and is just as tired. It has been the observation of the Commanding General, over many years of war service, that the so-called fatigue of troops is generally a reflection of a lack of determination and resolution on the part of commanders.

3. The Commanding General takes this opportunity also to deprecate most severely loose talk tending to aggrandize the potentialities of the enemy. He directs all commanding officers to deal harshly with every man who spreads such enemy propaganda, and especially enjoins upon all officers that demeanor of confidence, self reliance and assurance which is the birthright of all cultured gentlemen and the special trademark of the Army Officer.[6]

MacArthur's duty was to keep his troops on the battle line, as Roosevelt had ordered, ''as long as humanly possible.'' MacArthur did not waver. He confided his plans for the future to the officer who commanded the harbor defenses. If the forces on Bataan collapsed, as eventually they must, he would move the Philippine Division to Corregidor to man the beach defenses. Bivouac and hospital facilities were to be found for their use. MacArthur ordered him to hold enough food for 20,000 men on half rations so that the defense of Corregidor could be maintained until June 30.

I believe that MacArthur intended to die with the garrison. He had no illusions about the future. He told two reporters, Lee and Jacoby, that it would end only in blood and death.[7]

One afternoon MacArthur and Sayre walked together just outside the hospital entrance to the tunnel. Suddenly shells began to whistle over their heads. Sayre records: "... almost unthinkingly I dropped [to the ground]. But not the General. He believed that death would take him only at the ordained time and was fearless of shellfire; he remained standing ... his expression never changed."[8]

No one knows, of course, what MacArthur believed about death. Everyone knows that he hid his feelings under iron will and self-discipline. He may have been as frightened as anyone else. He simply refused to show it.

VI

Alamo, February–April 1942

Defense of Malaya; fall of Singapore; Quezon evacuated; Wainwright; MacArthur ordered south; evacuation

20

ABDACOM

The Australian-British-Dutch-American (or American-British-Dutch-Australian, depending on one's authority) Command (ABDACOM) developed during the strategic discussions of 1940-1942.

MacArthur was charged with the defense of the Philippines, all of it. Seen in retrospect, this does not seem to be a matter of great consequence, but in view of the thinking of the four decades that had preceded the decision of July 1941, it represented a considerable revolution in strategic planning. At least a decision had been made not to let the Commonwealth go by default. The importance of the Philippines was enhanced by the fact that the Filipinos were to have a significant role in its defense. MacArthur watched young Filipinos marching into training camps that were being built by Filipino laborers. He heard the roar of the heavy bombers that were landing on the new fields being constructed throughout the islands. He foresaw sleek coastal defense guns being installed behind parapets at the critical entrances to Philippine waters. He heard the whine of his minuscule patrol of PT boats. All of these were elements of his command intended to keep frontiers of the Philippines inviolate. It was not part of his assigned responsibility to give very much consideration to the broader aspects of regional defense.

MacArthur gave perfunctory attention to Singapore. He received several visits from British Air Chief Marshal Sir Thomas Brooke Popham, who had sent warm congratulations at the time of MacArthur's appointment and had received warm thanks in return. MacArthur did not return the visits. Contacts with the Dutch were less frequent.

Admiral Thomas Hart, who commanded the Asiatic Fleet, had been involved with the problem of regional defense for some time. It had long been understood that defense of the South China Sea would be a matter for naval forces of which he was the resident U.S. representative. Hart had advised MacArthur of the joint discussions in which he had been involved and attempted with less than successful results to arouse some enthusiasm on MacArthur's part. MacArthur continued to concentrate his attention on defense of the Philippines, recognizing that Hart would steam away to the south if the Japanese moved. He had grudgingly acquiesced in the directive from George Marshall that army air forces would be committed, with Hart's fleet, to the joint defense of the area. Beyond that, MacArthur was outside the framework of international strategic planning, which was dominated by the British and U.S. chiefs of staff at the highest level of authority. They knew, and MacArthur knew, that when the time came, MacArthur must carry out any orders they sent him.

Two days before the Japanese struck, George Marshall wrote to MacArthur concerning the coordination of MacArthur's air forces with naval operations in the South China Sea. He traced out the difficulty encountered in setting up an international command structure that would be acceptable to the various governments. The agreement gave strategic control of the area to the British. A later meeting at Singapore failed to solve the problem of command, principally because of objections raised by the U.S. Navy representatives. No other solution had been found. Now, on the brink of disaster, the goal of solidarity had been reinterpreted to mean "Each man for himself." Marshall urged upon MacArthur the necessity for cooperation in the planning and conduct of operations. He also warned him that the principle of unity of command would certainly be applied to naval control of air units.[1]

The events of the second week in December made it all a moot question. All air forces in the area were effectively gutted, and the sinking of the *Prince of Wales* and *Repulse* by land-based dive bombers demonstrated the limitations of naval opposition to the Japanese advance. They also provided a quick solution to MacArthur's qualms about unity of command. The Philippines had been isolated, and the center of action dropped to the southwest, at Singapore, and to the southeast, at Rabaul. By this time it was obvious to all but Churchill that Singapore would fall.

Under the pressure of events a command structure was hastily thrown together. Two areas were sketched out on a map of the Southwest Pacific: the ABDA area and the ANZAC. ABDACOM included Formosa, the Philippines, Burma, Malaya, Borneo, and the Netherland East Indies. The ANZAC command included Australian New Guinea, the Solomon Islands, New Caledonia, Fiji, New Zealand, and Australia. By the time the commands were organized, the Japanese had control of the ABDA area and were pushing relentlessly from Rabaul southeast toward Fiji and New Zealand.

The ANZAC area did not receive much consideration because attention was centered on Singapore and Manila Bay, at least until the middle of February 1942. When the Japanese finally occupied the Malay Barrier, and after MacArthur broke through that barrier and arrived in Australia, attention was focused on Australia and its approaches from the east. By late 1942 the ANZAC area became a center of great action and the focus shifted to it.

ABDACOM was given a British supreme commander, General Sir Archibald

Wavell, although his title did not properly reflect his command authority. "Supreme coordinator" would have been more realistic. The Americans, Dutch, and British retained control of their national forces. MacArthur was beyond the reach of Wavell's authority, although technically he was subordinate to Wavell. At any rate, a holding command had been provided to give the appearance of Allied unity while the Japanese destroyed the separate elements at their pleasure. No other command structure was possible and, given the circumstances, it did not make much difference. In 30 days its purpose had been served, and the command was dissolved. ANZAC survived until the Pacific had been reorganized under U.S. control.

Wavell established his headquarters in Java on January 15. All naval units in the area were placed under U.S. Admiral Hart. Ground forces were placed under Dutch General ter Poorten. Air forces were commanded by British Air Marshal Peirse. It was a loose organization, loosely commanded, with no clearly defined strategic goal. A limited force was thinly stretched over hundreds of miles. Wavell's deputy commander was U.S. General George Brett.

The decision had been made to abandon the Philippines and to concentrate the defense on Singapore, in the hope that Singapore would provide an obstacle to Japanese control of the Netherland East Indies. Wavell radioed MacArthur: "Have just arrived Singapore. I hope to meet Hart shortly and ask him what we can do to assist you in your gallant defense which we all greatly admire."[2]

MacArthur replied with a restatement of his understanding of the strategic problem:

The fall of the Philippines will inevitably result in the loss of Borneo, all or a large part of the NEI and of Singapore. . . . It is essential that Allied land, sea and air forces halt the hostile southward drive by securing NEI bases, by driving enemy air and naval elements out of the Davao region and by occupying that island in force. Northward progress from the Malay Barrier would be beset by enormous difficulties but would be relatively easy from Mindanao.[3]

Wavell replied that it would be hard going merely to halt the Japanese drive: "There is little I can do at present to help your magnificent defense except organize supply of ammunition and food to you. . . . All good luck to you and your gallant troops."[4]

On January 13 MacArthur was notified of the formation of ABDACOM. Wavell would coordinate operations, allocate reinforcements, require reports from subordinate commanders, issue communiqués, and organize task forces for specific purposes. His basic mission was to be strategic coordinator of the land forces that would arrive from India and the Middle East, the air forces that would fly across the Pacific, and the naval forces that were assembling to keep the Japanese out of the Netherland East Indies. Wavell had been instructed to re-establish communications, presumably both sea and air, with the Philippines. Marshall did not say so, but Wavell had been chosen because Churchill was afraid that anyone else he sent would divert British forces from the defense of Singapore to the Philippines and the air force as well.

Wavell later reported in his official despatch:

I could see no prospect with the resources available, of sending support to General MacArthur. The recent occupation by the enemy of Tarakan in North Borneo and of Menado in the Celebes had increased the difficulty of reaching the Philippines with air forces from the N.E.I. even had sufficient aircraft been available. Admiral Hart had arranged for a submarine to go to Manila loaded to capacity with the types of ammunition of which General MacArthur was running short.[5]

Wavell, like MacArthur, had found a great discrepancy between the air forces that had been promised and that were delivered. He also learned that airplanes alone were not enough:

The air forces in sight constituted on paper a formidable force. The United States authorities had placed under orders for the ABDA command, according to information given me by General Brett, well over 1,000 aircraft to arrive within the next two or three months. The British contribution was on a more modest scale but was quite a considerable reinforcement. If all the aircraft promised to ABDA command had arrived safely and up to time, and had we succeeded in establishing sufficient well protected aerodromes to receive them and in providing the ground organization to service them, all would have been well. I have always maintained, and still do, that the Japanese air force is comparatively weak and can be overcome whenever the Allies manage to concentrate a sufficient air force under favourable conditions.[6]

Toward the end of January, MacArthur asked for dispatch of two or three squadrons of fighters and dive bombers from Wavell's command to the Philippines. Wavell replied with a message of great despair. Washington had assured and reassured MacArthur that three bombers per day were leaving the United States for the Southwest Pacific. Wavell told him: "The American Air Force has 16 P–40s (fighter) and 10 four-engined bombers. Bombers double crewed and operating continuously against Jap installations. . . . "[7]

Wavell's command was falling to pieces. Two days after he radioed MacArthur of the state of his air forces, the defenders of Singapore pulled out of Malaya, across the Johore Strait, to the island of Singapore—Fortress Singapore—for a last desperate stand.

In reality Singapore was not a fortress at all but a naval base situated on a rather small island at the very tip of Malaya, not protected, as Manila Bay was, by natural barriers but open to the sea. On the north it was separated from the mainland by a narrow, shallow strait of water, wider than a medieval moat but not appreciably deeper. The naval base proper was covered by a system of coastal defense guns located on each end of the strait. They were far less in number and power than those at the entrance of Manila Bay. Perhaps it is too much even to say that Singapore was a naval base, because it had no facility for repair of battleships. One observer had written about the proposal to fortify the island, "It is the worst of all possible courses to put out at Singapore a halfway house and then half garrison it."[8] He showed remarkable prescience, for that is precisely what happened.

Discussion had begun in 1921. Britain could not afford to station a main battle fleet in the Pacific to protect its colonial interests, and was led to accept the more economical alternative of providing a base that would shelter a detachment of the Home Fleet when events would require a display of force in the Far East. The decade was not propitious for much action. The horrors of the Great War had led to the illusion that in the future collective security would eliminate the need for any effort on the part of individual nations. Most citizens of England apparently failed to recognize that collective security required something more than pious slogans if there was to be any security at all. In England, as in the United States, the line of pacifism was made more attractive by the illusion that nations could be isolated from the threat of war. In the United States the two oceans seemed to present a barrier. In England the illusion was based upon a considerably less substantial body of water.

Moreover Germany had been defeated, disarmed, and reduced to economic disaster by reparations. Japan, the only conceivable naval threat to Britain and the United States, seemed to constitute not much of a threat. In any event, all three had signed a naval limitation treaty that brought great satisfaction to the two Western powers but a sullen show of resentment by Japanese naval officers.

The 1920s brought great economic instability and political upheaval. Economy and pacifism dominated policy, and the great powers ceased to be militarily great. Military and naval budgets were cut in England and the United States but not in Japan. By the end of the decade it suddenly became evident that peace and collective security could no longer be taken for granted. After ten years of talk and inaction, efforts were made to fortify Singapore.

The effort represented a compromise between uncertain need and tight budgets, and all that came of it was the construction of base harbor facilities on the north side of the island. At the eastern and western entrances to Johore Strait two coastal batteries were installed. To meet the threat of the growing presence of air power, three airfields were built. Barracks were constructed to house the necessary defense and maintenance garrisons.

The entire project had been assembled on the basis of a strategic probability that any such attack would take the form of a naval assault from the sea. Such a view was plausible when the harbor defenses of Manila Bay had been established. By 1930 it was no longer realistic in Singapore, where it became increasingly probable that any attack would come down from Siam and the northeast coast of Malaya, and would strike Singapore from the north. If such an attack were made, the coastal defenses would be useless even if they had a complete circle of fire. A defense in depth would be needed with proper air support. While MacArthur as chief of staff was pleading with Congress for military funds, his British counterparts were waging a comparable campaign in Parliament.

When war came in Europe in 1939, Malaya was as inadequately defended as the Philippines. Moreover, it was obvious that only overt attack would justify the diversion of a fleet to the Far East. Even if Japan attacked, Australia and New Zealand must have priority in defense. Unfortunately, Britain unaided did not have sufficient force to justify even its bravado, much less effective opposition.

The discrepancy between needs and resources became increasingly unbridgeable in the two years that followed. The problem was intensified by the inability and the unwillingness of England's greatest potential ally to make a public commitment of support. U.S. politics would not stand much talk of war, especially in defense of "tottering colonial empires"—even the one in the Philippines. The British pleaded unsuccessfully that the United States send carriers to support the defense of Singapore, arguing that Singapore must be defended even at the expense of "island possessions" of the United States.

By that time the Japanese had control of Camranh Bay, the only viable harbor on the coast of French Indochina, which looked threateningly across the South China Sea to Malaya and Singapore, and were menacing Siam. The military commander in Malaya prepared a plan to occupy Siam if an attack by Japan seemed imminent. A move to the beaches in northeast Malaya would be made to throw back a landing attempt. The plan rested upon the frail reed of U.S. public opinion. Churchill could not approve a preemptive strike without losing Roosevelt's support. Roosevelt could not take action until the Japanese had committed the first hostile act.

On the night of December 7, 1941, when I settled down in Manila for my last sleep of peace, the defenders of Malaya, like the defenders of Luzon and Hawaii, were pinned helplessly in place to await the whims of a force that was already in motion.

At about the same time Japanese planes screamed into Pearl Harbor, a force of Japanese transports dropped anchor at Khota Baru in northeastern Malaya and unloaded their troops. At the end of the day less than half of the British air force was operational. The remainder had been wiped out in the air and on the ground by Japanese bombers. More galling to British pride, two ships, *Prince of Wales* and *Repulse*, steaming north to find the Japanese, were attacked and sunk by land-based Japanese bombers. A Japanese contingent streamed south out of Siam.

The withdrawal of the British down Malaya required some six weeks. The terrain was mountainous, covered with jungle and perforated with marshes. It was easier to defend and more difficult to attack than Luzon, where there were no natural points of defense. Moreover, it was a longer road, some 350 miles. The first four days of the action had been the decisive ones. It turned out to be a dress rehearsal for Lingayen. Two battalions of Japanese infantry and a tank company drove an Indian division out of well-prepared defenses in less than one day. In all areas the British units, which were manned by Indian soldiers, disintegrated and disappeared. In rain, mud, and confusion, without communications, Indian troops led by English officers pulled south, often fighting

stubbornly but to no avail. On January 20 they steamed across the causeway
that separated Malaya from Singapore, and the final stage of the defense began.

By this time MacArthur had settled into the defenses of Bataan and Corregidor.
He had assured Roosevelt in December that Bataan could hold for three months
and Corregidor longer. Roosevelt met with Churchill in January and undoubtedly
passed along the encouraging news. Churchill now was confronted with the
heroic defense of the Philippines. He apprehensively warned the British chiefs
of staff: "Beware lest the troops required for the ultimate defense of Singapore
Island and the fortress are not used up or cut off in Malay Peninsula. Nothing
compares in importance with the fortress."[9]

The British chiefs of staff must have winced with the realization that Churchill
did not have even the slightest hint of the disaster for which he apparently was
totally unprepared. Churchill had spoken frequently of the "fortress" at Singapore. Now he would be disenchanted. He thought of a great citadel, pierced
with subterranean chambers, capable of sustained defense by a relatively small
garrison against a relatively large force of attackers.

On January 15, when Churchill was in conference with Roosevelt, he asked
Wavell what fortifications existed for the defense of the island of Singapore.
Wavell replied bluntly: " . . . all plans were based on repulsing seaborne attack
on the island . . . little or nothing was done to construct defenses on north side
of Island to prevent crossing Johore Strait."[10]

Churchill was overwhelmed by this revelation and exclaimed in despair:
" . . . that the gorge of the fortress of Singapore, with its splendid moat half a
mile wide, was not entirely fortified against an attack from the northward. What
is the use of having an island for a fortress if it is not to be made into a citadel?"[11]

He hastened to propound a plan for the determined defense of Singapore "to
the death":

I want to make it absolutely clear that I expect every inch of ground to be defended,
every scrap of material or defenses to be blown to pieces to prevent capture by the enemy,
and no question of surrender to be entertained until after protracted fighting among the
ruins of Singapore city.[12]

Fortunately the generals were more sensible and more merciful than Churchill.
When General Tomoyuki Yamashita's infantry closed an iron ring around the
city, which was filled with 3.5 million helpless civilians, the British commander
surrendered to save the city from pillage and rape by Japanese soldiers. Churchill
would not have a Stalingrad, which must have caused him some anguish when
he had to confront Stalin and Roosevelt. To his great credit, Yamashita refused
to let his three infantry divisions enter the city, sending only selected groups of
technicians and engineers to restore public services and to keep order.

It has reasonably been asserted that the decision to defend Singapore was an
act of great foolishness, based in part on Churchill's erroneous view of the nature
of the fortifications and of the strategic importance of the base. It was defended

because it was erroneously believed to have strategic significance. Had the base been a great citadel, had it been defended bitterly through a siege of 48 months, the war in the Pacific would not have been affected. On February 15, the day of the surrender of Singapore, the Japanese landed on Sumatra. In late February, Bali, Timor, and Java fell. During the month the Allied naval force was destroyed in four futile battles. ABDACOM was dissolved on March 1.

MacArthur, who had warned of the end result of a diversion of forces on such a broad front, had brought the Japanese to a standstill and was holding.

On February 15 I recorded the simple fact that "Singapore falls at 7:00 PM."[13] On the following day Sutherland dictated to me a message that MacArthur had dictated to him:

The unexpectedly early capitulation of Singapore emphasizes the fact that the opportunity for a successful attack upon the hostile lines of communication is rapidly vanishing. If this enemy victory is followed by further success in the NEI the sensitiveness of his lines of communication will largely disappear due to consolidation of his positions in the south. A determined effort in force made now would probably attract the assistance of Russia who will unquestionably not move in this area until some evidence is given of concrete effort by the Allies. The opportunity still exists for a complete reversal of the situation. It will soon however be too late for such a movement.[14]

The collapse of the fortress at the tip of Malaya came as a great surprise only because the world was ignorant of the astonishing fact that its early collapse was inevitable if the entire Malay Peninsula could not be made secure against the Japanese. Except to those who were involved in its defense, it had become the symbol of an indestructible bastion that, like the great fortress of Malta, would endure a prolonged, heroic siege. The troops involved in the useless exercise could have been used to much better advantage in Burma.

Roosevelt and Churchill were masters and slaves of great illusion. They could weave words in tapestries of fantasy in which they sometimes became entangled. It cannot be said that they created the war with Japan; the Japanese needed no assistance in that direction. But after 1940 it was quite obvious to both men that the decisions they made and the positions they took, admirable and necessary as they were, led relentlessly to the final act that had been seen and discussed for two or more decades. Tens of thousands of Filipino and Indian boys were sacrificed to create an image of heroic resistance to a common foe, but the end result of their sacrifice was easily predictable and had been foretold. The cause seemed to be clearly defined, but the precise meaning of the resistance and the misery it inflicted is difficult to find.

21

Bitter End

In mid October 1941 the state of events in the Far East had impelled President Quezon to write to President Roosevelt an expression of his support for General MacArthur and Admiral Hart in their preparation for hostilities. He repeated assurances he had given to Roosevelt in the past.[1] These were brave words, and they were meant in good faith. Filipino young men were marching into their training camps to prepare for battle.

On December 12 MacArthur visited Quezon to prepare him for a possible Japanese capture of the Philippines. MacArthur did not seem to believe that affairs would work out in such a manner, but Quezon nevertheless understood that he should be prepared to leave Manila at any time on very short notice.

A meeting was held a week before Christmas to discuss responsibilities of civilian authorities during the occupation. All present wanted to be evacuated from Manila with Quezon when the time came. There were two reasons why that could not be permitted. First, there would not be enough space on Corregidor for them. More important, they would be needed to protect the people against the Japanese. MacArthur was asked for some rule to govern their behavior during the occupation. He replied: "Do what you think necessary except one thing— Take no oath of allegiance to the Japanese. If you do, when we come back, we'll shoot you."[2]

On Christmas Eve at 9:00 A.M., Huff called Quezon to say that MacArthur had ordered the evacuation of Manila. The vice president, the chief justice, the secretary of defense, the president's aid, and his secretary gathered to accompany Quezon, his wife, his son, and his two daughters. In the afternoon Sid Huff and Manuel Roxas arrived at the Malacañan Palace to escort the Quezon party to Corregidor. High Commissioner, Sayre, and his family were on board the ship, awaiting Quezon's arrival. The party arrived at Corregidor at dusk, about the time the *Don Esteban* with MacArthur was leaving Manila.[3]

Quezon was taken to the lateral in Malinta Tunnel that had been set aside as quarters for the Quezons, the MacArthurs, Huff, Colonel and Mrs. Carl Seals, and Roxas. Two rooms, seven by nine feet, had been prepared for each family. Two small houses east of Malinta Hill were set aside for the Quezons and the MacArthurs when artillery and air activity permitted them to live there. By January 26 we built a tent platform for Quezon outside the hospital entrance to the tunnel; he resided there between air and artillery attacks. More and more of this time was spent in the hospital area, where quarters were arranged for him and his entourage. MacArthur came by daily before noon to report on developments of the campaign and on activities in Washington.

On December 30 Quezon was inaugurated for his second term as president of the Commonwealth of the Philippines. It was a bleak and solemn experience with no embellishment of bunting, music, or audience. In his hands he held a copy of the proclamation issued by President Roosevelt the day before, which read in part: "I give to the people of the Philippines my solemn pledge that their freedom will be redeemed and their independence established and protected. The entire resources in men and materials of the United States stand behind that pledge."

A day later Quezon finally felt the significance of the phrase "will be redeemed." He asked MacArthur for a precise interpretation. Did Roosevelt mean to say that all was lost, that no help could arrive in time? MacArthur fudged and suggested that the word had been garbled in transmission. He apparently had no doubt as to its significance. When Quezon sent the message to the troops, he changed "redeemed" to "supported."[4]

Quezon met with MacArthur, Sutherland, Charles Willoughby, and Sayre on January 1. MacArthur read a telegram from George Marshall that suggested the evacuation of Quezon. The war cabinet was convened to discuss the matter with Quezon, who records: "The Cabinet decided that I should refuse to make the trip for they were very hopeful that before Bataan and Corregidor were forced to surrender, sufficient help would come. . . . I was doubtful if help could come in time even with my presence in America."[5]

Quezon wrote to MacArthur, neither accepting nor declining, expressing a willingness to conform to any action deemed necessary by Washington. The triumvirate (Quezon, Osmeña, Roxas) must not fall into Japanese hands. This was obvious from the beginning. They must be evacuated. But when?[6]

MacArthur radioed Washington that the evacuation of Quezon was too hazardous to attempt. He left it to Marshall and Roosevelt to interpret his meaning of "hazardous." Certainly there would be hazard to Quezon and his family that was real and not inconsiderable. Second, the evacuation of Quezon could result in alienation of public opinion in the Philippines, causing the people and the interim government to turn to the Japanese. Finally, it was difficult to measure the impact of Quezon's departure on the Filipinos manning the battle lines on Bataan. The cry "Betrayed!" has brought an ignominious end to more than one battle. The evacuation of MacArthur's family or of MacArthur himself might be even more destructive. There could be no talk of evacuation for the present.[7]

In February, MacArthur insisted that he did not fear for the courage of the Filipino troops. He counted upon them to hold to the end. But this was written after 30 days of battle and a successful withdrawal to the final battle line. In January he might not have been so certain.[8]

The end of the dream had become a nightmare for Quezon. As the bombs rained down on Corregidor, the triumvirate sat silently in the hospital lateral. Quezon, wiry, his fiery nervous energy dulled by tuberculosis, but not extinguished, fretted with unrestrained signs of frustration. Osmeña waited patiently, with resignation. Roxas, younger than the others, dark and sullen, radiated the anger and bitterness usual to his nature, now intensified by the humiliation of the circumstances in which he found himself. Mrs. Quezon waited by her husband's side, and his son and daughters chattered to hide their nervous anxiety.

Some forty years earlier, Quezon had laid down his sword before Lieutenant General Arthur MacArthur to take the oath of allegiance to the United States to bind his destiny to that of his conqueror. Osmeña had done the same. Their paths had joined in a common effort to find independence through cooperation. Setting aside the bitterness of insurrection, they had turned to politics.

Now the bitter end had come. Quezon knew his own life was already measured out. Osmeña, whose inscrutable face hid whatever ambition still smoldered in his heart, might still see better days. Both had tasted power and glory. Roxas had yet to hold the reins of power. With the others he had run away before the enemy. It seemed too late now to go back. The dark walls of Malinta Tunnel seemed to mark an ignominious termination to a stillborn glory. He had reason for bitterness.

The long debates over the defense of the Philippines had led to no conclusion. The Great Protector, on whom they had staked everything, was resolved to send its forces not west to the Philippines but east to the European theater. While Filipino boys were dying in a useless defense of Bataan to keep the U.S. flag flying a while longer, paying for a show of U.S. pride with Filipino blood, supplies were being spilled into the cold waters of the North Atlantic by German submarines. The logic of the matter, which seemed so obvious in Washington, London, and Moscow, seemed more dark and uncertain in the hospital lateral.

Quezon had not been happy with the events of December and the loss of the Philippines. All during his presidency the thorny problem of defense of the islands had been a constant irritant. There had been considerable doubt that they could be defended at all, and only MacArthur's insistent assertion that he could construct a successful defense machinery sustained Quezon's frequently reluctant support. Even granted the feasibility of a defense, the cost was very great. MacArthur's defense preparations required a very high proportion of the national budget—far greater, relatively, than was being spent in the United States—and Quezon's opponents had gained political advantage from the fact.

Quezon had wavered from enthusiastic support of MacArthur's position, through lukewarm enthusiasm, to outright rejection. But he was trapped by a dilemma. The position of the Philippines Commonwealth was ambiguous. Not quite independent, it was independent enough to lead Japan to feel that the United States might give Quezon freedom to work out a solution with Japan.

The decision to provide a U.S. fail-safe defense was made half a year too late. The crack of opportunity should have remained open until the spring of 1942. Had Japan waited three additional months, or had the United States moved three months sooner, U.S. regiments would have manned the Lingayen beaches and perhaps would have given the Filipino forces a will to fight. But the attack came, and Quezon was forced to choose a disagreeable alternative.

He felt that his show of defense had been betrayed by the unwillingness of the United States to make an honorable attempt to support his action. Now on Corregidor he was a virtual prisoner, cut off from his people and from the outside world, under absolute control of MacArthur. Coughing out his lungs in the dust of Malinta Tunnel, he sat sullen and frustrated.

Sometime toward the end of January, Sayre, who had talked with Quezon for six weeks about evacuation, appealed directly to Roosevelt, asking that he and his family be evacuated. Sayre was told that the matter was in the hands of MacArthur.[9]

On January 28 the Japanese announced the formation of a new government council of Filipinos who had been left behind by Quezon. Sayre suggested that Quezon publicly rebuke the men involved and warn them of possible retribution for their service to the Japanese. Quezon wrote to MacArthur, defending the motives and loyalty of the men in question:

Everyone of them wanted to come to Corregidor but you told me that there was no place for them here. . . . They are virtually prisoners of the enemy . . . they are only doing what they think is their duty . . . they are not traitors. They are the victims of the adverse fortunes of war . . . America should look upon their situation sympathetically and under-standingly. . . .

Has it already been decided in Washington that the Philippine front is of no importance . . . that, therefore, no help can be expected in the immediate future? . . . I want to decide in my own mind whether there is justification in allowing all these men to be killed, when for the final outcome of the war the shedding of their blood may be wholly unnecessary.[10]

MacArthur passed the message to Roosevelt, who replied with a long, inspiring message of understanding but he did not give much ground for hope:

While I cannot now indicate the time at which succor and assistance can reach the Philippines, I do know that every ship at our disposal is bringing the southwest Pacific the forces that will ultimately smash the invader. . . . Every day gained for building up our forces is of incalculable value.[11]

On February 3 came another suggestion from Washington that Quezon, Sayre, and Mrs. MacArthur be evacuated.[12]

Quezon was beginning to rebel. On February 6 he suggested to MacArthur that it might be appropriate for him (Quezon) to return to Manila to lead the people in defiance of Japanese authority. MacArthur responded that the Japanese would hold Quezon prisoner in Malacañan, would deny him access to the public, and would promulgate their own statements in his name. Quezon agreed to think about the matter.[13] Two days later Quezon prepared a message for Roosevelt. My diary records my own summary of the document on February 7:

Radio Quezon to Roosevelt. Suggests following plan: America grant Philippines independence; withdrawal of American and Japanese troops from islands; make Philippines neutral; Philippine foreign trade relations to be determined by Filipinos; American nationals to be removed with troops. Situation as described by MacArthur.[14]

There was great consternation among Quezon's advisers. None of them agreed with the proposal, arguing that it would inevitably put him and his family in the hands of the Japanese, who would know only too well how to use him. Osmeña reminded Quezon of what his daughters might expect at the hands of Japanese soldiers. Time, exhaustion, and reason cooled his passion, and he agreed to let his proposal die. It had been a shout of defiance and he had made his point; but his fate was sealed.[15]

MacArthur forwarded the dispatch to Roosevelt with an endorsement of his own and with Sayre's evaluation of the situation. MacArthur reported:

. . . troops have sustained practically fifty percent casualties . . . they are capable now of nothing but fighting in place on a fixed position. . . . All our supplies are scant and the command has been on half rations for the past month. . . . There is no denying the fact that we are near done. . . . Nothing . . . can prevent their utter collapse and their complete absorption by the enemy.[16]

Sayre advised: "If the premise of President Quezon is correct that American help cannot or will not arrive here in time to be availing I believe his proposal for immediate independence and neutralization is the sound course to follow."[17]

Washington, afraid that the effort in the Philippines would be weakened, again ordered Quezon's evacuation. The problem, as seen in Washington, perhaps was the possibility that Quezon might refuse to leave.[18]

Roosevelt replied to MacArthur:

I authorize you to arrange for the capitulation of the Filipino elements of the defending forces, when and if in your opinion that course appears necessary. . . .

American forces will continue to keep the flag flying in the Philippines so long as there remains any possibility of resistance. . . . It is mandatory . . . that the American determination and indomitable will to win carries down to the last unit. . . .

If the evacuation of President Quezon and his cabinet appears reasonably safe they would be honored and greatly welcomed in the United States. . . . This also applies to the High Commissioner. Mrs. Sayre and your family should be given this opportunity if you consider it advisable.[19]

Roosevelt also reminded Quezon of the faithful assistance of the United States.

. . . carrying out to the people of the Philippines a pledge to help them successfully . . . in their aspirations to become a self-governing and independent people. . . . Whatever happens to the present American garrison, we shall not relax our efforts until . . . we . . . return to the Philippines and drive the last remnant of the invaders from your soil.[20]

In a separate message to MacArthur, Marshall ordered, in Roosevelt's name, that Quezon not be permitted to release any public messages without Roosevelt's approval. He further asked for advice concerning the evacuation of Quezon by submarine.

Quezon was writing for history. There is no doubt that MacArthur understood the depths of Quezon's anguish and felt more deeply than anyone in Washington the bitterness of the complaint that loyalty cannot be demanded when protection is not given. MacArthur's addition to Quezon's statement is a straightforward, realistic appraisal of the military situation, the facts of which were already known in Washington. In early January, MacArthur set a term of three months: "It is estimated that this garrison unsupported can survive serious attack for possibly three months at most."[21] One of the months was already gone.

Sayre's contribution to Quezon's message shows that a new and unprecedented peak had been reached in unity of purpose between MacArthur and the high commissioner's office. Sayre was pushing for his own evacuation and had a personal stake in the matter.

Quezon was not MacArthur's prisoner, nor was he treated as such. He was dealt with as head of state, and within the seriously prescribed means available his wishes were implemented. Where such a strong community of interest exists, one need not seek out a conspiracy. Both men, of course, would have welcomed a change of policy in Washington, but they were reasonable enough to know that this particular suggestion would not carry more weight than previous appeals.

A forceful reply to Quezon came immediately: "The President of the United States is not empowered to cede or alienate any territory to another nation. . . . You have no authority to communicate with the Japanese Government without the express permission of the United States Government."[22]

On February 11, MacArthur notified Roosevelt that he would arrange for the evacuation of Quezon.[23] MacArthur told Marshall on February 12 that Quezon had declined on several occasions to make a trip by submarine because his advisers felt such a trip would kill him.[24] Sutherland began to work out the arrangements that would require another six days.

On February 13 at 3:00 P.M. MacArthur came into the lateral, motioned to Sutherland, and the two men began to pace up and down the narrow aisle in the rear of Lateral 3. He walked and talked with Sutherland about "highly secret matters of policy." Sutherland listened intently, but he did not have much to contribute to this matter, which had never crossed his mind. He raised a few questions.[25] At 3:30 MacArthur left the lateral. Sutherland sat down to work on his "in basket," a euphemism for documents that did not need much attention. He mulled over what he must write. At 4:00 he pulled over a yellow pad and a pencil and began to work on "important Executive Order for President Quezon." He was still working at 7:45. At 8:00 he left the lateral for ten minutes, returned, and picked up his work.

It is apparent that Sutherland had been caught flat-footed. If he had known before, he would not have needed 30 minutes to decide what to do or 4 hours to complete the task. Undoubtedly in the 3:00 meeting with MacArthur the basic outlines of the text had been agreed to. This was the usual pattern. Sutherland's present task was to get the exact wording. He did not work rapidly at such jobs, laboring over the organization and wording, with long pauses for thought.

MacArthur and Quezon may have reached an agreement during the regular noon meeting, but there is no way to know when they actually made the arrangement. It could have been anytime prior to the evacuation to Corregidor or later. They could have agreed privately to the fact and let the timing wait until the inevitable evacuation of Quezon.

Shortly after 8:30 Sutherland called me over to dictate his result. He seldom gave me a handwritten draft for typing and I would have noted the exception. I seem to remember several papers in my hands. I remember sharply the discrepancy between the dates, wondering what had happened and momentarily debating whether I should ask. Sutherland would have had the typed copy in his hands about 9:00. He would have had to clear it with MacArthur but did not leave his desk before 11:00 or so.

The document was Executive Order Number One, dated January 1, 1942, prepared for the signature of President Quezon. It awarded $500,000 to MacArthur for his service with the Military Mission. In the same order provisions were made for payment to Sutherland of $75,000, to Richard Marshall of $45,000 and to Huff of $20,000. The payments were to be made in U.S. currency.

Sometime after 11:00 P.M. I made the daily entry in my diary. I had been on duty since 7:30 A.M. It had been a long day with a large surprise. I was caught in a bind because I had been instructed on a previous occasion that I was not to make a record of MacArthur's financial affairs. With some hesitation I decided to record the event. Trusting to memory to recall the actual amounts, I changed MacArthur's $500,000 to $50,000. Then I changed Sutherland's $75,000 to $45,000, to keep it in line with my revision for MacArthur. The amount given to Marshall was reduced to $40,000. Huff's $20,000 was not changed.

It was not very cleverly done, but it satisfied my sense of honor. With one exception I did not discuss it during the war. I had been accepted into a position of trust, and I would not violate the obligation of my position. I merely noted: "God! I would like to be a general."

At 10:30 A.M. on February 14 MacArthur came into the office and talked with Sutherland until noon. The conversation ran over into MacArthur's customary meeting with Quezon. He had scheduled instead a 2:00 P.M. meeting with Quezon, Sayre, and Sutherland. As MacArthur left, I remember clearly a statement he made to the effect that the amounts hardly covered the losses they had incurred by staying with the Military Mission.

As soon as MacArthur had left, Sutherland called Richard Marshall on Bataan to discuss routine matters. Sutherland would not have dared to give any more than a veiled hint that something exciting had happened. He then went down to the hospital lateral and Quezon's quarters for the scheduled meeting. The men talked two and a half hours about "disposal of money and securities and on matters of high policy." Sutherland did not return to his desk until 8:00 P.M.

Sometime during the day I typed the cable to Chase ordering transfer of funds. I have not found a copy but I clearly remember the fact, the names, and some of the banks.

There was an uproar in Washington. The radio went from Marshall to Stimson. After some discussion the request was transmitted to Chase National Bank for action, and a copy was sent to the Department of the Interior. Ickes apparently refused to sanction the transfer, and the action seems to have been taken over his head. On January 18 Chase confirmed that the transfers had been made.

On Corregidor there was some sense of urgency in view of Quezon's imminent departure. There is no detailed record of the events that followed, but $1,280,000 in Philippine treasury certificates was segregated, placed in a footlocker, and delivered to Huff (who acted for MacArthur) with the understanding that it would be returned to Roxas if the transfer was completed. The receipt was signed on February 19. Quezon had radioed Chase National on February 18, asking confirmation that the transfer had been made. Quezon left Corregidor on the night of February 20. Five days later the necessary confirmation was received on Corregidor. The box of currency was returned to Roxas for Quezon, who by then was in Panay. Quezon was notified on February 27 that the confirmation had been received.

The transfer of currency made no more sense than my diary entry. If Roosevelt had not approved the transfer of funds, the entire affair would have been annulled. Mere physical possession of a box of currency would have raised significant legal problems. Eventually the large amount of money would have to be presented for redemption and difficulties would have been encountered. MacArthur and Sutherland surely must have known this. Like my diary entry, the useless stratagem relieved everyone's sense of honor.

On the day of his departure Quezon wrote a letter to MacArthur that was intended as a personal statement of the emotions that had motivated Executive Order Number One:

Although I have given official recognition to the services you have rendered to the Government of the Commonwealth and to the Filipino people in my Executive Order No. 1, series of 1942, I feel that I must write you this letter, which partakes of an official as well as private character, in order to tell you how grateful I am, my own family, and the members of my whole staff for the kindness and generosity with which we have been treated here; and to ask you to convey to all the officers within your command, particularly to General Moore, our deep gratitude.

As I have already told you, I would have remained here to the very bitter end, if you deemed it necessary for me to stay. I am going only because you and I have agreed that the cause for which we are fighting can be best promoted by my being in the unoccupied territory where I could render you help and assistance by keeping up the morale and determination of my people to stand by America. But I am leaving you with a weeping heart, for you and I have not only been friends and comrades; we have been more than brothers. My thoughts will always be with you and your dear wife and my godson. If better days should come to all of us, as I hope they will, I expect that the memory of these hectic days will strengthen our friendship and cooperation even more. I am leaving my own boys, the Filipino soldiers, under your care. I know that you will look after their welfare and safety and that, above all, you will see to it that their names may go down in history as loyal and brave soldiers.

With my love to you, Jean and the boy, in which all my family joins, I say good-bye till we meet again. May God ever keep you under His protection.[26]

In Quezon's memoirs there is a fragment that may be revealing: '' . . . the Filipino returns lavishly, with a loyalty that knows no bounds, the affection and confidence of those whom he has elevated to high office.''[27]

MacArthur left an oblique reference in his *Reminiscences*. During his term as chief of staff an attempt was made to reduce General Pershing's pension. MacArthur appeared before a Senate committee to speak in Pershing's behalf:

. . . spoke of the tribute accorded to General Douglas Haig in England. Haig was Pershing's counterpart during World War I. After the war, Haig was promoted to field marshal and received, in addition to a life trust of nearly $9,000 a year, a trust fund of nearly half a million dollars, yielding an income of about $30,000 a year.[28]

I accept these statements at full face value subject to my customary observation that motivation is quite complex and frequently is never articulated or even recognized.

One suspects that MacArthur and Quezon were laying down a deliberate challenge. They knew that the order to Chase National Bank was going to raise a fuss. Chase was required to notify the War Department. MacArthur and Quezon knew that Stimson would have to go to Roosevelt and that Ickes would have to give formal approval or accept the fact without it.

The challenge may be stated succinctly: ''I am the President of the Commonwealth. These are Commonwealth funds. Do you challenge my authority to give them away?'' Quezon was not squeamish about money, asking for it and accepting it easily, and giving it away just as easily, as long as it did not come out of his own pocket.

MacArthur was an old soldier and knew the traditions. Soldiers are never paid enough, and a general is entitled to a reward. It was a common affair. Marshal Haig in England had received such a bequest only a few years ago. Certainly MacArthur was entitled to as much as Haig, both in kind and in amount. Quezon would have been unwilling to be less generous than the British had been. MacArthur was a stickler for getting exactly what his position demanded, and would later lecture Curtin on such fine matters.

Both men knew that Ickes would protest in vain, and they were happy at the thought. Stimson and Roosevelt knew very well that it was worth $640,000 to get Quezon out of Corregidor and safely to Washington, and to keep him happy in the meanwhile. They certainly did not want him to slip away into the jungles of the Visayas and to get into God knows what kind of trouble.

Roosevelt already had a guilty conscience for the turn of affairs, had pondered, probably with some pain, the complaints about betrayal and abandonment. Since he could not do anything else, as he was told by the War Department general staff, he probably smiled quietly and gave the order. It would be good for Ickes' sanctimonious self-righteousness. There is no record that Ickes ever concurred in the act.

Rogers had his doubts for a long time, although he could never pin down the difficulty. Was it the fact, or the amount, or simply the ease with which such things were done? My diary seems to indicate that I only wanted an equivalent share. When Bothne came into my office in late 1943, I showed him the order, which was stored in my office. Bothne shrugged and observed that it was quite commonly done, was not cause for excitement, and the Old Man certainly deserved it.

One last question is whether Sayre knew or ever told. I cannot say.

Sutherland, of course, was quite happy to get $75,000. He felt the burden of long overdue doctor's bills lifted from his shoulders. Most of all, he had visions of a comfortable retirement that was only four years down the road. He called Marshall over from Bataan on February 15. The next morning Marshall came into Lateral 3 and read all the strategic radios, which that no doubt included those involved with Executive Order Number One. He and Sutherland surely talked about their good fortune.

To keep all of this in context, it was no great affair, buried in the constant flow of activity. All of the money was locked away in the States. None of the men on Corregidor could be sure they would survive to spend it. They could not discuss their good fortune with their best friends or gloat about it to their most objectionable enemies. It was very nice but of no present use at all, and therefore easily set aside.

MacArthur and Quezon very likely had the greatest private satisfaction. They had found a way to make Washington give them something and pushed a hard wad down the throats of the War Department general staff.

By February 16 arrangements had been made to move Quezon to the Visayas and eventually to Mindanao. MacArthur asked for a submarine to be used for this purpose. The same submarine would then evacuate Sayre to "the far south." Marshall advised that Roosevelt had approved the proposed evacuations and that submarines had been ordered to Corregidor for the purpose.[29]

The Quezon party finally left Corregidor on the night of February 20. Sayre followed four days later. There must have been a deep sigh of relief in Washington. My own diary notes only: "Quezon and family left for south."[30]

Early in the morning of February 22, *Swordfish* rendezvoused off the coast of Panay with the motorship *Don Esteban*, which had left Corregidor three days earlier. Quezon and his party transferred to *Don Esteban* and were taken to hiding.[31]

Quezon would soon be in exile.

22

Battling Bastards

For MacArthur the Bataan force was a defensive shield. Its function was to delay. It would be the abrasive that wore down the Japanese drive against Corregidor, the center of the entire campaign where the bloody sacrifice would be offered up.

The officers and men who fought on Bataan believed to the end that they had been defeated. Be that as it may, they had fought according to plan in a battle they were never expected to win. They were expected only to hold for three months, and that is precisely what they did. The victory of "Orange" was simply to fight and to hold back for the prescribed time. Whatever the Filipino soldiers lacked in the way of training and experience, they fought, and they fought well. The Japanese had not found their task an easy one.

It was only some 3 miles from Lateral 3 to Mariveles on the southern tip of Bataan; only some 25 miles to Mount Natib, which was the keystone of the main battle position; and only 12 miles to the rear battle position on the Orion-Bagac line. The action was very close, as battles go, to Lateral 3. Yet, for me, it was very far away, not seeming to be any closer than the more distant battles in Malaya and the Netherland East Indies or, for that matter, Europe. Unlike Corregidor, it never registered in my memory as a personal experience.

I had been on Bataan less than an hour at the time of our evacuation, and I cannot recall any emotional or intellectual reaction to the fact. That short visit was enveloped in events that centered to the south, and I never remember the small dock as the end of the Corregidor experience but as the beginning of everything that followed. Bataan and Corregidor raise visions of glory but not of joy.

During the first week at Topside on Corregidor, I met a Filipino soldier named Olivas. He was a small, middle-aged, and mild-mannered man who seemed overwhelmed in the presence of U.S. soldiers, even young ones. A day or so after the big air raid terminated our Topside existence and sent us scuttling downhill to safety in Malinta Tunnel, Olivas was ordered to Bataan. There is an entry in my diary to mark that event. I felt a sharp twinge of apprehension that such a quiet man was going into harm's way.

On January 20 Sutherland went to Bataan for an inspection trip. My entry for the day notes: "General Sutherland to Bataan presumably to stay." I did not expect to see him again. He had made visits before this one, including one on January 10 with MacArthur, but for reasons I cannot recall, this visit seemed to be a permanent relocation. I asked permission to go with him, but he told me curtly that it would not be possible.[1] Actually Sutherland returned in several days and my world was reestablished, but for the moment I felt lost and alone.

Bataan was never a part of my world. It existed only as a shadow world during my ten weeks of duty on Corregidor. I cannot write about the Bataan experience except as an outsider, but to make the story complete I must trace out the sequence of events there. I am sure that for those involved, it was Corregidor without Malinta Tunnel, a long siege that could end only in defeat but endured in the open air with some room for maneuver.

Advance echelon USAFFE was nestled in a wooded area some seven miles northwest of Mariveles, a mile or so off Trail 7 on the southwestern slope of Mount Bataan. The compound was an unimposing assortment of shacks, built in native style and set under the trees, hidden from Japanese reconnaissance planes. To avoid drawing attention, Sutherland had forbidden construction of any road closer than half a mile to the spot. A battalion of Philippine Scouts was bivouacked around the perimeter to provide security. The officers, 35 of them, slept 4 to a hut while the 70 enlisted men slept 25 to a hut. Separate messes were constructed for officers and men, as were separate baths and latrines, to preserve the traditional but not necessarily natural distinction between gentlemen officers and more ordinary enlisted men. Four small nipa shacks provided office space for various staff activities. Akin's signal office had a small radio.[2]

It was an advance echelon from the viewpoint of Corregidor. On Bataan it was located well in the rear area, separated by ten miles from the hospital and quartermaster areas at Mariveles. It was some dozen miles from the main battle position on the Mauban-Abucay line and some half dozen from the final battle line on the Bagac-Orion road. Several small rivers in the area drained from Mount Bataan down to the ocean.

There was no impregnable shelter like Malinta Tunnel. On the other hand, the compound did not constitute an inviting target, and it is likely that the Japanese never knew of its existence. Advance headquarters personnel must have heard artillery fire along the battle line and certainly would have heard the firing during the battle for the Points in early February. Even when the front collapsed in April, the Japanese advance drove down the eastern slopes and coastal plains of Mount Bataan, and Bataan was surrendered before Japanese soldiers penetrated to the headquarters area. All in all, advance echelon or not, it was cleaner, lighter, healthier, and more pleasant than Corregidor, where there was a constant foreboding and actual presence of destruction and death.

The advance echelon was set up as a field unit with very primitive accommodations. Looking at it from the viewpoint of the stone walls of Lateral 3, I once asked one of Richard Marshall's clerks whether he felt slightly exposed. He replied that it was much preferable to Corregidor because the sun, open sky, and fresh air gave a feeling of great freedom and release.

Advance echelon was MacArthur's eye on Bataan. Marshall acted as Sutherland's deputy and reported to him regularly. It was Marshall's duty to coordinate the actions of the various commands on Bataan. He transmitted orders received from Sutherland to Parker and Wainwright and reported back on action taken. MacArthur had "eyes" other than Marshall's. All of the senior staff officers went regularly to Bataan and reported back to Sutherland, who then reported to MacArthur.

Two mountain humps form the spine of the Bataan Peninsula, Mount Natib on the north and Mount Bataan on the south. Two river valleys run between the mountains, east to Manila Bay and west to the South China Sea. The two peaks are about 15 miles apart. It is roughly five miles from the peak of Mount Bataan to the southern tip of the peninsula, where Mariveles nestled in a cove just opposite Corregidor, three miles across the mouth of the bay. The scene of the battle filled an area some 20 miles long and 12 miles wide.

The forward battle line, intended to provide only a temporary barrier, was drawn along the river valleys from each coast up to the peak of Mount Natib. The main battle line, the final position, ran through the valley that separated Mount Natib from Mount Bataan. Along the east coast a flat plain ran five miles from the bay up to the foothills of the two mountains. It provided a natural avenue of attack and required heavy fortifications. The west coast was a wilderness of rocky points covered with impenetrable vegetation.

A line drawn north and south from Mount Natib formed the boundary between II Corps (Parker) on the east and I Corps (Wainwright) on the west. A line over Mount Bataan defined the northern limit of the service command, which contained headquarters, supply depots, hospitals, and other service installations.

II Corps carefully prepared defenses in the coastal area where the approach was easiest and the most likely to be used. I Corps ran a defensive line from the west coast toward the peak of Mount Natib until they could no longer find water. There was a break of some five miles in the center of the defensive position. In spite of Sutherland's orders, it was never closed.

Homma had a difficult choice as his troops cleared San Fernando and the junction of Highway 7. He could pull off on the Bataan road, maintain constant pressure, and prevent the fortification of Bataan. Or he could march directly into Manila to give his troops a rest. Homma moved to Manila and gave USAFFE two additional weeks to fortify. The time was not wasted.

When Homma's advance force finally moved into position, it faced the "strongest sort of field fortifications." Along the coastal plain they found barbed wire entanglements before all positions. On Mount Natib rifle pits and machine-gun emplacements had been constructed with fields of fire cleared around them.

Map 7
Bataan

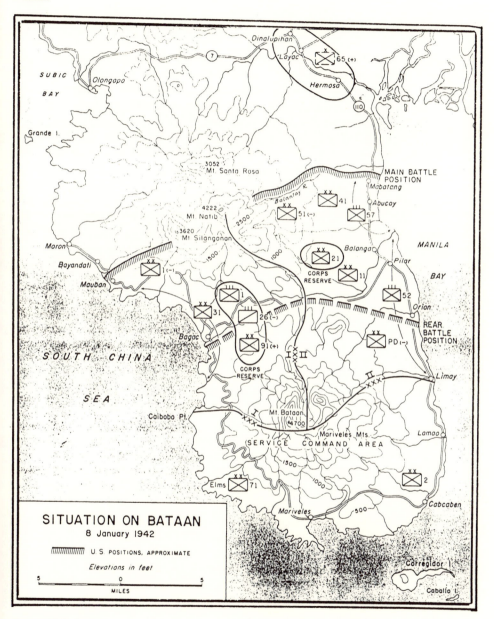

SITUATION ON BATAAN
8 January 1942

|||||||| U.S. POSITIONS, APPROXIMATE

Elevations in feet

5   0   5
MILES

Source: U.S. Army.

Everything was carefully camouflaged. Artillery covered the entire coastal plain area, and fire could be brought to bear quickly against any point. Observation posts had been placed to direct artillery fire. The Japanese who reported the above facts found no fault, from a soldier's point of view, with the defenses that confronted them.[3]

The environment was the same for both armies. The temperature was hot during the day but became cool or even cold at night. Underbrush, cane fields, and rice paddies made travel difficult. The trails into the mountains wandered aimlessly with no obvious destination. In low areas and river valleys there were muddy banks, swamps, jungle growth, and fish ponds. Drinking water was scarce and diarrhea was rampant.

The Japanese 48th Division had been transferred from the Philippines to Java just after the Lingayen landing. Homma thought that he was confronted by only 40,000 exhausted, starving, defeated troops who would not fight. He underestimated the defensive positions that faced him, believing that there would be a small action on the forward battle line, a USAFFE withdrawal to the rear battle line, another small battle, and surrender of both Bataan and Corregidor.

Homma's forces were finally regrouped by January 8 just north of the thin outpost line of the forward USAFFE positions. Orders were issued for an attack to begin on the following day. Under intermittent but heavy artillery fire from II Corps the Japanese made final preparations. All day on January 9 the Japanese troops sat nervously waiting for zero hour.

The attack began at 7:00 P.M. with an artillery barrage from the Japanese positions. Parker's batteries replied in kind. In the first few rounds a direct hit was made on the Japanese artillery headquarters, and most of the staff was killed instantly. Smoke and jungle obscured the field of battle. The Japanese began their approach. As they advanced down the highway, USAFFE troops pulled back from the outpost line without any attempt to oppose the attacking enemy. The Japanese hurried forward to press the attack and ran ahead of their wire-laying units. When night fell, the Japanese were sure they had an easy victory. It would simply be a repetition of Lingayen.

The USAFFE artillery barrage resumed with morning light on January 10. It was heavier than the day before. The Japanese could not locate the artillery positions, and they had no signal communications with the advancing forward units. They could not do anything to soften the destructive impact of the intense artillery fire. Bridges had been destroyed and could not be repaired under fire. Japanese tank units were immobilized.

As the Japanese infantry moved forward, the opposition stiffened. The vision of easy victory began to dissipate. By nightfall the attack had not reached the main USAFFE defensive position. On January 11 the resistance to the Japanese was even more stubborn. By nightfall the Japanese commanders reported that the tank unit had been stopped by artillery fire and that the USAFFE positions were impregnable. Japanese artillery was still unable to find the USAFFE positions, which continued to dominate the artillery battle.

Wainwright's front was quiet. A Japanese unit marched west all night across Bataan to occupy Olongapo, which was not defended. By the night of the 10th they had regrouped south of Olongapo and were preparing to move forward against Wainwright's positions at Mauban.

MacArthur made his first and only visit to Bataan just as the battle got under way. He toured the forward areas with Sutherland, talked with the two corps commanders, and made a short speech to the assembled officers that was published as a ''message to the troops'' five days later. This message is a coldly logical appeal. There is no trace of melodrama or cheap sentimentality, no appeal to patriotism or glory. It is a simple statement of fact and an appeal to common sense. The first paragraph, remembered with bitterness by many, was an accurate statement. MacArthur told them that reinforcements were on the way. He then told them what they all should have understood in any case: ''The exact time of arrival of reinforcements is unknown, as they will have to fight their way through Japanese attempts against them.'' The remainder of the message appeals to the commonsense rule of self-preservation:

Help is on the way from the United States. Thousands of troops and hundreds of planes are being dispatched. The exact time of arrival of reinforcements is unknown as they will have to fight their way through Japanese attempts against them. It is imperative that our troops hold until these reinforcements arrive.

No further retreat is possible. We have more troops in Bataan than the Japanese have thrown against us; our supplies are ample; a determined defense will defeat the enemy's attack.

It is a question now of courage and determination. Men who run will merely be destroyed but men who fight will save themselves and their country.

I call upon every soldier in Bataan to fight in his assigned position, resisting every attack. This is the only road to salvation. If we will fight we will win; if we retreat we will be destroyed.[4]

Wainwright asked MacArthur whether he wanted to see the huge 155 mm guns. It is reported that MacArthur replied shortly: ''I don't want to see them. I want to hear them!'' There have been other transcriptions of this remark, but this one gets close to the heart of the matter.[5] Sutherland walked up to the peak of Mount Natib, where Wainwright's right flank was supposed to be pushed tightly against the left flank of Parker's corps boundary. He found that the five-mile gap had not been closed. There were reasons for this violation of tactical good sense: There was no water on the ridge; it was an impenetrable thicket far from the main centers of action; there were not enough troops, and they were already too thinly spread. Yet Sutherland again ordered that the gap be closed.

During the week that followed, the gap in the defenses on Mount Natib became an increasing point of weakness. By January 14 the Japanese attack had drifted over from both flanks, found the hole, and drove through it. After a week of heavy fighting in an attempt to restore the main defensive position, it became obvious that a withdrawal would have to be made in Wainwright's sector where

I Corps also was in trouble. All reserves had been committed to the action, and the battle had become one of attrition. Sutherland came to Bataan on January 20, and on January 22 he issued the order to withdraw to the Bagac-Orion line.

The withdrawal was made during three successive nights. The troops, exhausted but not broken, moved into the rear battle position. It had been a retreat but not like the one at the Lingayen beaches. These troops had fought to complete exhaustion, but even in retreat they continued to fight. MacArthur advised Marshall that since there could be no further retreat, "I intend to fight it out to destruction."

Radio MacA to AGWAR. Enemy has settled down to attrition because of his unopposed command of the sea. Our losses have been heavy—35% of our forces. We will soon be forced to withdraw to our final positions here. Stand will be made to destruction. He laid it to the charge of Washington to keep our fame and glory alive. In case of his death he recommends General Sutherland as his successor.[6]

Phase One had ended. Philippine Army troops had become soldiers. The withdrawal was not a rout but an organized retreat. Units ordered to hold a defensive screen for withdrawing units did hold and fight. They pulled back in good order though dazed, exhausted, eyes glazed with shock and fatigue. MacArthur radioed Washington that the operations had been completed without loss of troops or supplies.

The Japanese report on the action concluded that their greatest difficulty had been terrain that offset the general deficiencies in training and combat quality of the Filipino troops. The fortifications had been well laid. Infantry fire, when prepared in advance, was skilled and the ability to shoot was "formidable." The artillery was well disposed and effective although not very flexible. As in the case of infantry fire, against prepared positions "wonderful results are possible," but they were poor against unprepared targets. Under attack the Filipino troops, instead of "withdrawing hastily from the position," defended it until the end and continued firing at the attacking force's flank and rear. The Filipinos did not fear attacks from the rear, and when Japanese attackers broke their lines, they continued to fire. However, their will to fight was not strong, and when caught unexpectedly in the open, they were at the mercy of the Japanese.

The troops had not yet settled into the new positions on the main battle line when Homma's second thrust began. He continued to maintain pressure along the main line and made a major attempt to turn the western flank.

The west coast of Bataan is studded with rocky promontories. A successful landing along these wild fringes of land, followed by occupation of the ridges behind the coast, would give control of the service area to the Japanese. Depots, hospitals, and the service areas of Mariveles would be held hostage.

Homma decided to use amphibious landings to bring down the Bataan defenses. Landing craft were assembled at Olongapo to move three infantry battalions down the coast. There would be two phases in the assault. The initial wave would be directed against Longoskawayan Point, at the very tip of Bataan. Mariveles lay about a mile away, and if the Japanese were successfully lodged there, the entire Bataan effort would be jeopardized.

On January 23 Marshall informed Corregidor that Japanese troops had landed on the coast just west of advance echelon. It was thought to be a small party, and efforts were under way to mop them up. He called a day later to report a second landing, and on the 25th he reported a third. On January 26, Marshall suggested that advance echelon should be moved.[7] It had become a serious matter.

Fortunately for the defenders, the Japanese ran into difficulties even before they reached the landing areas. The sea was high, the tides were treacherous, and in the dark the rocky points all looked alike from the sea. The trip down from Subic Bay was a rough one. Then, as they approached the southern tip of Bataan, PT–34, commanded by John D. Bulkeley, stumbled on the landing force. He sank the barges and the force split. About a third of the troops finally struggled ashore at Longoskawayan Point and the rest at Quinauan Point. They were completely disoriented.

The task of destroying the Japanese fell to Selleck, who still commanded the 71st Division. At that time it consisted of a rude assortment of sailors, marines, air force troops, constabulary, and remnants of the 71st Division that had run at Lingayen. Fortunately for Selleck, the landing force was scattered in disorganized units all along the coast. His motley crew moved in to attack. The Japanese were confused by the strange antics of these "suicide troops" who sat down in the open, lighted cigarettes, and talked loudly to induce the Japanese to betray their positions by opening fire. They might have been more confused to know that they were being attacked by sailors and a pursuit squadron.

Eventually, when it was obvious that Selleck's command would need more professional support, Philippine Army units and Philippine Scouts were called up. Mortars on Corregidor were permitted to fire against the entrenched Japanese. It was the first and only time the huge coast artillery batteries on Corregidor would see action. The Japanese could not understand what was happening to them as the huge shells screamed down from the empty skies, exploding with a roar.

MacArthur's concern is reflected in the fact that during this period he stepped into the tactical situation to issue personal orders to the corps commanders. For 9:50 A.M. on January 27 Sutherland's diary records: "General MacArthur directed that corps commanders be notified that patrolling be active and that the present line must be held at all costs."

At 10:45 a special message went to Wainwright: "General MacArthur directed that Major General Wainwright, I Corps, be notified to take charge personally of eliminating small enemy beachheads in his sector prior to nightfall."[8] Wainwright received the order with some sense of desperation. The Japanese pockets along the coast had not been cleared. At the same time his front battle line was beginning to feel pressure.

There are very few documentary remains of MacArthur's direct involvement in tactical operations during the war. One, preserved in the records of Lateral 3 on Corregidor, permits a detailed sketch of how MacArthur dealt with his field commanders. Wainwright received special consideration in Headquarters USAFFE. I can only presume that his seniority and service had earned him special respect that was not accorded to any of the other field commanders. Sutherland treated him with studied deference that was not displayed in his dealings with others. Wainwright was not known for aggressive independence. Moreover, his training as a cavalry officer gave him a tactical viewpoint different from that of the other officers, who had been trained in infantry rules of battle. This is not intended as a judgment of the man but as an introduction to the event described here.

As pressure began to mount toward the end of January, Wainwright became nervous about the stability of his front. He had cause for concern, but he was not alone in his discomfort. At any rate, he recommended a change in position, a withdrawal to a more advantageous defensive line. His request was sent not to MacArthur but to Sutherland. The fact demonstrates that Sutherland's authority over operations was accepted even by Wainwright. Wainwright's special position is revealed by the fact that Sutherland took it to MacArthur for decision. I do not know of any other field officer who would have received such deference.

Sutherland's diary indicates that MacArthur dictated to him a reply to be sent to Wainwright. Sutherland dictated to me, from his own notes, his record of MacArthur's dictation of the reply to Wainwright. When I typed the message, I simply set in the margins of MacArthur's quoted message. Sutherland carefully inserted quotation marks to emphasize the fact that he was transmitting a message from MacArthur, not from himself. Nevertheless, he emphasized in the first paragraph that Wainwright's request had been given the joint consideration of both MacArthur and Sutherland. He assured Wainwright:

We thoroughly understand the grave difficulties that confront you. There is no position that we can take that will shorten your line except the mere beach-head. Were we to withdraw to such a line now it would not only invite immediate over-whelming enemy attack but would completely collapse the morale of our own force. Sooner or later we must fight to the finish. Heretofore we have been maneuvering, falling back from position to position until we have now reached our last ditch. Our only safety is to fight the enemy off. He is not in great strength and if you can once really repulse him you will obtain relief from his pressure. He will continue to apply pressure, however, just as long as we continue to yield to it. If you clear him out on the coast his threats there will always be small. You must, however, hold on your front and there is no better place we can find than the one you are now on. Strengthen your position constantly. Organize your defensive groups in depth and prepare each one to attack either to the right or to the left. Cover each beach and trail and do not let the enemy penetrate your main line of resistance. Call for volunteers from each unit to compose a sniper company such as was ordered some time ago and such as that which fought so successfully in the II Corps under Funk. Explain constantly to your officers and men if they run they will be doomed but that if they fight they will save themselves. The few days which we will have now before the enemy can make a serious attack, if vigorously employed by all officers, may spell the difference between victory and defeat. Drive everything hard in this period of lull. Make the maximum use of artillery; it is your most reliable arm and its efficient use saved the II Corps on the original battle position. Every available resource at the disposition of this Headquarters has been committed and you must depend largely upon what you have. Once again I repeat, I am aware of the enormous difficulties that face you and am proud, indeed, of the magnificent efforts you have made. There is nothing finer in history. Let's continue and preserve the fair fame that we have so fairly won.[9]

MacArthur confided to Sutherland that Wainwright was trained as a cavalryman and therefore thought in terms of shallow defense. He went on to say, with great emphasis, that only a defense in depth was the key to Bataan.

By this time the Japanese had broken through the main line, again at the boundary of the two corps areas, between Wainwright and Parker. Three pockets formed as the Japanese drove through the defenses. It had not been particularly easy to break through the line, and it proved to be impossible to withdraw. USAFFE infantry closed in behind the Japanese and cut them off. After a week of hard fighting, with tanks and artillery, the Japanese were finally obliterated, killed to the last man.

Then came a lull of almost seven weeks. Homma had been brought to a complete standstill. The last of the Japanese soldiers at Anyasan Point died of starvation in the jungles, abandoned by their commanders, who could do nothing for them. Homma estimated that only three infantry battalions of his force were capable of action. He testified later that a concerted counterattack at that time would have driven him out of Bataan and out of the Philippines. He asked for reinforcements and sat back to wait for their arrival. Before the end of February, while Homma waited, Singapore and Java fell, and the entire Netherland East Indies and the long line from Singapore to Rabaul was welded into a continuous Japanese bastion. The only flag flying in defiance of the Japanese conquerors waved over the slopes of Bataan and Corregidor in the very center of the Greater East Asia Co-Prosperity Sphere.

Half a dozen messages written during this period reflect great pride in the achievement of the past six weeks of fighting and a grim appraisal of what lay ahead.

Sutherland wrote to Chynoweth in the Visayas on February 19:

With reference to the situation here, we have stopped the Japs cold on Bataan, inflicting very heavy casualties. The Filipino troops, some of whom were very bad at the beginning, many running away disgracefully, are settling down into first-class fighting units. His combat value varies directly with the discipline imposed upon him and with the quality of leadership. Well-disciplined and well-led, he is a first-class fighting man, and has proved it to everyone's satisfaction. You should use your American officers to the absolute maximum in troop commands because at first contact you will find many of the troops very uncertain. Returning to our situation, the Jap is going to have to put in a lot more troops up here to push us around any. He has established batteries on the Cavite shore, however, and is maintaining a disagreeable harassing fire on all of the fortified islands using 105 mm and 150 mm for this purpose. We counterbattery with everything we have and knock him out from time to time but the cover is so good that we have not yet been able to silence his fire. Damage, of course, from there amounts to very little and casualties have been light.[10]

MacArthur's estimate to George Marshall and Roosevelt on February 8 was more grim than Sutherland's letter. Sutherland could not have been as open with Chynoweth as MacArthur was with Marshall:

The troops have sustained practically fifty percent casualties from their original strength. Divisions are reduced to the size of regiments, regiments to battalions, battalions to companies. Some units have entirely disappeared. The men have been in constant action and are badly battle worn. They are desperately in need of rest and refitting. Their spirit is good but they are capable now of nothing but fighting in place on a fixed position. All our supplies are scant and the command has been on half rations for the past month. It is possible for the time being that the present enemy force might temporarily be held, but any addition to his present strength will insure the destruction of our mobile force. We have pulled through a number of menacing situations but there is no denying the fact that we are near done. Corregidor itself is extremely vulnerable. This type of fortress, built prior to the days of air power, when isolated is impossible of prolonged defense. Any heavy air bombardment or location of siege guns on Bataan or even on the Cavite side would definitely limit the life of the fortress. My water supply is extremely vulnerable and may go at any time. Every other vital installation can be rapidly taken out. Since I have no air or sea protection you must be prepared at any time to figure on the complete destruction of this command. You must determine whether the mission of delay would be better furthered by the temporizing plan of Quezon or by my continued battle effort. The temper of the Filipinos is one of almost violent resentment against the United States. Every one of them expected help and when it has not been forthcoming they believe they have been betrayed in favor of others. It must be remembered that they are hostile to Great Britain on account of the latter's colonial policy. In spite of my great prestige with them, I have had the utmost difficulty during the last ten days in keeping them in line. If help does not arrive shortly nothing, in my opinion, can prevent their utter collapse and their complete absorption by the enemy.[11]

On February 11 MacArthur clarified the intent of his dispatch of February 8:

My plans have already been outlined in previous radios; they consist in fighting my present battle position in Bataan to destruction and then holding Corregidor in a similar manner. I have not the slightest intention in the world of surrendering or capitulating the Filipino elements of my command. Apparently my message gave a false impression or was garbled with reference to Filipinos. My statements regarding collapse applied only to the civilian population, including commonwealth officials, the puppet government and the general populace. There has never been the slightest wavering among the troops. I count upon them equally with the Americans to hold steadfast to the end.[12]

After the middle of February, the plans for various evacuations absorbed MacArthur's attention. He advised Marshall on February 24:

The lack of visible support for the Philippines has created here a very difficult situation which I have been able to meet only through the peculiar confidence placed in me by the Filipino people and army on the one hand and President Quezon on the other. The intent of the enemy in this area is not yet clear. We may be approaching the stalemate of positional warfare but it is possible that a major effort may soon be made to break my Bataan front; his plans will shortly become evident. I am of the opinion that I can throw back an attack if made with the troops now available locally and can then restabilize the situation. I am not in possession of information regarding your developments in Australia but it is apparent that there must be a great deal of organizational work accomplished in the accumulation of forces and in the building of an SOS before offensive action will be possible.[13]

To Clark Lee and Annalee and Melville Jacoby, civilian reporters who asked MacArthur's permission to leave Corregidor in an attempt to break through the line and escape to the south, MacArthur's picture of the future prospect was grim indeed: " . . . if we don't get reinforcements here the end will be brutal and bloody."[14]

23

Evacuation

The fall of Singapore pushed the British line back to the Burma frontier and the British fleet to Colombo, Ceylon, deep in the Indian Ocean. There was no longer any talk of British involvement in the South China Sea. If Washington had ever entertained any serious hope of a thrust up from Singapore, the hope was now dead. Mindanao, on the southeastern flank of the long battle line, was the only conceivable link between the Bataan garrison and the supply base in Australia. The line of airfields that had been constructed during the fall and winter was centered in Del Monte on the Bukidnon Plateau of Mindanao. Although the Japanese controlled Davao and were pushing leisurely up the escarpment, the complex of fields was still open and would remain open until May.

The lines of communication with Australia ran in two directions through Mindanao. Blockade runners from Australia delivered their cargoes at isolated ports along the coast. The cargoes were transshipped to Corregidor. By February the flow was running thin. Now Del Monte was the center of an escape route that ran from Corregidor and Bataan. Headquarters of Far East Air Forces had moved down this route and had reorganized in Australia. Air force pilots and other personnel followed. Nurses eventually were evacuated through Del Monte.

The long message that Sutherland began to dictate during the first big air raid at Topside, and that he finished the following day in Lateral 3 of Malinta Tunnel, was a directive to Sharp on Mindanao. The directive emphasized the strategic importance of Mindanao:

The basic strategic concept in this Theatre is based upon the retention of Mindanao, preventing the development of enemy air and ground installations. The retention of Mindanao and the establishment of air bases will protect the N.E.I., permit the landing of an expeditionary force and greatly facilitate the counteroffensive in the northern part of the Philippine Archipelago.[1]

When this was written MacArthur still believed that reinforcements would flow north from Australia through Mindanao and eventually reach Luzon. Now, six weeks later, Mindanao was still important but only as an escape route.

Quezon was gone. Sayre had followed. Wavell had dissolved ABDACOM. Brett and Brereton had flown back to Australia—Brett went to Melbourne, which was as far as he could get from the action. The Dutch had surrendered, and the chief military officers had evacuated to Australia. The only centers of resistance in the entire South China Sea area were on Bataan, Corregidor, and Mindanao. Guerilla units already were forming in the jungles of the Philippines. The decision made in 1941 to center the opposition to Japan on Singapore had been played out to the end of the hand. That game was over.

Of the original partners of ABDACOM, only Australia and the United States remained. A new command would have to be organized, with the United States as the strategic head, to coordinate future operations in the Pacific. The supreme commander would of necessity be a U.S. officer. In the roster of ranking officers there was one obvious choice. MacArthur had the rank, he had been a field marshal of the Philippines and was now a full general of the U.S. Army; his tenure as general officer was longer than that of anyone else available; his troops had held the Japanese, and would continue to hold for two months more; he had a flair for self-confident command.

The decision to evacuate MacArthur was debated in Washington in January. On February 3 Marshall inquired about any plans MacArthur had for evacuating Mrs. MacArthur and their son, young Arthur, to safety. On February 4, MacArthur was notified by Marshall:

The most important question concerns your possible movements should your forces be unable longer to sustain themselves in Bataan and there should remain nothing but the fortress defense of Corregidor. Under these conditions the need for your services there will be less pressing than other points in the Far East.[2]

Marshall suggested two alternatives. MacArthur might move to Mindanao for a short period, then proceed to the south, where he would reassume command of USAFFE. Or, alternatively, he might go directly to Australia.

There was an interval of intense activity caused by the neutrality proposal of Quezon, which resulted in the first direct order to evacuate Quezon and his family. It was also suggested by Roosevelt that MacArthur's family be evacuated. MacArthur immediately replied, "I am deeply appreciative of the inclusion of my own family in this list but they and I have decided that they will share the fate of the garrison."[3]

On February 14 Marshall urged that the General reconsider his decision not to leave Corregidor. MacArthur acknowledged the message the next day, without giving any reply about the matter of evacuation.[4] Richard Marshall was called over from Bataan to discuss with Sutherland the evacuations of Quezon and Sayre and the message just received from George Marshall. MacArthur had told

Sutherland that he was reluctant to leave until he had done all he could to prolong the defense of Corregidor. According to Sutherland preparations for leaving were to be made soon.[5]

Several conferences were held during the night of February 15 and during the next day. On the morning of the 16th Marshall read the file of secret radios (the Secret File) that had occupied MacArthur and Washington during the previous two weeks. Later in the day MacArthur, Sutherland, and Marshall discussed the various aspects of the complicated situation. The evacuation of Quezon and Sayre must have had high priority. It is also quite likely that they discussed MacArthur's own evacuation.

The evacuation of Quezon and Sayre occupied everyone's attention for several days, but as soon as the two parties were safely away, George Marshall renewed the discussion of MacArthur's departure, this time with a notice that there would be an unequivocal order to leave.[6]

Roosevelt's order came on February 23. A commander was needed in Australia, and MacArthur was no longer needed in the Philippines.

The President directs that you make arrangements to leave Fort Mills and proceed to Mindanao. You are directed to make this change as quickly as possible. The President desires that in Mindanao you take such measures as will insure a prolonged defense of that region—this especially in view of the transfer of President Quezon and his government to the Southern Philippines and the great importance the President attaches to the future of the Philippines by prolonging in every way possible the continuance of defense by United States troops and the continuance of the active support of the Philippine Government and people. From Mindanao you will proceed to Australia where you will assume command of all United States Troops. It is the intention of the President to arrange with the Australian and British Governments for their acceptance of you as commander of the reconstituted ABDA area. Because of the vital importance of your assuming command in Australia at an early date, your delay in Mindanao will not be prolonged beyond one week and you will leave sooner if transportation becomes available earlier. Instructions will be given from here at your request for the movement of submarine or plane or both to enable you to carry out the foregoing instructions. You are authorized to take with you your Chief of Staff, General Sutherland.[7]

MacArthur replied on February 24, requesting a temporary delay in the departure. He advised Marshall that he intended to use surface craft and bombers for the evacuation because movement by submarine would be too time-consuming.[8] I vividly remember the preparation of the dispatch of February 24. MacArthur and Sutherland pored over the matter, Sutherland sketching out a reply that was dictated and typed. There were several changes, but it was finally approved. Sutherland handed it to me for delivery to the signal office, saying, "When this comes off, you will stay with me."

On February 26 the date was set in a radio to Marshall:

Suggest you request Navy Department order submarine immediately to Corregidor. If navy has doubt as to probability of arrival here suggest two be sent to insure arrival.

Also suggest directive to Brett to dispatch planes on call. Anticipate possibility of execution of plan about March 15.[9]

Roosevelt agreed to the delay and left the details to MacArthur. During the next four days arrangements were made for the movement of submarines to Corregidor. I typed a brief outline of information about Australian cities for Huff in the form of a memorandum to MacArthur.[10]

There is a strange series of entries in my diary from February 9 through February 27.[11] The entry for February 9 is the cryptic "Look for something on 15–3." Sutherland had made a remark to me at the end of that day in Lateral 3. I have never doubted that the numbers referred to March 15. I expect Sutherland said, "the fifteenth of next month." On February 10 I wrote:

Repeated radio of 7th to General Marshall. Reported that an attack will be made on Japs 153 first in Biri Buoy as a feint then in south. Our naval striking forces are three cruisers and some destroyers. Two of the cruisers have been damaged by Japanese air raids. Need fighting planes. Repeated firing from Hughes and Drum. Drum has been fired on frequently.

I have searched in vain for documentary references to the sentence "Reported that an attack will be made on Japs 153 first at Biri Buoy as a feint then in south."[12] All other elements of the entry have been traced to specific documents. Perhaps I read a document that contained this information. It seems to be a précis of a formal statement.

On February 11 the diary reads: "Rumors as to our offensive 315." The next day there is a record that Roosevelt's reply to Quezon's thunderbolt had been received, with the added note: "Still sweating out 153." On February 15: "No go on info of Feb. 9." The day before, Marshall had urged MacArthur to reconsider his refusal to leave Corregidor. On this day MacArthur acknowledged without any reply.

On February 24 my diary noted: "Radio MacArthur to Washington regarding reassumption of command of troops in the Far East and move to south. MacArthur recommends that the departure be delayed to permit proper psychological and physical adjustments here. I will stay with General Sutherland at his orders."

Between the day of MacArthur's reply to Marshall and March 11, nothing was said to me concerning the matter. On February 25 Roosevelt gave permission for MacArthur to select the time and method of departure. The next day MacArthur finally notified Washington of his decision to leave Corregidor. I remember typing this radiogram.[13] My diary records on February 27: "415 MacArthur plans to 324." I vividly remember making this entry. The date 153 is buried in the two sets of numbers. The 4 and 24 had no meaning. The rearrangement was intended purely as a deception; I was too cautious to record any specifics. As for the vague references to an occurrence to be expected on March 15, which first came into my records on February 9, I am sure that they referred to the date of our evacuation from Corregidor.

MacArthur certainly knew from the beginning that at the end a final, un-equivocal order would come. He would have known by February 4 that Singapore could not hold. He regularly received reports from Wavell, some of which I saw. He knew enough of the situation to understand that he alone stood in line as the leader of a reorganized command even before Marshall spelled it out for him.

MacArthur records his reaction to receipt of the order to leave the Philippines: "My first reaction was to try and avoid the latter part of the order, even to the extent of resigning my commission and joining the Bataan Force as a simple volunteer. But Dick Sutherland and my entire staff would have none of it. . . . For two days I delayed a final decision."[14]

Frazier Hunt records a conversation with MacArthur in the 1950s that gives more detail of MacArthur's feelings at this time. MacArthur's account was written a decade later.

I fully expected to be killed. I would never have surrendered. If necessary I would have sought the end in some final charge. I suppose the law of averages was against my lasting much longer under any circumstances. I would probably have been killed in a bombing raid or by artillery fire. . . . And Jean and the boy might have been destroyed in some final general debacle.[15]

MacArthur's reference to his "entire staff" presumes a knowledge of the actual workings of his headquarters. "Staff" was used very loosely by Mac-Arthur, here and elsewhere. It never referred to the collectivity of the officers assigned to him and acting formally as a body. No such staff meetings were held, especially for top-secret strategic problems. In this particular context it referred to Sutherland, who was continuously at MacArthur's side during this period. Richard Marshall might well have been included, but he was isolated on Bataan except for limited visits to Lateral 3. The allusion to "entire staff" must refer only to Sutherland's understanding of what the individual members would agree to "if they had been asked." There is no indication that any others were asked, even individually. Akin, as signal officer, personally handled the "eyes only" messages, but as a messenger not as an adviser.

Certainly MacArthur sent for Sutherland, and the two men thrashed out a reply together. The debate over the matter rested on MacArthur's subjective, emotionally charged understanding of what honor demanded of him, on the one side, and the demand of prudent rationality, on the other. MacArthur spoke for honor, Sutherland spoke for duty. The outcome was perfectly predictable. It was not just bombast on MacArthur's part; he meant what he said about the obligation imposed upon him by his "special situation." He also was a soldier and knew that in the end prudent rationality would define duty.

MacArthur was not haranguing Sutherland or Washington, he was addressing himself. He knew what the result must be, and the feelings that tormented him must be exorcised. As he walked and talked and gesticulated, the wind of reason

cooled emotion. Unlike the others, MacArthur carried not only a present responsibility for events of this moment but also the dread of facing the opprobrium
of the future, when others would say he had led his troops into a death trap from
which they could not escape, and then had run away to personal safety and
personal glory.

I suspect that MacArthur talked of the betrayal of the Philippines, gesticulating
in despair, complaining of Roosevelt's refusal to move, as honor had dictated,
to the relief of the Filipinos. He must have grimaced with disgust and even
revulsion as his words warmed his passion. He must have asserted at least once:
"Dick, I will resign my commission. I will go to Bataan as a civilian and stand
with the troops until the bitter end."[16]

Then, as the physical effort of the walk began to cool MacArthur's emotions,
he listened to Sutherland's commonsense reply: Such an action would be inconceivable; it would destroy MacArthur; it would deprive the Filipinos of any
hope of relief if there were any hope at all; it was too late to repair lost opportunities, the line of action now hovered over Australia, and MacArthur was
needed there. No one would understand a resignation, and it would cause more
harm than the evacuation. The entire staff would oppose a resignation. The
discussion then moved to the question of precise details, and they began to work
out the reply to the president's order.

The discussion of evacuation began in January and intensified during February.
It is quite likely that all recollections of the discussions have been compressed,
perhaps disjointed, and tangled. One basic fact emerges: Sutherland was the
organizer of the evacuation. More important, he was MacArthur's chief support
(aside, of course, from Jean MacArthur).

I typed a message to Brett on March 1:

You have probably surmised purpose of mission. Request detail best pilots and that best
available planes be placed in top condition for trip. B–24's if available otherwise B–
17's. Ferry mission only. Desire if possible initial landing on return to be south of combat
zone. Anticipate call for arrival Mindanao about 15.[17]

On the morning of Wednesday, March 11, Sutherland came into the lateral
and handed me a copy of Special Order 66. It was dated March 11 but had been
written some days earlier. My task was to type a copy for each officer listed on
the original. The typed list included all of the officers who had been selected to
leave Corregidor. At the bottom Sutherland had written in M/Sgt. Paul P. Rogers
with my serial number. The first copy directed General Douglas MacArthur to
proceed from Fort Mills to undesignated points. Major General Richard Sutherland's copy followed, on through Brigadier Generals Marshall, Akin, and
others.

While I was typing, the headquarters commandant, a captain whom I had seen
just once before, walked up to my desk, agitated and flushed with anger. He
said, "Rogers, God damn you, I didn't want to do this. I told them I wouldn't

do it, but they made me. Take these damned things, hide them, and keep your mouth shut.'' On my desk was a set of master sergeant's chevrons. I put them in my pocket without saying anything, not knowing what would be appropriate under the circumstances, and returned to my work. The captain strode angrily away. I was startled at this interruption of my work, but I understood his anger. I had been promoted above men with greater rank and longer service. Shortly thereafter I reached the bottom of the list and typed the order for Master Sergeant Paul P. Rogers, Infantry. I had sat down a private, and I got up a master sergeant of infantry.

I delivered the papers to Sutherland. Neither of us said a word about the promotion. He told me to get my barracks bag and to get ready to leave that afternoon.

I looked around the room at the men who would be left behind with a feeling of shame, guilt, and regret. God knows, I would be glad to leave—but in a different way. I finally decided I could perform at least one service. I found two friends and told them to pass the word that I knew of a fellow who could get letters out of Corregidor if he could have them before three o'clock.[18] Soon I began to receive letters, always without comment, and I threw them in my barracks bag. Colonel Seals came to my desk with a small, grim smile. ''Rogers, I hear you know of someone who can deliver letters. Will you see that he gets this one?'' Then the time came! Marshall stopped by my desk and said, ''Rogers, it is time to go.''

I picked up my barracks bag and walked out of Lateral 3, not daring to look at the men who sat at their desks, performing, or pretending to perform, the tasks committed to them. Nothing was said. We turned down the main tunnel, then went out the west entrance. Jeeps took us to the North Dock. MacArthur, his family, Sutherland, and Huff remained a little longer.

The rest of us, headed by Marshall, boarded an admiral's launch that rolled gently as each of us stepped down into it. I was the last man aboard. Before I had sat down, the navy chief cast off the line and the coxswain turned the launch out across the channel, toward Bataan.

I sat on the seat of the launch just opposite Diller. For the first time I was able to look at my new stripes. I pulled them from my pocket and spread them out on my leg to look at them. Diller smiled and asked, ''Rogers, what did you get?'' I replied briefly, ''Master.'' Diller thought: ''My god, he's awfully young to be a master sergeant.''[19]

Mariveles Mountain loomed in the foreground, and we approached a small dock at Sisiman Cove where two torpedo boats were lined up on either side. We walked onto the dock and broke into groups. Wilson told me to follow him. With Willoughby and Diller we boarded PT–35. When all passengers were aboard their respective boats, the lines were cast off, the boats backed slowly away from the dock, then strained forward out into the channel.

PT–32 had waited at the quarantine dock at Mariveles to pick up Akin, Sherr,

Casey, and Marquat, who came down from advance echelon to embark. MacArthur and his family, with Sutherland, Huff, and Morhouse, drove down to the north dock and boarded PT–41, which waited there for his party. As soon as they were on board, it pulled out into the bay to rendezvous with the three other boats. The entire squadron moved out to sea.

The three officers on PT–35 moved forward. I went back along the torpedo tubes, where spare drums of fuel were lashed, to the aft section of the deck, and stood alone. The wind whipped the cool salt spray against my face, and I was soon damp all over. We pulled out around Corregidor, which loomed black against the sky. It was past sunset, and the dusk was being swallowed rapidly by the dark.

I followed the bulk of Corregidor as it passed across my field of view. Then, as it moved to the rear, in response to an undeniable impulse, I came to stiff attention and brought my arm up in a salute in honor of the friends I had left behind. It is recorded that on PT–41, up ahead in the dark, MacArthur also was standing at attention. The deck lurched as we picked up power. I dropped my arm and walked slowly forward.

MacArthur's decision to evacuate his staff raised questions at the time. Had he left Sutherland with Marshall and the remainder of headquarters USAFFE, Wainwright would have been overshadowed by a staff that remained loyal to MacArthur. MacArthur, on his part, would have arrived in Australia tired, sick, and dispirited, to be confronted by surly subordinates. It would have taken him a year or more to put together a replacement comparable with the USAFFE group, if he could have done it at all. As it was, MacArthur arrived in Melbourne almost without losing his stride, and he was able to set immediately to work. Of the two areas, Australia needed MacArthur more than Corregidor needed him. By the same token, MacArthur had greater need of his staff than did Wainwright.

Sutherland, not MacArthur, prepared the list of passengers. The number was determined by the space available on four PT boats and three B–17 bombers. The priority slots were easily filled: MacArthur, Mrs. MacArthur, young Arthur, his nurse, Ah Chu, Sutherland, Marshall, and Huff. Morhouse was called over from Bataan because a doctor was needed. Admiral Rockwell and Captain Ray were requested by the navy, and General George by the air force in Washington.

The higher-ranking officers had been chosen by Sutherland because of their proven loyalty, their predictable behavior, and their testing under fire. Sutherland knew their strengths and their weaknesses; they were tools sharpened by his use. MacArthur would need them in Australia. A commander can move freely only if he feels that he can trust his staff both professionally and personally.

Wilson and I were added by Sutherland, probably because we were "his." Wilson was Sutherland's assistant; I, his stenographer. In Melbourne, Richard Marshall once asked me if I knew why I had been taken out of the Philippines, suggesting with a grin that perhaps it had been the will of God. Having no better answer, I replied, "Yes, sir, I suppose it was the will of God." He snorted and replied, "Will of God, hell! It was Dick Sutherland who added your name to that list."

Wilson told several officers in my presence: "Rogers was chosen because he was doing his job. If the other steno in the office had been on the job as he should have been, he would be here and Rogers would be in prison camp." Later he wrote: "Master Sergeant Paul P. Rogers was selected by Maj. Gen. Sutherland to make the trip because of his speed and accuracy as a stenographer-typist. On March 11, 1942 he was promoted in rank to Master Sergeant. Before the war ended, he attained the rank of Second Lieutenant."[20]

A plan had been worked out by Admiral Rockwell for Motor Torpedo Boat Squadron 3. If we encountered the enemy, PT–35 would stand and fight to destruction. PT–32 and PT–34 would follow, in that order, to permit the escape of PT–41 with its important cargo. At any rate, in engaging the enemy those who were least would become first in the action. PT–35 was commanded by Ensign Akers, a quiet, unassuming young man who probably was not much older than I was. Passengers included Willoughby, Wilson, Diller, and finally Rogers, newly promoted to master sergeant, possibly the youngest master sergeant in the service at that time, a far cry at 21 from the traditional picture of a grizzled senior non-commissioned officer. I felt elated at my promotion, wondering at my good fortune but aware of the discrepancy between my experience and the authority imparted by the brand-new stripes.

The formation slowed as the boats picked their way through the mine field at the entrance to the harbor, moving cautiously along the tight lanes, then out again into the open sea. Sometime during the night PT–35 separated from the other three boats. We were traveling in the dark without lights of any kind, the weather had turned cloudy, the sea was rough, and Akers simply lost contact.

As a matter of fact, the entire squadron was separated during the night, and all wandered into the rendezvous at different times. MacArthur's boat was mistaken for an enemy ship by the other two and narrowly escaped being fired upon. PT–32 lost its reserve fuel tanks and was abandoned.

On PT–35 we went below to find our bunks in the dark. The pitching of the boat bounced me up and down, and the bunk finally gave way with a crack. Water drained down from all sides, and I lay there, cold and wet, waiting for morning. I had a bottom bunk on the left side of the cabin. Wilson had the one above. Diller was in the bottom bunk opposite me, under Willoughby. Diller awoke once or twice during the night to see Willoughby's white hand hanging delicately and lifelessly over his head on a limp arm that swayed gently with the boat's motion.

At daybreak we pulled alongside an island and rocked in the hot sun all day. I crawled out of my shattered bunk, climbed the short ladder to the deck, and walked back to the galley, where one of the crew was preparing breakfast. He grinned and asked how many hotcakes I could eat. I replied enthusiastically that I could probably eat a dozen. I had not had one since the luxurious days at the

Philippine Department mess. He asked if I would take three, and that is what I
got. After breakfast I took the new stripes out of my pocket, borrowed a needle
and thread from one of the crew, and sewed them on my shirt. The navy men
were surprised to see so many stripes on such a young arm.

During the long afternoon a fishing boat appeared from around the island,
creating uncertainty and excitement. We were afraid that the crew were Japanese
or would radio the Japanese of our whereabouts. They may not have been sure
of our status and intent, since we were running without any identification. Finally,
U.S. flags were waved by the Filipino fisherman and they came alongside. I
suppose they also had Japanese flags so they would be prepared for any even-
tuality.

We were not terribly far from the rest of the party, but we could never have
found each other. Late in the evening Akers took us to the rendezvous, only to
learn from PT–32 that we had just missed the other boat. We left water and
shotguns for PT–32 and proceeded to follow the others. We never did catch
them.

The next night we traveled on, rolling and pitching, soaked and uncomfortable.
We had difficulty finding Cagayan the following morning. Willoughby tried his
hand at navigation with map and ruler but without success. One of the crew
used flag semaphore to make contact with a Boy Scout on shore who gave us
the name of the village, also with flag semaphore. We were close to the end of
the first segment of our escape from Corregidor. We finally arrived at Cagayan,
Mindanao, where a truck was waiting to drive us to air strip Del Monte #2.

Four planes had left southern Australia. Only one left Darwin, in northern
Australia, for the trip to Mindanao. The others had dropped out because of
engine trouble or other difficulties. The lone plane flew north. During the night
someone threw the wrong switch in the dark, and 300 gallons of fuel were
dumped. The pilot flew on, knowing that he was in great danger. He almost
made it. Then, only a dozen miles from his goal, the engines died and the plane
settled into the ocean. Two men died in the crash, and all the others were injured.
They struggled a mile through the surf to the beach and were taken up the ridge
to Del Monte shortly before MacArthur arrived.[21]

Sutherland talked to the pilot and then took him to see MacArthur, who
remarked, ''Anyone as lucky as you are can serve with me.'' Henry Godman
thus became the first GHQ staff pilot and was added to our small group.

Lieutenant General George Brett, now commanding general of the U.S. Army
forces in Australia, received a specific order from MacArthur. I typed the document at Del Monte:

Arrival Del Monte today with Admiral Rockwell, his chief of staff, fourteen army officers,
and my own wife and child. Upon arrival here discovered that only one of the four planes
dispatched here had arrived; and that with an inexperienced pilot, no brakes and super-
chargers not repeat not functioning. This plane was returned to you by General Sharp
since it was not repeat not suitable for the purpose intended. It is necessary that only the

best planes and most experienced pilots of adequate service be employed for the transportation of such a party. This trip is most important and desperate and must be set up
with absolutely the greatest of care lest it end in disaster. Properly functioning B–17s
must be obtained from Hawaii or the United States if they are not otherwise available.
As my presence at Del Monte must be kept secret, radio me full information addressed
as usual to Fort Mills. Be careful not repeat not to send clear text addresses or text
signatures which would disclose my presence here.[22]

Brett took this as a sharp rebuke, and he was correct!
   Another message went to George Marshall:

I have made hazardous trip successfully by naval Motor Torpedo Boat to Del Monte
Mindanao. In order to expedite movement I did not await submarine. Upon arrival
discovered that Brett had sent four old B–17s of which only one arrived and that not
repeat not fit to carry passengers due to inoperative supercharger. Failure of three planes
to arrive not repeat not due to enemy action. The other plane took off for return trip
before my arrival. I am informing Brett but request you inform him of group to be
transported and order him to dispatch suitable planes if on hand, otherwise that you make
such planes available to him. I am accompanied by my wife and child and fourteen
officers, Admiral Rockwell and his chief of staff. The best three planes in the United
States or Hawaii should be made available with completely adequate and experienced
crews. To attempt such a desperate and important trip with inadequate equipment would
amount to consigning the whole party to death and I could not accept such a responsibility.
I am in constant communication with Corregidor and request reply to that station in usual
manner. I am continuing to function in command of all forces in the Philippines. My
presence in Del Monte should be kept completely secret and every means taken to create
belief that I am still in Luzon. Pursuant your order I did not inform Brett of mission and
it would appear that he was ignorant of importance.[23]

   We were taken to the Del Monte plantation, where we were quartered until
we could be evacuated. It was a nervous experience. Japanese patrols had been
seen only 30 miles down the road, unaware how close they were to a great prize.
The air strip was held by some 500 air force personnel. A young major took me
under his wing and gave me a tour of the immediate area. He showed me a
cave, telling me it would be a good place in which to hide the general if the
Japanese attacked.
   In the officers' quarters I noticed a collection of Moro knives hanging on one
bunk. I expressed admiration and asked where I could get one. My guide took
one and handed it to me, saying the owner would not mind. He was wrong. The
owner did mind, and came to find me later in the day to raise a heated objection.
I apologized and returned the knife. It was my first meeting with Captain Henry
Godman, neither of us knowing that we would spend two years of our lives in
close company.
   I do not think I saw MacArthur more than once at Del Monte before we
boarded the B–17s for the trip to Australia. He was secreted away in one of the

bungalows on the plantation. Sutherland set up a small, informal office in the clubhouse, where I took dictation and transcribed it.

Our secret mission turned out to be not so much of a secret after all. On the second day of our stay, a Filipino woman arrived on foot, to the consternation of everyone demanding to see General MacArthur. She knew he was there and had come to obtain information about relatives in Manila. I suppose every Filipino in the area knew also, but how they knew was beyond our understanding at the time. Now, of course, I know that radio and telephone are not the only means for long-distance communication among "primitive" people who find other ways to pass along information.

In between working I wandered around the area. I found pineapples, bananas, and oranges growing in the fields and orchards. I picked and ate them; I had not had fresh fruit since the USAFFE mess at One Calle Victoria. It was easy to let Corregidor, my world of just two days before, fade away. Here on Mindanao there was sunshine, fresh air, lush tropical vegetation; in the officers' club were pineapples, tea, coffee; and, most of all, a great sense of freedom and release.

While we waited at Mindanao, we slept on cots in the plantation clubhouse area. We were spread over several rooms. Morhouse, Wilson, and I, relatively junior members, shared a room. I retired early and was lying on my cot when the other two came in. Morhouse was a very recent addition to the General's group and was learning his way around. Not aware or not caring that I was present, he asked Wilson, "Who is this Rogers, anyway?" Wilson replied, "He's a fine young man; a perfect gentleman. The General thinks a great deal of him." The same question was being asked in Australia.

Finally, on March 16, just before midnight, two planes arrived. We were hastily divided into two groups, threw our luggage on the ground, and climbed into the bellies of the planes, which took off for the return trip to Darwin. These B–17s had been borrowed from the navy in Australia—so we were saved by the navy in both segments of the journey.

It was a cold, dark trip. We sprawled out along the aluminum hulls of the bombers, with only one blanket each against the cold metal that drained the heat from our shaking bodies. We slept fitfully, turning constantly to find warmth and relief from the aches that came with cold and stiffness.

The formation pulled east, then droned south, bending around Timor to escape detection by the Japanese, who now held that island, then pulled back on a direct line for Bachelor Field at Darwin, the northernmost settlement of Australia. Upon arrival we climbed clumsily from the planes, stretched our legs, and drank up the warm sun. MacArthur and his family were hurried to a nearby building to wash, rest, and change clothes. MacArthur had stripped down to his long underwear when Sutherland came in to report that planes were available for the remainder of the trip to Melbourne. MacArthur lashed out that he would not fly. Sutherland tried to explain that the only alternative would be a truck caravan over the desert to Alice Springs, the nearest railhead to the south. MacArthur was obstinately furious and refused to budge.

Marshall came in to tell Sutherland that Japanese bombers from Timor had been sighted on a bearing from Bachelor Field and Darwin. Sutherland had reached the end of his powers. He took Morhouse, the medical aide, aside and told him that he must find some way to make MacArthur change his mind. Morhouse found the right approach. He told MacArthur that the long trip by truck caravan would be extremely injurious to young Arthur's health. The argument carried the day; MacArthur yielded and allowed himself and his family to be gently hurried to the airplanes. He had not been told about the Japanese bombers. The rest of us clambered aboard, and the pilots hurriedly cleared the field just minutes before the bombers made their first run. After droning south in the sun over the Great Australian Desert, we arrived at Alice Springs, which provided a night's rest and rail connections with Melbourne, still hundreds of miles across the desert. We were billeted in the only hotel, a ramshackle relic reminiscent of a western movie set. I washed up, then walked around the town, which was filled with a motley collection of Australian civilians and soldiers who were not aware that the leader of Australian defenses had arrived in their midst.

With my new stripes almost shining on my arms, I walked into a pub where a dozen or so Aussie soldiers were belting away large mugs of powerful warm beer. I was still a teetotaler and finally ended up, to everyone's unrestrained surprise, drinking ginger beer. They looked at me with alarm, but nothing was said until one grizzled sergeant put his hand on my shoulder and growled, "Well, cobber, each mate to his own taste." I bought him a beer. There was heat, dust, and sand, and there were many, many flies.

At Alice Springs our party broke up. MacArthur and his family, with Sutherland, Morhouse, and Huff, waited a day longer for the arrival of a special train sent up from the south. MacArthur refused to fly farther. The trip would take several days longer, but he felt that he needed the rest, in any case; and he certainly did not want to fly.

The rest of us, headed by Marshall, completed the journey by plane and were in Melbourne perhaps eight hours or so later. We stopped to refuel in Adelaide, where I found chocolate bars in a small airport café. I bought a hat full. When I returned to the plane, I ate two and left the others in my hat on the seat. I went to sleep, and when I awoke, all the candy bars but one were gone. I think it was Diller who grinned and said, "Rogers, you're a master sergeant now. You'll have to give up that pogey bait."

The author en route to Manila, September 1941.

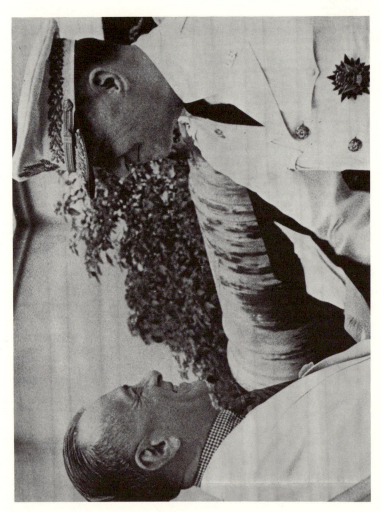

MacArthur and Quezon, Military Mission period. Photograph courtesy of National Archives.

MacArthur and Wainright, October 1941. Photograph courtesy of National Archives.

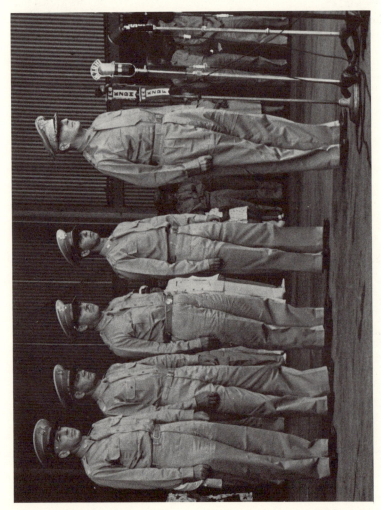

MacArthur and staff, August 1941. Behind MacArthur, left to right, are Sutherland, George, Marquat, and Diller. Photograph courtesy of National Archives.

General and Mrs. MacArthur, Corregidor, February 1942. Photograph courtesy of National Archives.

MacArthur and Quezon, Corregidor, February 1942. Photograph courtesy of National Archives.

MacArthur and Sutherland, Lateral 3, Malinta Tunnel, January 1942. Photograph courtesy of National Archives.

MacArthur and Sutherland leaving Malinta Tunnel. Photograph courtesy of National Archives.

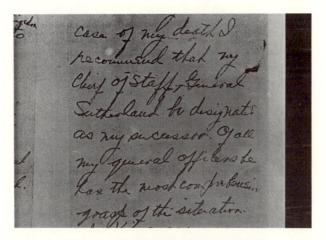

MacArthur's evaluation of Sutherland, January 1942.
Photograph courtesy of MacArthur Memorial.

The author, two weeks after evacuation,
late March 1942.

The author, 401 Collins Street,
Melbourne, late June 1942.

Departure from Melbourne, July 1942.
Front: Wilson, Godman, and Sutherland;
rear: Marquat and MacNider.

The author, Port Moresby, September 1942.

Government House, Port Moresby, December 1942.

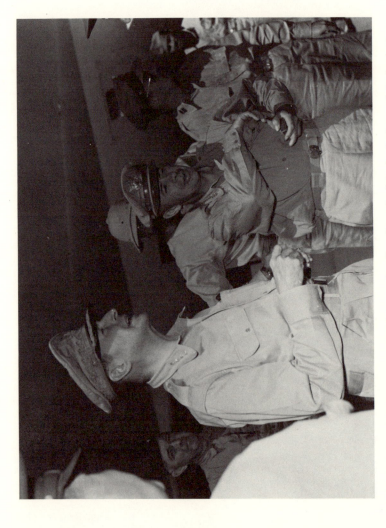

MacArthur and Kenney arrive in Brisbane, signaling the end of the beginning and the beginning of the end, January 1943. Photograph courtesy of National Archives.

VII

Hospitable, March–July 1942

MacArthur dispirited; Sutherland's increased role; new headquarters and personnel; romantic adventures; fall of Bataan and Corregidor; MacArthur orders fight to death

24

I Shall Return

The bulk of the Bataan Boys flew south from Alice Springs to Melbourne. Our C–47 transport flew from Adelaide, where I had purchased my chocolate bars, and landed late in the afternoon at Essendon Airport north of Melbourne. The officers went in several cars to their billets at the Menzies Hotel. I rode alone in a staff car through the city to a small hotel in St. Kilda. The driver left me at the door. Tired and hungry, I went in to find my room. I have a very vague memory of talking to the woman at the desk and of climbing the narrow stairs to a small room. I showered, changed clothes, and went down to get something to eat. The dining room had closed, so I walked down the street and found a small café. I was the only customer. Yanks were still a rarity in Australia and were looked upon as curiosities. I asked for, and got, apple pie, ice cream, and milk. I ate my fill. A new kind of war was under way! The code name applied to Melbourne certainly was selected by someone who felt as I did; Melbourne was truly "Hospitable."

The next morning I was driven to Robertson High School, where a temporary headquarters was being set up. When I arrived, Wilson already was there, supervising the crew who were moving tables, desks, and chairs into offices. Wilson and I were talking when there was a sharp roar. We hit the floor, just as we had done at Topside on Corregidor. It was an involuntary reflex. When we got up, we looked sheepishly at each other. Someone had dropped a desk.

A special train was sent from Melbourne to give MacArthur relief from flying for the remainder of the trip. The general needed the rest badly. The trip had been the final agony of the four months of defeat that lay behind him and the certain knowledge that the next four months would not give much improvement. With him went his family, Sutherland, Huff, and Morhouse.

The black engine with its two coaches stood at the platform at Alice Springs while the passengers boarded the train. They settled into their seats, the trainmen signaled that all was ready, the whistle sounded in reply. Steam hissed from the valves as the pistons drove back against the drivers, straining to move the wheels forward, pulling with them the weight of the engine and the two coaches. Wheels spun on iron rails, caught, spun again, then settled into steady motion, the connecting rods now synchronized with the motion of pistons and drivers in slow, powerful rhythm. As the engine inched forward, the slack in the couplers tightened, one after the other, with a slight jerk and a great rattle and groan. Then, taut and steady, the entire train, now a single unit of force and energy, began to glide gracefully down the twin ribbons of steel that stretched south into the red sand of the desert. Already the heat shimmered over the desolate waste, like glass in the distance. Heavy smoke plumed from the stack as flame consumed coal in the fiery furnace below, caught in the larynx and lungs, and sprinkled a layer of grit and grime over everything, inside and outside the iron boxes.

The passengers settled gratefully into the padded seats, stretching legs into the wide aisles, and lounged in comfort in the wide seats. The coach was practically empty, and they had the feeling of a luxurious expanse of space and comfort. The heavy panting of the engine, the steady clacking of wheels on rail joints, and the occasional exultant wail of the whistle were a welcome relief from the cramped, cold interior of the B–17 that had flown them from Del Monte to Darwin. Now they could cluster in groups to talk or simply to sit in silence, adjusting with the miles and the minutes to the realities of the new life.

The Old Man looked drained, and for the first time his younger officers saw the signs of his age—and perhaps read into it more than was warranted. He was tired and almost haggard. The strain of three months of unremitting erosion of responsibility marked his face and body. The jaunty show of bravado that he wore like a uniform had wilted. Worn by the exasperation of an anxious delay, he had dreaded the flight to Australia. It had not been an easy one for him or for his family. He belonged to the age of the luxury passenger coach and the luxury steamer. Planes were not then, or ever, a part of his life.

He was still tired, irritable, and, most of all, torn with doubt about the future. What would it be like? The mercurial, outgoing Quezon who had been his partner in arms was hiding in the jungles of Cebu; the long trail they had walked together had come to an end, separating them forever. Ahead was a new trail with a new partner, a Labour Party working man's prime minister—plain, earthy, undramatic, leader of a raucously independent party that led an equally raucously independent nation.

The Old Man sighed with discomfort at the recognition that behind him lay defeat, and perhaps more and greater defeat lay ahead. If laurels of victory were to be had, neither he nor anyone else could guess if and when he might wear them. He raised one foot and propped it on the seat opposite him. His eye ran ruefully down the long, skinny shank draped in his grimy uniform. It could still carry him, but he was not sure how far and how long. He let his eye slide over the paunch that was only partly hidden by the pleats in his uniform trousers, an affectation that did not reflect elegant taste but an urgent necessity to conceal this sign of advancing age.

Today he felt his age, all sixty-two years of it, as well as the years ahead that hung over him like a great heavy shadow of doubt. Some 100,000 young men had been entrusted to his care, and soon they would rot in Japanese prison camps, at least those who survived the final bloody battle that he saw at the end of this campaign. He had drawn the battle order in his mind, and when the day came, he would give it. On Bataan, in defeat, the command would drive forward in one final attack to permit the escape of a fortunate few into the mountains. The others would die, or surrender and die, and a few would survive. He had no illusion as to what they might expect from the Japanese. On Corregidor there could be only bloody, brutal destruction at the end. He would order it coldly. He would order it without tears or remorse. He would feel guilty only that he was not there to share it.

The train rocked, lulling him into a doze and finally into sleep. His head dropped on the small shoulder beside him. Suddenly his entire frame relaxed; he rolled to his side and let himself slide into the warm comfort of the companion who had sheltered and comforted him through the great travail even when she knew that he would have destroyed her and her son in the great killing.

Sutherland, across the aisle, watched out of the corner of his eye as the Old Man slid off to sleep, thankful that sleep had come and hopeful that it would be a long one. The Old Man's wife had borne half the burden, the personal one. Sutherland had borne the official half. He took it in the stride of a young lion who knew how to carry such burdens. He had run the operation—under the Old Man's eyes, to be sure—pretty much in his own way. The Old Man had set a few firm guidelines, but within them Sutherland arranged the details. There was not complete freedom; the large problems had to go to the Old Man. The Old Man wrote his own operations reports and gave them to Sutherland to be dictated and typed. The major policy messages were discussed by the two men, MacArthur doing most of the talking in these months, Sutherland noting down what the Old Man said, interjecting suggestions or warnings when enthusiasm began to outrun cold logic. Then Sutherland dictated, Rogers typed, and the Old Man approved.

Sutherland gazed at the Old Man, propped on the small shoulder. The Old Man was fourteen years older than Sutherland; the small shoulder that supported him was decades younger. Sutherland's wife might have been Jean MacArthur's aunt; Sutherland's daughter, Natalie, might have been her younger sister. It had been more than a dozen years since Sutherland had watched a diaper being changed. It had been hardly that many months since MacArthur had watched Ah Chu change young Arthur.

Sutherland had become a soldier against the wishes of his family. He had let them go. MacArthur had been held by his mother after his father's death, through one impossible marriage, until he was in his mid-fifties. Not until her death had he been released. Only then did he find a true marriage partner and settle into the routines of domesticity.

It was not domesticity as Sutherland had known it. No sense of domestic responsibility, for that was not part of MacArthur's married life. MacArthur did not find household management a financial problem with outgo pushing hard on or exceeding income, as had been the case with Sutherland and other ordinary men. Sutherland and Josephine had encountered, struggled with, and sometimes evaded such problems when the demands of ordinary existence pushed hard on a young junior officer's salary. There were still bills hanging over Sutherland's shoulders, but not MacArthur's.

Josephine had met Sutherland as an equal partner. There had been love, and events would demonstrate its durability. But Josephine had not addressed him as "Gen'ral" even after he became one. He was just "Dick" or "Dear Dick," a husband of the ordinary type, obviously one who would rise to routine success but never to become master of a sizable share of the population of Asia.

Sutherland knew he was a match for MacArthur except for one element he could not quite fathom. He was as intelligent as the Old Man, the only officer who could meet him head on in equal debate, parrying MacArthur's positive or even dogmatic exuberance with rapier thrusts of cold logic, forcing MacArthur to bend to reason. MacArthur acknowledged then and later that he needed this part of Sutherland even more than his administrative ability. Dick Marshall could move the machinery, but he could never outdebate either Sutherland or the Old Man.

Sutherland was tougher than the Old Man. He was, or seemed to be, the iron in MacArthur's velvet glove. It was Sutherland who kept subordinates wary, who forced them to hide growls of defiance and to march to his standard. MacArthur was considered an "old softy" by those who learned the secret and knew how to use it. Moreover, no one had to be told not to challenge the commanding general of a theater of operations. He was by definition above defiance, open or hidden. One had to hew to Sutherland's line but was free to growl behind his back to fellow sufferers. Sutherland held all the reins firmly in his two strong hands. MacArthur might specify "gee" or "haw," but Sutherland shouted the command and pulled the reins. Those in harness knew that Sutherland held the whip and would wield it mercilessly if he were pushed to it.

The one aspect of MacArthur's personality hidden from Sutherland was his tendency to wander off into dreams of destiny. It lay beyond Sutherland's own experience and, therefore, his understanding. Sutherland had been a student of history but in a different generation. MacArthur's intellectual development began on the great deserts of the Southwest with men who had charged at Shiloh and Cold Harbor. Men thought differently in those days.

Sutherland was pragmatic and predictable, politically as conservative as MacArthur and in social philosophy even more so. When MacArthur orated to Sutherland about the claims and rewards of destiny, Sutherland sat in respectful silence, in the early days perhaps not even daring to think "egomaniac." The day for expressing that blasphemy eventually would come, but only after long strain of battle.

Sutherland brushed away flies and watched the sand stretched out to the horizon. He could not have been too happy with events. Marshall, Rogers, and the rest were now in clean rooms with hot showers and fine food. He was shepherding the indomitable MacArthur on a long trip across an empty wasteland, a trip that would have taken eight hours by air.

The train chugged along the rails through an eternity of empty sand. The Old Man slept peacefully and long. The small shoulder that pillowed his head was patiently immobile, quietly content to comfort this huge ego that life had entrusted to her gentle care, not caring about destiny and empire, only that the man she cherished would be happy. When the train pulled into the station at Adelaide, at least part of the exuberance had been restored, and MacArthur left the train to read his message. Physically he was drained, but the dream sparkled clear and bright. What he wrote in fatigue, as a routine press statement, rang like a trumpet in a wilderness.

MacArthur had emerged from the dark shadows of Malinta Tunnel into the brilliant glare of public attention. The escape from Corregidor created an image the public could not resist. Some, though not many, might see the matter as a skulking retreat. The affair was carried off with elegance and style. MacArthur chose the only option available (except the submarines), the remnants of the torpedo boats that had been built at his insistence during Military Mission days and the remnants of the 19th Bombardment Group, which were now operating out of Darwin. The mission had been carried out, with some delay, in five days.

The announcement that MacArthur had arrived, almost miraculously, came as a thunderclap. There had been real danger that no one could deny. At the time I had not been concerned for two reasons. First, I was too ignorant to be aware of the hazard. Second, I had very little to lose. Now I know better! Looking back at all the things that might have happened, I view the matter with more understanding.

The public had not recovered from the shock of the news of the evacuation when they saw the pictures of MacArthur, obviously worn by fatigue and the erosion of battle, his stained hat drooping over the dull glitter of the braid and oak leaves but head erect, voice firm and resonant, swinging his cane jauntily as he had done on Corregidor—a picture of resolute determination.

They read the bold, simple message, "I shall return." The message written and delivered was not as bold as it appeared to be in banner headlines. MacArthur knew full well that the return was not a matter in which he had undisputed jurisdiction. He could not have felt sure that the pledge would ever be redeemed. The Japanese were still masters of Southeast Asia. They had not yet been re-buffed. The delay at Bataan and Corregidor had been just a nuisance, not causing a significant pause in the rapid advance to the main targets farther south. It was not certain yet where the Japanese would be brought to a halt, if indeed they could be.

When the train that carried MacArthur from Alice Springs pulled into the station at Adelaide, MacArthur read the short message from the rumpled sheet of paper on which he had written it. Neither the style nor the delivery was dramatic. MacArthur read in a subdued voice that he had been brought to Australia to organize a U.S. offensive against Japan. The primary objective of his mission was to liberate the Philippines. The final sentence was read without that emotion of which MacArthur was capable: "I came through, and I shall return." It was not meant as bombast but as dedication.

The simple statement seems to demand a theatrical pose, and so it has come down through four decades, a gesture for comic burlesque, quoted by children who cannot know the events that inspired it and repeated by buffoons as a pratfall because it easily causes an ignorant laugh. For me it evokes the smell of blood, of acrid smoke, of decaying bodies stacked like cordwood in the tropical sun, of beautiful buildings shattered, the reverberation of guns echoing over the tropical ocean, up into the hills, with clouds of dust. It also evokes an undeniable feeling of glory, a terrible irrational glory, and tears for lives wasted.

As General Sam Houston led his collection of fronteirsmen in retreat across Texas, hounded by the uniformed pride of Mexico, the cry "Remember the Alamo" did not seem to have much meaning. At San Jacinto, in a small meadow at the fork of a small river, where a battle had to be fought because there was nothing left to do, Houston's army gave the slogan a meaning and transformed it from a desperate memory of defeat into a great shout of victory. MacArthur was standing on the edge of his own San Jacinto, defeat behind, uncertainty ahead. He found a battle cry that gave purpose to the next three years of the war.

Many could not understand the message, Admiral Ernest J. King most of all. "I shall return" did not conform to the navy's idea of how the war in the Pacific would be fought. The navy plans provided for an island-hopping approach through the Central Pacific. The Philippines would be bypassed. Later one of King's admirals recorded: "He (King) ended our talk with the sarcastic remark that MacArthur seemed more interested in making good on his promise to return to the Philippines than in winning the war."[1] King had reason to be wary. A very large shadow had fallen over the navy plans for victory. Behind the slogan stood the man.

Sutherland immediately stepped into the task of rebuilding a headquarters. It would be more difficult than at One Calle Victoria because the scale would be larger. More complications would emerge, especially since no decisions had been made as to MacArthur's official role. Nevertheless, whatever mission would be assigned, there must be a headquarters to carry it out, and that was the first order of business.

Robertson High School would not do for the headquarters MacArthur and Sutherland had in mind. A more suitable arrangement was found at 401 Collins Street, the office building of a large Australian insurance firm. MacArthur's headquarters moved in as fast as offices on the middle floors were hurriedly vacated. It was catch as catch can for several weeks while the space was re-modeled. My first office was in a rather small closet on a main hall, farther from Sutherland that I had ever been. It was large enough for a small typing table and a straight chair. Willoughby's office was just down the hall. MacArthur's own office was hurriedly arranged, but Sutherland was in temporary quarters for almost a week.

The General disliked telephones. When his office was being prepared in Melbourne, several telephones were routinely installed on his desk. Richard Marshall, MacArthur's deputy chief of staff, came in to examine the office and asked, "Do those phones ring?" He was told that they did. Marshall remarked with a smile, "You'd better get the bells out. If those phones ring, the General will throw them through the window." Sutherland would have said "Take the bell out!" MacArthur seldom used the telephone, and then only with some discomfort. On one occasion he was required by courtesy to talk with Manuel Quezon, president of the Philippines, who arrived in Melbourne on March 27 and was to leave for the United States three weeks later. MacArthur hardly needed the phone. His voice reverberated up and down the hall as he shouted, "Manuel, is that you, Manuel?"

New officers poured in to take the place of those who had been left on Corregidor and to fill newly created positions on the new staff. Stephen Chamberlin, who had been Brett's chief of staff, came in as G–3 in charge of planning and operations. Lloyd Lehrbas was an aide to MacArthur with specific duties in press relations as an assistant to Pick Diller. Lehrbas had been a foreign correspondent and had known MacArthur for years. He was at the station to meet MacArthur on his arrival, hoping to become press relations officer. Diller already had the job, and Lehrbas had to settle for a lesser position. Lester Whitlock was G–4, and Burdette Fitch was adjutant general.

In a week or so the arrangements began to fall into place and a routine developed. Sutherland's new office was finally completed, and we were installed in it. I had a space between Sutherland's office and MacArthur's. A solid wall separated me from MacArthur, but there was only a glass partition between me and Sutherland. The partition covered the space from perhaps four feet above the floor to the ceiling. I could see Sutherland's head as he worked at his desk, and he could see me.

As befitted my new rank, I had a large desk, a bookcase, and a window behind me that looked down to Collins Street. The long days began at 7:30 A.M. and ended twelve or more hours later on some nights, but usually around 6:30. During the second week new clerks were added to my office. A second stenographer was brought in for the aides, and three other clerks for general office duties. I did not know what to do with them and suggested to Wilson that three clerks were too many. I had not yet learned army ways. He replied that if someone somewhere had decided we needed three men, he was not going to take the responsibility for returning them to a combat unit. He told me to put them on a schedule. So I did; half a day each on duty and a day and a half free. It was good duty. The three were with me until the return to the Philippines.

The old office routine collapsed. Both MacArthur and Sutherland were head over heels in a new situation. Affairs did not always run smoothly and sometimes were not very well coordinated. Late in May, MacArthur received a letter from Prime Minister John Curtin, who referred to a copy of a message he had sent to Roosevelt. The copy had been sent to MacArthur ten days earlier. MacArthur could not remember seeing the message and feared it had been lost. He wrote to Curtin: "I have not received it and would be glad indeed to have a second copy."[2]

Three days later MacArthur wrote again to Curtin:

On receipt of your letter I had another most careful search made to see what had become of the first copy as I feared there might have been some interception between your office and my own. I am glad to say that I have located it and the fault was in this office. It was filed in our secret safe and, indeed, with such secrecy that it had been kept even from me.[3]

Wilson had put the letter in Sutherland's office safe. It was too important to circulate in the office of the adjutant general.

On the first day at 401 Collins Street, MacArthur arrived at his usual 10:00 A.M., missed the rush, and got into his office without any difficulty. Departing that evening was another matter. He left earlier than he usually did, just in time to encounter the five o'clock rush. The General stood at the elevator with Morhouse, who pushed the "down" button. One elevator, fully loaded, passed down. Another, empty, rose past the floor. It came down fully loaded and passed the General by. The first elevator passed on its second trip up. Then down again. MacArthur said to Morhouse, "Doc, we're not getting very far this way. Let's walk." So they walked the several flights down to the street. The General was not particularly upset, but Morhouse was. Thereafter, an elevator was waiting when the General arrived and departed. He never again left his office until long after the evening rush hour.

In this office Henry Godman and I were educated to democratic ways. We both spoke to Sutherland in third person, as we had been taught. Godman had the first lesson. I heard him ask Sutherland, "Does the General want to fly today?" Sutherland retorted, "Godman, don't address anyone in the third person except the secretary [of War]." Godman thereafter used the second person, "you."

I got my lesson two days later. I was not sure that master sergeants had the same rights in this matter as captains, who, after all, fell into the same genus as generals, both being commissioned officers and therefore gentlemen. I asked Sutherland late one evening, "Does the General have anything else?" Sutherland replied with deep irony, "No, Rogers, the *General* doesn't have anything else tonight." I understood, and thereafter used the more democratic form of address, aware that it did not imply any greater democracy in our relationship.

I was in MacArthur's office in Melbourne only once or twice that I can remember. I recall many occasions when MacArthur wandered through my office into Sutherland's.

Memories of Melbourne reflect my interests at the time. I had returned to civilization alive and healthy, with an appetite for enjoying life again. MacArthur and Sutherland might run the war. I had other interests—when I could get out of the office to cultivate them. It was not easy.

One young officer harbored a deep resentment toward the Japanese in general and concentrated his antipathy on the one man he held to be the architect of all our misfortunes—Tojo. The officer was a decorated combat veteran of the Philippines and Netherland East Indies, and had good reason for his antipathy. He ordered a rubber stamp "You Son of a Bitch, Tojo" and stamped every document that came through the office with this insult. Finally the adjutant general complained to Sutherland. Sutherland smiled when he saw the evidence but told the young man that he would have to forgo that particular form of revenge.

Carlos Romulo made the last escape from Bataan to Melbourne. He had been editor of the Manila *Herald* before the war and was an enthusiastic supporter of the United States in the Philippines and Asia. When the war broke out, he was commissioned a major and served in Diller's press relations office.

Romulo had been left behind when Quezon and MacArthur were evacuated from Corregidor. When Bataan fell, he was able to commandeer a dilapidated airplane that flew him from Bataan to the Southern Islands just as the Japanese stormed down in their last triumphant attack. He was picked up by submarine and finally arrived in Melbourne. I did not know anything of his civilian status prior to the war. About all I knew at the time was a small, quiet, polite Filipino officer with an innocent face who moved quietly around Lateral 3. I do not recall that I ever talked to him.

Later, when Romulo arrived in Melbourne, I met him in my office. His eyes were red. He told me that there had been a party of celebration the night before for those who had escaped from Corregidor. He said that he just could not go. He had cried in his room all night.

He was now a colonel, wearing a GI uniform with a black wire belt buckle. I had a shining brass buckle on a tan belt. He asked where he could find one like mine. I told him, "You need it more than I do; take mine." I unbuckled my belt and we exchanged.

I confessed my feeling of guilt about the promotion over other men who deserved it as much or more. I expressed concern for what they had thought. Romulo smiled and said I needn't worry about it any more. My promotion had broken the table of organization, and every man had been promoted one rank after I left. That knowledge did not satisfy me very much.

25

April in Melbourne

It was April, and change was in the air. The wind began to shift from north to south, picking up the cold, crisp air from the ice caps of the South Pole. It was that ambiguous time of the year when morning chill fades easily under the warmth of noonday. In the Blue Ridge of Virginia, winter was blossoming into spring. In Melbourne summer was fading into autumn. For those of us who had crossed the equator, it brought a delicious, tantalizing thrill of anticipation. Our entire beings, out of the tropics where fall and winter never come, were suspended in uncertainty, caught in feelings that yearned for spring, felt autumn, and were distracted by the contradiction. For us, spring and autumn had merged into one experience.

We were alive. No one in Melbourne knew as well as we did what that meant. MacArthur had brought us with him. Between us and our past lay a gaping hole of forgetfulness. I was never able to cross back over that chasm. It forever separated youth from manhood. I had gone into the chasm a Puritan, and I came out a Puritan. But there was an eternity of difference between the two states of grace. Corregidor had taught me to understand the inscrutability of Divine mercy and justice and to wonder, like Job, at the apparent capricious injustice of God's ordering of the universe. I had no inclination to prate dogmatically of the fact that God had saved me. I remembered too well more deserving souls who had not been saved but had been destroyed. The burning question became the purpose of my salvation—if there was any purpose.

MacArthur settled into the old domesticity and valued it all the more because he had recognized that he was, after all, an old man. The mask of complete self-assurance was now more difficult to wear. The year had begun in disaster and might very well end in even greater disaster. During the next nine months his publicly confident assertions were supported by the inner knowledge that destiny was a trying taskmaster who did not give rewards as easily as the "very perfect model of a modern major general" had believed just four months ago.

The fact that he was in Australia gave him the right to believe that destiny still carried him forward. But how many Corregidors must he endure before the triumph? He had his wife and his baby. Domesticity cradled him in the warm blanket of love. He needed it badly to support a public facade of command and self-assurance upon which others could anchor their hopes for the future.

Sutherland was not ready to acknowledge even the possibility of old age. He had a woman younger than MacArthur's, a woman of blazing passion who had taught him, to his surprise, that he could probably match the performance of any of the young studs in his command, enlisted or commissioned. If he chose, he could sire himself a son or many sons. Again he felt burning passion, not of youth but of maturity that has pushed all hope of such passion aside, burying it in work and men's games. He was in love, not as a young man who looks to the future he has not known, but as one who looks to the past, in the illusion that the present passion recovers what has gone before and has been lost. Sutherland deluded himself that he was young, just as MacArthur deluded himself that he was old. Both were wrong.

Sutherland suffered another, more serious delusion. Less than ten days after his arrival in Melbourne, he attended a party given by one of Melbourne's leading social lights. At the party he met a young Australian matron who had returned to Melbourne from England with her infant son. Her husband had fought in Malaya for the defense of Singapore and was now in prison camp. Like Sutherland, she was lonesome. The two were attracted to each other. Within two weeks the clerks in GHQ were gossiping about this affair, and others as well. Sutherland no doubt thought he was the master of his new passion just as he was master of his golf clubs and his plane. He would never know what was happening until it was too late.

I, of course, was young, inexperienced, and an inept learner. There was not much time for experimentation. With blind faith that all good things come to those who have a stout heart and fine intentions, I leaped into the most complicated of all human relationships totally unprepared and untrained for any single aspect of it. There would be bitterness, but surprisingly, after a very long time, bittersweet understanding and friendship based on past failure.

MacArthur and his family moved into the Menzies Hotel and picked up their life in less luxurious surroundings than those they had left behind in Manila. The General preserved an even greater social isolation in Australia. The staff also moved into the Menzies. Officers began to find solace for the dreary days on Corregidor.

I moved into Scott's Hotel, a dignified old establishment that was a favorite resting place for sheepmen from the Outback on visits to Melbourne. The place bristled with propriety and good breeding. I was the youngest tenant. There was no place in the Menzies, where the officers of USAFFE were billeted with MacArthur, for an enlisted man. I would not have wanted to be there, in any case. Scott's gave me privacy.

The stay at Scott's Hotel provided an education in itself. I still remember my first meal in the quiet, sedate dining room. An elderly, dignified man served as waiter and instructor. The table had been set in full service, complete with finger bowl, and I was baffled as to proper use of each piece of flatware. The waiter coached me with patient dignity, I think sincerely concerned for my proper education. I will not forget the large bowl of Scotch broth, thick and spicy, the steak and potatoes, and the apple pie that followed. For breakfast there were eggs and broiled kidneys, or steak and eggs, or grilled lamb chops and kidneys, with muffins and, inevitably, tea.

Later I was moved to the Victoria Hotel, which still stands above Swanson Street in Little Collins Street, also a dignified bastion of Victorian elegance, which was much upset by the influx of U.S. enlisted personnel who were not particularly dignified and whose mores reflected a different set of values.

For several months before my decision to enlist I had dated a young lady, one of three or four over two or three years. She had finally called a halt to our arrangement. I admit that by my son's standards I must have been a "klutz," whatever that may be (I interpret it to mean inept where young ladies are concerned). After our arrival in Melbourne with its subsequent publicity, I received a heavily perfumed letter that lamented the earlier decision and proffered a resumption by mail, with other, undefined rewards to follow when I returned. I could never decide whether the letter was the result of a return to sanity on her part or simply of the realization that, "klutz" or not, I had become something of a celebrity and might be worth a gamble.

She was two weeks too late. Had I received the letter sooner, her perfume and my memories would have produced a reconciliation by mail and I would have spent the last three years of the war pining by mail for her. Fortunately, or unfortunately, depending on how the matter is viewed, I had already met another. So I had a conscious small revenge of telling the young lady that she had thought too long; I was already spoken for.

During the last two weeks of March I made my way around Melbourne, sometimes alone, sometimes in the company of one or another of the men who had been assigned to my office. About the middle of April, on a pleasant Saturday afternoon, Jim Larkin and I visited the zoological gardens in Royal Park. We walked around, then stopped in front of the lions' cage. Perhaps a dozen yards down the path were two young women. We proceeded to photograph the pair, who smiled at the attention. The ice was broken. We talked and walked together, my friend with the brunette and I with the blonde. During the afternoon both of us arranged separate dates. Because I was scheduled for duty on Sunday that week, I arranged to meet Nancy on the following Monday at a tea shop on Collins Street not far from GHQ. I set the time for 7:00 P.M. on the chance that Sutherland would be away from his desk by 6:30, as had been the case for almost a month.

It was a miscalculation. At 6:00 on Monday Sutherland still sat at his desk. At 6:30 he was still at his desk, and it was obvious at 6:45 that he would not be gone before 7:00. I went in desperation to Wilson, who looked dubious and told me I had better ask Sutherland. I asked Sutherland's permission to leave, stating that the other steno would be available. He looked at me coldly and said, "No." I came as close as I ever did to open insubordination. I had never argued with him before and never did afterward, but that night I stuck to my guns. He finally relented on my grim assurance that there would never be a repetition. There never was. Sutherland was a demanding master.

The arrangement with Nancy proceeded swiftly to a foreseeable conclusion. She had become the center of a very fashionable courtship with more than a little glamor involved. I visited her home with Jim Larkin the next weekend, and he told her parents of our high station in life at GHQ. The father was convinced that he and his family were the butt of a certain soldierly tendency to exaggerate. The following day the Melbourne papers carried a story about the "Bataan Boys" who had come to Australia with MacArthur. My picture was included. Nancy and her parents were impressed.

On my birthday, April 18, I had another encounter with Sutherland. A young lady I had met at a party before I met Nancy had decided to remind me of her existence. Three weeks after the party she had set out to learn where my office was. I was sitting at my desk, while Sutherland worked at his desk behind the glass partition that separated us. His phone had an extension on my desk. I never used it because Sutherland always answered his own calls. I had never had any calls—until today. A messenger had just come into my office with a package. Sutherland, hearing the commotion just outside his door, looked up. The package contained a birthday cake.

As I opened the cake, the telephone rang and Sutherland answered. Looking annoyed, he said loudly, "Rogers, it's for you." I managed to express my thanks and to assure the young lady who had sent the cake that the conversation must come to an immediate end. Sutherland called me in later to say that there would be no further social calls on his telephone. I tried to explain but quickly let the matter drop, saying it would never happen again. It did not.

Later I had the pleasure of listening to one of the aides, caught similarly in a social bind because he could not get away from the office, explaining to his friend over Sutherland's phone on my extension why he could not possibly honor his obligation. The conversation ran pretty much on his end to "Yes, dear" and "No, dear." I handled my problem as well as he did his own.

By the middle of May, Nancy and I had an understanding, and it was agreed that we would announce our engagement on her birthday or when I left Melbourne, whichever came first. The days flew by, two evenings a week and either Saturday or Sunday afternoon through a delightful fall season.

By the end of June, I knew I would be leaving Melbourne in less than two weeks, and we announced our engagement. Wilson read the notice in the paper and took it to Sutherland, who came out with a grin to congratulate me. A letter home remarked:

He said he had seen my "ad" in the paper and put out his hand. I was rather proud; master sergeants don't get many chances to shake hands with major generals. It must

have gone the rounds for most of the other officers that came out of the islands have
been around [to congratulate me].[1]

I left Nancy and Melbourne on July 21. It was a lush time. Corregidor and
its despair were behind me, not forgotten but not much thought about. I had a
certain prestige, especially after newspapers carried the story and photographs
of the "Bataan Boys," in which I was included as staff secretary. I was pointed
out as I walked down the street or entered a hotel or restaurant.

I had money for the first time, and because my tastes were inexpensive I did
not feel a financial constraint, which has never been the case since. Books were
my only vice, and they could be obtained in inexpensive editions. The Oxford
Classics and Everyman's Library provided far more than I could hope to read
and digest. I learned to appreciate Cadbury's chocolate in great quantities—to
no great disadvantage since I was quite thin. I stumbled upon a philatelic shop
upon Collins Street and made an extravagant expenditure on the paraphernalia
needed for the hobby—the best, of course. Marshall—who frequently waited in
my office to see Sutherland—watched me working with it one day and remarked,
"By God, when you do something, you do it in style, don't you?" Marshall
also at one time or another picked up my World Classics edition of Gibbon's
Decline and Fall—a very small volume with minuscule type—and commented,
"Rogers, you are going to ruin your eyes if you keep this up." I did keep it
up, and I haven't yet ruined my eyes. I will not attempt to evaluate the long-
term benefits of the reading, but it certainly gave me short-run satisfaction and,
I hope, elevated my intellectual equipment.

Nancy provided the impulse and the companionship for social activities, mostly
theater and tea rooms and small restaurants. We found Gilbert and Sullivan
performances—*Yeoman of the Guard, The Pirates of Penzance, Gondoliers*, and
others, but never *The Mikado*, since Australia was at war with Japan and the
company demonstrated its patriotic fervor by refusing to perform an opera that
dealt with the emperor of Japan, even a fictitious one.

Occasionally, leaving Flinders Street Station, instead of turning left we turned
right across Prince's Bridge to walk through Alexandra and Queen Victoria
Gardens or along the Yarrah River. We spent only some three months together,
probably six Sundays and twenty or so evenings.

General Headquarters was located at 401 Collins Street, about two blocks
below Swanston Street. I could leave GHQ, walk rapidly up Collins Street, turn
right on Swanston toward the Yarrah River for two blocks, and quickly be at
the entrance to Flinders Street Station. Then I could run up the stairs to the ticket
cage, then down the stairs to the platform to catch the train out to Blackburn,
(Nunawading), the other extreme of my existence, ten miles east on White Horse
Road, a major highway to Canberra and Sydney.

At Blackburn I left the station, walked below the tracks in an underpass, went
two blocks to White Horse, and turned left several hundred steps to 114, "Y-
Tarri," where I found the warm comforts of home.

Our engagement was a hasty jump into an uncertain future, taken with great expectations and with little thought of any possibility of sorrow to follow. Later the marriage, having very little shared experience to build on, fell to pieces. But that is not part of this story.

The first official GHQ staff plane carried the name BATAAN emblazoned across the nose over a map of the Philippines, as a pledge for all to see that we would surely return. It was not the name the plane first carried. The call letters on the C–47 were VH-CXE.

One morning MacArthur was driven to the airfield to inspect the plane. He was photographed standing under the nose. Above his head in splendor lounged a scantily clad young woman of overwhelming anatomical endowments with the name "SHINY SHELIA" spread above it all. MacArthur must have seen it but with dignity he stood, smiling, while the photographs were taken, then walked to his waiting limousine.

The photographs were processed and delivered. With great horror on his face Diller hurried to Sutherland's office. "Look what Godman has done!" Sutherland looked and shouted, "Get Godman in here." Godman could not be located in the office. Sutherland then called for his car. Godman recalled later: "General Sutherland came out to the field and looked at the painting and said for me to remove it—NOW!"[2]

Later in the week MacArthur returned to the field to pose again, this time under a more dignified emblem. He had never said a word about the matter. I suspect he appreciated "SHINY SHELIA" as much as Godman and enjoyed even more the knowledge of the turmoil it would create. The plane thereafter was always referred to as "Sexy."

MacArthur received fan mail in Melbourne, and he always read it himself. The envelopes were cut across one end to save the General the trouble but he removed and read the contents and saw to it that each letter received a reply, written either by himself or the aides. Some letters were from parents whose sons had been left in the Philippines, and these received special attention from MacArthur himself. Some were from relatives who had not heard from sons, grandsons, or nephews; these young men received instructions from the commander in chief himself, sent down through channels, to observe the conventions required by familial piety. One case involved a young man in the G–2 section only 20 feet down the hall. He received a personal directive from MacArthur, in MacArthur's office, to write immediately to his grandmother.

26

End of a Command

We were in Melbourne for four months. During that time MacArthur was occupied with the collapse of the Philippines; with the development of working relationships with the Australian government; with the determination of how much in the way of forces he could wheedle, cajole, or bully out of Roosevelt; with his own emergence as a public figure who had a great following and certain tantalizing prospects; and with the organization of the new command.

The evacuation of MacArthur to Australia relieved Washington from anxiety in two respects. In Australia, he was now the "distant" commander of the beleaguered forces in the Philippines, charged with their supply and their relief. With the shoe on the other foot, George Marshall no longer had to face the barrage of importunate demands for actions. He could use MacArthur as a buffer. MacArthur, caught between Washington and Corregidor, was powerless to do anything with his limited means. He was on the defensive with respect to both Wainwright and Marshall. He had been effectively checked for the moment. The ploy also blunted political pressures from MacArthur supporters in Congress and elsewhere. Their hero had been placed in charge of the effort. Certainly if he could not do the job, no one else would be able to do so.

The evacuation thus provided Washington with a series of personal, political, and military benefits, and solved a number of immediate problems. With respect to Wainwright and his beleaguered garrison, MacArthur would be the stern "naysayer." Roosevelt and Marshall could appear to offer what MacArthur could not or would not deliver. At the same time, Wainwright reported directly to Washington and MacArthur's control was more apparent than real, formal command to the contrary. It had been neatly arranged.

MacArthur was not relieved of his duties as commanding general USAFFE, nor was Wainwright designated as his successor. Roosevelt and Marshall worked on one set of assumptions. MacArthur relied on another. Roosevelt and Marshall simply assumed that by the fact of his departure MacArthur had vacated the command and that it had passed to Wainwright, although this would not necessarily have to be the case. Indeed, MacArthur assumed, in view of the statement in a February 4 dispatch that told him he would "reassume command of all Army forces in the Far East," that he was still commanding general of USAFFE and that Wainwright was still a subordinate. Perhaps Roosevelt thought it easier to let the ambiguity resolve itself.[1]

At the time of his departure, MacArthur had intended to retain direct control of operations in the Philippines. He left behind four independent commands, two in the Southern Islands, the Harbor Defense Command on Corregidor, and the Luzon Force, which included the forces fighting on Bataan and as guerrillas in northern Luzon. It was the Luzon Force that he had assigned to Wainwright.

Headquarters USAFFE at Corregidor was left as an advance echelon of the headquarters to be established by MacArthur in Australia. Under MacArthur's arrangements he would retain overall command of the four independent forces in the Philippines. Each would report directly to him through the advance echelon Headquarters USAFFE on Corregidor.

There were good reasons for this arrangement that MacArthur did not care to discuss openly with anyone. Those who did not know his reasons might assume that only personal vanity was involved. MacArthur was hedging against the day when, in spite of Roosevelt's orders to him, and his orders to Wainwright, the command must collapse and surrender. With the four forces operating independently under his command, surrender of one would not tumble down the others. When Corregidor surrendered, as it must in spite of the orders from the White House, two forces would still be free in the Southern Islands to fight on as guerrillas.

Washington did not understand MacArthur's arrangements, assumed that Wainwright had filled the vacuum left by MacArthur's departure, and treated him as MacArthur's successor in command. There were thus two commanding generals USAFFE. MacArthur by his own arrangements, and probably by right, since no orders had been issued to formalize transfer of his authority, intended to act in that capacity in Australia. Wainwright was addressed by Washington as commanding general USAFFE in dispatches to Corregidor that ordered him to report directly to Washington. Roosevelt promoted him, believing he was MacArthur's successor.[2]

On March 19, a day after his arrival in Melbourne, MacArthur questioned Wainwright about the command structure, and Wainwright confirmed that he had assumed command on orders from Washington. On March 21 MacArthur advised Washington of the arrangements he had made at the time of his departure. He attempted to avoid a written statement of his doubts about Wainwright's ability to deal with the huge burden that had been entrusted to him. He could only imply and ask that his judgment be trusted in the matter. This was lost on Marshall, or perhaps it merely hardened his heart; and Roosevelt supported Marshall. MacArthur acquiesced and turned to the organization of his new command.

When the collapse came, we had settled into our new lives in Melbourne and watched the events as observers rather than participants. The collapse on Bataan moved swiftly, rather as MacArthur had anticipated. As the Japanese cut through the final defense positions, there was one desperate flurry of radio exchanges among Corregidor, Melbourne, and Washington. The roar of Japanese artillery announced the attack as waves of fresh troops rushed forward against the center of the Orion-Bagac line, which folded back and broke. By the night of April 6 the Japanese had reached Mount Samat and had forced a deep wedge through the breach, poised for the final destruction of the forces on Bataan.

MacArthur wrote to Marshall on April 1, expressing opposition to a surrender:

I am utterly opposed, under any circumstances or conditions, to the ultimate capitulation of this command. . . . If it is to be destroyed it should be upon the actual field of battle taking full toll from the enemy. . . . I would be very glad if you believe it advisable to attempt myself to rejoin this command temporarily and take charge of this movement.[3]

Marshall, of course, notified MacArthur that he should not return to the Philippines. I was relieved to see this reply, whatever MacArthur felt about the matter.

On April 4 MacArthur radioed Wainwright that there must be no surrender under any circumstances. He spelled out a plan to be used when it had become obvious that the defense would collapse. "If food fails you will prepare and execute an attack upon the enemy." I Corps on the west would deliver a heavy artillery bombardment to convince the Japanese that an attack was being made on that front. Then II Corps on the east would drive forward with all tanks still available, supported by artillery. It would drive north to the junction with the Olongapo road, then turn west toward Subic Bay. Then I Corps would drive forward. Olongapo would be caught between the two corps, and its capture would provide food and other supplies. If Olongapo could not be taken, some of Wainwright's forces could slip through the Japanese lines and escape into the Zambales Mountains, where they could operate as guerrillas.[4]

On the surface this order seems to be a complex plan of maneuver. In reality, all of the instructions for marching and flanking hide a very simple idea. Since there was no room for further retreat, the only escape lay ahead, toward and through the enemy lines, into the mountain wilderness. Several officers, who had not seen MacArthur's order, asked their commander, Brougher, for permission "to take off into the dark and make their way through Japanese lines to the north" on the night before the surrender. They succeeded, and led guerrilla groups in the mountains of Luzon. That is precisely what MacArthur intended for the entire command. Who can say that the troops would have suffered more than they did in prison camp?

Late in January 1942, during the first withdrawal from Mount Bataan, an officer of the 26th Cavalry led a small group of officers and men north through the Japanese lines to organize resistance in the mountains east of Clark Field.

When it became obvious that the end was near on Bataan, two others, also with the 26th Cavalry, made up their minds that "our military situation was hopeless" and "decided to escape rather than surrender." When the surrender order came, the officers pulled away from their units and walked north through the jungle to the crater of Mount Mariveles and over Mount Samat. On the night of April 14 they crossed the Orion-Bagac road between Japanese columns. Then they went north about two miles west of the main coastal road, where the prisoners of war were being marched up to Cabanatuan and prison camp. The two officers joined the growing resistance movement. One was captured in 1943, tortured, and executed. The other survived to write the history of the resistance effort in Luzon.[5]

I remember typing MacArthur's order, recoiling at the General's ruthless determination to destroy his command, if necessary, to prevent a surrender. The reader is reminded that Roosevelt had issued mandatory "no surrender" orders to MacArthur on February 9 and to Wainwright on March 23. The order had not been withdrawn.

On April 9 the War Department, which understood what Roosevelt had done (although he probably did not), persuaded Marshall to educate the president on the peculiarities of the military vocabulary. Roosevelt authorized a radiogram to give Wainwright authority to make any decision he felt appropriate. The message was sent through MacArthur for redispatch to Wainwright "only if you concur both as to substance and timing." By the time MacArthur received the message from Roosevelt, Bataan had surrendered. MacArthur held Roosevelt's message without action. He did not concur in its content, and the event had made the message irrelevant.[6]

Roosevelt had created a dilemma for MacArthur, who had acted single-mindedly under the orders originally sent down in February and confirmed in March. General Edward King had already surrendered on his own initiative, convinced that he would end his life branded as a traitor. Wainwright could not have changed the matter.

The only effect of Roosevelt's order was to excuse actions that had already been taken. Roosevelt's message would involve MacArthur in this belated repudiation of orders that had governed all of MacArthur's actions on Corregidor and Bataan. It gave MacArthur the choice of seeming to say to the world that all sacrifices made between December and April were now to be set aside, that his orders to Wainwright of April 4 had been repudiated, and that the original "no surrender" order had been merely a stratagem to keep troops in senseless battle to meet some timetable determined by Roosevelt's sense of what political reality would bear.

Whatever MacArthur felt about Wainwright's actions, he had little cause to mend Roosevelt's political fences. The surrender involved a technical violation of existing orders. The annulment of those orders had arrived after the fact of the surrender. MacArthur, acting on orders, had been led into an extreme position. He was not one to give Roosevelt public support for an action that might

have been taken as easily two or three months before. Roosevelt had wanted
only the appearance of the Alamo. MacArthur had been willing to give him the
reality.

Captain Jimmy Ray, a naval officer who had left Corregidor in the MacArthur
party, was called into MacArthur's office on the morning of the surrender.
MacArthur paced the floor, "tears streaming down his face," and told Ray that
he had asked permission to return to Corregidor but had been refused.[7]

The month that followed was a hell beyond the imagination even of those
who had been there. After Bataan surrendered, the full brunt of the attack fell
on Corregidor. All remaining surface installations were leveled to the ground.
Air attacks were no longer the dreaded danger. Artillery bombardment became
the great killer, delivering a steady fire against every target that could be found.
The Japanese fired from morning until noon, and from three in the afternoon
until midnight.

The tunnel, always crowded when I was there, was now closed at both ends
and filled to capacity. Water and food supplies were being depleted, and rations
were reduced.

The Japanese assault finally was made on the night of May 5. The bitter end
of "Orange" had come. The flag came down, and the white banner of surrender
was raised. The men, too tired to complain, sat staring silently into space, or
fell asleep to await whatever fate held for them. They had held longer than any
other force in the face of the Japanese. They had held long enough.

At the last minute Wainwright tried to undo the consequences of his reorganization of MacArthur's command. He hoped to restrict the surrender to the force
on Corregidor, leaving all other commands free to fight. Homma was not taken
in, and demanded the surrender of all U.S. forces in the Philippines.

Wainwright was not in a position to bargain, but he tried. He told Homma
that he commanded only the harbor defenses; that the forces in the south were
under MacArthur's direct command. Homma replied that he himself had seen
the general order issued by Wainwright to announce his assumption of command
of all the forces in the Philippines. Wainwright replied that only a few days
before he had released Sharp, the southern commander, from his control. Homma
refused to accept a piecemeal surrender of the various forces, and Wainwright
yielded to save the garrison on Corregidor from massacre.

MacArthur had foreseen the impact of the changed command, however rational
it might appear in Washington. If the two southern commands had been left
independent of Wainwright, reporting directly to MacArthur in Australia, they
could have refused to surrender with complete legality.

Chynoweth and Christie, who had garrisons in the Visayas, challenged the
decision to surrender. Christie radioed Sharp: "I must have MacArthur's okay
otherwise it may be treason. I do not see even one small reason why this unit
should be surrendered because some other unit has gone to hell or some Corregidor shell-shocked terms are issued."

Sharp responded with another order to surrender. Christie replied:

Your radio of surrender of my forces sounds totally unnecessary and for me to comply tends to treason without sanction of [War Department] through MacArthur. Can surrendering of one island automatically do same for others that are in good order?

Finally Sharp's messenger arrived and explained that Wainwright believed the Japanese intended to massacre the Corregidor garrison unless all forces surrendered. Christie agreed to comply with Sharp's order.[8]

After the war Chynoweth wrote to MacArthur that he had been told by Sharp that MacArthur had authorized surrender, and he had acquiesced for that reason:

... When Sharp sent an officer with written orders, to contact me in the mountains of Cebu, we were informed that General MacArthur had authorized Sharp to act according to his own judgment. When I first met Sharp on a prison ship, he informed me that the surrender was unavoidable under the circumstances and orders. The surrender was abject, requiring us to comply with every order of the Japanese General. Sharp told me that nothing else could have been arranged.[9]

If MacArthur's original intention had been adhered to, major forces would have operated in the Philippines for much of the war. Certainly the history of the guerrilla movement would have been different. MacArthur's concept of the defense was keyed to Corregidor. Bataan was to serve as a screen to delay the final assault on Corregidor. It was his intention to stock enough food on Corregidor to sustain the defense until the overwhelming force of the Japanese would finally bring it all down in destruction. Bataan was peripheral to this main objective. MacArthur measured the importance of Bataan in terms of the survival of Corregidor.

Wainwright saw the campaign from the opposite viewpoint. He was tied physically and emotionally to the Bataan sector. He could not grasp MacArthur's intention nor understand its reason. Like a great many others, he saw the hoarding of food on Corregidor as an act of self-indulgence that deprived the fighting soldiers on Bataan of food they desperately needed. When MacArthur was evacuated, Wainwright immediately ordered the movement of food from Corregidor supplies to the forward area. And so it was with the command. Sutherland told Wainwright of MacArthur's command arrangements but did not explain why they had been made. It would have been difficult to do so.

There were a few lingering mementos of the Philippines. Records were sent from Corregidor by submarine. They reached my desk for Sutherland. I remember looking at the musty parcels of papers wrapped tightly in oilskin, smelling of dank death. Thoughts of Malinta Tunnel tumbled in my mind. I looked away.

A request came from Washington suggesting that MacArthur recommend Wainwright for the Medal of Honor. MacArthur refused, on the grounds that there was no evidence of a specific act to justify the decoration. He felt there were other officers who had contributed more than Wainwright to the defense of the Philippines but would not qualify for the Medal of Honor.[10]

Before the surrender of Corregidor I wrote to my parents about my life in

Melbourne, expressing evident remorse about my present good fortune: "Somehow the weather, the steaks and the good times here don't seem so desirable when I think of the fellows who are still on the 'rock'; especially since Bataan fell. I have a lot of good friends there."

My guilt and concern for the feelings of those left behind was not unfounded. Hundreds of miles to the north, in a prisoner of war camp, General Brougher wrote on April 1: "A foul trick of deception has been played on a large group of Americans by a Commander in Chief and small staff who are now eating steak and eggs in Australia. God damn them!"[11]

I cannot blame Brougher for his bitterness. Nevertheless, it is a naïve general who believes that he may be asked to fight only for glorious victory. There were men who were not professional soldiers, who had been conscripted into military service and had more reasonable cause for complaint. No one in prison camp would have been any better off had I been there with them, nor would MacArthur's presence have lessened their bitterness. It had been seen and ordained from the beginning in Washington. MacArthur was more useful in Australia. He, like all the rest of us, was under orders.

MacArthur would not let the rest of us forget. We had a mission to fulfill and he kept the mission before us. The switchboard in GHQ was the "Bataan" switchboard. "Bataan" was given as a name to MacArthur's staff planes, one after the other. Always Bataan, never to be forgotten. Those who had never been in the Philippines were constantly reminded that others had been, and that we all shared the same calling—we must return! The will of others might waver. MacArthur's never did.

VIII

SWPA, March–July 1942

Negotiations with Australia and SWPA; MacArthur plans for offense; organization of new command; role of GHQ defined; new title; MacArthur's roles; Sutherland and the staff

27

New Command

It is commonly held that MacArthur was stunned on his arrival in Melbourne by the forces available—or, rather, *not* available to him. He had been told on February 4 that a strong base was being established in Australia and that he would act in the capacity of commander of all army forces in the Far East. Given everything that had happened in the interim, MacArthur can hardly have been convinced that a great deal had actually been accomplished in the course of six weeks. I do not think there was much surprise, although it undoubtedly was painful to face a reality that would limit his course of action for some undefined period into the future.

MacArthur knew fairly well the state of affairs on December 8. He had served as chief of staff and should have been able to estimate rather accurately what could be done with forces available in 1941. He knew of the fate of the ABDA forces and could easily surmise the true strength of naval forces available and expended in defense of the Malay Barrier. The trip out of Del Monte demonstrated what he could easily have guessed about the nature of air force strength in Australia. He had been told bluntly by Washington that the major thrust would be made toward Europe and that the Pacific area would occupy a secondary role.

Nevertheless, Roosevelt and Marshall had ordered him out of the Philippines to defend Australia and to prepare for an offensive. That implied considerably more than was warranted by the forces they intended to make available in 1942. The discrepancy between the statement of intent and the forces already present and those scheduled to be made available left MacArthur on the thin edge of a cruel dilemma. To publicly acknowledge the mission and to say nothing about lack of forces would make nonperformance of the mission seem to rest on his shoulders.

The dilemma could be resolved by accepting the mission, thereby binding Roosevelt and Marshall to it as well, and complaining about the lack of forces to accomplish it. This was the essence of his position until well into 1943.

Roosevelt could not withdraw the mission, and perhaps he could be persuaded, cajoled, or pressured into making forces available.

In reality, the matter of the organization and mission had not been defined any more realistically than the matter of forces. A commander normally receives a directive that defines his strategic objectives and authorizes the command structure required for the implementation of those objectives. MacArthur had neither. He was in limbo with respect to the future situation in Australia.

Washington did not share the sense of urgency that drove Australian Prime Minister John Curtin. Curtin sincerely believed that the Japanese would soon descend to rape the cities of Australia as they had done in Nanking. Roosevelt did not share MacArthur's compelling need to return to the support of the beleaguered garrison in Manila Bay and to redeem the promise he had made on arrival: "I shall return!" MacArthur meant sooner rather than later, and preferably much sooner rather than much later.

March was filled with bitter debate in Washington that was not resolved until the middle of April. For a full year or more London and Washington had wrestled with the problem of the proper allocation of forces in a two-front war. Churchill, speaking for the British, demanded a firm commitment of all forces against Germany, which he considered to be the essential enemy. He was particularly apprehensive that the Russians, who were suffering horrible losses, might lose the will to fight, as they had done in 1916–17, and withdraw from the war. Stalin used the possibility to demand that he be supplied without fail. Stalin did not relent until the losses caused by German submarines and air on the long run to Murmansk became so serious that even he was forced to admit that the effort was futile.

Roosevelt shared the concerns of Churchill and Stalin but was constrained by events in the Pacific, by the reaction of Americans to those events, and by the urgent entreaties of MacArthur and Curtin. He could not ignore the Pacific theater, nor could he risk the possibility that the Japanese might break through the Malay Barrier and penetrate into Australia and New Zealand. He did not want to diminish the flow of supplies to Europe, but something must be done for the Pacific. When Churchill pressed obdurately for complete commitment to Europe, Roosevelt took out the proposal submitted by MacArthur from Corregidor that the European war be held in abeyance to permit an immediate, full-scale reduction of Japan.

In the end an agreement was reached as to relative distribution of forces and the terms of the directive to be issued to the Pacific theater commanders. Churchill agreed on March 18 that the United States would be responsible for the war in the Pacific. For the remainder of the month the discussion involved negotiations between army and navy as to the proper division of the Pacific. The navy wanted substantial control, but it had to reckon with MacArthur. MacArthur was in Australia, already commanding in reality and impossible to ignore. He had the support of the Australian government, and he must have a significant area of operational authority.[1]

The joint chiefs of staff divided the Pacific between MacArthur and Nimitz. A small shatter zone was created between them to dissipate the force of any collision. MacArthur's area included the Philippines, the Netherland East Indies, Australia, and most of the Solomon Islands. Nimitz had everything else in the Pacific. Nimitz's command was complicated on paper but quite simple in practice; he ran it all, and King in Washington ran Nimitz.

Grand strategy would be defined by the combined chiefs of staff of the United Kingdom and the United States. Operational strategy would be controlled by the U.S. joint chiefs of staff. It is not known what the combined chiefs and joint chiefs contemplated with respect to timing. MacArthur believed at the time that he was in limbo, and I have not seen anything since to contradict his view. I feel now, as I did then, that Washington and London would have been content to have him settle down into the leisurely pattern that dominated military life in Melbourne, accepting the limitations of forces, waiting patiently for future developments. Certainly Washington and London saw the holding mission as the immediate concern. An offensive was somewhere in the vague future. MacArthur saw the matter differently. He preferred to take the initiative in the immediately foreseeable future as the means for holding Australia and for destroying enemy shipping and bases in the process.

MacArthur carefully kept these views to himself and his immediate staff. He hid them from John Curtin for a full year. Curtin would later assert that in 1942 MacArthur had no intention of taking offensive action. He did not understand MacArthur as well as he believed.[2] Whatever MacArthur intended in 1942, every decision he made from the day of his arrival in Melbourne, involved a forward movement, looking to an offensive action. From Melbourne the Malay Barrier seemed to be far away. For my part, a holding operation in that lovely city might be maintained forever. Others shared my view; MacArthur did not.

Most of the territory in the Southwest Pacific Area (SWPA) was in Japanese hands. Only Australia, New Zealand, and Papua remained free. There was no evidence that Japanese ambition or potential had found a limit. An attack was expected at any time; first on Papua, then on Australia.

SWPA was tiny only in relation to the entire Pacific Ocean area taken as a whole. Willoughby once prepared maps comparing it with the continental United States to emphasize the difficulty of MacArthur's assignment. SWPA stretched from east to west for a greater distance than the span from Washington, D.C., to San Francisco. From south to north it would cover the span from Guatemala to Alaska. It was a mighty field for action filled with islands, dense populations, and rich resources. Moreover, it constituted the gateway to the Philippines and Tokyo.

At the time of MacArthur's arrival it was commonly assumed that available Australian forces could defend only a part of Australia. A defense perimeter had been defined as the "Brisbane Line," which would cut off the coastal area from Brisbane through Adelaide, the southwest corner of the continent, where the majority of the population and the great cities were located. The Japanese would

Map 8
Pacific Areas

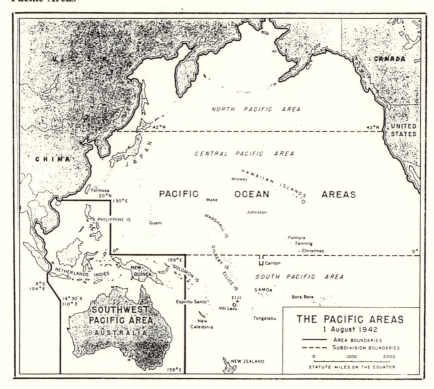

Source: U.S. Army.

be left with the dry desert of central Australia and the sheep runs of the Outback. The mountains that formed a spine behind the coastal cities would make a defensive barrier.

The idea was repugnant to MacArthur. He had just been removed from Bataan and did not relish the idea of another Alamo. It is characteristic that in every situation his gut reaction was to find a way to attack the enemy. He refused to think defensively any longer. MacArthur maneuvered to create a situation in which the Australians would have to agree to an offense. He intended to move forward, not to the defense of Brisbane but to an attack against the Japanese in Papua.

MacArthur wrote about the situation that confronted him:

The new Southwest Pacific Area was finally established yesterday after a series of delays and discussions in Washington. I have been operating in the interval by good will and coordination with the Australian Government and the situation is at last beginning to assume some definite form. I am trying, of course, to pass from the academic blueprint stage to an actual operational basis and the way will probably be long and dreary. . . .

I have established a headquarters on Collins Street and hope to have it running smoothly in a short time. I, myself, am planning to go north in the Townsville area very shortly for probably a month and, of course, longer if the enemy pressure increases.[3]

MacArthur's command structure in the Philippines had been simple and cleanly defined. The Philippine Army units had been called into the U.S. Army. The air force was an integral part of the army. The navy was completely independent of any local authority. MacArthur, as commanding general, USAFFE, commanded all ground and air forces. He and Quezon were bound by long ties of intimate friendship. Whatever complications had existed before the Japanese attack, Quezon accepted MacArthur's authority in military matters afterward without any apparent reservation or opposition.

Organization of SWPA involved more complications. The British were no longer a major factor, having abdicated their Pacific responsibilities to the Americans. New Zealand was sliced off into Nimitz's Pacific Ocean Area, so that complication was eliminated from the game. The Philippines were written off with the presumption that Quezon would soon be safely in Washington, where he could be controlled and isolated from interference in Pacific operations. The Dutch had no forces to contribute and therefore little to demand in policymaking. Australia had significant ground, air, and naval forces and was the most obvious target of future Japanese activity. Australians could, and did, demand recognition as an equal partner in command.

SWPA was organized along federal lines. The supreme commander would not have direct control of any national force. He stood at the peak of the structure, isolated by one tier of authority from direct command of troops. His essential function was to coordinate activities of three service commanders. These, in turn, would coordinate the activities of the various national forces that were assigned to them. The framework was essentially that of ABDACOM.

Australian General Sir Thomas Blamey commanded the land forces. When MacArthur's directive was issued in April 1942, the Australians had the preponderance of ground forces in Australia. Two U.S. divisions were en route to Australia, but this force was outnumbered by Blamey's divisions. The two U.S. divisions arrived in April and May and spent the summer in Queensland. They were not assigned to any particular higher unit of command. Technically they were part of Blamey's Allied Land Forces, but in practice they were controlled by GHQ.[4]

Lieutenant General George Brett, an American, commanded the air forces. In this matter Americans had, or at least would soon have, the overwhelming preponderance of numbers. The Royal Australian Air Force was brought into the Allied Air Force structure. Brett's chief of staff was an Australian. There was great scope for friction in the Allied Air Forces. As U.S. units were assigned to airfields in the forward areas of northern Australia and New Guinea, they found themselves subject to the unaccustomed tight control of Australian officers who commanded the regional defenses.

The Allied Naval Forces were commanded by a U.S. admiral. Elements of the Royal Australian Navy seemed to fit comfortably with their U.S. counterparts, and there was little cause for friction because there was little intimate contact between the two national components.

These three commands with their respective headquarters comprised the combat command structure of SWPA. In addition there was a service of supply to provide logistical support for operations. MacArthur designated the supply command as USAFFE, of which he was commanding general. This arrangement made it possible for him to carry out certain legal functions enjoined upon the commanding general USAFFE. The structure had some considerable emotional value to him, and might be useful at some future time when operations would grow out of the chrysalis of present needs.

MacArthur conceived of the entire top structure of the command as a single unit. To counteract a natural tendency on the part of each service to split away, he brought them together in a single location, at least the air and navy commands that were headed by Americans, who could not easily escape. Blamey occupied separate quarters, on the grounds that he was not only commander of Allied Land Forces but also the ranking officer in the Australian Army. The others were crowded cheek by jowl into 401 Collins Street in Melbourne and later in the AMP Building in Brisbane. They were not always comfortable and happy in their communion, but they were readily accessible to MacArthur, to Sutherland, and to each other.

GHQ was an operational headquarters, stripped of all superfluity, spare and lean. The base section commands could settle easily into a sense of relative permanence. GHQ was poised for movement to battle.

A letter sent to Blamey late in 1942 refers to the arrangement of GHQ:

One of the great advantages of having General Headquarters and the headquarters of the Allied Land Forces, Allied Naval Forces and Allied Air Forces in close proximity is the immediate interchange of information . . . all pertinent messages are made available to Land, Naval and Air Forces regardless of the sources from which the messages are derived. Each operational staff is thus enabled to analyze and interpret the messages with obvious advantage.[5]

In late 1944 Sutherland wrote to George Marshall:

We have developed here a method of operation which has yielded unbroken success. General Headquarters determines the objective to be attained and develops a plan which is submitted to ground, naval and air commanders to implement, giving each untrammeled latitude in the execution of the mission save where it is necessary to effect complete integration of effort and to insure the attainment of the objective. Thereafter the commander-in-chief insures complete and harmonious coordination of ground, naval and air components. It is our concept that that is the elementary and inescapable function of General Headquarters in this type of operations.[6]

Another message of July 1943 describes the organizational principles that governed the structure of GHQ. MacArthur had received inquiries as to the integration of the national commands and the various service commands. Marshall looked upon the matter in terms of equal numbers of officers from each group, so that all interests would be represented in debate. MacArthur resisted the idea of numerical equivalence or quotas. Sutherland wrote to Marshall, emphasizing that general headquarters was precisely that, a headquarters that represented all nations and all services. Its function was to achieve complete unanimity of purpose and action.

. . . land forces, air forces and naval forces each operate under a commander with completely organized staff. Naval and air commanders and staffs are in the same building with general headquarters and land commander and staff are nearby. These commanders confer frequently with the commander in chief and principal members of his staff and in addition to complete functions as commanders operate in effect as a planning staff to the commander in chief. When operating in forward areas the same condition obtains. Air officers and naval officers are detailed as members of general headquarters staff and function both in planning and operations on exactly the same basis as army officers similarly detailed. The problem in this area is complicated by the fact that it is an allied effort and Australian and Dutch army, navy and air officers have been similarly assigned. The personal relationships established and the physical location of land, air and naval headquarters at General Headquarters make possible a constant daily participation of the staffs in all details of planning and operations. Every member of general headquarters from the commander in chief down is in intimate daily contact with appropriate members of the three lower headquarters. GHQ is in spirit a general headquarters planning and executing operations each of which demands effective combinations of land, sea and air forces and has successfully developed an attitude that is without service bias. It must be understood in contemplating such an organization that although the physical location and staff procedures of all four elements are of the utmost importance it is the indomitable determination that general headquarters shall act as such rather than as the headquarters of a single service that will produce the unanimity of action and singleness of purpose that for the successful conduct of combined operations is essential.[7]

28

MacArthur's Headquarters

The directive designated MacArthur as supreme commander of the SWPA. He refused to accept the title and used instead "commander in chief." I recall hearing him complain to Sutherland that he did not care to be referred to as "El Supremo;" the title was too flamboyant for the command. He found several reasons for his opinion, not the least of which was that the public would "think the title to be somewhat tinged with military egotism."[1] To the best of my knowledge the title "supreme commander" was used just once during the war.[2]

MacArthur had dual roles at GHQ. One was purely ceremonial; he received important civilians, extended to them the courtesies of his command, and briefed them on the state of affairs in the area as they related to the interests of each visitor. MacArthur always received the guests but did not, to my knowledge, leave his headquarters to return or to make calls. He was always a gracious host, making his friends feel that they were honored and welcome. He was always knowledgeable and always the dominant partner.

The other role involved his official position as commander in chief of a theater of operations. MacArthur did not take the role lightly. He had worked out in his own mind the precise configuration of his position in the hierarchy of power and was determined to meet the obligations and to demand the rights established by tradition for that position.

MacArthur did not regard the title of commander in chief as an insignificant one. He was very proud to be commanding general of a theater of operations, and correspondence of late 1941 refers to his pride and understanding of his new role.

Late in 1942 MacArthur wrote to Curtin:

The hierarchy of award to Commanders-in-Chief has been fixed by practice of long standing and I would not want to violate the prestige of such a distinguished office by failure to abide by the standard generally accepted by military men throughout the world.

To do so would not only cheapen the office of Commander-in-Chief but would defeat the very intent of the award.[3]

He refused to demean himself and his position. When he received an angry letter from Blamey, he sent it to Sutherland with a handwritten notation: "Letter shows too much heat for a high commander—tone is too intemperative to make any reply advisable—no action. File. MacA."[4]

MacArthur dealt directly with heads of state in matters of military policy. Quezon and Curtin met him as an equal in this respect. MacArthur extended to them the deference due their position, treating them with studied courtesy and genuine respect, and they reciprocated. His affairs with the two governments were characterized by open dealings and frank statements. MacArthur dealt directly with Curtin, who acted as his own minister of defense in order to retain complete personal control of military affairs.

MacArthur acted as the agent of the secretary of war in the execution of the directives that were sent to him by the War Department through its chief of staff. He did not hesitate to appeal directly to the president, knowing that he would receive a fair hearing of his views. His immediate superior was George Marshall, chief of staff of the U.S. Army. The chief of staff was the supreme authority in the army chain of command. He spoke for the secretary of war, dealt frequently with the president, and served as chairman of the joint chiefs of staff, who had final authority—when they could agree—in matters of operations and command.

The issue that divided MacArthur and Marshall then was a question of strategic priorities. MacArthur posed a constant threat to Marshall's European strategy. During 1942 this was a crucial matter, because public opinion might easily be swung to MacArthur's position by reversals in the Pacific. Marshall had no reason to demand personal loyalty from MacArthur and no reason to believe that he could coerce him. The two men regarded each other with cold detachment and suspicion in the constant battle for strategic policy. They were so equally matched in power that neither felt he must acquiesce, but neither could be sure that he would be the master.

MacArthur had a special claim on both Secretary of War Stimson and Roosevelt, and his relationship with them was rather different from Marshall's. MacArthur's tie was more personal in both cases. His view of the obligation of the United States to the Philippines was an emotionally charged commitment that Roosevelt could understand. The cold, practical views of Marshall reflected traditional War Department dislike, distrust, and distaste for the Filipinos and the Philippines. He could not see any great breach of faith in delaying the liberation of the Philippines. Roosevelt would have seen the question as MacArthur saw it, accepting the War Department view as a regrettable necessity. It was Roosevelt personally, not the War Department, who had insisted that MacArthur must come out of Corregidor to Australia, knowing that only his personal direct order would overcome MacArthur's reluctance to leave.

When all is said, Marshall displayed great equanimity all during this relationship. There were two or three instances when messages from Marshall contained comments that could be read as reprimands, but it is not certain that Marshall wrote them or saw them. MacArthur did not at any time descend from the high peak of strategic policy debate, although on several occasions he made helpful offers of sympathy and assistance that may have caused Marshall to pause.

The men were not close friends and did not pretend to be, but each accorded the other the courtesy and temperance demanded in high command. They worked harmoniously together during the war. There is no evidence of deep personal attachment or relaxed exchange. On the other hand, there was no bitterness.

Some have found signs of acrimony in the correspondence. When I typed the documents, they seemed to be dramatic and emotional. As I read them now, I have a different reaction. The documents are formal in nature, written by men who held widely divergent views of global strategy. They are proper, devoid of any personal feeling. I have found only one or two isolated instances of sharpness on either side.

In addition to official duties that tied him to the War Department, MacArthur was charged with full responsibility for all activities within his area. In reality, of course, although his responsibilities were defined in sweeping terms, his authority and duties were more limited. He made policy decisions, and he had ultimate responsibility for planning and execution of operations. All details were in the hands of a chief of staff who reported directly to MacArthur. Under the protocol that governed the relationship between the two men, MacArthur could intrude into the detailed administration of the command only by removing his chief of staff or by taking advantage of his absence from GHQ—when MacArthur, by the nature of things, acted as his own chief of staff.

After the move to Australia, MacArthur was involved intimately and personally in tactical planning at all levels, both in GHQ and in lower commands. He was briefed by Willoughby and Chamberlin about plans formulated in GHQ. As lower echelons developed their own tactical plans to implement GHQ directives, the army commanders or their subordinates briefed MacArthur. He entered freely into the details of the plans, expressing whatever his thoughts happened to be. He did not spare his own staff and was known to take public exception to their positions even in discussions with lower command echelons. MacArthur frequently went to headquarters of tactical units to hear and see for himself what they proposed to do and how they proposed to do it.

MacArthur's references to his "staff" do not have much meaning unless one understands the context of the situation. "Staff" could properly mean what happened to be in MacArthur's mind at that given time. Typically it meant Sutherland and Richard Marshall or simply Sutherland. These two men were his closest and most trusted advisers between July 1941 and September 1945. In his memoirs, MacArthur states that on one occasion his staff would not permit him to take a certain course of action. He meant only that if he had raised the issue with Sutherland or Marshall, either man would have refused to concur in it on the grounds that it violated common sense.

On Bataan and at Buna, Sutherland ran the forward operations, subject to MacArthur's ultimate direction. After Buna this changed. MacArthur, with a small advance echelon, rode forward at the head of the action, subjecting it to his personal supervision and control. Sutherland became MacArthur's emissary in strategic planning outside the area and the central figure in planning.

MacArthur operated within a very narrow span of personal control. This was necessary because his proper activity was very-long-range strategic planning. His thinking ran far beyond the current operations, or even those projected for the near future, into matters that lay beyond the narrow definition of operations. Civil affairs in the Philippines, problems of integrating policy with Curtin and Quezon, the long-run role of his command in relation to the total war, and musings of destiny were matters that could not be delegated to others.

MacArthur consciously and assiduously coached Sutherland, not for present duties that he had mastered, but for a future career at the peak of the army command. He felt that Sutherland eventually should be, and would be, chief of staff of the U.S. Army, holding high commands in the interim. He tutored Sutherland in the fine arts of acting as commander in chief. In daily conversation he coached Sutherland about matters of high policy.

Only two formal staff conferences that I can identify were called for the entire staff to discuss policy. Both of these were held in Manila just after the war began. MacArthur and Sutherland apparently concluded that they were clumsy and futile, and held no more. In Australia and later, "staff meetings" were meetings of principal commanders only, to discuss and to reconcile differences. Preliminary meetings were chaired by Chamberlin and Sutherland. The last and ultimate test would be held in MacArthur's presence, to get the final decision. These were basically rehearsals of operations, most details of which had been agreed to.

Sutherland talked with staff chiefs individually. If there was a conflict, the interested parties assembled in his office to present their views and to receive his verdict. These matters never came to MacArthur's attention. MacArthur's diary shows that individual commanders came frequently to his office to present their views. Less frequently Chamberlin and Willoughby came—to inform, not to discuss. But the staff belonged to Sutherland. MacArthur's office was an empyreal height that few scaled—as was proper and necessary.

MacArthur and each commander had a staff. The staff was organized around four major functional areas: personnel, intelligence, operations and planning, and supply. There were special sections for communications, administration, engineering, antiaircraft, and others. Each staff section had habitual patterns of action, governed by army regulations and practice. For each section in GHQ there was a corresponding section in the War Department that monitored the

subordinate unit. Most of the daily work involved routine reports and correspondence about the current status of plans and operations. It was the duty of
the chief of staff to direct and to coordinate the various staff functions.

MacArthur's chief of staff was the second most important man in the official
hierarchy of authority. He reported directly to MacArthur and could be replaced
only by MacArthur. For practical purposes the chief of staff was one member
of a two-man team that exercised a common command function. The relationship
between MacArthur and his chief of staff ran far beyond a mechanical demar-
cation of authority. The two men acted together on the basis of close cooperation
and discussion. They represented one mind where official matters were concerned.

MacArthur made policy, although in only a few cases did it come to that. He
seldom stepped in to give his chief of staff a directive. In almost all cases policy
represented a common effort in which Sutherland participated actively. Mac-
Arthur acknowledged what everyone knew. Sutherland was the only officer in
the command who could meet MacArthur head-on in open debate, testing the
Old Man's intellectual processes and bending them. He alone of MacArthur's
generals was accepted by MacArthur as an equal partner. As it was with respect
to policy, so it was with planning and operations. MacArthur consulted others
for information; he consulted Sutherland for active discussion and advice.

Sutherland supervised all the details of the command. He controlled GHQ.
All promotions and appointments were made by him. My field commission in
1945 came to me directly from MacArthur, but only because Sutherland was
absent from GHQ and MacArthur was acting as his own chief of staff. Had
Sutherland returned, he could have blocked the promotion. MacArthur's only
recourse would have been to replace Sutherland, a very unlikely course of action.
Sutherland was too valuable to MacArthur to be released. He also coordinated
the activities of the force commanders, who, like it or not, found that what
Sutherland ordered, MacArthur ordained, either before or after the fact.

All details of two commands led ultimately to Sutherland's desk. He was chief
of staff of GHQ by official designation. He was also chief of staff of USAFFE
by usage. Thus he sat at the controls of the operational headquarters (GHQ
SWPA) and of the administrative headquarters (USAFFE). Richard Marshall
was designated as deputy chief of staff USAFFE. He was charged with the
immediate control of USAFFE affairs, but he came to Sutherland as his immediate
superior for final decision and direction.

Charles P. Stivers was an anomaly in the structure. Officially he was assigned
as G–1 in GHQ. The duties of his assignment were not particularly demanding.
As a result he also served, like Sutherland, in a dual role, one aspect of which
was ignored in the formal organization charts. Stivers acted as Marshall's assistant in USAFFE without any official appointment in that headquarters. The
arrangement provided backup for both Sutherland and Marshall. When Sutherland left GHQ, Marshall moved into the empty chair, Stivers moved into Marshall's empty chair, and Stivers' assistant picked up the slack. Sutherland coached

Marshall about operations and plans. Marshall kept Stivers informed of current policy both in GHQ and in USAFFE.

The other staff chiefs occupied well-defined areas of responsibility with clear-cut boundaries of control. They knew their positions and reported to the appropriate chair, regardless of the occupant, in carrying on daily business. Everyone knew that Sutherland was the boss and that Marshall was next in line. Stivers was never considered a candidate for either of the two top slots.

Roger Egeberg later wrote about Sutherland:

General Sutherland was tough. He was a loner and allowed himself few friends or social life. He was considered to be General MacArthur's hatchet man, and the question was, did he relish that? I was spared his hatchet personality but I didn't think at the time that it disturbed him to dress a man down or to fire him. He did it in a flat, on-the-line way. No apologies or explanations, no softening up, just one or two reasons.[5]

Had someone repeated to Sutherland Egeberg's question, "Did he relish that?" Sutherland would simply have smiled at the inability of Egeberg's civilian mentality to come to grips with military reality. Sutherland did not relish his actions, nor did he regret them. He did what was required in a manner consistent with his status as an officer, a general, and the highest authority once removed in the theater. Affability was not expected from him by professional soldiers, who treated their own subordinates as Sutherland treated them. In the broad array of personalities Sutherland was proper. He was never warm and intimate except with Richard Marshall. He was official, abrupt, and efficient. Given his work load and responsibility, and the necessity for keeping under control men who had higher rank and command authority, this is a comprehensive attitude.

Weldon Rhoades has written that, like MacArthur, Sutherland was not easily approachable, but for a different reason. Sutherland was required to take responsibility for unpopular decisions, sometimes not his own, that disturbed ambitious egos with seemingly needless harshness. Many, like Robert Eichelberger, believed that he was intentionally sadistic. Sutherland felt, perhaps, that sooner or later he would make a mistake that would weaken him; so the tougher he was, the tougher he had to be in order not to reveal weakness.

It must be remembered that the army, certainly before and during World War II, was a baiting, goading, even abusive system. The purpose of the system was to develop strong personalities who would not wilt under the most severe pressure and to weed out gentle souls who could not adapt to such an atmosphere. No tenderness was expected, and none was given. The surprising thing is that men like Sutherland, who could haze their own kind without mercy, were able to treat outsiders differently.

The razzing Sutherland imposed upon Godman and Rhoades implied their acceptance as equals and trust in their sense of propriety. He knew they would never display familiarity outside the magic circle. Sutherland needed a command in which he could stride over his subordinates, as MacArthur did, confidently and unquestioned. The greatest chink in his personal defense was the knowledge that he could speak only "by command of General MacArthur."

Sutherland was given to irony, a characteristic of men with finely tuned intelligence, a feeling of superiority, and a sense of being at odds with immediate and remote surroundings. Irony is dangerous because prosaic and pragmatic souls never understand it until it is too late, if at all, and therefore feel that they have been offended or at least taken advantage of. Those who must suffer it continuously from the same person soon take it as sarcasm, and more often than not interpret even innocent and well-meaning remarks as intentional slurs, assuming that, having missed the true meaning of other equivocal remarks, they should not be misled by more obvious ones. The offender is unable to give up the irony, which is his only defense against the idiocy of the situation in which he finds himself. Knowing that he does give unintentional offense, he withdraws into proud isolation, ignorant of how to establish a more congenial pattern of conversation.

Sutherland not only was suspect for his detached irony and air of superiority, he was feared as well. After 1937 he had real power over other men that grew steadily during the war years. His subordinates, for he had no equals in the area, knew that his judgments would be translated into efficiency ratings. Upon his judgments rested assignments, promotions, and decorations.

Sutherland was obviously and avowedly intolerant of mediocrity. Most men, even if born with equal status, generally feel that they have lost it under the pecking of siblings, playmates, and (as adults) social rivals. They are easily convinced that an arrogant man's judgment of mediocrity may have some foundation in fact. Whom they fear, they distrust, even when there is nothing to distrust.

Sutherland's powers of concentration were overwhelming. He could sit hour on hour, bent over smudgy documents filled with dry data, in almost any surrounding, absorbed in the mastery of their contents, cataloging, collating, analyzing, interpreting, then translating them into action. During the hours appointed for work he worked, resenting interruption even when MacArthur was responsible for it. He did not stop for coffee or tea, though sometimes he drank a glass of water. Occasionally in the field, when hours stretched from dark to dark, he had a single scotch and water before dinner. He ate sparingly but preferably with elegant accoutrements, with dignity and decorum. Until 1945 he slept soundly but not long. It was not easy to waken him, but he woke in full command of his facilities. Then he returned easily to sleep. His physical processes seemed to run with the same precision that characterized the processes of his mind.

Every aspect of Sutherland's behavior reflected the unrelenting submission of all physical and intellectual processes to the pressure of overpowering will. He imposed fierce discipline upon others but to an even greater extent upon himself. Sorrow, chagrin, joy, elation, fear, dread, anxiety, anger—none of these ever broke the iron band of control that he threw around them. Late in the war sheer exhaustion of body and will cast over him an obvious pall of ennui and the appearance of physical deterioration. But even in exhaustion he was controlled. The mark of his suffering was not anger and resentment but a softening of habitual responses, revealing gentleness and tenderness where before only steel had been displayed.

Sutherland's was a voice of command, with a ring of steel blade on steel: sharp, clear, precise, clipped. Without emotion his words marched out of his mind in purposeful order, none redundant, always appropriate for the need, without gloss of elegance or brilliance, just sufficient for rational presentation of relevant fact or argument. He did not waste words in anger or frivolity. Like MacArthur, he did not use profanity, but for a different reason. MacArthur did not want to spoil the artistic effect created by the roll and thunder of his rhetoric, which billowed out and up like the great towering clouds of the Pacific, flashing with light and shadow, blazing red and gold, reverberating with Olympic splendor. Sutherland simply did not want boorish or uncultivated words to detract from the sophistication his mind displayed to the world through every aspect of his behavior.

Sutherland's mind was an orderly catalog of facts and ideas, filed neatly away in proper drawers, which he could locate and recall precisely and correctly. Precision was the master here. One was always one, two was always two; he would not tolerate any metaphysical mumbling of "oneness" or "twoness" or a shading of one into the other. His mind drew sharp, clear boundaries that made the clean cuts of a steel blade pulled sharply through a formless mass. It was always tied to present reality. Today's date was the most important one of all time for Sutherland because it was the center of his activity. Only once or twice he mistook tomorrow's date for today's and expressed great chagrin at his failure. My mind was quite cluttered, and in it Thermopylae crowded in easily with Borodino and settled down side by side with Bataan, and while the precise date of Thermopylae might be firmly fixed, today's might easily be lost between yesterday and tomorrow.

Sutherland found greatest delight in activities that require precision and intense control of body by mind. He was a golfer, he was a cabinetmaker, he was a pilot. All of these activities in which a man is measured against himself and constantly attempts to meet the boundaries of his innate potential. All can be done alone; there is no room for bluff or chance. All depends upon a clear mind in control of a steady hand. Those who played golf with him or flew with him were not competitors but simply physical occupants of the surrounding space, perhaps observers of Sutherland's contest with himself. For Sutherland a drive in the countryside was an exercise in navigation as he sat with map and compass, controlling the moves of his chauffeur as if he were a pawn on a chess board, the object of the game to arrive at a given point at a given time.

All of this aside, Sutherland saw natural objects in the surrounding world rather than cartographic coordinates. He saw sunsets, as others did, and appreciated their beauty. He heard music, and it brought emotional response. Such feelings, however, usually were carefully hidden and seldom displayed.

MacArthur's diary does not given any indication of the great role exercised by Sutherland. There are few entries to indicate that Sutherland visited Mac-Arthur's office. Sutherland's diary gives a better record. The flow of visits usually ran from MacArthur's office to Sutherland's. Sutherland did not visit Mac-Arthur's office until he was summoned. It was characteristic of MacArthur simply to walk into Sutherland's office from time to time during the day, as business or boredom required.

The aides were assigned to the office of the commander in chief; that is, they were responsible directly to MacArthur. Huff was senior in terms of tenure and rank, but he acted as Mrs. MacArthur's constant assistant and companion and was seldom seen in GHQ. During the Corregidor period a number of aides were appointed. Diller was both aide and press relations officer in the Philippines.

In Melbourne five aides were assigned: Huff, Wilson, Romulo, Lehrbas, Morhouse. George Marshall complained that this was too many, not understanding that three of them had duties that were not normally assigned to an aide. Wilson was detailed as Sutherland's assistant, in reality a military secretary. Romulo had been detailed to Quezon in Washington. Lehrbas worked with Diller in public relations. Morhouse was the only true aide, and he was the physician as well.

During 1942 Morhouse and Wilson occupied desks in the outer office that housed the office personnel. In late 1943 Lehrbas was given a desk in the office. Early in 1944 Morhouse was reassigned to the United States (his tour of duty had expired), and he was replaced by Egeberg. Egeberg and Lehrbas thereafter served as the two personal aides. Neither cared much for Sutherland.

A certain amount of restrained tension existed between Sutherland and the aides. Sutherland might object to them, but he could not do much about it without very good cause. The aides, although protected by the official lines of authority, nervously considered the possibility that some indiscretion might give Sutherland an opportunity to step in. The tension was exacerbated by the fact that the parties were in daily close contact. One could not avoid the other. Wilson, a career army officer, was posted as Sutherland's assistant. He had learned to ride rough water. The other aides were civilians and had more difficulty. MacArthur usually was gentle with them. Sutherland was abrupt and official, and they were not used to such treatment. They did not realize that the man who trembled before Sutherland on his own turf was equally tough with his subordinates.

Morhouse was MacArthur's physician, not Sutherland's; Sutherland found other medical assistance. He sensed, accurately enough, that a medical aide is likely to find himself caught in a conflict of interest. The confidentiality the doctor owes to the patient may be overwhelmed by the loyalty the aide is required to feel for his immediate superior. MacArthur used his physician to check potential difficulties of his staff. Egeberg was asked to keep an eye on the physical and psychological condition of MacArthur's generals. It may be presumed that Morhouse had been given a similar charge. Sutherland preferred to protect his privacy in this essential matter.

Sutherland had blood pressure problems and an erratic pulse. It was a difficulty shared by his mother, who had become something of a medical celebrity because of it. During Military Mission days Sutherland had a spell in the hospital, apparently in connection with this problem. Thereafter he was seen to take his own pulse. I recall watching him do so although at the time I did not understand the significance. One day Morhouse noticed that Sutherland was measuring his pulse, and with the familiarity permitted a physician, asked, "Well, how is it?" Sutherland was taken by surprise, caught in a display of weakness, and was offended by the unprecedented familiarity. He replied sharply, "I have never asked your advice or your assistance about the state of my health. I never intend to ask your assistance. I expect you to mind your own business and to leave me to mine."

Morhouse flushed red with anger and chagrin, and walked away. He had not meant any harm or insolence. He had failed to understand Sutherland's qualms about letting MacArthur's aide have free access to the state of Sutherland's health. Morhouse kept his distance thereafter and despised Sutherland.

Half a dozen staff pilots were assigned to GHQ over the years as MacArthur's fleet grew to five planes. Hank Godman was the first chief pilot and continued in that capacity until October 1944. Dusty Rhoades joined MacArthur's staff early in 1943. He was a civilian pilot with long experience and served until December 1945. There were others whose names I have forgotten.

The clerical staff in Manila consisted of Master Sergeant Turner and Private Rogers. Turner served, I think, with the Bataan echelon of USAFFE; Rogers with the Corregidor echelon. In Australia, Rogers was joined by H. B. Curtis. Curtis was replaced in mid 1943 by Edwin Bothne. Fred Harrison and Vernon Lewis were assigned in January 1945.

One steno was assigned with the aides to the office of the commander in chief. After the move to Brisbane the assignment did not reflect the reality. Sutherland's dictation ran beyond the capacity of one steno. Sutherland began to usurp the second steno and left Morhouse to private indignation and resentment. The aides did not dictate very much. After arrival in Brisbane, the second steno served Sutherland as a principal duty and the aides as he was needed by them. There was one clerical office, of which I was chief clerk and master.

James D. Larkin, John F. Kitka, and Joseph R. Kozlowski joined the office in Melbourne. Kozlowski moved to G–2 in 1944. Jim Larkin kept the MacArthur/Sutherland Secret File and a large miscellaneous file in addition to other duties. At one time he was delegated to sign MacArthur's name to certain letters.

29

MacArthur as Commander

MacArthur's command philosophy was simple and uncomplicated. It rested on a firm perpetual assertion of his ultimate authority. No one ever doubted that MacArthur was in command. He defined the mission but he seldom interfered in the execution. His commanders had unprecedentedly wide latitude and independence in carrying out their tasks. If they were successful, they were rewarded. If they failed, and not a few did, they were relieved and replaced with another man. Commanders who accepted the ultimate authority of MacArthur had great freedom of action in detail. Their freedom grew as they proved themselves in battle.

MacArthur was a master at motivating subordinates. He could reach each man's character to find the most basic center of appeal. MacArthur played them all—ambition, self-fulfillment, glory, desire to serve. In each man, great or small, he found the core of character and used it. Most of the men called upon to serve MacArthur directly had been screened through a rigorous selection process to establish their capacity for dependable, predictable service in the task to which they were assigned. They knew what to do and how to do it. Most of MacArthur's effort was simply to reassure them that they could perform the most difficult task. Then he let them do it.

MacArthur was a realist where men were concerned. He would have preferred the finest but did not always get what he preferred. He accepted each officer and enlisted man with his limits and weaknesses until they ran beyond the limit of reasonable tolerance. An officer who performed his duties well would be given much in the way of other factors. MacArthur looked to results, not to personality.

Barbey's evaluation confirms what the others had learned:

It was a pleasure to listen to MacArthur. He had the voice and manner of an orator and though I was but an audience of one, he spoke deliberately as if what he said would be recorded for posterity. He was convincing and exhilarating. . . . General MacArthur proved to be the finest commander I had ever worked for. He delegated authority far more than do most commanders. He gave his subordinates a job and then left to them the details of how it was to be done. If the job was not being done to his satisfaction, he simply found another man to do it.[1]

No attempt was made to impose rigid patterns upon individual commanders. Success in battle was the ultimate criterion of performance. Later in the war Kenney expressed to ''Hap'' Arnold a philosophy that reflected MacArthur's own:

Air tactics and techniques of the Fifth and Thirteenth Air Forces differ in many respects. I do not interfere as long as they shoot down Nips and sink ships. . . . The soundness of our system for the war against Japan can hardly be open to argument as long as we are winning.[2]

MacArthur wrote to Blamey: ''I think you will realize from your own long experience that no Commander-in-Chief, present on the field of operations as I am, could have given greater latitude to you.''[3]

Of one officer who was considered to be an ''arrogant and mean S.O.B.'' MacArthur said: ''But he does his job well . . . and whom could I take away from any other job that would do as well? And—you know what I'd get if I asked Washington for a replacement.''[4]

MacArthur was predictable, gentle, sensitive, and sympathetic, a characteristically quiet man. This portrait will surprise many who have seen only the MacArthur of press and screen. All of this notwithstanding, he could be as brittle as obsidian where duty was concerned, ruthless in the demand that soldiers fight to the death if necessary. He sat quietly for hours on end, then erupted like a volcano with enthusiasm, pouring out the fruit of meditation in hot emotion, and cold logic, with perfect syntax and elocution, covering the entire range of human feeling with the dramatic force of a prophet in ecstasy.

During the years I knew him there was a conscious struggle against age. The events of Corregidor and the evacuation had intensified his apprehension, and for a while he was afraid to test himself too far before his troops. He made a first tentative move with the airdrop over Nadzab, without disastrous results. He put his hand on the shoulder of Henry Godman, the pilot, and remarked with restraint that it hadn't been too badly done for an old man. By the time he returned to the Philippines, he was running with the hounds of war, leading his aides and staff relentlessly into great physical exertion and great peril, a testing that found its climax in the final landing at Atsugi airport in Japan.

MacArthur was fair and had a fine sense for righting the wrongs that inevitably result from pride and arrogance. He was able to find a finely tuned correction which satisfied the injured party that his wrong had been redressed without undue humiliation of the wrongdoer. MacArthur stepped into those situations which came to his attention with benevolent authority and a marked touch of irony and humor. The wrongdoer bit his tongue. Everyone else smiled in satisfaction that fairness had triumphed.

Obdurate recalcitrance would be met with reasoned, measured retribution. MacArthur would say quietly, "You will do your duty. Perform, and I will forget it all and reward you. Persist, and I will humiliate you. But you will perform your duty."

I saw MacArthur daily, in defeat and victory, tired and vigorous, drained and ebullient, bored and filled with excitement. I watched the outpouring of emotion and the cool reason that always had the upper hand.

The vocabulary that deals with character and emotions is very poorly defined and very carelessly used. In daily experience most of us are aware that emotional reactions display a very wide range of intensity. The physical actions that accompany them are quite complex and do not necessarily give an adequate measure of the intensity of feeling that produces them. Words like "angry," 'happy," and "courageous" are used as very rough indications of an emotional and physical reaction to a situation. They do not convey any understanding of the mutual interaction of emotion, will, and reason. But some such understanding is necessary if one is to have an adequate picture of a given event.

Those who observed MacArthur in World War II were not given to making nice distinctions about such matters. Most had not thought deeply enough to verbalize subtle distinctions, although they recognized very well that one situation was not quite like another. Unfortunately, events they reported in writing or in conversation give no hint of the details that are required to determine the intensity of feeling or the physical reaction resulting from it.

MacArthur had a predictably even disposition. To those who saw him daily, year in and year out, he was even-tempered. He reacted within the normal range of civilized usage to the incidents that upset his habitual flow of emotions. He was not given to violent extremes of reaction. He was an extremely disciplined person and held his physical actions under firm control. There had been several times in his life when emotion had driven him to nausea and vomiting. He feared that they might recur in the presence of the troops.

In the ordinary routine of the day MacArthur was the epitome of courtesy, consideration, and sympathetic understanding. Habitually he behaved with civility. On the other hand, when he had convinced himself that reason would not produce the desired result, he could conjure up a premeditated fury, and on one occasion he provided a spectacle of anger in full view and hearing of the troops for the benefit of an officer who intentionally and publicly had defied him. Typically, however, on the very few occasions when he was caught unprepared in a vexatious situation, he would hold his emotions under tight control until he could find a temperate release.

MacArthur was an intellectually restless man. It was difficult for him to confine himself behind a desk. I expect he was bored mightily by the daily budget of reports that he was required to read. In most cases he knew very well what a situation was likely to produce and had already anticipated the day's development.

The daily duties imposed upon MacArthur were not particularly strenuous. He was freed of all of the nagging irritations that confront lesser men. He did not have to worry about paying bills, getting his laundry done, or ordering the regimen of his personal routine. All that was taken care of. Doors were opened for him, elevators awaited his arrival and departure, all others stood aside to watch his coming and going. It was an effortless existence in that respect. In the official duties of his day events moved with comparable ease and dispatch. If things went wrong, he was not required to express displeasure. An aide or staff officer would step in to deliver a reprimand and set things straight even when MacArthur would not have bothered to give one or when he did not particularly want to give one.

MacArthur's time and energy were conserved for duties that centered on the highest level of command responsibility. In the day-to-day exercise of these duties, he was a predictably affable, approachable, understanding master.

Barbey wrote after the war:

MacArthur was never able to develop a feeling of warmth and comradeship with those about him. He had their respect but not their sympathetic understanding or their affection. He could not inspire the electrifying leadership Halsey had. He was too aloof and too correct in manner, speech, and dress. He had no small talk, but when discussing military matters he was superb.[5]

MacArthur would have replied:

That is all well and good. Halsey certainly has a style. But I am a commander in chief. Halsey is a field commander. I deal directly with heads of state in a position of higher authority than Halsey's. He deals with troops. I deal with governments. My actions must be more restrained.

At any rate, electrifying or not, MacArthur was considered easy to live with. Every officer knew what was required of him. If he performed his obligation, he would have a happy existence with MacArthur. If he did not, he would be replaced. Of all his commanders, Brett gave MacArthur the greatest possible exasperation. Yet MacArthur treated him gently, all things considered. I do not recall that MacArthur ever personally castigated Brett, although he was irritated enough to have done so.

Carpender and Kinkaid, MacArthur's naval commanders, were another source of exasperation. On separate occasions both of these men, one at Buna and the other at Mindoro, refused at an extremely critical time to support ground force operations. Kinkaid, at Mindoro, compounded his sin by refusing to support operations and target dates to which he had previously agreed.

From the beginning to the end of the war, MacArthur was master of his command. He wrote to Curtin: " . . . The only one who is conversant with every phase of the operation and who has ultimate knowledge of the whole strategic position is myself."[6] This was not a hyperbolic statement. I expect that Sutherland and Richard Marshall might have had greater knowledge of details of the command than MacArthur, but MacArthur was the only one who could see the structure of strategy in long-range perspective, each broad element clearly defined and accurately measured with respect to all other elements. MacArthur never revealed himself completely to anyone; no one ever knew all the cards in his hand. He confided to each man exactly what that man needed to know to perform his function. He withheld even from Sutherland, his most trusted adviser, matters that were not essential to his duties. Not much, admittedly, was withheld from Sutherland, but I am certain that he never had taken MacArthur's full measure.

Part of the magic of high command is mystery. The mystery derived from a feeling of ignorance about the true breadth and depth of the commander's knowledge. It is enhanced by reserve and isolation. None of those in MacArthur's office—the chief of staff, the aides, the clerks—had a complete view of MacArthur. The aide who was probably closer to him than any other was Roger Egeberg, his constant companion for 18 months or so. During the Philippine campaign of 1944–1945 Egeberg was the general's intimate confidante—or, as Egeberg says, with characteristic puckishness, he was "MacArthur's wife." He meant that he filled all the lonesome pockets of emptiness during the campaign. With a fine intellect, the curiosity and sharp discernment of a physician, and warm human understanding, Egeberg observed MacArthur when his reserve was let down. He probed and tried to penetrate the inner workings of MacArthur's spirit. Yet even he was never satisfied that he had a complete understanding of the man.

Close as he was, Egeberg seldom saw official documents, and MacArthur never discussed official matters with him. Such matters were not essential to Egeberg's function. I, on the other hand, saw the documents and was involved in their preparation, but had only occasional glimpses into MacArthur's personal existence and never penetrated into the circle of intimate conversation. Those who thought they understood MacArthur were lacking in wisdom. They had seen only what MacArthur revealed to them, generally with deliberate intent, to make a record. The reserve with which MacArthur shielded himself had a price that he no doubt recognized and properly assessed.

30

MacArthur's Men

The Bataan Boys moved from their respective positions in USAFFE to corresponding roles in GHQ: Sutherland, chief of staff; Marshall, deputy chief of staff; Charles Stivers, personnel (G–1); Charles Willoughby, intelligence (G–2); Spencer Akin, signal officer; Hugh Casey, engineer; William Marquat, antiaircraft; LeGrande Diller, public relations. The rest of us, who were less exalted, continued to serve our respective superiors. To this contingent were added Stephen Chamberlin, operations and plans (G–3); Lester Whitlock, supply (G–4); and Burdette Fitch, adjutant general. Junior officers and enlisted personnel were added to fill out a relatively small mobile operations headquarters.

Those who had been in Australia when we arrived fretted at the concentration of power in the hands of the Bataan Boys, and complained then and later that they were excluded officially and socially from this select group. Perhaps they were. They charged that the Bataan Boys were aloof from their colleagues in Australia, filled with pride in the fact that they had seen combat while their less (or more) fortunate colleagues had not. The charge is not entirely groundless, especially during the first several months. Joe McMicking later took offense at the charge, asserting that no one in the group, except perhaps Sutherland, had such feelings. McMicking did not feel that any of us had been in combat. One may, of course, reasonably debate the proper content of the word. I was very willing to agree that I had never committed a violent personal act against a Japanese soldier. I also would insist that I had been the object of such acts. Although the combat had been unilateral, I felt that I had been intimately and hazardously involved in the process. I suspect that for a while we must have worn our memories openly, to the offense of our brethren who had none. That soon passed.

On the other side of the coin, we had the feeling that the behavior of those in Melbourne arranging our evacuation might reflect a reluctance to see the arrival of MacArthur, who might, and eventually did, unsettle more than one paradise. Brett's failure to send operational planes and Leary's refusal to provide substitutes might lead a nervous soul to believe that we were not particularly welcome. We were all nervous, and the conclusion was properly drawn.

A certain mutual distrust and disdain colored relationships for a very short time, but when GHQ finally left Melbourne, the emotions had faded into insignificance. We were all in MacArthur's headquarters and were all Bataan Boys, the only difference being that while some of us would "return" in the proper sense, all would make the trip and share in the honors.

The Bataan Boys had been tested in battle. Whatever their military specialties might be, their most important role was their service as MacArthur's personal emissaries on the field of battle. All of them had exposed themselves to danger far beyond the demands of their official headquarters assignments. At a time when MacArthur did not visit the front at all, these officers went forward on his behalf to observe, to correct, and to inspire the troops. They were the eyes and the ears and the voice of MacArthur and Sutherland on the battlefield. This would continue to be the case for the remainder of the war.

On Bataan and at Buna they were desperately needed. Both of these battles were fragile, susceptible of disintegration at some unpredictable moment. Careful control was essential. "Cartwheel" and "Reno" were less likely to produce significant surprises. By the time MacArthur returned to the Philippines, he could rely more heavily on the personal efforts of his commanders—Krueger, Kenney, Kinkaid, and Eichelberger—without so much oversight.

Sutherland already has been identified as the most intimate extension of MacArthur's command personality. He was "another MacArthur" insofar as GHQ was concerned. Officially he had no other personal identity. He was MacArthur in action. MacArthur himself was MacArthur in decision.

All of the subordinate commanders held steadfastly to the view that Sutherland wanted to keep MacArthur in an ivory tower. They felt that he was responsible for the requirement that they come to him before he sent them on to MacArthur. This was not the case; it was MacArthur's own policy. He preferred not to be bothered. When he wanted to see the men, he wanted Sutherland to sound them out so that he would have advance notice of what was coming. Sutherland usually would have preferred not to be bothered with the chore.

When someone slipped directly into MacArthur's office, the Old Man accepted the intrusion with his usual affability, talked to the intruder as if he were a welcome friend, gave every impression that he was happy with a fortunate turn of events. In this way the visitor left convinced that the barrier was raised by Sutherland. Sutherland received the butt of their resentment, while MacArthur appeared to be a good fellow who was sheltered by the jealousy of his chief of staff. Some officers felt it to be an assertion of importance to walk past Sutherland and directly into MacArthur's office. GHQ officers, of course, knew the rules and understood where they were made. Some of them disliked Sutherland, but because he was a demanding, unrelenting master who would not tolerate mediocrity or slipshod performance.

Many believed that Sutherland alone held up promotions MacArthur would gladly have made had he known of the matter. I find this difficult to believe. Promotions were tightly controlled by regulations and policy, and I suspect Sutherland merely accepted responsibility for decisions that were forced upon him by policy.

Krueger could not abide Sutherland. In planning conferences and in other such matters he had to march to Sutherland's command because Sutherland spoke for MacArthur and could not be ignored. In other situations Krueger strode resolutely past and around Sutherland in icy silence. When he visited GHQ, as he did infrequently and probably reluctantly, he marched directly into Mac-Arthur's office, leaving his chief of staff to talk with Sutherland.

Next in line of importance was Richard J. Marshall, deputy chief of staff, Sutherland's backup but really more who reported to Sutherland, went to him for resolution of conflicts, and kept him advised of developments within the supply organization that was Marshall's chief responsibility. Nevertheless, Marshall was not quite subordinate to Sutherland. There was a very small gradation of authority and responsibility between them. MacArthur knew that Sutherland was far more capable than Marshall. But as MacArthur tutored Sutherland to step into his position if he, MacArthur, should die, so he tutored Marshall to replace Sutherland if that became necessary. The three top positions in the area were thus buttressed with a deep reserve of men who could step in to fill a high-level vacancy. Or, if an outsider was installed, Sutherland and Marshall could ease his transition to power and maintain a continuity of planning and operations in the area. Any outside replacement of MacArthur would have found himself dominated by his newly acquired chief of staff and deputy chief of staff.

Marshall could afford to be more affable and slightly more relaxed in demeanor than Sutherland around GHQ. He was a tiger at Headquarters USAFFE, where he was top man. Those in GHQ compared him with Sutherland, some thought he was "namby-pamby" but they erred in their judgment. Nevertheless, I think he was more pliable, more amenable, more "human" than Sutherland. In the daily work of Sutherland's office, one could not really know which of the two men was in the office. When Marshall sat behind the desk in Sutherland's absence, nothing changed. Documents dictated by Marshall cannot be differentiated from those dictated by Sutherland. The degree to which MacArthur, Sutherland, and Marshall had fused their intellects is astonishing. The men could be separated by 10,000 miles and without any communication, but in any single situation all three would come up with the same solution in remarkably similar style and expression. No one else in GHQ ever achieved as much.

A rather wide gulf separated these three men from all the other staff chiefs, none of whom rose appreciably above the other. Chamberlin, perhaps, was the acknowledged leader of this pack, although he was far from its most conspicuous member. Chamberlin, G–3, was an outstanding staff planner: quiet, unassuming, methodical, determined, aggressive in defending his position when challenged. He had a fine sense of timing and integration. He manipulated his three separate planning teams to move down parallel paths toward the same objective or, when necessary, to move along divergent paths to map out a change of direction.

Once an objective had been defined in long-run terms, Chamberlin and his planners set the basic sequence of events. All major commanders participated in the planning process, with Chamberlin coordinating and adjusting to smooth out conflicts. Considering the huge distances involved and the necessity for working in the humid heat of equatorial islands, the performance was stupendous. The apparent ease that characterized the operations reflected the thoroughness of the planning process. On those occasions when MacArthur required a sudden and pressing shift of direction, Chamberlin delivered, not always with great patience. The deadlines were met with a finely turned operational plan.

His patience had limits. The only subordinate who dared to go over his head was immediately expelled from G–3. Chamberlin generally was a quiet man but could be forced into anger or disdain if sufficiently pressed. This was not characteristic; typically he bore himself with a quiet determination.

A fatherly man, Chamberlin was almost gentle when dealing with his clerks. He was courteous to a fault. Not handsome, he was stocky, and had a boyish pockmarked face and a huge, bulbous nose that gave rise to ribaldry among certain soldiers. He had the loveliest civilian female secretary in Melbourne, a ravishing young woman who would have followed him—indeed, begged him to take her—from Melbourne to Brisbane. Chamberlin, patiently refused and left her at home, showing great good sense at a time when others were more foolish. No one ever suggested that she was more than his secretary.

Chamberlin's deference to MacArthur was so great that to some observers it seemed that he figuratively "saluted while sitting at attention" in any meeting with the General. Yet no one ever interpreted this as a fawning display of ingratiation. Chamberlin's great capacity for work and the ferocity with which he held to staff decisions gave the lie to any such charge. MacArthur was the only person to whom Chamberlin deferred so intently. He was a workhorse who pulled the harness with patient, enduring steadfastness, apparently never feeling pain or discomfort, or even the pangs of boredom. He had the capacity for burying himself completely in the task. Chamberlin was different in this respect from Sutherland, to whom the daily chore of administrative routine was burdensome both physically and mentally. It usually was obvious that Sutherland preferred to be elsewhere. Chamberlin never seemed to have such feelings.

The MacArthur literature sometimes reads as if Chamberlin had constant contact with MacArthur. The two men did talk, but occasionally and incidentally, about some particular situation where Chamberlin's knowledge was needed. But basically Chamberlin had very limited access to MacArthur, dealing with Sutherland instead. Very late in the war, in July–August 1945, Chamberlin sat at Sutherland's desk as acting chief of staff and during that period, of course, saw MacArthur on a regular basis. This short span is not representative of the previous four-year stint of service.

Probably next in the hierarchical pecking order was "Sir Charles" Willoughby, G–2. He was handsome, affected, and articulate. He looked like an exiled Prussian aristocrat, proud but nervously uncertain. He stooped to petulant needling for very specious reasons and passed to subordinates the anger he felt when rebuked by a superior or ridiculed by his peers. On three occasions I was the butt of unwarranted nastiness.

Willoughby had a fine intellect. I heard him use three languages fluently, and he probably knew more than that. He had a great desire to display erudition. He was well read, and he knew who the masters were. In GHQ he had first honors in this category. He aspired to literary style. Willoughby was always groomed immaculately, a handkerchief tucked under the cuff of his sleeve. He had a great ambition for roles and statuses that were beyond his powers. He was a polished courtier who could change with the wind, gracefully unconsciously and quickly.

He appeared to fawn before MacArthur, but it may be unfair to say so. He had spent 28 years of his career waiting for destiny to call him. Much of the duty had been as instructor in military history at the Command and General Staff School. The subject he taught fed his ambition, and he made repeated attempts to attract MacArthur's attention. Then, just at the end of a long career, his request for assignment to the Philippines was granted and he found himself identified with the most heroic figure in the army hierarchy.

Willoughby knew that destiny had finally called. He was a faithful disciple of MacArthur for the remainder of his service, as he had been for more than a dozen years before. It was not so much that Willoughby served MacArthur's vanity as that Willoughby's vanity and self-esteem were fed by his close association with MacArthur.

Willoughby was fearless, especially since he sought glory, unlike some of the other staff officers who found it forced upon them. His only duty was to serve MacArthur, and to this duty he gave himself without reservation or limitation.

Charles Paul Stivers, G–1, was Willoughby's opposite. He did not cut an imposing figure. Like Marshall, Stivers was a far cry from Sutherland. Where Marshall was langorous in appearance, Stivers was simply nonmilitary. Where Sutherland, Chamberlin, and even Willoughby exuded an air of military command, Stivers exuded the concern of a businessman whose overdue payroll exceeds his current cash balance. He was not as heavy as Marshall, but whereas Marshall's fat was evenly distributed over his frame, Stivers had a small roll of fat across the belly that protruded from an otherwise thin frame.

In spite of Stivers' unassuming appearance and undramatic duties, he was the number four man in the hierarchy of command. He understudied Marshall and supervised the bulk of administrative matters for the area. He was assigned to GHQ as G–1, a relatively innocuous duty, but his real worth was in USAFFE, where he had no official assignment. In mid 1943 MacArthur recommended Stivers for a second star. George Marshall in Washington asked for an explanation of the discrepancy between the apparent assignment and the recommendation for promotion. Sutherland replied, for MacArthur, that Stivers would soon be designated deputy chief of staff USAFFE, to release Richard Marshall for duty as deputy chief of staff GHQ.

Stivers could be a tiger in defense of regulations and administrative propriety. He took on George Kenney regarding the delicate matter of decorations for combat crews. Kenney had sent up the recommendations, and Stivers had denied them perfunctorily. Now it came to Sutherland for adjudication. Kenney out-bravadoed Stivers. Ignoring the letter of the regulations, he went to the heroics of the matter, his voice rising inversely to the strength of his logical position. It was a good performance.

Stivers sat, his mustache quivering with exasperation, until he could stand it no longer. He rose in fury, outshouting Kenney: "God damn it, George, your people didn't do anything heroic. On the basis of your own recommendation they threw out everything in the God damned plane to save themselves."

This had been the case. With three engines out, the crew of the B–17 had dumped everything they could pry loose, including guns and ammunition, to keep the plane airborne. They struggled into Dobodura, tearing the tops off the trees on the way in. It was a matter of self-preservation. Stivers won the debate. Sutherland asked for more time and held the papers on his desk.

Diller had first been MacArthur's aide. Then, as the war got under way, he became press relations officer as well. With the creation of SWPA he was assigned as public relations officer, a considerable expansion of responsibilities. He continued to supervise the activities of the press contingent that was assigned to GHQ, a considerably larger, less tractable, and more critical group than he had found on Corregidor. The new group had not seen MacArthur on Corregidor. Some were tainted with the "Dugout Doug" syndrome and an anti-MacArthur attitude that survived from the Hoover years.

As chief censor, Diller managed to soften the impact of the encounter between MacArthur's ego, on the one hand, and the collective ego of the press, on the other. His inherent integrity, good humor, and patience were tested by many trials. Others might have found the duty to be an impossible task, but Diller carried the duties with apparent ease and good feeling toward all concerned. He seldom displayed irritation, and then in a controlled, commanding manner.

Diller always had a boyish appearance. I thought he was quite young, although he was older than Egeberg. Sometimes his face bore an anguished, disturbed expression, but this was infrequent. I sometimes fell into familiar joviality with him, daring to make ironic comments. He never took offense, tolerated my breaches of etiquette, and sometimes returned my easy humor in kind. Perhaps he remembered the two nights we spent in opposite bunks on PT–35. Diller was a gentleman, a dedicated officer, who worked long hours in great discomfort to serve MacArthur.

Diller served up the daily ration of military information in MacArthur's com-muniqué. His censors frequently took away what Diller had given. Reporters were not permitted to read into the communiqué any hint of interpretation. The communiqué *was* the interpretation. There could be no embellishment of the single source. Diller permitted correspondents to come to him for final appeal when a story was hopelessly mangled by the censor. On more than one occasion he was hauled out of bed in the wee hours by a desperate correspondent whose deadline for a radio newscast was only a few hours away. The two men would sit with the blue-penciled manuscript as Diller separated the permissible from the prohibited, working out a compromise version that would meet the minimum requirement of both the reporter and the censor. It was not an easy task.

Lloyd Lehrbas provided a bromide for MacArthur's seeming vainglory. He had been a newspaper man, and had come to Australia just prior to MacArthur's arrival from the Philippines, hoping to be public relations officer. He served for a while under Diller, then came upstairs as aide.

Lehrbas appointed himself guardian of MacArthur's public image. As a newspaper man he knew the value of legend and understood very well what goes into the making of legend. He and MacArthur simply had a different concept of what the image should be. Lehrbas preferred a personality that would accommodate itself to the behavior of a cooperative and willing subordinate. He regretted MacArthur's political maneuvering, preferring disciplined heroics that never created disorder or disarray. For the press he would have preferred a more conciliatory MacArthur, one who would bend at least slightly to their pride, meeting them, if not as equals, at least as legitimate workers in a common vineyard. Lehrbas fretted in vain. He wanted an Eisenhower; he had a MacArthur!

Of them all, Joseph McMicking was the perfect specimen of Hollywood casting for the hero of a war movie. He was tall and dark, a large smile exposing gleaming teeth beneath an elegant, neatly trimmed mustache. Mysterious and quiet, he exuded pleasant goodwill. Gentle eyes sparkled with good humor. Once I saw them red with tears that welled up and flowed down a face torn with anguish. His family has been massacred by the Japanese defenders of south Manila. At first assigned to Willoughby, he was later attached to Quezon in Washington. He came back to GHQ in late 1944 for the return to the Philippines.

Spencer Akin was a product of VMI. He was MacArthur's signal officer, a specialized calling. Akin felt constrained, and tried several times to obtain a transfer from the signal corps to a general staff assignment or a troop command. He remembered World War I and the fate of officers who remained in the service after 1918. He foresaw a greatly reduced army after the end of World War II and the demise of the signal corps. He felt he would be forced into retirement. Instead he rose to become chief signal officer of the U.S. Army.

Akin was relatively tall, slender, not particularly handsome, but certainly pleasing in appearance. He was quiet and unassuming, but his face was stern. Under the stern face was a gentle, humorous man and a sensitive one. He was one of the few who ever attempted subtle humor with MacArthur. He sent up a half sheet of paper with a typed doggerel verse: "The queen bee is a noble soul who doesn't believe in birth control. That is why one always sees so very many Sons of Bees!" The General noted, "Yea Bo. MacA." I kept it for my own file.

Marquat and Wilson have been described elsewhere. The others are indistinguishable in my memory.

In general, each staff officer went his own way, Marshall with affability, Willoughby with elegant volatility, Stivers with quiet determination, Akin with stern kindness, Chamberlin with unobtrusive, dedicated attention to details of his work, Kenney and Marquat with profane, lighthearted good humor, Fitch with unrestrained bad humor. I have tried to characterize their essential personalities. They were all fine soldiers, dedicated to their work, on duty 24 hours a day, with few periods of relaxation.

Personal conflicts did not interrupt the requirements of their work, nor did they interfere with coordination of planning activities. Confrontations and disagreements were the exception. The rule was simple acceptance of each other's whimsies and peculiarities.

IX

Settling in, April–September 1942

Australians accept censorship; the communiqué; problem of unity of command; collisions with Navy; new air force commander

31

Censorship

When the two B–17s that had carried us from Del Monte touched down at Darwin on March 17, General George Brett, the ranking U.S. officer in Australia as commanding general U.S. Army forces in Australia, in the name of President Roosevelt called John Curtin, the prime minister of Australia, to inform him of the arrival of an important guest. The Australians had not been told of Mac-Arthur's arrival because of the need for secrecy to protect the evacuation that was then under way.[1]

Curtin, who had requested in February that MacArthur be appointed supreme commander in Australia, responded with apparently genuine relief and proceeded to support MacArthur. The new command structure had been in the making since January. The details were hammered out in the weeks after I first learned of the impending evacuation from Corregidor.

It may be true that at the level of government MacArthur's arrival and designation as the new Allied commander were accepted enthusiastically. However, among the citizens of Australia there was some doubt not only about MacArthur but also about the invasion of Yanks. Much of this amounted to no more than friendly competitive jealousy, fostered, perhaps, by the apparent affluence of the Yanks. As I talked with people, a refrain was sung that reflected the underlying problem: "Yanks are overpaid, oversexed, and, worse yet, over here!" There was invidious comparisons on both sides. Yanks had their fair share or more of Australian girls, both maidens and wives, which made some Australians happy and others angry. It may be added that Australians in Canada were in about the same situation as the Yanks in Australia.

MacArthur was often referred to disparagingly as "Dugout Doug" or "Doug"—or, in the array of Australian obscenity and profanity, much worse. The display of pomp and circumstance and the aloof dignity that he assumed went against the grain of Australians, who leaned to informality and equality. To many Australians, MacArthur was a foreign general imposed upon them, their generals, and their sons, and it created resentment. MacArthur, however, received less critical attention than a member of the royal family might have received.

MacArthur faced a new reality in Melbourne that would test him in a way he had not been tested before. Manila had been an easy post. As former chief of staff, he could dominate any U.S. officer who came his way. The authority, actual and potential, that came automatically to the military commander in the Philippines had permitted him to cow Hart, Sayre, and Quezon, but Melbourne was another matter. The old regimental tie of past association would not give him an edge of precedence. One or two missteps would pull him into an abyss of controversy from which he could never rise.

John Curtin, head of the Labour Party and prime minister of Australia, was a hard-working, serious man, not given to frivolity or to mercurial displays of emotion. He was a parliamentarian, an aggressive, tough-minded trade union leader. It would be impossible to charm him, to delude him, or to outwit him. He was frank, open, and practical. The warmth, fun, and enthusiasm of Quezon simply were not there. By an even greater irony, MacArthur, who had come to serve Curtin's government, would be the Labour Party general. Aristocratic style to the contrary, he must stand shoulder to shoulder in a highly unlikely alliance with the trade union leadership and rank and file. His otherwise natural allies in the opposition would attack him viciously, using any tactic available, in the hope of embarrassing Curtin and bringing down his government. The imposition of censorship and the daily communiqué were the focus of opposition for almost 12 months.

There would be trouble in another quarter. In Manila, MacArthur had good-naturedly badgered Tommy Hart to "get yourself a fleet." It was simply a ploy to establish the proper scale of priorities in his theater of operations. He and Hart had long been friends. Now in Melbourne, MacArthur was faced by two navies, the U.S. and the Australian. Out along his supply line, over which troops and supplies must sail mile after mile, stretched a growing armada of fighting ships commanded by admirals who did have a fleet, or even fleets, and were not likely to be dominated by good-natured badgering. They were MacArthur's powerful competitors in a winner-take-all game. He would have to fight in open debate to have his way. Destiny and honor would not be accepted as admirable arguments. The Pacific had been organized to foster the competition. Former chief of staff or not, he would have to meet the admirals as equals and fend off as best as he could their personal and intellectual hostility in order to enforce the principle of unity of command.

Finally, MacArthur's long-standing reputation as the enemy of air power, the incongruous U.S. command structure in Australia, and the bitterness of an air force that had driven itself to destruction in hopeless battle in the Philippines and the Netherland East Indies would continue to create an impossible situation within his own headquarters command structure. All in all, MacArthur would have his hands full for his first 120 days in Australia.

The first test with the Australians came over censorship. Everyone knows that censorship is a bad thing, except when it is necessary and possible to use it to cover one's own difficulties. It is one of those institutions that, correctly, is considered to be insidious, suspect, and therefore reprehensible. But there are times when it is necessary. The extent to which the censorship actually imposed corresponds to the needs of a given situation are necessarily debatable.

Military officers give themselves great latitude, since all information is of some potential value to a wily enemy. Those who are the object of censorship, on the other hand, whose livelihood consists of informing, are more likely to view the matter differently. For them, the privilege to know is a stout bulwark buttressed by economic necessity, and they are inclined to argue that a wily enemy will know everything anyway and that the public should share every secret.

Contrary to popular opinion, imposition of censorship was pressed by Roosevelt and George Marshall. MacArthur expressed reluctance to intrude into what he considered a highly explosive issue. The initial shot in this particular affair came from Marshall in early 1942. In reply MacArthur gave a detailed lecture on censorship in Australian practice. He asserted that Prime Minister Curtin himself had absolute control over all Australian military information. Curtin and members of his government met daily with the press, and freely and openly discussed military operations and strategy. It would be very difficult to impose U.S. control. Even when MacArthur was confirmed as supreme commander, he would not have any control over censorship of high government officials. Moreover, MacArthur continued, British press representatives were completely outside his control. MacArthur advised Marshall: "For the past ten days have been endeavoring by conference to remedy the situation. I shall continue to do everything possible along this line but I am certain that a completely satisfactory solution will not be achieved."[2]

Marshall complained several weeks later: "Censorship of news emanating from Australia including that from your headquarters is in need of complete revision. You are directed to take necessary action at once."[3]

MacArthur replied immediately that censorship would violate Australian law and policy. He suggested that solutions to the problem must be found by "an authority superior to my own," which of course meant Roosevelt:

Elements of the highest sovereignty of government are involved which far transcends the mere mechanics of censorship. I shall do everything I can to comply with your instructions but to attain the efficiency you desire far exceeds any powers which have been placed in my hands.[4]

Roosevelt then entered the fray: "The only difficulty I am having here is a good deal of loose newspaper talk coming out of Australia, and I suggest you do all possible to get a censorship on outgoing messages from Australia and possibly New Zealand also.''[5] New Zealand was not part of MacArthur's command, so one must infer that this was meant to be an ironic suggestion.

Another request came from Marshall on May 10 because of a complaint raised by Admiral Nimitz about Australian publicity concerning naval actions.[6] Again MacArthur stated that he could not exercise unilateral control of publicity. Australian citizens could not be denied news about Australian forces fighting in Australian waters.[7] In the meantime Curtin had moved the levers of Australian governmental machinery. The Australian war cabinet on May 6 issued a minute imposing censorship. It was sent to MacArthur.[8]

On May 15 MacArthur reported to Washington that he had raised the matter with Curtin. MacArthur had urged that the Australians provide a self-imposed solution. He had emphasized to Curtin that the issue was raised to protect the military situation. It was not intended that censorship be controlled by U.S. authorities. MacArthur advised that he had been given ''partial control over the Australian censorship. This has been done in such a way that our own government is not in any way involved and no allegation can be made that it is attempting to impose its will in any way upon that of the Australians.''[9]

Several months later MacArthur, with ''the utmost reluctance,'' complained to Curtin about two articles prepared for the press. They had been written by important Australians and contained information that could have come only from the War Council, the highest body for discussion of strategic policy. MacArthur urged:

I beg of you to take steps to suppress this type of sabotage and espionage. . . . If some degree of self restraint is not practiced here I believe that parliamentary and legal methods should be applied to produce that degree of silence which will enable military plans to be carried out without previous exposure.[10]

John Curtin must have watched the transformation of the process of military policymaking with astonishment. The proud, independent, vociferous members of Parliament at Canberra considered this to be an inalienable part of their domain. Imperceptibly they were excluded from the process and even the public discussion of the process. At the time of MacArthur's arrival, strategy had been openly debated. Three months later the strategic decisions were hammered out behind closed doors, and the commander in chief took care that the details would be handled only by his headquarters.

Parliament might fret, but they had to take what they were given. The Australians did not have sufficient forces to hold back even one of the potential threats, and were debating what portions of Australia should be sacrificed to the enemy and which should be held.

Tension between the Australians and Churchill was not new and certainly had not originated with MacArthur. As the Japanese drove south and spread across the Malay Barrier from Burma to Rabaul, the Australians began to evaluate the Japanese potential in terms of Australia. A command structure was laid down in February. The matter of an international command with a U.S. commander was under discussion when MacArthur arrived. Force requirements had been identified in detail for each of the potential target areas.

The Australians took their demands for increased assistance to London, the center of British decision making. They felt that their position would be strengthened if it was supported by their newly arrived commander in chief. The Australian representative in London touched the match to the powder keg in a cable to Curtin:

On this it would be very helpful if a short analysis of the position could be prepared by General MacArthur in cooperation with our Service Chiefs. . . . The documents should emphasize the probability of immediate attack and the inadequacy of our means. . . . Of course, they can make official report to General Marshall if they prefer but if they do I would like some statement from them in addition.[11]

MacArthur was notified of this request. He sent Sutherland and Brett to meet with the Australian service chiefs to prepare the information that had been requested. Curtin then transmitted the military information back to London for presentation to Churchill. Curtin reported to Churchill that "the commander in chief . . . is bitterly disappointed with the meagre assistance promised for the Southwest Pacific Area for the performance of the tasks imposed upon him by his directive."[12]

MacArthur, to cover all bases, radioed George Marshall asking for information on the nature of the offensive that was contemplated for SWPA, the size of the forces to be made available, and the date on which the operation would begin. A copy was sent to Curtin.[13] The request was reasonable enough, but Marshall had no desire to specify that the reply to all three points, as of that date, was "none." Almost at the same time Marshall received a message from Roosevelt, who had just heard from Churchill of MacArthur's involvement in the Australian pressure to obtain more forces. Churchill resented having been bothered. Like Marshall, his only answer could be "none at all." Churchill, moreover, had handed the problem of Australian defense to the Americans and did not want to be troubled with it.

Marshall batted the ball back to MacArthur, insisting "that all communications to which you are a party and which relate to strategy and major reinforcements be addressed only to the War Department."[14]

MacArthur replied that his position in Australia was a delicate one. He was required to provide Curtin with complete information regarding the situation. MacArthur noted that his responsibility to Curtin was equal to his responsibility to Roosevelt. He had replied freely to all of Curtin's requests for information. Nevertheless, he wrote: "I have endeavored to observe scrupulously proper channels of communication . . . I am not conscious, even by indirection, of any taint of disloyalty."[15]

MacArthur argued that he must discuss military matters with Curtin: "I apparently at the present have the confidence not only of the Australian government but of the Australian people which is due largely to the lack of any attempt on my part at intrigue or reservation.''[16]

Roosevelt replied directly to MacArthur in order to pour oil on the troubled waters:

I am especially trying to avoid any future public controversies between Mr. Churchill and Mr. Curtin. . . . I see no reason why you should not continue discussion of military matters with Australian Prime Minister, but I hope you will try to have him treat them as confidential.[17]

MacArthur wrote to Curtin that discussion of strategy should

. . . properly be a matter of conference between you and myself . . . the only one who is entirely conversant with every phase of the operation and who has the intimate knowledge of the whole strategic position is myself. I propose, as I have previously stated, to keep you fully informed.[18]

Curtin acknowledged his agreement to the arrangement. The matter had been arranged to the satisfaction of all parties without creating friction between MacArthur and Curtin. It is a tribute to the determination of each man to find a rational solution to a very complex problem.

The evidence available from other sources confirms my memory that genuine mutual friendship and respect existed between MacArthur and Curtin. I do not recall ever hearing any remark from either Sutherland or MacArthur that could be taken as a slight of the prime minister. Parliament, of course, was Curtin's responsibility, and in the Australian system, as in England, the prime minister headed and spoke for the party in power in Parliament. As long as Curtin and MacArthur stood shoulder to shoulder, there might be heckling from the opposition or the back benches, and there usually was, but the party stalwarts arrayed in the forward seats were required to support Curtin—and therefore MacArthur.

32

Communiqué

During June 1942 a committee of Parliament, after discussing the problems of censorship and communiqués, sent a statement of complaint to Curtin. The complaint concerned the communiqué more than censorship, but the two matters were closely interwoven. Members of the press had complained to the committee that figures given in the communiqué did not always coincide with those provided by intelligence reports. The discrepancies cited in the statement related to losses of Allied airplanes in operations. It was asserted that the communiqué systematically understated Allied losses. The committee recommended that either Curtin or MacArthur meet in person with representatives of the press to discuss the matter. Curtin sent the complaint to MacArthur, requesting his comment. In reply MacArthur sent a four-page letter that is the only firsthand statement of his views of the proper nature of a military communiqué. The draft was written personally by him. The letter is quoted in full.

Dear Mr. Prime Minister:

I have read your letter of June 26th embodying the complaints against the official communique issued by this headquarters.

Censorship and communiques in a democracy are questions which will always be debatable. On the one hand there is the insatiable desire for fullest detail and on the other the reluctance to assist in any way the intelligence service of the enemy. In the present complaint the general charge is made that the communiques have presented an over-optimistic picture and cite several instances in which losses have occurred which were not included in the official communique. The allegation of over-optimism is not, in my opinion, tenable. A careful examination in the light of full facts will show an understatement of our successes rather than an overstatement. Since these communiques commenced, the war picture with reference to Australia has immeasurably improved. Our air battling in the north has not only dislocated the enemy's aggressive plans, but has resulted in markedly greater losses in enemy materiel and men than in our own forces. The Coral Sea Battle was one of the really brilliant engagements of the war on our part. The transformation of Australia from a condition of practical unpreparedness to the present armed strength which now exists, together with the corollary efforts appertaining thereto, represents an inspiring picture indeed to me, who above all others, would have reason to complain of inertia or complacency. The truth is that Australia has passed from a position of acute danger and crisis to one of local relative security. Yet no note of over-confidence, no overstatement of braggadocio, can be found in any communique that has been issued. Much indeed has been said as to the restraint and composure reflected in these official statements. In reality criticism of the communiques, if criticism is properly levelled, would be to the effect that full credit for what has been done has not been claimed.

The second charge, that certain losses on particular days have not been carried or that some general statement that "our losses were light" rather than figures, has more basis of realism. The exact knowledge of losses that our forces sustain would be of real benefit to the enemy. As a consequence the communiques report only those losses which have actually occurred in combat action and which the enemy consequently knows. No losses are reported in the communiques of our planes which crashed not in enemy action but through the natural vicissitudes resulting from flights. For instance, if fifteen planes engaged the enemy and four were shot down and four others not due to enemy action crashed, the four that were shot down would be reported in the communique, being known to the enemy. The other four which crashed from natural causes and unbeknown to the enemy would not be reported in the communique. This practice, however, presents no distorted view as compared to the enemy's losses, as we do not claim or attempt to claim the crashes and wastages in his forces due to these same natural causes. We report only those planes of the enemy which are destroyed or damaged in actual combat. The communique, therefore, presents the same picture for both sides. This is the present practice and is a modification of the original policy not to report our own losses. The original policy, I may say, was that of the American Government until modification some weeks ago. The great majority of the air forces employed were American and a great preponderance of losses were of that nationality.

The actual details of air losses are dependent upon the operational reports that are received from pilots and others engaged in the action. For many reasons it is quite possible, and even probable, that inaccuracies occur, but in so far as the officer who prepares these communiques is concerned, his endeavor, within the limitations I have stated, is to present an unbiased and uncolored picture of events. It is not the purpose or desire of military authorities to use the official communique for propaganda or to affect in any way the free flow of public opinion. Under no circumstances should the communique be regarded as a substitute for energetic and thorough reportorial effort. They are historical records which are written from the standpoint of globular perspective and have little relationship with the emphasis which animates a local press. They are designed to influence the policy of the press and to control it just as little as possible.

The communiques here when compared with communiques on other fronts show a far greater liberality than is normally practiced. As a matter of fact, I have received a number of admonitions from Washington with regard to the liberality of censorship from this area. The situation is thus presented in which the United States thinks too much information is given and Australia thinks there is too little. Perhaps a reasonable balance is being achieved. The enemy countries solve the question very simply. They completely suppress a free press and their communiques are issued entirely for propaganda purposes. When they express the truth, it is merely coincidental. The gravest care is being taken at this headquarters that nothing of such a pernicious practice shall be allowed to develop.

I may be wrong, but it seems to me that I detect in the complaints that are being made an endeavor to unduly pessimise the situation here, either to discredit the war efforts that are being made or, what is more probable, to attempt to accelerate the effort through the utilization of a factor of fear which the successes of the past few months do not properly warrant. Communiques form only a small part of the picture and must be appraised in conjunction with the official statements of the responsible heads and ministers of government. I have carefully noted the statements made by the Prime Minister as Minister of Defense and those of the members of the War Cabinet. Taken as a whole in conjunction with the communiques, I personally do not see how a fuller and fairer picture could have been presented to the Australian people. They are certainly more accurately and completely informed than either the people of the United States or Great Britain.

The request that has been submitted to you asking for a conference with me, would seem to imply that I had not been available. This is entirely misrepresentative as I am always ready and glad to see such representative groups.

Whatever may be the merits or demerits of this question, and as I have indicated, there are two conflicting points of view which must be synchronised, it is deplorable in my opinion that it should have been made a medium of controversial and acrimonious public discussion by high personages to the delight and satisfaction of the enemy. In contrast, I commend most heartily the action of the committee headed by the Right Honorable Mr. Scullin in presenting this matter to you for clarification. In time of war a due sense of responsibility should be exercised by everyone, even a free press, unless the enemy's destructive efforts are to be indirectly aided and abetted.

I do not wish you to infer from anything I have said that I believe our communiques are not susceptible of improvement. Others might well do much better, but I merely wish to say that they constitute the best that we can do within the limiting policies I have explained. Whatever their standard of efficiency, they represent nothing but our most honest effort and there is nothing of guile in them.

In the last analysis the questions involved are ones of judgment upon which men of honest intent and purport may frankly disagree. When such temporary disagreement occurs, the opinion of those who are temporarily vested with the responsibility of government must necessarily prevail. There is always the recourse in a free country of changing the individuals if the country so wills it.

If there is anything further that I can offer in answer to your query, please command me.[1]

When I typed this letter, I paused over the verb "pessimise." It did not seem proper to me, yet I did not feel that I could question MacArthur's use of the English language. I checked the dictionary without success. Finally I took the draft to Sutherland and asked his opinion. Sutherland paused from his own work, read the paragraph, looked up at me, and said, "Rogers, you're right. There isn't any such word. But that is what the General wrote and I expect that is what we had better type," MacArthur had a better dictionary. It is a proper word.

A week later Curtin wrote to the Parliamentary Committee, sending a copy of MacArthur's observations. He reminded the committee that "In accordance with the cordial and cooperative relationship we have established, he has furnished a very reasoned reply,''[2] Curtin shunted aside the proposal that MacArthur should be asked to meet with the committee ''in view of his special standing in this country.''

Sixty days later the matter of the communiqué was raised again by the Defense Committee. MacArthur replied more curtly:

Its [the communiqué] nature must be understood in order to understand its proper niche in publicity. It is not intended in any way to be what might be termed "news copy"— it is a historical report of the events which have occurred in the past twenty-four hours— with due perspective in relation to the war as a whole and on other fronts. It merely serves as an indication to the press of the operations which may be subjects for their reportorial writings. It is in no sense a substitute for the press.

Each day the relative importance of news items of a paper is determined by what occurs in that short cycle of time and with due reference to its own local and special interest. Communiques, on the contrary, have no concern with anything but the briefest historical records placed in proper perspective to the historical events of the war that day. They have the further limitation of not conveying information that might be of value to the enemy. They are completely dependent upon what actually occurs. When there is no action, it is impossible, if integrity is maintained, to report anything but the fact that there is nothing to report.[3]

The daily communiqué and the special press releases issued by MacArthur are the best-known of his literary productions. I use the term ''literary production'' advisedly, in the sense that he gave great care to their formulation and endeavored to embellish them with a unique style that could not be mistaken for another's. Almost everything he wrote—whether a simple note or a routine check sheet, a notation on an operations report that passed over his desk, a congratulatory message to a commander, a reprimand to an erring subordinate or a reproach to a superior, a formal report or an entreaty—bears the hallmark of MacArthur's determination to leave the imprimatur of his personality. Nothing was trivial because he, MacArthur, had touched it; and in this sense even the most mundane minutiae acquired an aura of destiny.

MacArthur's prose was phrased in the patterns of nineteenth-century elegance. It was quite natural and familiar to him. The books of his library were written in that style. If he had read only a fraction of the volumes, he would have absorbed the styles of their authors. The aristocratic, flowing expression with long, rolling sentences, phrases cascading to a polished conclusion, was not artificial or stilted in his hands but a sincere use of an accustomed idiom. His literary style was just one aspect of aristocratic good breeding, the hallmark of a gentleman.

The communiqués and press releases attained greater notoriety in this respect because they were issued with predictable regularity and were widely disseminated. They were subject to the criticism of those professionals who were masters of style in their own way but not given to majesty. Readers of the daily press usually are offended by apparent displays of what they consider to be feelings of God-given superiority.

Communiqués and press releases received especially careful attention, and I doubt that a single document in this category ever escaped his attention. Several were written by Sutherland in his absence, but it was expected that the Old Man would certainly read them on his return to the office.

The routine at USAFFE in the Philippines was not as elaborate as the one in SWPA days. When the war broke out, MacArthur routinely wrote the drafts for the releases. An entry in Sutherland's diary for December 21, 1941, records that Sutherland discussed with Diller the organization of a press section and the press releases. There are no details of what was said.

The entry marks the absorption of the press function into the official headquarters routine, which was Sutherland's domain and subject to his supervision. As an aide Diller reported directly to MacArthur, completely outside the sphere of Sutherland's authority. As press officer Diller was a part of Willoughby's intelligence staff section and an integral part of the headquarters staff. While the press was MacArthur's domain, he did not want to deal directly with the members of the press, choosing an intermediary who could absorb and deflect some of the heat that inevitable frictions would produce. As the war in the Philippines entered a serious stage, it was felt that control should be tightened over the press function, which would acquire a greater significance.

Three weeks after the arrival on Corregidor, Diller reported to Sutherland concerning a news story that involved some problem. Thereafter Sutherland regularly read and supervised the press releases and worked out administrative problems of Diller's operation. On February 1, 1942, there was a discussion of how photographs could be sent from Corregidor to the United States.

The daily press release was viewed as an adjunct of the official operations report that was sent to Washington every morning. The press release carried two sections. The first was a report of operations that was coordinated with, but understandably not identical with, the official operations report. The second was a story written by one of the press officers. The style of the two elements is so different that they cannot have been written by the same person. The "story" was not necessarily related to the operations section and was avowedly designed for a more emotional impact.

A dispatch of January 2, 1942, warned Washington of a possible discrepancy between the daily operations reports and the daily press release:

In addition to my daily operations report I will endeavor from now on to send daily reports for your press release section. This report may at times contain propaganda and where it differs from my operation reports the latter will be accurate. From now on I must rely entirely on your efforts as regards influencing public opinion, not only in the Philippines but elsewhere.[4]

This message was an extremely unfortunate one. It was written just after advance echelon had been blasted out of Topside and was not yet settled into

Malinta Tunnel. There were two crowded days as Quezon was inaugurated and his evacuation was discussed. I am sure that neither MacArthur nor Sutherland wrote it. Probably someone was instructed to write the message, after being given the general outline of what was desired. It left an indelible impression in Washington that communiqués misrepresented the truth. This was not the case, either on Corregidor or in Australia. On Corregidor I typed both items.

After we moved to Australia, the communiqué procedure was modified, and thereafter communiqués and operations reports were very strictly coordinated. The special story disappeared. Whatever the message cited above meant on Corregidor, it had no significance at all for Australia.

On January 19, 1942 on Corregidor, Diller had reported to Washington that "Press relation reports [are] practically composed by General MacArthur."[5] In Australia the procedure changed but MacArthur's personal control did not.

The daily communiqué became an important item of business. The deadline was noon of the day it was issued. That particular time was selected to allow for the time differential between SWPA and the United States. The General tried to give a prompt, accurate accounting of military events. I do not know of any cases where statements in the communiqué contradicted facts as they were reported by appropriate commanders on the day the communiqué was written and I was in intimate contact with the communiqué process from the beginning.

Early each morning Willoughby prepared a special packet for the day's communiqué. On the left side of the legal size folder he stapled the operations and intelligence reports that provided the basic information considered important for release. To the right side of the folder was stapled a draft of the communiqué. This folder was delivered to Sutherland, who immediately reworked the draft. I typed Sutherland's revision. On occasion Sutherland made subsequent revisions and the draft had to be corrected again.[6]

When MacArthur arrived at 10:00 A.M., he read and reread, sending successive drafts back to Sutherland for rewriting until he was satisfied. Sutherland found the job more and more demanding, frequently occupying his time until noon. This process continued for quite some time. I suspect that at first Sutherland may have been startled. It must have seemed strange to him that while he could prepare an important dispatch of half a dozen pages that MacArthur would approve with only minor changes, the communiqué of a dozen or so lines required far greater effort. After a while he may have sensed that he was involved in a game in which he would never be the winner. I have often wondered, as I did at the time, whether MacArthur wanted direct control of the project but hesitated to ask for it. He waited, instead, until Sutherland tired of the effort and asked to be relieved.

Sutherland was an exceedingly stubborn man, not given to yielding ground, and he persevered, but with increasing discomfort. Finally, in frustration, he asked that be be relieved of the task, on the justifiable grounds that it interfered with matters of greater importance. The General agreed, I suspect with satisfaction. Sutherland complained to me, "Rogers, the communiqué takes too much of my time. No matter how I do it, I can't seem to satisfy the General."

Sutherland's retreat from the task opened the way for Willoughby to have direct contact with MacArthur. At first MacArthur found it necessary to call Willoughby in for clarification of one item or another. An even more direct contact was then devised by Willoughby, who could be seen poised in the door of the G–2 office, waiting for MacArthur to pass by as he arrived for work in the morning. The General, seeing Willoughby, would remark, "Good morning, Charles. Do you have something?" Willoughby always did have something, and could then walk into the General's office, bypassing Sutherland.

As MacArthur turned to Willoughby for direct assistance with the communiqué, he picked up mannerisms that irritated Sutherland. Everyone but Willoughby used anglicized pronunciation for all place names. Willoughby had several elegancies that set him apart. "CommuniKAY" became "commiNEEK." Lae, which everyone else pronounced LAY, was LIE to Willoughby. MacArthur picked up Willoughby's usage.

MacArthur's communiqué was criticized, ridiculed, or lamented by many. Most critics failed to understand that MacArthur did not write the communiqué for the benefit of his troops, the press, or the politicians in Canberra, London, and Washington. He wrote it for the American public, whose opinion could influence political forces in decisions of strategic planning and control.

He wrote his communiqué to focus the attention of the American people on SWPA and its needs. He made himself the single concrete personification of all the forces of his command, of the prisoners of war in the Philippines, and of the Filipino people, presenting himself as the one central reality that objectified the amorphous whole. How much of this was intuitive and how much was contrived is anyone's guess.

To attempt to interpret the communiqué, and all other aspects of MacArthur's activities, in terms of pure, unrestrained ego is a gross simplification and underestimation of the General's complex character and of his intellectual capacity. He thought deeply, and he analyzed the effect of his actions. He seldom did anything without considering its ultimate impact.

The communiqué was a daily chore that taxed ingenuity to the limit. Frequently there was little to say or the events merely repeated what had happened yesterday. Sometimes the facts were not clearly known or could not be completely revealed.

The special releases, on the other hand, constitute the ultimate MacArthur. Written to commemorate a unique event, they sparkle with light and flash with lightning, rolling in grandeur like the magnificent clouds of the Southwest Pacific. MacArthur gave them the care of a sculptor, carefully choosing the words that would provide the proper balance of light and shadow, highlighting the deed that the words would transform into eternal legend.

Working at his desk, with yellow pad and pencil, MacArthur wrote carefully, erasing neatly when changes were to be made, sending the releases to the typist for first typed copy, then correcting, and refining, sometimes through half a dozen or more versions until he was satisfied.

There is in the file a copy of MacArthur's draft of a statement issued in April 1943 on the anniversary of the fall of Bataan. MacArthur handed the draft to Courtney Whitney, who had just arrived from the States, for comment. Whitney's reply is a very good index of his habitual dealings with MacArthur:

This is superb. It has the classical quality of imperishable statements. I predict that, some day, it will be carved in stone, on monuments in the Philippines. I predict a tremendous emotional effect. American history is shot through with the power of such words and slogans "Remember the Alamo." . . . This has the dignity of distinguished literature. I take the liberty of inserting one single word, "again," in the last line.[7]

The statement is quoted in full:

A year ago today, the dimming light of Bataan's forlorn hope fluttered and died. Its prayers by that time, and it prayed as well as fought, were reduced to a simple formula, rendered by hungry men through cracked and parching lips, "Give us this day our daily bread." The light failed. Bataan starved into collapse. Our flag lies crumpled, its proud pinions spat upon in the gutter; the wrecks of what were once our men and women groan and sweat in prison toil; our faithful Filipino wards, sixteen million souls, gasp in the slavery of a conquering soldiery devoid of those ideals of chivalry which have so dignified many armies. I was the leader of that Lost Cause and from the bottom of a seared and stricken heart, I pray that a merciful God may not delay too long their redemption, that the day of salvation be not so far removed that they perish, that it be not again too late.[8]

33

Navy

Underlying many of the most perplexing problems that confronted MacArthur in SWPA was the principle of unity of command. This principle is the basis of the command structure of the military services and any other hierarchical structure. It requires that only one line of authority, responsibility, communication, and command link the various units. A subordinate reports to only one superior; there cannot be overlapping of command authority or responsibility. Communication must not cut across lines of command.

MacArthur was tied directly to George Marshall, from whom he received orders. He could not communicate officially with anyone in Washington except through Marshall. Within MacArthur's command all lines of authority ran down through channels from MacArthur and all communication flowed up and down the same channels. MacArthur could refuse to tolerate the presence in his area of any individual or unit that did not work through the prescribed command/communication channel. Normally he could not communicate directly with other area commanders, nor they with him.

The area commander was restricted to those activities which could be carried out within his own command, the boundaries of which were clearly defined. For command purposes the territory was inviolable. The principle of unity of command forbade overlapping jurisdiction of competing and aggressive officers and services. Only one four-star general or general of the army was permitted to be assigned to any given area, in order to preclude any debate as to priority of rank. All messages coming into the area must be addressed to its commander even when it is expected that he would never see them. All outgoing messages must have his signature although, in reality, most were never seen by him. He was responsible for failure of any component and for success, even though he could very well sleep through it all and contribute nothing except the authority of his physical presence. In practice, commanders could not sleep through it all unless an unprecedented run of success and victory seem to indicate that the results proved the merits of this unlikely method of command.

No commander in the Pacific slept through very much. Their physical and psychological presence permeated their own commands and lapped over the boundaries into other areas. Men who rise to high command do so because they have demonstrated a great capacity for controlled aggressiveness and competitive zeal. They are neither required nor expected to be meek and mild-mannered. Excessive courtesy is likely to raise doubts.

In SWPA, MacArthur was confronted with threats to the integrity of his command from several directions. One overwhelming difficulty arose from the fact that the command had been created by international agreement. The government of Australia was tied by direct lines of obligation to the imperial network that fanned out from London. Australia did not feel deep bonds of affection for England, but habit, tradition, and mutual economic interest had prevailed even after it had become obvious that England could no longer protect the far-flung dominions. England assumed the role of an indigent, despairing parent, demanding filial loyalty from robust offspring in a time of dire need. The Australian government was involved in overlapping and frequently conflicting relationships with MacArthur and imperial councils in Westminster. MacArthur was caught in the web of multiple lines of authority. The principle of unity of command entailed consequences that were never foreseen and created situations that caused some embarrassment.

An English officer, a citizen of Manila before the war, was commissioned and served as liaison between MacArthur and the British during the Corregidor period. With MacArthur's permission he had left Corregidor, had served as liaison for MacArthur with Wavell, and after the collapse of Wavell's command had gone to Washington. MacArthur held him in highest personal and professional esteem, and had assumed that he would occupy a position on MacArthur's staff in Australia, where his specialized knowledge would be of value.

It turned out that the officer was an agent for a British intelligence agency and intended to use his own personal codes to communicate with London and the British army. With obvious regret MacArthur barred him from GHQ on grounds that "one channel would circumvent the Australian's contact with the British government and the other would violate MacArthur's to [Marshall]."[1]

The British wanted to set up a British air force mission in Australia "to help in maintaining for the United Kingdom authorities the prompt supply of information as to operational plans." MacArthur reported to Marshall that it would

violate the normal channel of communication to the Joint Chiefs of Staff and would provide a bypass of information direct to the Prime Minister of the United Kingdom which would not be subject to the knowledge of the Australian Government or the Joint Chiefs of Staff or myself. . . . Our own practice does not permit of a war department representative operating within the headquarters of a command and reporting on the commander, his staff, and his subordinate commanders and his troops through secret channels of communication not known to the commander himself.[2]

MacArthur was on good ground. Even representatives of George Marshall on observation visits to SWPA sent their reports through MacArthur, using his codes. I frequently typed such messages.

During 1942 MacArthur was caught between Canberra, Washington, and the navy about collisions of command authority. Australian ships served with U.S. task forces in the Coral Sea and at Guadalcanal. When Australian ships were sunk, difficulty inevitably arose. MacArthur's position inevitably was that Australian interests were entitled to equal consideration with those of the U.S. Navy:

This is an action in Australian waters involving Australian forces and the very fate of the Australian people and continent and it is manifestly absurd that some technicality of administrative process should attempt to force them to await the pleasure of the United States Navy Department for news of action.[3]

During the Guadalcanal fighting the Australian cruiser *Canberra* was sunk. Curtin complained, justifiably, that

. . . no information with reference to the Solomons action except the official communique of the Navy Department furnished to him for the secret information of his War Cabinet and War Council. He receives corresponding communications always from the British Government. I have informed him that it is beyond the scope of my authority.[4]

The matter dragged on until the survivors of the *Canberra* arrived at Sydney. MacArthur notified Marshall that there could be no further delay and issued his own communiqué to prevent embarrassment to Curtin.

Another source of difficulty in maintaining the integrity of command involved the navy directly. Under ordinary circumstances the army and the navy could avoid direct collisions because the army marched on dry land and the navy sailed on deep ocean waters. Their paths, by the nature of things, hardly crossed. There might be difficulty where land and water met or when armies had to be transported over oceans. In the war with Japan most of the action occurred where land and water met and where large groups of men required naval transport. The customary petty bickering reached Jovian heights as general was pitted against admiral, or admiral against general in a mighty defense of long and bitterly held prerogatives.

The navy's position concerning Pacific strategy was built on the sound premise that such a large body of open water provided an avenue only for large fleets. Masses of ground troops would have no place on its broad expanse except incidentally, as a garrison for the defense of naval bases. No real thought was ever given to the kind of war that actually developed in the archipelagos and islands that were surrounded by the Pacific on its southwestern boundaries or on the continental mass that was lapped by the calmer waters of the South China Sea.

The navy planners saw only great armadas of battleships with clustered satellites of cruisers and destroyers sailing into battle line, the crescendo of countless turrets of great naval rifles spitting out tons of steel and fire. Bases were built for, and would be defended by, naval forces while army garrisons would watch with envy and admiration. In the case of the Philippines the image was marred by the realities of economic stagnation and by the airplane. Japan built ships. England and the United States did not, they even scrapped units. When the critical hour came, no ships were available to defend the bases.

There was the airplane, the potential of which had been foreseen but not actually tested in battle. It added a third dimension to the Euclidean world of traditional strategy and tactics. It flew above land and water with equal facility. The juncture of water and land at the beach, which had served as a comprehensible boundary in the past, suddenly became irrelevant. During the 1930s and early 1940s the debate waged as to which of the two service units should control air units. Unable to come to grips with the implications of Lobachevskian space, Euclidean minds simply tried to extend the water line vertically into the air, arguing that when a plane of the army air force flew on the land side of this invisible vertical boundary, it would be controlled by the army. On the water side the navy should have command.

MacArthur's Allied Naval Forces was commanded by a U.S. admiral who also commanded the U.S. Seventh Fleet. Technically he was commanded by MacArthur, but in reality his promotion and assignments came from the commander in chief, U.S. Navy, which made him understandably sensitive to Admiral Ernest King, holder of that title. He had a community of interest with Admiral Chester Nimitz in Honolulu. Both King and Nimitz frequently forgot that by the rules of the game they must address the commander of the Seventh Fleet through MacArthur. On one occasion they had to be reminded that they could not interfere with MacArthur's air force units. Every violation brought a protest from MacArthur.

The navy, in turn, resented release by MacArthur of information concerning Australian units assigned to areas controlled by King and Nimitz. The navy was equally determined to preserve its own prerogatives. Only two days after the official formation of SWPA, the navy was confronted with the problem of multinational command. Australian ships were attached to U.S. naval forces for tactical missions. Customary practice required that the senior naval officer present in a joint task force exercise command. King and Nimitz suddenly realized that command of U.S. forces conceivably could pass to an Australian officer, and hurried to eliminate such a threat. King notified MacArthur of his objection:

While I accept the general principle that command should be exercised by senior officer present when US and Australian naval forces cooperate tactically this cannot derogate the higher principle that COMINCH and CINCPAC always retain the power to appoint as Task Force Commander any officer under their command regardless of rank. In particular, operations of Pacific Fleet carrier units in SOPAC and SWPAC areas have been predicated on understanding that Commander thereof commands the Combined force when Australian vessels cooperate tactically, regardless of relative rank of officers concerned. In view necessity that officer experienced in carrier operations be in control may I ask that you confirm this understanding with reference to future combined activities.[5]

The particular problem they had in mind was the command of U.S. carriers (the Australians had none) in joint forces. They wanted to be sure that only those officers who had carrier experience would command operations that involved carriers.

One might suspect that the matter of commanding carriers was a convenient argument in support of the "higher principle." The Australians did not have carriers, and therefore no Australian naval officer would be qualified to command a joint task force of significant size.

When Daniel Barbey reported to MacArthur in 1943, MacArthur warned him: "Since you were on Admiral King's staff, I assume you will write to him . . . it is well to remember that echoes of what you say will come back to me."[6] Barbey, otherwise impressed by MacArthur, was affronted by this remark, suspecting that MacArthur feared "that some future historian might find in my letters some improper comment."

Perhaps, but more likely MacArthur was telling Barbey what everyone who came into his area was made to understand: "This is my command. The rule of unity of command is enforced. You will communicate with outsiders only through me." Barbey's right to communicate directly with King was acknowledged. Barbey did not understand that MacArthur had made an unprecedented concession.

Unity of command is an organizational principle. When MacArthur hammered on the anvil, it was because he feared the consequences that would follow from its violation:

I wish to reemphasize the necessity of all ground operations in this area being under my direction. To bring in land forces from other areas with a view to their operation under naval direction exercised from distant points can result in nothing but complete confusion and such a lack of coordination as would probably jeopardize the success of the movement. The very purpose of the establishment of the Southwest Pacific Area was to obtain unity of command.[7]

On occasions during the war the refusal of the joint chiefs of staff to come to grips with the problem posed by the principle of unity of command led close to disaster—almost irrevocable disaster at Leyte Gulf.

Early in June 1942 Nimitz sent a directive to commander, South Pacific Area, directing him to coordinate his operation directly with commander, Seventh Fleet, passing over MacArthur. MacArthur protested that the dispatch should have been addressed to him. Nimitz immediately responded that action had been taken to ensure that future messages would be directed to him. He added a final courtesy:

I am taking steps to insure that it is well understood that despatches pertaining to coordination of your forces are addressed to you. When the task now at hand is completed I shall take pleasure in concerting with you some operations which will curb and eventually drive back our enemy.[8]

Several weeks later, in a long statement to Marshall that outlined MacArthur's plan for an attack on Rabaul, MacArthur complained that Admiral King, Marshall's navy counterpart, had violated proper channels of communication. Marshall replied that the problem was being discussed, and suggested, "Therefore, do not concern yourself with the question of command for the proposed operation at the present time."[9] MacArthur was not deterred. On the day following he radioed Marshall, complaining of another violation of channels. Nimitz had ordered Leary (commander, Seventh Fleet and Allied naval forces) to send Nimitz photographs of enemy positions and an estimate of how much of MacArthur's air force would be available to support the navy's Tulagi operation. MacArthur protested to Marshall, generalizing from a relatively minor incident to warn of a broader and more critical threat:

It is quite evident in reviewing the whole situation that the navy contemplates assuming general command control of all operations in the Pacific theatre, the role of the army being subsidiary and consisting largely of placing its forces at the disposal and under the command of navy or marine officers. By using army troops to garrison the islands of the Pacific under navy command the navy retains marine forces always available giving them inherently an army of their own and serving as the real basis for their plans by virtue of having the most readily available unit for offensive action. This navy plan came under my observation accidentally as far back as ten years ago when I was Chief of Staff and senior member of the Joint Board. The whole plan envisioned the complete absorption of the national defense function by the navy, the army being relegated merely to base training, garrisoning and supply purposes. I cannot tell you how completely destructive this would be to the morale of the army, both air and ground units. It is of course unnecessary to point out the deleterious far reaching effect of such a program. In the instant case and based upon my own experience as Chief of Staff I would anticipate the possibility of unilateral presentation by the navy of their plan in an endeavor to secure presidential approval without your prior knowledge. I shall take no step or action with reference to any components of my command except under your direct orders.[10]

In this message one finds a key to the attitude that may have colored relations between Washington and MacArthur during the entire war. MacArthur's references to "ten years ago when I was Chief of Staff and senior member of the Joint Board" and "my experience as Chief of Staff" raise the problem that baffled Tommy Hart. How does one deal with a former chief of staff? MacArthur was an anachronism and a flaw in an orderly hierarchy. His present assignment placed him under the command of men who had been his subordinates—very minor subordinates. It was impossible for MacArthur to ignore his real status and his experience. It was impossible for them to accept his tutelage. He could not be eliminated, because he was acknowledged to be the most capable commander for the task at hand. He knew too much to be ignored, and he could not be dominated. He could not be cajoled with a friendly drink and a wry anecdote. The dilemma created tension from which there was no reasonable escape. There was truth in MacArthur's statement about navy intentions, and before many months Marshall would have to acknowledge the fact.

One should note King's final message in this exchange. Again, directly addressing the Seventh Fleet commander instead of MacArthur, he directed him to do the following:

Say to General MacArthur that I regret to have given any occasion for his misunderstanding of my intentions in sending to you despatches informative of contemplated operations especially that one which inadvertently omitted specific direction afterward corrected to you to show them to him. Chief of Staff Army.[11]

King was not known for graciousness!

Finally Marshall suggested that MacArthur go directly to the neighboring navy commander with future requests for naval escort units needed by MacArthur in New Guinea. MacArthur asked: "May I infer that I am now authorized to deal directly with Nimitz and Ghormley. . . . Since such direct communication would be an exception . . . I request confirmation."[12]

MacArthur perhaps remembered from his own experience that not all dispatches signed with Marshall's name had necessarily been seen by Marshall, and he addressed his question to Marshall personally. A reply came from Marshall for MacArthur's eyes only: "You are encouraged to communicate with Ghormley and/or Nimitz in effecting mutual support of operations."[13]

Thereafter the barriers between MacArthur and Nimitz began to dissolve. The fundamental dispute, however, persisted until the end of the war.

34

Two Georges

In the middle of February 1942, before MacArthur left Corregidor, Brereton and Brett concurred that the bulk of the air force in Australia should be moved to India. On February 22 a convoy left Australia with 3,000 troops, 37 P–40s, and air force ground troops. All B–17s en route from the United States were ordered to India. Brereton headed the contingent. Like Eisenhower, he had been drawn to a brighter star. Brett could not leave so easily. By the time MacArthur left the Philippines, there was very little of the great force that had been promised him.

On March 21, filled with uncertainty and apprehension, Brett waited at Flinders Street to meet MacArthur. He was aware of MacArthur's feelings about the arrangements he had made for the evacuation. He had been warned that MacArthur was not happy with him. MacArthur's coolness at the first meeting did nothing to reassure him. The coolness, of course, may have reflected only the fact that MacArthur had just completed a journey that covered the seven most uncomfortable and distressing days of his life. He was tired, dispirited, covered with the grime of a long rail trip, anxious to have a hot shower and a rest before he settled into the routine of business. Brett should have understood this much.

Brett had problems that probably were understood by everyone. MacArthur arrived as a senior officer in the area without any formal command status. The fact created great confusion in the Philippines and in Australia as well. Brett was commanding general of U.S. Army Air Forces in Australia and was independent of MacArthur. Their relationship was not clearly defined, and his own future was uncertain. He knew he would no longer be the highest authority, and he could not find any consolation that as eventual commander of Allied air forces he would have a much greater command than the one he now held. Brett had been the second highest officer in the U.S. Army Air Forces before his appointment as Wavell's deputy, and had been the personal representative of George

Marshall in the negotiations that had created MacArthur's new command. It would be difficult to step down to second place.

In the past Brett had been accountable only to himself for the sad performance of his forces. Now he had a taskmaster who was filled with a hot passion to return immediately to his lost command, to avenge defeat. The taskmaster could not be mollified because Brett could not reach him. That is precisely why Sutherland had been appointed MacArthur's chief of staff. He relieved MacArthur of the arduous toil of driving subordinate commanders to do what they were told.

Less than two weeks after MacArthur arrived in Melbourne, he sent Sutherland to Brett to direct him to make a strike over the Philippines. The mission was not designed to produce any significant tactical result but was intended to remind the Filipinos on Bataan that they had not been forgotten. Brett provided the only record of this meeting, and a wise historian would note the fact.

Brett, a lieutenant general, was not prepared to take orders from a major general, an officer without command authority over anyone except his own staff. He bridled at the suggestion, and, with a complete lack of understanding, replied that the Philippines were already lost and a mission would be merely wasted effort. A more sensitive and prudent man would have realized that Sutherland might believe this line of reasoning had been considered earlier, in connection with other lackluster attempts to provide air support in the Philippines. Brett went on to assert that his exhausted pilots and worn-out planes had all they could do "to keep the Japanese out of Port Moresby." He presumed to teach tactics to his commanding officer.

Sutherland spoke for MacArthur and in MacArthur's name. He was not given to open challenges to the source of his authority, and in a voice that tolerated no refusal he tautly stated: "General MacArthur wants the mission accomplished." And so it was. Brett could not expect much sympathy for his plaints about exhausted pilots and worn-out planes. An entire command was perishing on Bataan and Corregidor, fighting in exhaustion to self-destruction.

Brett reports that the confrontation took place in his office. This is a remarkable demonstration of Sutherland's intention to be agreeable and to defer to Brett's feelings. Brett's successor would go to Sutherland. Brett believed that he already had difficulties with MacArthur, which undoubtedly is true, but everything he did thereafter compounded the difficulty. He was not capable of adapting to the new situation and always seemed to drag his feet, to temporize, and even to maneuver in petty intrigue.

Two months earlier Brett had been Wavell's deputy supreme commander in ABDACOM. Now he must face the fact that, at most, he would be MacArthur's air commander. He had already felt the icy indifference of MacArthur. He had two options: He could accept the reality and adapt to the new situation, or he could sulk in petty resistance to protect his own ego. That new situation included Major General Richard Sutherland, who spoke for MacArthur. It was a hard pill to swallow, and Brett gagged on it.

Sutherland was not an outsider where Brett's command was concerned. On the trip out of Mindanao he had added Henry Godman to the GHQ staff. Godman had been a pilot with the 19th Bomb Group and had been decorated for his missions in Java and the Philippines. He became the first GHQ staff pilot. He also was Sutherland's direct contact with the pilots who flew missions. Sutherland obtained a great deal of information through him.

During the first 30 days in Australia, Sutherland made frequent visits to the bomber and fighter commands. He identified colonels in Brett's command who had a reputation for slackness and inefficiency. In spite of George Kenney's blustering about Sutherland's interference in air force affairs, when he replaced Brett and assumed command of Far East Air Forces, he promptly replaced the colonels in question and pushed others as head of the fighter and bomber commands.

In the file there is a copy of an organization chart for Brett's newly created Allied Air Forces. The note that accompanies the file indicates that it was prepared by an Australian woman who served as Brett's secretary. It states that "General Brett furnishes the attached for your information." It is dated 6/4/42 (April 6, 1942), about one week after Brett's first unhappy encounter with Sutherland. Apparently Brett had decided not to have any further direct contact.[1] Future formal communications were handled by Brett's chief of staff, who was Sutherland's counterpart.

MacArthur personally wrote a reprimand to Brett. Two days later Sutherland requested clarification of a report made by one of Brett's subordinates that P–39 and P–40 fighters were not dependable for long-range missions over Lae and Salamaua. One the same day Sutherland sent Brett a summary of B–17 heavy bomber operations during May. Sutherland took the trouble to make the calculations himself. He concluded: "The above tabulations indicate that there is something basically at fault with the equipment, maintenance or operation of this type airplane."[2] On the same day the adjutant general was instructed to request that Brett make prompt recommendations for decorations. Burdette Fitch signed the letter but the initiative was Sutherland's as indicated by the fact that he received a copy for his file.

Late in May the Japanese began to concentrate a large fleet of naval and air forces in Rabaul, in preparation for what turned out to be the Battle of the Coral Sea. This was a direct and obvious threat to New Guinea. Brett had stated to Sutherland in March that he could not order a mission to the Philippines because "his exhausted pilots and worn-out planes had all they could do to keep the Japanese out of Port Moresby." Now it turned out that a mission could not be mounted even for that purpose.

On June 4 Sutherland dictated to me a directive ordering that Brett comply with instructions issued on May 29. The order called for a bomber attack on Rabaul. Sutherland listed the missions that had been carried out on the four preceding days and concluded: "No attack has been made upon the airdrome at

Rabaul . . . It is desired that action be taken without delay to execute that order.''[3] MacArthur was under heavy pressure from Washington to deliver the strike.

On June 5, Sutherland wrote to Brett to acknowledge a dispatch in which Brett complained that U.S. fighters were not suitable for intercepting Japanese bombers. Sutherland cited an air force operations radio which indicated that Japanese bombers had been intercepted and damaged by those fighters.[4] That same day Sutherland received reports from Brett's chief of staff concerning the deficiencies of P–39 and P–40 fighters. There was also a report concerning the failure to attack Rabaul.[5]

Five days later MacArthur entered the affair. He signed a letter, written by Stephen Chamberlin for his signature, that requested the facts of bomber operations in the forward areas of New Guinea. The letter ended with a direct order: ''You are directed to attack that target with all available planes without further delay.''[6]

Finally on June 10, almost two weeks after the original order had been issued, Brett reported to MacArthur that six B–17s had been sent north for an air attack on Rabaul.[7]

The next day MacArthur received a long report on the factors that had made it impossible to comply with the original directive. The report documented in detail ''pilot fatigue'' and ''unserviceable equipment.'' The five pages of explanation ended with a request for modification of MacArthur's original order.[8]

On May 17 Brett was asked for a staff plane, preferably a B–17. One might expect, after the problems encountered with B–17s at the time of the evacuation, that Brett and his staff would give unusual concern to the matter. Almost a month later a follow-up letter was sent over the signature of Fitch. The next day a memorandum was sent by Brett's chief of staff, offering a B–17 or a DC–3 (C–47) transport. Godman reported to Sutherland:

B–17C was shot up very badly in December. I personally counted over 400 holes in the ship . . . has been in the depot for six engine changes . . . The electrical system is makeshift . . . is continually ''OUT.'' Most instruments are faulty . . . radio equipment is unsatisfactory. . . . The ship is considered to be ''lemon'' by *all* pilots.[9]

Sutherland wrote to Brett, repeating Godman's evaluation in more dignified terms. Eventually the DC–3 was chosen as more suitable and flew me north and south many miles.[10]

All of this had reached a level of absurdity. In later days these matters would involve merely a telephone call from Sutherland along the following lines: ''George, what happened to that attack on Rabaul?'' Kenney would have replied: ''Dick, you know what it's like up over Rabaul. But my boys will kick their behinds or I'll know why. I'll call you back.''

The end was near for Brett, and he may have known it. On June 26 MacArthur reported to Marshall on the situation in terms that would be understood by both

Marshall and "Hap" Arnold, Brett's air force superior.[11] There was a prompt reply inquiring whether Brett should be replaced, to which Sutherland immediately replied in the affirmative.[12]

A battle came over the movement of GHQ from Melbourne to Brisbane, which had been ordered for late July. On July 5 MacArthur received a typical Brett reply to an order:

The Director of Communication indicates that he does not consider sufficient communications can be made available . . . he does not consider sufficient trained signal personnel is available . . . a great deal of trouble in finding suitable accommodation for the personnel now on duty.[13]

He concluded that the proposed move would jeopardize the successful completion of operations against Rabaul.

Sutherland replied on July 11:

It is desired that you and the American echelon of your headquarters . . . comply with existing orders with reference to the forward movement of General Headquarters. . . . This confirms the conversation between the Commander Allied Air Forces and the Chief of Staff Southwest Pacific Area on July 10.[14]

I recall smiling when Sutherland dictated the last paragraph. The call had been far more colorful and less diplomatic than the letter.

On July 14 Brett received the letter from MacArthur announcing his replacement by Kenney.[15] The transfer of command was the result of the complete failure of Brett to accommodate to GHQ. He did not have many planes and he had his problems, but the greatest problem was the impression that he was not really trying and that he was obdurately resisting legitimate authority. Headquartered in Melbourne, thousands of miles in distance and thought from the war, Brett refused to budge. Most of us assumed that he was merely reluctant to leave the lovely city with its lovely streets, lovely parks, and lovely ladies. We could sympathize, because we all enjoyed Melbourne's pleasures. When the order came to leave, only Brett resisted.

George Kenney did not present a very imposing figure when he came to MacArthur's office to report and to make his first contact with the Old Man himself. He was a small man whose head tended to roll warily, his eyes seeming to search nervously for some unseen target or some hidden adversary, as if he were still in the cockpit of a World War I fighter patrol over enemy territory. There was no show of bravado; he appeared apprehensive, ill at ease, and nervous.

Kenney's first stop was my office, where he waited until he was escorted across the hall to meet with Sutherland. Sutherland gave him the first taste of the cool superiority he assumed was suitable for this occasion. He intended to set the proper tone for Kenney's encounter with MacArthur, where there would not be much cordiality. There would be no "flowers in May" in this greeting. Kenney must understand that he and his air force were going to have to shape up.

Kenney had known Sutherland since 1933, when they were together at the War College. He saw Sutherland much as others did:

> . . . a brilliant, hard working officer, Sutherland always rubbed people the wrong way. He was egotistic, like most people, but an unfortunate bit of arrogance combined with his egotism made him almost universally disliked. However, he was smart, capable of a lot of work, and from my contacts with him I had found he knew so many of the answers that I could understand why General MacArthur had picked him for chief of staff.[16]

Sutherland immediately began to express his great concern about the unspectacular performance of the bedraggled Allied Air Forces of SWPA. As Sutherland talked, Kenney began to feel the accumulated burden of reproach that should have been heaped on the head of the absent Brett.

The next day Kenney returned to visit MacArthur. He stopped first at my office, then Sutherland's, and was told to go in to see MacArthur. MacArthur picked up where Sutherland had left off and recited the deficiencies of Brett's performance. At the end he spelled out the ultimate defect: " . . . the air personnel had gone beyond just being antagonistic to his headquarters, to the point of disloyalty. He would not stand for disloyalty. He demanded loyalty from me and everyone in the Air Force or he would get rid of them."[17]

Kenney decided it was time to make his case. He acknowledged that performance of the air force had not been good, but "from now on, they would produce results." He assured MacArthur that he had never been disloyal to others and would never be disloyal to MacArthur, nor would his command.

Kenney would remember later:

> The general listened without a change of expression on his face. The eyes, however, had lost the angry look that they had had while he was talking. They had become shrewd, calculating, analyzing, appraising. He walked toward me and put his arm around my shoulder. "George," he said, "I think we are going to get along together all right."[18]

Kenney walked out of MacArthur's office subdued and thoughtful, with no particular sign of anger or frustration, but without any air of exaltation. He had received his orders, and now he must go downstairs to his office and begin to reconstruct MacArthur's air command.

I suspect Kenney's real mission in SWPA was to get along with MacArthur. The General, on his side, was very happy to find an agreeable working relationship with Kenney. The difficulties with Brett made MacArthur anxious to have a better arrangement with Brett's successor. Kenney never found it difficult to get direct access to MacArthur, and he became a constant visitor and companion in the field. His rough qualities were expected in air force pilots and could be overlooked.

After Kenney's arrival the air force began to give evidence of a new era. It was obvious, at last, that a spirit of confidence was sweeping the air command. Kenney received planes and spare parts where Brett did not. Successful missions became the rule rather than the exception.

Kenney never quarreled with MacArthur, and MacArthur never quarreled with Kenney. He did not have to. Sutherland stood between them, dealing with matters where controversies emerged. Sutherland was the one who said "No" to Kenney, leaving to MacArthur the happier role of acquiescence. Kenney achieved a special status with MacArthur because he produced results.

Kenney and Sutherland butted heads, and Kenney was not always the winner. I overheard a heated debate one day in Sutherland's office. I cannot recall the subject, but the outcome is still vivid in my memory. Sutherland, reaching the limit of his patience, and perhaps of logic, told Kenney:

George, you are right. You are an air force commander. I am only MacArthur's chief of staff. I am a staff officer, and I cannot give you an order. But I will tell you exactly what I can do. You are going downstairs. I am going to call in Rogers and dictate my suggestion in the form of an order. When it is typed, I will sign it "Richard K. Sutherland, By Command of General Douglas MacArthur." Then, by God, it will be an order and you damned well will execute it.

That is precisely what happened.

Kenney worked feverishly to eradicate the negative image Brett had left behind him. He learned that "the boys were really bedded down to stay" in Hospitable. Kenney concluded that "the tendency seemed to be to keep everything in the south on account of the probability that the Japanese would soon seize Darwin and land on the east coast of Australia."[19] Everyone seemed to speak of the coming evacuation of New Guinea. Besides MacArthur, only Thomas Blamey "really believed that we would hold New Guinea."[20]

Kenney hurried back to Melbourne to look over the supply headquarters. He spent the night at the house leased by his Melbourne staff: "A beautiful place, full of good-looking furniture, rugs, and paintings. Excellent meals and nice comfortable beds. No wonder the boys didn't like to give it up."[21] Kenney issued orders that the entire installation would move north to Townsville. By the end of August the move was under way.

During the 60 days following Kenney's assumption of command there is only one item of written correspondence between Sutherland and Kenney. A memorandum was sent by Sutherland on August 29 to ask why torpedoes had not been used in an attack on Japanese shipping. Kenney's reply was succinct and direct, without any taint of defensive resentment, a simple note written on the bottom of Sutherland's memo: "Ten torpedoes were at Milne Bay. B–26's tried to get into Fall River twice to load them but they were prevented by weather. By the time they could make it the target was gone. . . . Kenney."[22]

By September, MacArthur had become an uninhibited Kenney fan:

General Kenney, with splendid efficiency, has vitalized the air force and . . . is making remarkable progress. From unsatisfactory, the air force has already progressed to very good and will soon be excellent. In comparatively few weeks I confidently expect it to be superior. Excepting George in Bataan, I have now competent, energetic and effective air force general officers for the first time since my assumption of command in the Philippines.[23]

X

Threat, July–September 1942

GHQ moves north; all commanders under one roof; office routine; roles of MacArthur and Sutherland; Japanese at Rabaul; Japanese into Papua and the Solomons; Corregidor surrenders; Battle of Coral Sea; Battle of Midway; bases at Port Moresby and Milne Bay; plans to occupy Buna; Australians driven back; Guadalcanal and Milne Bay; MacArthur warns of possible defeat; plans for evacuation of New Guinea; Eichelberger arrives

35

Brisbane

It was a lush time in Melbourne, but in spite of that, or more likely because of it, MacArthur decided to move. Stephen Chamberlin had been working since March on plans for the occupation of the east coast of New Guinea, which was scheduled to begin on July 13. Melbourne dissipated martial ardor and suffocated any faint stirrings of the passion for glory, to which I could attest. It was too far from the action that was developing in New Guinea, some 2,000 miles with 2 refueling stops and 15 hours of flying time. Melbourne was not an ideal location for an operational headquarters.

Townsville was a very small city on the upper coast of Queensland above Brisbane. The flight to Port Moresby could be made from there without refueling. It had a tropical climate and few distractions, and would have been ideal except for lack of communications. MacArthur yielded to reality and settled for Brisbane, which was larger than Townsville but much smaller and less metropolitan than Melbourne. The move was ordered and made.

GHQ was divided into two echelons, a practice that was followed in all moves thereafter. On July 20 the headquarters at 401 Collins Street was dismantled. A special train had been assembled to transport the headquarters. A private car awaited MacArthur and his family. Four coaches were assigned to staff and three baggage cars were for equipment. Two flatcars carried the limousines that were assigned to MacArthur and Sutherland. Just before 2:00 P.M. the general, with his aides and family, entered their private car for the long journey to Brisbane.[1]

At Albury the train left Victoria and entered New South Wales. Railroad gauges were not the same, so the train halted at the junction and all the passengers and cargo were unloaded, carried across the tracks, and reloaded on another train that would continue the move to Brisbane.

MacArthur sat in his coach during the process. Other passengers scrambled to the crowded lunch counter for a cup of tea and, perhaps, steak and kidney pie. Two MPs guarded each end of MacArthur's coach. The transfer was finally completed and the stragglers were herded into their new accommodations. MacArthur and his family and aides, flanked by guards, crossed the platform and entered the opposite coach. The journey was resumed as the engine belched smoke and soot, and groaned north into the great Australian expanse.

I had a less dramatic trip. I remained one day longer in Melbourne with Sutherland. Early in the morning of July 21 I drove to the airfield with Willoughby, Marquat, Wilson, Henry Godman, and several other staff officers for the flight to Brisbane. Sutherland's car drove up; he climbed out and began to talk with the other officers. A young civilian woman slipped out of the car and walked quietly and unobtrusively to the plane and boarded, taking a seat in the rear. We arrived in the late afternoon, just before the General's train pulled into the station at Brisbane.

I was driven with the others to Lennon's Hotel, which had been designated as the billet for GHQ staff officers. I was flanked by stars and eagles going in, and had no difficulty. Leaving was another matter. I tried to go out to find something to eat but was stopped at the door by a burly MP who informed me brusquely that the hotel was off limits to enlisted personnel. I threatened to call down a star or two to establish my right to be there. The MP gave way before the show of force. Getting back into the hotel provided the occasion for another show of strength because in my absence the guard had changed. A day or so later I was moved into a barracks.

Brisbane was to be our home for the 24 months between July 1942 and July 1944, when we finally left for the invasion of Leyte. A full half of my military service was spent there.

We had moved away from the land of the lotus eaters and forward to action, or as close as MacArthur could get to it and still maintain the headquarters operations on the scale the war now required. He could stage forward to the very front any time he wanted to. It was a rough compromise between an operational front line headquarters and a base area completely divorced from the war.

GHQ and the base area command were both quartered in Brisbane, but they were two different worlds. GHQ was an operational headquarters. Distance from the war did not diminish the feeling that we were an intimate part of it. The war was the essence of our existence. The base area command was tied in spirit to Brisbane and had a feeling of permanent attachment to the area, or at least it seemed that way to me. Life in Brisbane was an orderly pattern of office routine and not much else. Letters from Melbourne were my only contact with the paradise I had left behind. Books and movies were pretty much my only escape.

Brisbane was a far cry from Corregidor, but it was also a far cry from Melbourne. It was a halfway house between grim despair, on the one hand, and carefree escape from all thought of war, on the other. In Brisbane one knew that the war still continued and felt its pressures, but there were sufficient amenities of city life to soften its impact. The war was only six or eight hours away by air, a sufficient separation to give a comfortable sense of remoteness yet a recognizable proximity that could be bridged without difficulty. One could be catapulted from almost civilian comfort into direct combat with frightening ease.

MacArthur's entire headquarters, except for Thomas Blamey's staff, was concentrated in the AMP building. MacArthur and G–2 were on the eighth floor; other staff sections occupied floors four through seven. It was crowded.

MacArthur's office, and therefore Sutherland's and mine, was in a suite remote from the elevator shaft that ran up the other side of the building. We walked from the elevator down a hall past Willoughby's office, turned right, then to the end of the hall. Sutherland had an office in the corner on the left-hand side. A small connecting room separated Sutherland's office from MacArthur's, which was about three times as large. Before GHQ appropriated the building, MacArthur's office had been occupied by the president of an insurance company. Sutherland's had been used by the president's secretary.

Across the hall a suite of three modest rooms had been the office of the company doctor. The aides took one of the rooms, I took another, and the junior stenographer occupied the third. My office did not have any outside windows, and I always felt shut in.

My office served as a waiting room for all the visitors to Sutherland and MacArthur. On a given day there would be half a dozen general officers or admirals sitting in nervous impatience. I generally was busy transcribing dictation, too busy to be gracious. When I was not typing, I read. I remember Kenney and Willoughby using Jim Larkin as a sounding board for some idea they were rehearsing for presentation to the General.

The office routine followed the pattern that had been established in Melbourne. I arrived at the office daily at 7:30 A.M. to be there when Sutherland arrived at 8:00. MacArthur did not come in until around 10:00, giving the staff time to prepare daily reports. Sutherland regularly went out to fly in the morning and frequently did not arrive until 9:30 but I could not depend on that.

MacArthur remained in the office until 2:00 P.M. or so, then went home for a late lunch and nap. Sutherland had his lunch at the same time but came back an hour later. The General came back about 4:00. Lunch was specially prepared for them. I was not so fortunate. I ate where I could find an open restaurant (they typically closed at 1:30 in Brisbane) or I did without, sometimes sending out for tea and sandwiches.

MacArthur and Sutherland worked late, seldom leaving before 6:00 and frequently as late as 8:30 or 9:00. Again, eating was no problem for them but I found it difficult since restaurants closed at 7:30. Fortunately, I found a Chinese restaurant that was open until midnight. I was in bed around 10:30 and up again at 6:30.

The General's room was about 20 feet wide and 30 feet long. His desk, at the far end of the room, faced the entrance. There was a sofa along the wall to the left of the entrance. The right-hand wall contained windows that looked out on the city. Along that wall was a massive table, the center of which was occupied by a large wooden chest inlaid with designs of exotic woods and filled with a collection of fine Cuban cigars, a gift from an admirer in Havana. A large metal supply cabinet in the anteroom between MacArthur's office and Sutherland's contained a substantial supply of cigars that had been sent as gifts to MacArthur by other faithful admirers. Ranged around the box in an arc was a display of corncob pipes, also gifts, that grew with time into an imposing array. There were other pipes as well. Several armchairs were placed around the office, and a rug covered the hardwood floor.

On top of the desk lay a small array of precisely arranged mementos that included a rusting set of dividers that MacArthur prized very highly. Above the table and the cigar chest was a large poster that contained a folksy poem extolling the virtues of youth. The poem gave solace to the General's awareness that he was no longer a young man. He made too much of the matter, I suspect, and Sutherland, who was reaching the peak of maturity, began to take it seriously— to his own eventual downfall.

Every morning the General walked into the anteroom, put his hat and jacket on the rack, then went to his desk to read the staff reports that waited for him, moving rapidly to the communiqué, which was his great concern. After the work was done, and in the process of doing it, MacArthur paced the floor. When messages from Washington required serious attention, he came to the door and called Sutherland. I could hear him say, "Dick, come in and let's work this out." Sutherland walked through the small hallway into MacArthur's office, where he sat with a pad to record their thoughts. Sutherland interjected such comments or opinions as he felt necessary. In come cases the sessions required several hours.

Sutherland then walked back to his office and buzzed for me; I entered to take dictation, often finding him slumped in deep thought over his notes. They were written in a large hand with spaces between incomplete phrases. Sutherland dictated in snatches, working out phrases and sentences while I waited for the rapid, staccato delivery of the idea. Long dispatches could take six or more preliminary drafts before Sutherland presented the final work to MacArthur. Subsequent changes were made with more or less minor revisions of wording or arrangement until both men were satisfied. Sutherland and MacArthur initialed the dispatch, and I hand-delivered it to the signal office. No draft copies were kept, and no one except MacArthur, Sutherland, and Rogers ever knew how much of the work was MacArthur's and how much Sutherland's; and Rogers was not always sure.

MacArthur did not dictate to stenographers, preferring to write out drafts in neat longhand. He wrote until his material outran the dimensions of the paper. When pressed into a tight corner, he would carry a sentence to the right-hand side of the page, turn the paper, and continue up the edge, the letters becoming progressively smaller. I have seen drafts where the final sentences ran completely around four sides of the paper, the writing shrinking until it was hardly legible.

Yet it was always neatly written with precise penmanship. MacArthur's ideas seemed to form very easily into words. For a simple correction MacArthur would erase and rewrite, as if it were an exercise in penmanship for a demanding teacher.

MacArthur's voice had an emotional quality, as if every statement involved great events and the unrolling of destinies. It was natural and habitual with him, a rasping at the back of his throat and a slight vibrato. Those who met him just once sometimes felt that they were the sole cause or beneficiary of the effect, but they were not.

Sutherland's voice was commanding and even arrogant. I am not sure that he intended the effect of arrogance, but I am fairly certain he would not have changed it. His whole being was commanding. However, he was indeed in command, and perhaps the knowledge of that fact influenced the reaction of people who stood before him. He was not given to asking ordinary souls to sit in his presence, reserving the honor for those of equal rank and stature. Egeberg once growled to me that Sutherland never asked anyone to sit down while he talked to them. Egeberg took this as an affront, and perhaps he was right. As a civilian physician his stature was as high as Sutherland's.

Sutherland was not impressed with previous achievement. We once had a sergeant in the office who had been vice-president of a small company in the States. I commented to Sutherland that the sergeant's past record made some of the rest of us (me, in particular) look foolish. Sutherland said, without smiling, "Rogers, it isn't what you *were* that counts, it's what you *are!*"

MacArthur and Sutherland both were unapproachable, but for different reasons. With MacArthur you always had the feeling that except for his obvious stature and the patina of prestige that covered him, you could smile or tell a joke. You never did, nor did anyone else, because he *was* the General above whom there might be God or President Franklin Roosevelt, neither of whom, being far away, diminished the power of MacArthur's presence. In spite of that, to those around him MacArthur gave evidence that underneath his commanding presence was a gentle affability that saw and recognized individuals, and was responsive to their feelings.

Sutherland was not particularly gentle with the feelings of his staff, but chiefs of staff seldom are, I have been told since the war. On at least three occasions he sent me to deliver what must have been considered reprimands. I did not enjoy the task and was never sure how Sutherland wanted me to handle it. As a result, I simply told the officer involved, "Sir, General Sutherland asked me to tell you . . . " and then repeated the message verbatim. On one occasion Fitch, the adjutant general, then still a colonel, was recipient of the message. He was talking to his assistant. I knocked, interrupted, and delivered the message, which happened to be a sharp one, without ceremony or softening. Fitch put a letter of complaint in my file. On another occasion a general officer outside GHQ called me "sir" when I delivered such a message by telephone.

No one ever had coffee in the office. There were water carafes in MacArthur's and Sutherland's offices, but nothing else. The Australian officers always had tea morning and afternoon. Marshall's and Kenney's secretaries, who were Australian women, made tea or coffee for them. Sutherland and MacArthur did not drink coffee or tea until lunch.

Sutherland's office was smaller than MacArthur's, about 15 feet square. His desk cut an angle across a corner opposite the door. There were two side chairs by his desk. A small table stood in the opposite corner. A metal safe stood in the third corner.

Sutherland read more than 500 documents a day, as shown by a log I kept of items passing over his desk. He dictated two to three or more hours a day. He spent several hours of a typical day serving as coauthor and amanuensis for MacArthur. He generally received GHQ staff officers before they saw Mac-Arthur.

Sutherland's dictation ran the gamut from staccato rapidity to a slow, irregular pace with agonizing waits while he wrestled with a difficult sentence or idea. I was so used to him and his style that, more often than not, I could anticipate sentences as they developed. I took dictation standing. It amused Sutherland, who sometimes boasted to other staff officers that I could take dictation standing at attention better than anyone else could do it sitting at a table. I never objected to the publicity, although I suspect it cost me friends. I did plenty of sitting during the course of the 10- to 12-hour day and was glad for the change of position. Sutherland was demanding of stenographers, according to others who worked for him. Perhaps I satisfied him because he knew I was not afraid of him. After the air raid on Corregidor, I could look him directly in the eye. My courage had equaled his own, and he knew it.

In Brisbane, Sutherland represented the power before the throne, and few got to the throne without seeing him first. He read every dispatch and from his desk controlled all the details of the war. During this period only two staff officers managed to find constant independent direct contact with MacArthur: Willoughby and Kenney.

Sutherland did not always get his way with the staff. He once tried to improve the flow of staff work by drawing up special instructions for presentation of proposals, complete with illustrative examples involving initial statements, objections, rebuttals, and so on, with a prescribed form of presentation. I do not recall seeing any changes in the papers he received from the staff.

We arrived in Brisbane, having left the cold winds of Melbourne some thousand miles to the south, to find warm winds and hot days that persisted even during the depth of the Australian winter in July. We left the Melbourne airport dressed in winter wool and found it comfortable. In Brisbane winter wool was uncomfortable, and we changed to summer uniforms. I could still wear the chino uniforms that Sing Lee had made for me in Intramuros. MacArthur also wore uniforms from Manila days, although he could have had new ones tailored to meet his enhanced status. MacArthur was not given to novelty. The uniforms worn in Manila were one of those familiar continuities from the past into the present, and he was reluctant to give them up.

Approved wear for officers included light woolen uniforms adapted to summer in the United States and to the continual heat of the tropics. Most of the officers in Australia when we arrived wore these tan woolen uniforms as a matter of routine. MacArthur arrived in Melbourne wearing rumpled chinos, with an informal jacket that shielded him against the cool Melbourne winds. He and Sutherland soon shifted to warm winter wool.

I did likewise, although Wilson had to remind the headquarters commandant that I had been in Melbourne six weeks without an issue of appropriate uniform. This was one of the rare situations when Wilson had an opportunity to exercise his rank, and he appeared to enjoy it. I tried to intercede, explaining that I had not asked for uniforms, but Wilson was adamant. The headquarters commandant was required to see to the welfare of his men. He did not know of my efforts in his behalf. He heard only Wilson's hard cold comments. Thereafter, I was a persona non grata in his office.

As soon as Sutherland arrived in Brisbane, he placed an order with a local tailor for half a dozen lightweight uniforms. Some days later they were completed and delivered to his quarters. On the same day, shortly after MacArthur's arrival at the office, the General strolled into Sutherland's office and remarked, "Dick, up here in Brisbane I'm going to wear my Manila summer uniforms. We don't want any of those ice cream suits." Sutherland replied, "Yes, General," and there the matter stood. It would be half a year before he could finally wear one of the new uniforms. By 1943 the matter had been forgotten. After my promotion to warrant officer in late 1942, I had several uniforms tailored; and before my wedding I bought one of the new ice cream suits and was married in it.

Some of MacArthur's winter uniforms were adorned with a mass of ribbons, and others were not. The summer uniforms never had them. MacArthur wore the ribbons when expected guests merited such attention. On ordinary occasions he did not.

Just down the street from the AMP Building a warehouse was converted into a barracks for GHQ personnel. With the usual concession to rank, first-three-graders had rooms shared by two noncoms. I shared mine with a tech sergeant from G–2. It was not a large room and had a bunk on either wall with a small closet. First-three-graders, whatever their quarters gave them in the way of privacy, got none at all in the latrine and showers, where everything was shared pell-mell. No one wore stripes on underwear and so rank was inconsequential. This was generally the case in GHQ, where privates were more rare than brigadier generals. I remember hearing one GHQ soldier, referring to a new officer in headquarters, tell his friend: "Him, he's just a brigadier general."

An enlisted mess was set up in the barracks, much to the distress of all personnel. We had been given a monetary ration allowance in Melbourne, and the new arrangement was seen as a severe restriction of accustomed freedom and luxury. The War Department was the cause of it all. Complaints were made about the very large amounts MacArthur used for such purposes in SWPA compared with other areas. Generally I got to the mess after the regular meal at night. The first night I arrived after nine, I asked the mess sergeant if he could find some food for me. He looked belligerent, hesitated, and said that all he had was some stew cooking on the stove. I remembered Corregidor not so many months in the past, and smiled as I told him it would be fine. He served me mutton stew, heavy bread, butter, milk, and canned peaches. I ate it all with pleasure. The mess sergeant told me, "Gee, a master sergeant eating in my kitchen."

When my own office personnel complained, I was hard-nosed about it, remarking that I knew fellows farther north who would be very glad to have their share. I had learned to accept food for what it was and not to quarrel if I had any at all.

I do not remember much else of the barracks experience, which lasted less than two months. On October 21, almost exactly one year after my first meeting with Sutherland at One Calle Victoria, I was appointed warrant officer (junior grade). I hurried to find uniforms and was moved to a small hotel on Grey Street, across the river from Roma Street Station, where I stayed until 1944.

36

Australia Threatened

Yamamoto had run wild for six months. Manila and Hong Kong fell on Christmas Day, 1941. Rabaul was occupied on January 2, 1942. A month later Singapore fell. Burma collapsed on February 23. Two weeks later the Netherland East Indies fell and Rangoon was occupied. Bataan surrendered on April 9 and Corregidor on May 6. The emperor's domain radiated in a great circle more than 2,000 miles from Tokyo, southwest to Singapore and southeast to Rabaul.

Australia sparkled below this line, a deceptively tempting target. It was only several hundred miles from the nearest Japanese base, on Timor, to the northern tip of the continent. It was much farther, over a great desert wilderness, to the great cities on the southeast coast. The problem was how to get there. There were three routes. One attack could be made out of Singapore on Perth, on the western coast of Australia. Then there would be 2,000 miles of desert to cross. The attackers would be threatened by the British fleet, which was waiting in Ceylon for better days.

An attack could be made out of Timor on Darwin, but again there would be 2,000 miles of desert. Yamashita felt the change of climate might be beneficial to the health of his troops, who were tired of the jungles of Malaya.

A better approach could be made from Rabaul. The Japanese were converting this sleepy lagoon into a great base. A Japanese force could move south out of Rabaul, under its own air cover much of the way, down a long archipelago of islands that led on the west to Australia and on the east to New Zealand.

The U.S. Navy had not yet made a serious attempt to control the waters that lay to the east. A move down this line might tempt it to become involved in a major naval action. The Japanese presumed they would have at least an equal, if not greater, chance of victory. The Japanese fleet then could move eastward into the expanses of the Pacific with some feeling of security and some hope of success. The fleet already was preparing a great action that would move simultaneously south, east, and north. It was destined to find great adventure there.

Map 9
Solomon Sea

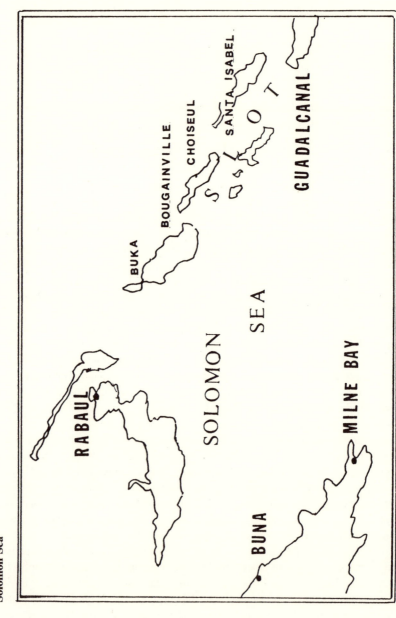

The move out of Rabaul into New Guinea and the Solomons concerned MacArthur because it struck directly toward Australia.

Rabaul had become a mighty naval base. Its harbor was protected on all sides. On its airfields were arrayed bombers and fighters. We believed Zeros were the world's greatest fighter planes. They were proven in air combat not only in Asia but over Britain as well. Allied pilots would not have a solution to them for another six months. The airfields and harbor were ringed with an array of antiaircraft batteries whose gunners fired with a consistent precision that soon became the object of grudging admiration and despair of Allied pilots. They reported regularly that antiaircraft fire had been ''heavy, intense, and accurate.''

The first move against Papua was made in March 1942. At the time I traded my watch for a piece of chocolate, just before the evacuation from Corregidor, a Japanese convoy sailed into the harbors of Lae and Salamaua and unloaded troops. They proceeded to move up the Markham River to Nadzab and its air strip. Crossing the Markham River, the Japanese moved toward the Wau and Bulolo gold mining centers. Trails from Wau led south over the mountains to Port Moresby. As the Japanese moved closer to Wau and Bulolo, the defense by Australian irregulars became increasingly bitter, and the Japanese advance came to a halt. It was soon obvious that an overland move to Port Moresby from this area would prove to be very costly—if it was possible.

The attack on Port Moresby and the Solomons was scheduled for early May. The geography of the islands inevitably led the Japanese to divide their forces in this critical area. One chain of islands, the Solomons, pulled southeast from Rabaul and led temptingly to Fiji and New Caledonia, which led still farther to New Zealand. If the Japanese could gain control of this line of islands, they could cut off all supplies to Australia and eliminate it as a base of operations for the United States. Southwest of Rabaul was Papua, the western section of the island of New Guinea. Port Moresby Bay, on the southern edge of Papua, would provide a base for air and naval control of northeastern Australia.

Thus the Solomon Sea offered both a great opportunity and a great temptation to move simultaneously in two directions, which inevitably would pull the two attacking forces farther and farther apart. The Japanese plan for the capture of Port Moresby fell into this trap. The Japanese could move simultaneously down each side of the wedge and a common covering force could move between them to protect, as events required, either or both flanks. One unit of the force could move southwest around the tip of New Guinea into Port Moresby. Another unit could move southeast down the southern Solomons to Tulagi. The force began to assemble at Rabaul.

Late in April, Nimitz warned MacArthur that intercepted Japanese dispatches indicated a possible attack: ''An enemy offensive in New Guinea-Solomon area is at present indicated for first week of May probably primary objective Moresby. May eventually include 3 or 4 carriers, about 80 heavy bombers and same number of fighters at New Guinea and New Britain air bases.''[1]

Three days later MacArthur warned the forces in New Caledonia:

Map 10
New Guinea Area

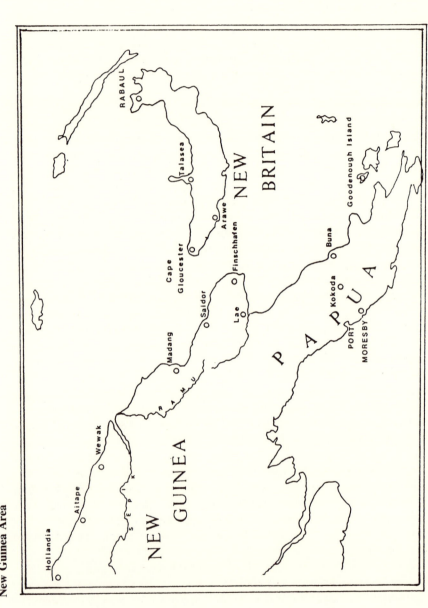

Transports now in vicinity Rabaul more than adequate to carry division. Land based aircraft in New Guinea-New Britain area being reinforced to probable aggregate 150 planes. . . . Estimate most likely objective Port Moresby and possibly Horn Island, York Peninsula, supported by land based aircraft. Time April 29 to May 3rd. Operation covered by heavy raids by carrier aircraft on cities, harbors, airdromes northeast coast Australia south to Brisbane.[2]

In anticipation of the threatened attack on Australia, MacArthur notified George Marshall of the weakness of his naval forces:

The surface element of the naval forces of this area is unbalanced because of the lack of integral air force and in consequence its value as a striking force is practically nullified, reducing it to the execution of subsidiary and minor missions. . . . I therefore urge that every effort be made to provide an air carrier even of the smallest type in order to make possible a more offensive attitude in the southwest Pacific area.[3]

Several days later MacArthur reported that two carriers would be preferable and informed Marshall that Prime Minister Curtin was trying to obtain an additional carrier from the British.[4] He received not carriers but a request for transfer of his own air units to New Caledonia to reinforce that garrison, even though the area lay outside MacArthur's command and in spite of the obvious threat to Australia.[5]

MacArthur responded with assurance that he would give all possible assistance, but added, "It is too late to attempt from here to build up [New Caledonia] air force under the immediate Japanese threat. Greater assistance can be given at this time from units based in Australia." He went on with a warning that the events would prove correct:

The threatened movement of the enemy along the boundary line between the South Pacific Ocean Area and the Southwestern Pacific Area emphasizes vividly the tactical weakness involved in the present boundaries of sectors in that a natural line of enemy advance is not completely encompassed in one area or the other.[6]

At about the same time a letter went to Blamey, advising him of the expected attack and asking whether it would be possible for land forces to take Lae and Salamaua if the Japanese could be driven back.[7] Blamey's reply is not in the file.

As the Battle of Coral Sea ended, and with the surrender of Wainwright in the Philippines, MacArthur again warned Roosevelt of the great strength of the Japanese and requested an increase in forces assigned to SWPA.[8]

The Japanese force, with two carriers and two heavy cruisers, steamed into the Solomon Sea. It encountered planes from the U.S. carriers *Lexington* and *Yorktown*. Neither commander ever saw an enemy ship. Targets were reached by carrier fighters and bombers, often flying at the limits of their range. After three days of action, the Japanese withdrew without rounding the corner of

Papua. They had sunk more ships but had suffered a strategic defeat. They left behind a seaplane base at Tulagi and returned to Rabaul to regroup for another attempt.

Brett's air force did not contribute very much to the combined action. Three B–17s out of Townsville flew over the area, sighted a U.S. destroyer, and dropped their bombs on it. The navy complained to Brett and suggested that a conference be held to develop proper recognition signals. Brett denied the bombing and refused to discuss the matter. I remember an air force operations report coming over my desk out of MacArthur's office. It reported that of seven planes available for a strike, only three reached the target area, where bombs were dropped without effect. Across the upper margin MacArthur noted in a neat, precise hand, "A very poor showing."

Thanks to the navy, Port Moresby was still open for development, and MacArthur moved rapidly to establish a forward base there. It was not a great day for MacArthur. His air force had contributed very little to the action, and Brett showed no determination to change that situation.

Far to the north Wainwright was surrendering Corregidor. "Orange" had come to the final gasp. While the machine guns at Infantry Point on Corregidor were firing against the Japanese assault barges, the guns of U.S. carrier fighters were blazing at the Japanese force in the Coral Sea. The Battling Bastards of Bataan and Corregidor, although they did not know it, had fought long enough to be in action on the day the tide turned.

A week after the battle ended, MacArthur warned Marshall that changes should be made in the kind of aircraft used against Japanese shipping, and that the command structure in the South and Southwest Pacific Areas inherently was weak and would cause grave difficulties:

There is an element of danger in the coordination of operations of this kind in that a task force commander is responsible only for immediate tactical execution but movements of this nature to exercise a successful influence must be oriented with the past and the future with regard to the campaign being carried out in the area affected. Coordination of effort between air and naval forces can be effected without difficulty, but in any case in which land forces are involved the operations must be handled both as to planning and execution by the commander of the area in which the operation takes place.[9]

MacArthur was warned by Marshall on May 14 that the Japanese were concentrating north of Truk in the central Pacific, far from MacArthur's command. Marshall assumed that the attack might move south toward the Solomons.[10] The Japanese, however, had more far-reaching goals, the most important of which were the destruction of the Pacific Fleet and the occupation of Hawaii.

As MacArthur had argued all during the Corregidor period, the Japanese defense in the Pacific was a lightly held line of bases that could be penetrated. The Doolittle strike[11] demonstrated the fact. The Japanese needed a deeper defense that would be able to hold the Pacific Fleet in and behind the Hawaiian

Islands. Such a defense could be had by occupying Midway. A strike at Midway could produce two positive results: a base might be gained, and the Pacific Fleet might be destroyed. Either result alone would be worth the effort. A simultaneous move against Alaska would serve as a diversion from the main effort and might give the Japanese a base there.

Toward the end of May, MacArthur was notified that the target would be Midway Island on the night of June 2. Nimitz's cryptographers had broken the Japanese code and had identified the ultimate objective. A simultaneous attack would be made against Alaska.[12]

A day later Marshall radioed:

Present information on organization, and indicated objectives of Jap concentration in home waters, develop an immediate and serious threat against United States territory, in Alaska, Central Pacific and the West Coast. It is clear that the Japs are endeavoring to maneuver our Pacific Fleet out of position and deliver damaging blows. The future of Australia will hinge on our preliminary deployment to meet this situation and our counter moves.[13]

MacArthur replied with another warning that naval forces must be concentrated in the Pacific:

The fatal weakness of our position is and has been since the beginning of the war lack of sea power in the Pacific. Every disaster in that theatre is due fundamentally to that fact and these disasters will continue and increase until a force is concentrated sufficient to challenge the Japanese navy. It is no longer a question of priorities of fronts or of maintaining the flow of supplies to critical areas. The enemy is concentrating his full power in the Pacific for a definite decision which cannot be avoided. By great good fortune we have become possessed of his plans in sufficient detail to enable us to concentrate to stop him. The Atlantic and the Indian Oceans should temporarily be stripped in order to concentrate a sufficient force for this special occasion to overwhelm him. There is still time for such a concentration on our part which can promptly be returned to present missions as soon as the stroke has been accomplished. If this is not done much more than the fate of Australia will be jeopardized. The United States itself will face a series of such disasters and a crisis of such proportions as she has never faced in the long years of her existence.[14]

In the action on June 4, the Japanese lost the battle and, in a manner of speaking, the war. Yamamoto's six months had run out. His four fast carriers lay shattered at the bottom of the Pacific. Their 250 planes were destroyed. The conventional ships were at the mercy of U.S. planes. Yamamoto ordered a withdrawal. Hounded in pursuit, the remnants of the Japanese fleet suffered more losses. Fifty U.S. carrier pilots had defeated the Japanese. Without carriers, Yamamoto's superior gun power could not be brought to bear against the aircraft of the two surviving U.S. carriers. It may have consoled Brett that at Midway air force bombers operating out of Hawaii were no more effective than his bombers had been at Coral Sea. The navy would continue to gloat over the fact.

Strike South was running out of momentum. Two Japanese attempts to reach Port Moresby had been blocked. Below Wau the Australians were still holding against steady pressure. The failure to take Port Moresby in May had established the difficulty of a naval move around the southeastern tip of Papua. The effort at Midway occupied Japanese attention during June. The third attempt would be made toward the end of July. It was to be an overland attack along the "road" that was marked on the map from Buna to Port Moresby.

The Battle of Coral Sea had demonstrated that the Japanese could be stopped. The fact had been decisively confirmed at Midway. Both MacArthur and Nimitz prepared for a counteroffensive. MacArthur, established in his new command at Melbourne, looked anxiously north more than 1,000 miles to Papua; beyond Papua northeast to Rabaul; and beyond Rabaul northwest to Mindanao.

Port Moresby was the key to it all in early 1942, both for the Japanese and for MacArthur. Whoever controlled Port Moresby controlled the northeast coast of Australia and Papua. Port Moresby was the Japanese gate to the south, and it was MacArthur's gate to Rabaul and to Mindanao. The first task for MacArthur was to fortify Port Moresby and to develop it as an air and supply base. This was Hugh Casey's assignment. During April and May he directed his engineers. Old strips were enlarged and new strips were built to handle bombers, and squadrons of C–47 transports. Supplies and equipment were moved forward.

The tip of New Guinea airstrips would be needed to cover the approaches to Port Moresby. Milne Bay was occupied by Casey's combat engineers and by a force of Australian veterans. The base was developed quickly under very difficult conditions. Over the Owen Stanley Mountains northeast of Port Moresby was a small airstrip on a coconut plantation at Buna. Airfield locations in the Buna area were not easy to find, and this one would have to be occupied. It would defend Port Moresby to the rear, and would give the airforce a forward attack base within range of Lae and Salamaua. Milne Bay and the Buna area must be taken and held if the Japanese were to be kept out of Port Moresby.

Chamberlin's planners worked out a scheme for the occupation and development of Buna, titled "Providence," that was put into effect in July. The 39th Australian Battalion, with a battalion of native constabulary and 600 Papuan bearers, set out to march over the mountains from Port Moresby to Buna. A second force would follow two weeks later. An airfield complex would be constructed, and all seemed to be moving smoothly.

On May 19 MacArthur issued an operations plan titled "Preparation for Counteroffensive" that directed the attention of his commanders not only to the forward area of New Guinea but also to Mindanao, which had been on his mind continuously since the dark days of Malinta Tunnel. He knew that the return would be far in the future. Nevertheless, this operation plan was the first step in that direction.

On May 29 MacArthur repeated to Marshall an exchange of radio messages between Nimitz and himself. Nimitz had available a marine raider battalion and suggested that it be used to reoccupy Tulagi. It was only a seaplane base and not of great importance, but it was a marker, a challenge in this great killing game, and as good an objective as any other.[15]

The navy planners had offered an extremely limited objective to be taken with an extremely limited force. It was a practical approach that looked to the immediate future and immediate prospects. MacArthur shared Nimitz's zeal for aggressive action, but he recognized that one marine battalion could not hold even Tulagi without air, naval, and ground units in support. Such forces were not available to MacArthur. Marshall readily agreed that additional forces would be needed. He left the matter to MacArthur.[16]

The matter rested. Then came the Japanese defeat at Midway. A new situation existed, and MacArthur proposed that it should be exploited. Broader horizons than Tulagi had been opened. MacArthur suggested that plans be laid for the capture of Rabaul. He would begin the offensive immediately if he was given sufficient forces. Marshall told MacArthur: "All decisions, including the extent to which you accede to any further proposal by [Nimitz] rest with you. Please keep me advised."[17]

A week later MacArthur radioed again that the new situation should be exploited. He proposed that the obvious objective should be Rabaul and stated that he would begin an offensive immediately if he was given sufficient force.[18]

Marshall replied that he was attempting to arrange for MacArthur to have the forces he needed. He was considering transferring to MacArthur two marine amphibious teams of 10,000 men, the 37th Division, two or three U.S. carriers, two British carriers, and additional bombers. He added, "Until I have had an opportunity to break ground with the Navy and British please consider all this personally confidential."[19]

MacArthur responded, "I comprehend fully the extreme delicacy of your position and the complex difficulties that face you there. Is there anything I can do to help you?"[20] The former chief of staff had intruded into the present, and Marshall may have winced. He may have felt a slight barb in this inoffensive courtesy. If nothing else, it reminded Marshall of the incongruity of MacArthur's place in affairs.

Two weeks later Marshall's hopes proved to be groundless. The British would agree to use their carriers only in an attack on Timor and only if land-based air support could be provided. The navy was reluctant to commit its forces to possible attack by Japanese land-based planes in MacArthur's area. Tulagi must be occupied first, to give proper air cover for naval units.[21]

MacArthur replied with two arguments. First, the navy had not understood his proposal. Rabaul would be the ultimate, not the immediate, target. MacArthur's attack would involve a series of steps that would precede the final assault. He acknowledged:

It would be manifestly impracticable to attempt the capture of Rabaul by direct assault supported by the limited amount of land based aviation which can be employed from the presently held bases. My plan which is now being worked out in detail contemplates a progressive movement.[22]

This plan eventually was "Cartwheel."

Three days later MacArthur warned that the Japanese were building up forces in Rabaul and were expanding airfields in the Lae-Salamaua area. This might be a prelude to offensive action or merely a consolidation of defensive position. In either case it altered the situation with reference to his own plans. He stated that he would need more planes.[23]

MacArthur continued to press the need for an offensive plan that would encompass an entire flow of events from Tulagi to Rabaul. He warned that occupation of Tulagi alone would create a dangerous salient that could not be held. He argued that the directive not be issued until he had been given an opportunity to defend his views.

Marshall informed MacArthur that his proposal would provide the basis of the directive and that command of the Tulagi phase would be given to the navy, with the remainder passing to MacArthur, who would command all subsequent operations up to and including Rabaul.[24]

MacArthur replied that the command arrangement proposed by the navy was open to serious objection:

The command setup proposed by King is open to the most serious objections. The entire operation in the Solomons-New Guinea-New Britain-New Ireland area should be considered as a whole in which successful accomplishment of the offensive will depend upon complete coordination of the land, sea and air components. A change in command during the course of tactical operations in which it is impossible to predict the enemy's reaction and consequent trend of combat would invite confusion and loss of coordination.[25]

The directive for the new operation, "Cartwheel," was issued on July 3. To make geography fit the navy's insistence that it control the Tulagi operation, the area boundaries were changed to move Tulagi from MacArthur's command to South Pacific Area. Marshall asserted this was the best that could be done.[26]

Marshall further emphasized that the navy had reserved the right to withdraw its units if necessity arose. MacArthur was cautioned that this reservation must not be interpreted as indicating an intention to suspend the operation with the occupation of Tulagi. One suspects that MacArthur was more concerned than reassured by the precautionary remark.

MacArthur had the directive for "Cartwheel." It was less than he asked for but probably as much as he had expected to receive. He could begin to move back toward the Philippines. Three tasks were assigned. Tulagi, Santa Cruz, and adjacent islands were to be occupied. The northern Solomons, Lae, Salamaua, and northwest Papua were to be taken. The Rabaul would be assaulted. Task One was assigned to the navy in the South Pacific with a target date of August 1. Tasks Two and Three were assigned to MacArthur. No target dates were given, but MacArthur began to move immediately.

Map 11
"Cartwheel" Area

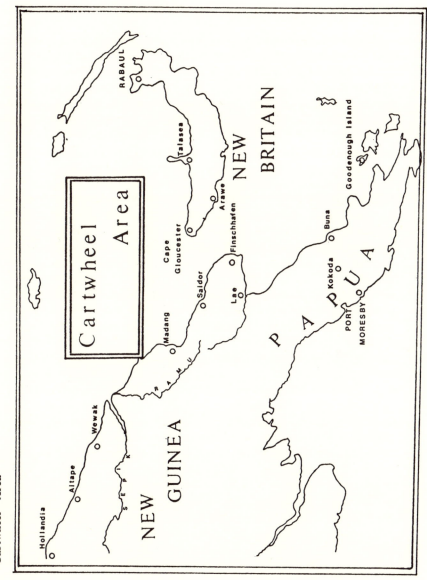

Hollandia

Aitape

Wewak

S E P I K

NEW GUINEA

Madang

R A M U

Saidor

Lae

Finschhafen

Cartwheel Area

Talasea

RABAUL

Arawe

Cape
Gloucester

NEW

BRITAIN

Goodenough Island

Buna

Kokoda

PORT
MORESBY

P A P U A

The navy sent the marines into the Tulagi area on August 7. Guadalcanal, rather than Tulagi, became the center of the action. At first it looked easy, and on August 15 King suggested that on the basis of the successful progress of Task One (Guadalcanal), it should be practicable to mount the operation against Lae and Salamaua immediately. Then came the grinding battles at Guadalcanal and Buna.

"Cartwheel" depended on "Providence" and the airfields at Buna; "Providence" depended on the Australians. Buna was Australian territory, and Thomas Blamey's Australian infantry would have the task of occupying and holding it. Nothing was there except a line of native villages along the coast, a mission station, and a plantation. Everything else was mountain or swamp. Even before the Australians began to march, MacArthur felt apprehensive. He reported his doubts to Marshall.[27]

MacArthur had reason to be apprehensive. On July 21 a Japanese transport with two destroyers and two cruisers delivered fire support for the landing at Buna, but it was hardly needed. There were no defenders. Landing craft moved soldiers from the ships to the beach. The soldiers rapidly found the trails that led up to Kokoda and over the mountains to Port Moresby. There were a battalion of infantry, a company of marines, some artillery, and antiaircraft units with engineers. This was the advance party. On July 22 more transports moved to the beaches at Buna, and troops landed to build airfields and a road to Port Moresby. Patrols moved out over the mountains. Two days later Australians met the Japanese moving up the trail toward Kokoda. "Providence" had been annulled by circumstances, and the battle for Buna had begun.

MacArthur felt a great bitterness that would gnaw at him for two years. Even as victory was in his grasp in 1945, he confided to Roger Egeberg the fact and cause of that bitterness. As "Providence" was set in motion, with shipping in short supply, Richard Marshall had suggested that Australian stevedores be asked to work overtime to accelerate the turnaround time. The stevedore unions adamantly refused to do the additional work, even for pay. Marshall then suggested that U.S. troops be taken out of training, or from any available source, as a substitute labor force. The unions balked at that solution.

MacArthur was asked to go to Curtin for help. He and Curtin had been involved in many problems during the spring and summer. This one seemed to invite a breach between Curtin and his own Labour Party. It would be difficult to arouse in Australians any sense of urgency for the Papuan adventure, which many of them already considered to be a lost cause. An open row in Parliament and the press would leave wounds that could not be healed easily. The matter was dropped.

The movement of troops and cargoes was slowed. The Australian march over the Owen Stanleys was delayed. The Japanese took the only airfield on the east coast of Papua, and six months of fighting were required to conquer it. The long chain of future operations was disjointed. A small delay in the beginning was amplified by an unknown magnitude of delay for the Philippines and Japan.

The battle for Buna had three phases, each of almost exactly 60 days. In the first phase the Australians marched over the mountains to meet the Japanese and were thrown back almost to Port Moresby. In the second, Australians and Americans assembled around Port Moresby and Milne Bay and moved over the mountains to the Buna area. In the final phase the battle for Buna was fought.

On the flanks of this action there were two other battles: at Guadalcanal and at Milne Bay. The Guadalcanal battle equaled the battle for Buna in intensity. Japanese success at either Guadalcanal or Milne Bay would have serious consequences for the battle at Buna.

It was inevitable that the main line of the action in the first two phases of the battle for Buna followed the Kokoda trail and other trail systems over precipitous ridges to the summit of the Owen Stanleys and down again to the coast. These trails were the only line of communication available. No airfield was available on the eastern coast, and there were very few sites for the construction of airfields. Until sites could be located and airfields constructed, cargo aircraft could not be used for movement of troops and supplies.

The possibility of sea communications was limited by reefs scattered through the area. Japanese aircraft controlled the skies. The navy was reluctant to commit ships even as small as destroyers because of exposure to hostile aircraft. During the early days of the battle, Japanese aircraft found holes in Kenney's fighter cover and destroyed several small convoys. It was felt that without naval support there could be no movement of shipping except for very small coastal craft.

For the moment any movement across the island had to be made on foot. Not even pack animals could survive the ordeal. It was a rigorous test of human endurance but not an insuperable one. Papuans regularly walked the trails carrying loads heavier than the 70 pounds considered a maximum tolerance for soldiers on the march. One 60-year-old Australian missionary priest regularly walked even the most precipitous sections. Nevertheless, it was an extremely difficult trail.

It was some 100 air miles from Port Moresby to Buna and, as any backpacker knows, that would be made at least three to five times longer by elevation changes and meandering of the trail along contours and around obstacles, as well as by switchbacks needed to smooth out steep grades. To the topographical hazards must be added extreme heat at lower levels and relative cold at higher altitudes. Heavy rain produced mud on the trail and humidity in the air. With heat and humidity came insects, leeches, and other torments.

The trail rises from sea level at Port Moresby to more than 7,000 feet at the summit, then drops to sea level at Buna. It crosses a succession of ridges that rise unevenly to the jagged summit. Over rocks and tree roots, along narrow ledges, up muddy banks, the trail presented one obstacle after another. Nevertheless, it could be walked, was walked, and would be fought over because there was nothing else to do.

None of the commanders chose the trail as the preferable route to a strategically necessary objective. They used it because it was the only route available. They

Map 12
Buna Trails

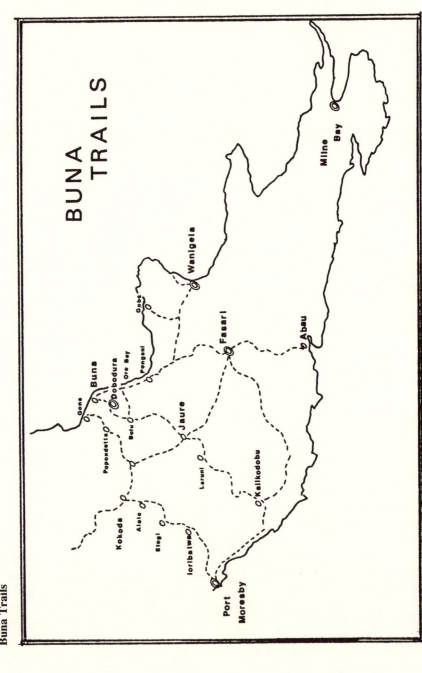

had been ordered to fight, and fight they must. This is the work of a soldier. There are no pleasant places for battle although some are better than others. This place was about as bad as a battlefield could be. This is where the armies met and this is where the battle for Buna would be fought. The Australians would cover the trail three times and the Japanese twice before the battle ended.

The advance patrol of the 39th Battalion at Awala waited all day on July 23 for reinforcements from the battalion base at Kokoda. The reinforcements came in late in the afternoon, just as the first Japanese patrol moved into rifle range. When the Australians opened fire, the Japanese fanned out on either side of the road and brought machine guns and mortars into action. They had seen this kind of fight before.

The Australians pulled back up the trail to the Kumusi River at Wairopi, where a cable bridge provided the only crossing. The Australians retreated across the river and destroyed the bridge. The Japanese advance was delayed for the night. The next day they pressed forward. For a week the Australians withdrew through Oivi and Kokoda to Deniki, where a stand was made.

By August 4 a telephone line had been laid to establish a connection with Port Moresby, and a drop site for air supply had been found at Myola. Kenney's transport aircraft out of Port Moresby moved supplies quickly to the forward area along the trail. For five days the 39th Battalion fought to hold the Japanese at Deniki but were finally forced to withdraw to Isurava, near the summit of the Kokoda Trail. A second detachment of Japanese landed in the Buna area. Some 8,000 troops with 3,000 naval construction personnel and 450 marines were now ashore, prepared for action. The entire area from Buna to Kokoda was in Japanese hands.

During the period August 13–21 the Australian 7th Division, a tough fighting infantry division that had been moved back to Australia from the Middle East, arrived in Papua. Two brigades were at Port Moresby and one at Milne Bay. The 21st Brigade immediately moved up the trail to reinforce the 39th Battalion troops at Isurava. By August 28, in spite of the arrival of 7th Division veterans, the Australians were pushed back past Ioribaiwa. On September 13 the 21st Brigade was relieved by the 25th and 16th Brigades, which were ordered to hold at Ioribaiwa at all costs. The Japanese were within 20 miles of their objective. They remained there for a week.

During this critical period with the first phase of the battle for Buna hanging in the balance, Sutherland came to Port Moresby to determine the facts of the situation, and I came with him. The plane landed at Seven-Mile Strip, and a bevy of officers awaited Sutherland.

As I left the plane, Henry Godman pointed to a jeep and I climbed in. The driver took off in a cloud of dust. I do not know precisely where I was. It was a camp provided for bomber crews who spent the night there on trips between Australia and targets in forward areas.

I found the orderly tent and made myself known. I was the only tenant in the camp and had my choice of cots. I put my bag on one of them and was set up

for my stay. I wandered around the camp, looking for something to do or someone
to talk with. Outside the cook tent three or four soldiers sat peeling potatoes. I
stood for a minute, then picked up a knife, sat down on an empty box, and
began to peel potatoes with the others. There was a startled silence until the
mess sergeant said apologetically, "Master sergeants don't have to peel potatoes." I replied that I had done worse in my military career, remembering the
urinals at Fort Des Moines, and that master sergeants also ate. That opened the
conversation, and during my stay I was treated as a friend.

Two days later, while I was sitting at the mess table, a crew came in headed
by a colonel, who sat down with his men to a plate of mutton stew. After the
customary remarks about the food, which led me to recall the opulent days at
Fort Santiago in Manila, the colonel remarked in a loud voice that he had to fly
some "goddamned general" to Australia the next morning. I walked over to his
table to say that I had arrived with a general and wondered if he was the same
person. I then asked if I could ride down to the strip with his crew. The next
morning we rode off together. No one said anything to me but watched me with
suspicion. At the strip Godman and Sutherland waited at the side of the plane.
As I walked up, Godman turned to Sutherland to say, "I told you he is a big
boy and can take care of himself." I am not sure Godman was necessarily right.

I regret to say I did not know much about the details of the situation. All I
knew then was that the Japanese were said to be 20 miles up the trail.

37

Down "The Slot"

The first task of "Cartwheel" was to occupy Tulagi and adjacent islands. As matters turned out, the battle came not on Tulagi but on one of the adjacent islands, and it is remembered as the battle for Guadalcanal. It was a great navy show, and "MacArthur's Navy," the Seventh Fleet, was transferred temporarily from his command to the South Pacific to strengthen the Guadalcanal effort.

There it had to stay, even with its Australian components, until the U.S. Navy released it. During the months that followed, the foolishness of this divided command nearly led to disaster in both areas, as MacArthur had warned. The transfer had been made on the interesting assumption that the Japanese would apportion their own effort to satisfy the provisions of the U.S. directive.

The naval task force assembled for Guadalcanal included a battleship, 3 carriers, 10 cruisers, numerous destroyers, and 21 transports. It was a sizable force, but before the battle ended it would not seem enough. This force covered the First Marine Division, which stormed ashore, established an airfield, then defended it against all comers.

The landing was not too difficult, but the defense of the position captured was another matter. The bulk of the marine division went ashore on Guadalcanal, easily dispersed the relatively few Japanese defenders, occupied the half-finished airfield, and settled down for their first night ashore. It was more difficult at Tulagi, but in 24 hours that island had been secured. The navy reported that "results so far achieved make every officer and man in the South Pacific proud of the task forces." It is well that the commendation contained the qualification "so far."

It soon became obvious that the Japanese intended to make the Americans fight. Their first move had been into Buna and across the Owen Stanleys. Whether they had intended it or not, the Japanese had blocked one important element of the Guadalcanal offensive. Air support from SWPA would be reduced for lack of an advanced airfield on the north coast of New Guinea. The Japanese move into the Buna area would hold MacArthur's attention for four months while his troops were locked in battle to drive the Japanese back into the sea. The Japanese fleet could look south from Rabaul with the relatively comfortable feeling that the U.S. Air Force, which had not caused them appreciable difficulty before, would be even less able to interfere, in the immediate future, with the move into the Solomons.

On August 9 the Japanese came down the line of the Solomon Islands like wolves, to drive out the marines. One convoy left Rabaul. Five Japanese heavy cruisers moved to rendezvous near Rabaul with three light cruisers, then sailed south down "The Slot" to inflict upon the Americans one of the worst defeats in their naval history.

The Japanese suffered very little damage. The U.S. force that opposed them was virtually demolished. The *Canberra*, *Astoria*, Quincy, and *Vincennes* were sunk after midnight of August 9. Had the Japanese pressed hard, when morning light came, they might have caught U.S. transports that were hurriedly unloading supplies for the troops ashore, a task not finished until the middle of the afternoon. It was perhaps a case of overconfidence, surprise, and lack of ability to meet a night attack, to which a naval historian adds luck, that unpredictable catalyst of battle. There would be five more naval engagements over the next five months: one more in August, two in October, one in November, and the last in January, when the long battle finally ended.

The marines ashore stood on the defensive, fighting bravely and stubbornly, holding their airfield against repeated attack, never in such dire straits as the Japanese cornered at Buna but never free from danger. They suffered bombs day and night, naval bombardment at night, field artillery bombardment at any time, rain, mosquitoes, heat, attack by Japanese day and night. Perhaps it is impossible to say that it was "better" or "worse" than for U.S. troops at Buna. Whether standing in defense or moving in attack, if the process is prolonged, the battle becomes an unimaginable hell.

On August 24 the Japanese fleet, led by Yamamoto himself in the great *Yamato*, stormed down from the north with three carriers, three battleships, five cruisers, and eight destroyers (plus four cruisers and five destroyers that joined later). On the U.S. side were a battleship, 3 carriers, 7 cruisers, and 17 destroyers. The big guns were the *North Carolina* and the carriers *Wasp*, *Enterprise*, and *Saratoga*. The purpose of all this naval might was, on one side, to land 1,500 Japanese soldiers on Guadalcanal, and, on the other, to prevent the landing. To that extent the Americans won the battle. No Japanese got ashore. The Japanese recognized that it would be difficult to reoccupy Guadalcanal.

By this time MacArthur and King had joined their voices in an attempt to attract the attention of Washington to an impending crisis in the Pacific. Sutherland and Kenney flew to Noumea to meet with Arnold and Nimitz. But in Washington all eyes were on North Africa. Nothing would be available for the Pacific.

The battle at Guadalcanal dragged on, neither side able to eliminate the other, in a bruising, bloody brawl. There were skirmishes at sea and the *Wasp* was lost. Nothing much had changed by October 10, when the Japanese moved into battle to prevent U.S. reinforcements from going ashore. The U.S. transports were covered by four cruisers and five destroyers. The Japanese met them with three cruisers and two destroyers shielding one transport with Japanese reinforcements. Two U.S. carriers stayed clear of the action. The Japanese were caught in the classical "T," and as they moved into the turning point, they were shattered by massed fire. Hard hit, they pulled away, pursued by U.S. ships that met heavy Japanese fire. Almost all ships involved on both sides took many hits and were damaged. The Japanese reinforcements were put ashore.

The Japanese had the last voice in this affair. On October 14 two Japanese battleships moved down "The Slot" during the night to give the U.S. Marines a taste of more than 900 rounds of 14-inch naval gunfire. The two ships withdrew after an hour and a half. They had destroyed half the planes on the airfield and killed 42 men. The attack continued for three more nights. On the morning of October 15 three Japanese transports, protected by fighters and destroyers, unloaded reinforcements before they were finally destroyed.

Nimitz radioed a message of despair: "It now appears that we are unable to control the sea in the Guadalcanal area. Thus our supply of the positions will only be done at night at great expense to us. The situation is not hopeless, but is certainly critical."[1]

Admiral William Halsey assumed command of the U.S. Navy forces three days later. He added his voice to those of King and MacArthur against the irrationality of risking forces already in combat for the benefit of future operations in Europe. The joint chiefs of staff deadlocked, Marshall argued steadfastly for no diversion of forces from Europe. Roosevelt broke the deadlock in favor of the Pacific.

The Japanese tried another attack on the airfield late in October, in support of the troops they had put ashore two weeks earlier. They could not budge the marines.

The Japanese fleet again assembled with Yamamoto on *Yamato* and other battleships, cruisers, and destroyers. The sailed out to meet Halsey's carriers, cruisers, and destroyers. The encounter, at Santa Cruz Island, was a deadlock. The Japanese had a tactical victory but were not able to exploit it. Nimitz's evaluation of the situation rose from "certainly critical" to "not unfavorable."

Mid November brought another collision of the giants. Again it was a deadlock, but the Japanese did not attempt to move down "The Slot" again.

U.S. reinforcements for the marines at Henderson Field and more planes were moved in. Patrols pushed out to find and destroy the Japanese. It would take ten more weeks to bring the action to an end, and there would be one more small naval battle. Finally, on February 9, 1943, the battle came to an end when the Japanese evacuated the island for good.

For three months the battle had raged. As in New Guinea, matters were suspended in the balance, causing Nimitz in Honolulu and MacArthur in Port

Moresby agonizing uncertainty as to whether either area could be held. The Japanese did not win in either case, although with a little more luck they might have had one or the other, or even both, of the battles. In the short run they blocked MacArthur's air out of Guadalcanal and Nimitz's navy out of the Buna action, and ground troops suffered for it in both battles. Had MacArthur's medium and heavy bombers been free to strike with undivided attention at the approaches to the Solomons, South Pacific forces would have had an easier time. On the other hand, if Nimitz could have provided just two or three destroyers to cover an amphibious landing at Buna, the campaign there would have ended in two weeks.

Milne Bay lies on the very tail of New Guinea. Like Buna, it was an assortment of huts, plantation groves, small piers, and a mission church, all connected by mud trails, with a small airstrip. In the prewar period it had been an infrequent port of call for tiny coastal steamers. When Casey began to develop Port Moresby as an air and supply base, he moved into Milne Bay for the same purpose. By the end of July three airstrips were under construction. During the first week in August the 18th Brigade of the 7th Australian Division moved into the area. U.S. engineers and antiaircraft troops built and defended the airfields there.

On August 26, the day the Japanese fleet moved down "The Slot" for the second great battle at Guadalcanal, a Japanese convoy sailed from Rabaul toward New Guinea. Early in the morning two transports left Kavieng and a force of seven landing craft followed, both moving southwest. The landing craft were seen near Buna, and P–40s left Milne Bay to intercept them. They strafed the barges to destruction. The survivors washed up on surrounding beaches.

The transports were sighted long before they approached the final destination, but they had better luck. Orders went out from GHQ to all aircraft in the area to find and destroy the Japanese task force. An array of B–17s, B–25s, B–26s, and P–40s lined up on the airfields in northeastern Australia, Port Moresby, and Milne Bay. They were to rendezvous that afternoon to join in a simultaneous attack. Then rain came and visibility dropped to zero. The planes from Australia could not find the target. The planes from Port Moresby and Milne Bay could not get off the ground. At ten that night the Japanese force slipped into Milne Bay, moved safely to the beaches, unloaded troops and supplies, and slipped away.

Once ashore, the troops moved easily up the trail against 7th Division troops. In two days the Australians had been driven back to the airstrip, where they were joined by U.S. engineer and antiaircraft units in a final defensive position. Fortunately, the rains that made it so easy for the Japanese to get ashore made it virtually impossible for them to move against the airfield. The bulldozers had cleared the area around the strip, and the rain had converted it into a mass of deep mud. Japanese tanks ground into it and came to a halt.

In less than three days, some 2,000 Japanese soldiers had slipped safely under the entire Allied air force, into the target area, and had driven 9,000 Australian infantrymen back to a defensive position. The Japanese were still attacking, and there was some danger that the entire complex of airfields would fall into their hands.

Sutherland wrote to Blamey in his own name, asking that the Australian commander be instructed to clear the area at once and to submit to GHQ a report of action taken with an estimate of Japanese strength there.[2] On the same day MacArthur sent a dispatch to George Marshall warning of a probable Japanese move against New Guinea (in addition to the one already in progress). He reported what Marshall already knew:

Due to the absence of all SWPA naval forces which are operating under the South Pacific Area . . . the enemy completely controls the sea approaches to New Guinea and when adverse weather hampers our air activity he is able to move transports directly into Milne Bay. If strong infiltration continues or if a major movement eventuates my situation will immediately become critical unless I am afforded Naval support.[3]

On August 30 MacArthur reported on the Milne Bay situation. More than 8,600 Australian infantry, supported by 1,300 U.S. construction service troops, were commanded by two Australian generals who had experience with their troops in the Middle East and were reputed to be the best-qualified men available. The Japanese strength was "very much less" than that of the Australian defenders.[4]

MacArthur began to have misgivings about a clouded future. He had seen the training reports on his U.S. divisions that indicated they still had not reached satisfactory levels of achievement. He had seen the Australians in action. When asked whether the Australians alone could drive the Japanese out of New Guinea, he replied shortly, "No. They won't fight."[5] His view of the U.S. divisions was similarly clouded.

On August 29 a second Japanese convoy succeeded in putting about 800 more troops ashore. The combined force attacked the Australian defenses all night long. The attack was repulsed with heavy losses, and the Japanese began to pull back. The Australians pursued them. During the night of September 4, 1,300 Japanese were taken aboard transports and evacuated to Rabaul. In a rebuttal to a final report made by the Australian commander covering the action at Milne Bay, MacArthur remarked: "Actually, only a fraction of our forces were engaged at any one time and an operation which should have been concluded with great promptness was allowed to drag along over a very considerable period of time."[6] This was a foretaste of events to come.

References have been made to the "optimism" of MacArthur. Casual comments made in idle moments to intimate friends hardly outweigh considered judgments. There were very few times in 1941–1942 when MacArthur's messages to Marshall reflected rosy optimism about the realities that confronted him.

In early September the Japanese were brought to a halt 20 miles above Port Moresby, on the last ridge that looked down to the sea. Milne Bay had been cleared of the Japanese. In New Guinea, at least for the moment, the situation seemed secure. The affair at Guadalcanal had not yet reached a climax. Two great battles had been fought at sea, and the marines still held Henderson Field, but the Japanese fleet had more blows to deliver. Japanese reinforcements were shipped into Guadalcanal almost as easily as they had moved into Milne Bay. It was hardly over in the South Pacific. No one had anticipated what might happen if Yamamoto turned his major force against New Guinea, and no one knew how it could be met or what it might achieve.

MacArthur, who had frequently expressed his reservations to Marshall, began to assemble forces to drive the Japanese over the Owen Stanley Mountains. He had no reason to expect extraordinary results from the two major forces that were available to him. The air forces had never been able to deliver consistently even a fraction of their potential force against the enemy in any given action. The perpetual naysayer Brett had not demonstrated ability or luck to any considerable degree. He had been replaced by Kenney, but in those days Kenney was far more subdued than he would be two months later. He had seen Brett's air force, which was now his, and was not sure that he could find the answers.

The land forces, Australia's best, had been driven back from Buna by an inferior Japanese force. At Milne Bay, outnumbered four to one, the Japanese had come ashore, maintained an attack for two weeks, and withdrawn as easily as they had come. There might be greater hope for the U.S. contribution to the show, but the 32nd Division had not been tested. It was an unknown quantity and did not give any evidence of ability to surpass Australia's best.

Moreover, Blamey was still bickering with GHQ over control of air force units. He wanted to exercise control of a kind that had been abandoned long ago by all U.S. Army commanders, MacArthur included. Difficulties had developed in the staff of the amphibious training program, and senior officers had been relieved. There were no landing craft nor transports. Amphibious assaults did not seem an immediate possibility.

There was a short exchange between MacArthur and Blamey over control of Japanese prisoners of war. MacArthur acknowledged Blamey's inquiry and then disposed of it peremptorily: "The number of prisoners of war from projected operations in this theatre in the near future is estimated to be so small that no additional accommodation need be provided at present."[7] MacArthur understood the situation correctly. At the end of 1944 only some 400 Japanese were held in POW camps. Their reluctance to surrender was matched by the reluctance of Allied soldiers to permit them to do so.

On August 30 MacArthur radioed Marshall, warning of impending difficulties as the Japanese moved their forces against the Southwest Pacific. He noted, perhaps with intended irony, that "holding areas must have sufficient force actually to hold." He warned that changing conditions required a change of action. He requested a review of the situation by the president, "lest it become too late."

I comprehend entirely the strategy that has been outlined, assigning present missions as holding ones to enable concentrations to be made elsewhere. It is fundamental however that holding areas must have sufficient forces actually to hold and that the strength of holding forces, with the initiative in the enemy's hands, can be determined only by a constantly changing accurate appraisal of the enemy's power. An arbitrary predetermined figure of strength will not ensure safety. Unless the strategic situation is constantly reviewed in the light of enemy current potentialities in the Pacific and unless moves are made to meet changing conditions, a disastrous outcome is bound to result within a short time. I beg of you most earnestly to have this momentous question reviewed by the President and the Chiefs of Staff lest it become too late.[8]

Marshall replied that everyone in Washington had indeed reviewed the matter, and assured MacArthur, "The defense of the Pacific areas particularly in air and naval matters will depend to a large degree upon the closeness of the cooperation and coordination of the forces now available to you, Nimitz and Ghormly."[9]

On September 6 MacArthur urged an immediate attack to clear the Japanese from the north coast of New Guinea:

In view of changed situation urge that attack to clear the north coast of New Guinea be undertaken as soon as possible. The plan outlined in my previous dispatches is no longer applicable. If defensive attitude only is maintained the situation will soon become serious. The enemy attack has developed and is now revealed as infiltration from the north in ever increasing pressure. Adverse weather and other conditions make it impossible to prevent his landing with great freedom on the north shore. The jungle trails are such that he can seep through to the south in volume. The Australian troops have proven themselves unable to match the enemy in jungle fighting. Aggressive leadership is lacking. The enemy's defeat at Milne Bay must not be accepted as a measure of relative fighting capacity of the troops involved. The decisive factor was the complete surprise obtained over him by our preliminary concentration of superior forces.[10]

MacArthur asked for an increase in naval forces to permit an amphibious landing to support the projected overland offensive:

Due to lack of maritime resources I am unable to increase ground forces in New Guinea as I cannot maintain them. I have temporary air superiority there. It is imperative that shipping and naval forces for escort duty be increased to insure communication between Australian mainland and south coast of New Guinea. If New Guinea goes the results will be disastrous. This is urgent.[11]

Marshall's reply was a cool suggestion that MacArthur seek aid from the South Pacific.[12] He would get no more aid from Washington. With South Pacific forces holding on by their teeth in Guadalcanal, he would get no more from that area.

On September 10 MacArthur was informed that simultaneous attacks would be launched by the Japanese against Guadalcanal and New Guinea. He replied with a question: "If the enemy launches a sea, air and land attack at New Guinea what assistance may I expect from the Pacific Fleet?"[13] Marshall suggested a joint conference of commanders to "serve as a means to reach a common understanding of each other's problems and future plans."[14]

Late in September, MacArthur renewed his request for naval support and landing craft. None were available, but Marshall assured him that some would be shipped from the United States in October, November, and December.

In mid October the Japanese fleet made another thrust down "The Slot" to Guadalcanal. Now it was Marshall's turn to plead for MacArthur's support:

Japs have outranged our artillery on Guadalcanal, keeping airfield under constant bombardment from land and occasional heavy bombardment from ships. Their naval superiority is preventing reinforcement and resupply, especially gasoline. Situation therefore most critical.

It is evident that supporting action of some sort must be taken immediately and at the moment we can only see possibility of increased frequency of bomber activity from New Guinea directed against naval task forces referred to. This apparently can only be managed by accepting the hazard of basing heavy bomber group at Moresby and operating medium bombardment from Milne Bay to maximum possible extent. Can this be managed and how quickly.

I suppose the foregoing proposal would mean some weakening, of air support of your ground operations in New Guinea. However the situation in the Solomons is so critical that such action seems imperative. Since the Japanese have committed themselves to the maximum effort in the Solomons can anything be done to expedite your operation to seize the airfields on the northeast Guinea coast?[15]

MacArthur noted in reply that he had been aware of the critical situation in the Solomons, had anticipated it, and had warned Marshall and King as early as July. He summarized the actions that had been taken by his air force over Guadalcanal and outlined the progress of forces in New Guinea. He closed with a warning:

I invited attention to the acute danger developing and begged review of the question by the President and Chiefs of Staff lest it become too late. . . . The situation anticipated then has now developed. It is now necessary to prepare action that must be accomplished beforehand in preparation for possible disaster in the Solomons. If we are defeated in the Solomons, as we must [be] unless the navy accepts successfully the challenge of the enemy surface fleet, the entire Southwest Pacific will be in the gravest danger. Information has already been derived from enemy sources that an attack on Milne Bay and possibly elsewhere in New Guinea is contemplated for mid November. I urge that the entire resources of the United States be diverted temporarily to meet the critical situation; that shipping be made available from any source; that one corps be dispatched immediately; that all available heavy bombers be ferried here at once; that urgent action be taken to increase the air strength at least to the full complement allotted for this area; that immediate action be taken to prepare bases for naval operations on the east coast of Australia; that the British Eastern Fleet be moved to the west coast of Australia.[16]

MacArthur ordered Chamberlin to draw up a plan for a possible evacuation of all Allied forces from New Guinea if a Japanese attack should make such a move necessary. Fortunately, events in Guadalcanal improved.

In the midst of all this uncertainty a corps commander arrived for the two U.S. divisions. MacArthur's first choice for the post declined the honor because he did not want to serve under an Australian command. As usual, MacArthur was given two additional names. He left the choice to Marshall, expressing a willingness to have either man.

General Robert L. Eichelberger finally arrived in Australia on August 25. He was met at the airport only by Major Morhouse, MacArthur's aide. A week later he visited GHQ to report to MacArthur. Finally, two days later, his new command, I Corps, came to official life.

Eichelberger had to walk a wary path between two vigilant commanders. His immediate superior was Blamey, but Eichelberger knew very well where to find his real boss. He had been instructed never to become closely involved with the Australians. He did not quite understand why, although in GHQ there was sufficient evidence to support MacArthur's counsel to stand clear of involvement. The real test would come in the Buna campaign.

XI

Buna, September–December 1942

Japanese fall back to Buna; Eichelberger over the mountains; troops airlifted; advance GHQ at Port Moresby; Kenney flies to glory; Bloody Buna; Navy refuses support; Eichelberger in command; Sutherland sent to Buna to relieve Eichelberger; I will relieve Sutherland; victory

38

Marshaling Forces

The objective was the Buna area, 100 miles over the mountains. The only airfield in the area was held by the Japanese. No landing craft were available for an amphibious assault. The navy refused to let destroyers escort small freighters to the beaches at Buna. Two supply bases were available, one at Port Moresby and the other at Milne Bay. There was hardly enough transport to supply the forces currently in New Guinea and certainly not enough to supply more. MacArthur faced three problems: How could two divisions be moved to the target area? How could they be supplied? Would the troops be able to drive out the Japanese? There did not seem to be an answer to any of the problems. MacArthur was not optimistic. The enemy was on the final ridge overlooking Port Moresby. Bad weather hid Japanese convoys from air attack, and reinforcements were being landed at Buna as easily as at Guadalcanal.[1]

There was no stopping in midstream to await better times. The Japanese were moving with unabated aggressiveness, showing no sign of diminished force, with a willingness to hammer with their entire strength at this corner of their new domain. They had to be met. A collapse of Allied efforts in either New Guinea or Guadalcanal in September would bring down the entire fabric in the South and Southwest Pacific Areas. MacArthur proposed an immediate advance in New Guinea. The issue must be brought to a head quickly. The test must be made.

One part of the assembly of force was relatively easy. One brigade of the 7th Australian Division was fighting the Japanese up the track from Port Moresby. The remaining brigades could be sent up the trail to drive the Japanese before them back to Kokoda, then Wairopi, and finally the last approaches to Buna.

The turn of battle coincided with the need. The Japanese at Ioribaiwa Ridge had come to their last reserve of energy and were no longer able to hold. They did not require even a push. The command at Rabaul ordered a withdrawal to the Buna beaches, where the Japanese could fight under more favorable conditions.

On September 20 the 7th Division charged forward and found the Japanese position empty and silent. There was fighting during the withdrawal but only delaying skirmishes, not bloody battles. One month after the Australians had moved out, MacArthur radioed Blamey: "Press General Allen's advance. His extremely light casualties indicate no serious effort yet made to displace the enemy. It is essential that Kokoda airfield be taken."[2]

Two days later MacArthur spelled out for Blamey the seriousness of the situation in a long letter. The basic argument was that Japanese control of the sea-lanes might permit them, with only a few small torpedo boats, to cut Blamey's supply lines. The Japanese seemed able to bring in reinforcements wherever they chose, so Allied forces must be prepared to withdraw at any time. They would have only supplies that could be carried on their backs or the backs of Papuan carriers, or that could be moved by air. The advance must be planned to permit a withdrawal, and supplies should be assembled at key points. Kokoda must be taken.

MacArthur's admonition notwithstanding, the Australians did not take Kokoda airstrip until the first few days in November. Finally, six weeks after they had walked through Ioribaiwa, they controlled the Kokoda Trail and could move into the final assembly area.

Shortly after the Australians began their drive, the 126th and 128th Regiments of the U.S. 32d Infantry Division were moved to New Guinea, the 126th by sea and the 128th by air.[3] The problem was then to move across the mountains to Buna. The Kokoda Trail could not accommodate the movement of these regiments in addition to the Australian brigades.

Eichelberger was asked to make a recommendation. He and his staff studied the topographic maps and accepted what nature and long years of Papuan walking offered. The 32nd Division would move forward in two columns. The right column would walk from Abau to Jaure. Eichelberger concluded that the Abau Trail would be the easier one: "I anticipate no great difficulties in this matter except the inertia of those who will sit and wait for the Japanese to drive them into the water at Port Moresby." He asked that Americans be kept under nominal control of Blamey because "He may enter into the spirit of supply for American troops more wholeheartedly than if American troops entirely divorced from his command."[4] MacArthur sent an engineer team to reconnoiter the Abau Trail, hoping that it could be developed as a jeep road. No fighting was expected along either of the two trails.

Private Sam Brown, Company E, 126th Infantry, stepped down from the army cargo plane, sweating in the tropical heat at Jackson strip, where a convoy of trucks stood ready to move him and his company forward to Kapa Kapa. Already his skin burned as perspiration soaked his uniform. It had been tan two days ago, but now was a mottled, dirty green. Brown's skin was showing signs of irritation from the dye. Brown did not know, nor did anyone care very much, that the dye was poison and was already being absorbed into his system. It seemed a minor problem. Considering the various probabilities in the events that lay ahead, the poison might be a relatively minor peril. He soon would face more imminent ones.

Brown picked up his rifle and pack and climbed into the truck, which jolted down the gravel road, past three B–17s that had just been loaded with bombs for a strike against the Japanese base at Buna. A flight of P–40s was just coming into the field after a strafing run at the Japanese positions only a few miles up the road on the Kokoda Trail, where the Australians were fighting a heavy defensive action.

Company E had been selected to explore and build a trail from Kapa Kapa, a native village on the beach, to Kailkadobu (which Company E promptly renamed Kalamazoo), to be ready for the arrival of the 2nd Battalion of the 126th Infantry. This force would make a reconnaissance over the mountain to Jaure, which would be used as a staging area for advance on Buna.

Two weeks later a rough jeep trail had been hacked out with the help of Papuans up toward the village of Nepeana. Advance elements of the 126th began their march, cheered and jeered on by the men of Company E, who had been in Papua long enough to consider themselves hardened veterans, especially since they were not worried about having to make the march themselves. The village of Jaure was more than 75 map miles over the mountains at more than 7,000 feet elevation. Between Kalamazoo and Jaure stood the imposing ridge of the Owen Stanley Mountains at more than 9,000 feet.

The 126th Infantry set out with 100 Papuan carriers to reconnoiter the trail. The Papuans were uneasy because the trail led up to Laruni and Ghost Mountain, which held imprecisely defined but very real terror for them. Several days out on the trail, as the party set up camp for the night, 35 haggard Australians struggled down the trail into the campsite. They had been forced off the Kokoda Trail on August 30 when the Japanese had occupied Alolo. They had traveled cross country up the Kumusi River to Jaure and over Ghost Mountain. The Papuans were frightened and ran away, leaving their burdens to the Americans.

The soldiers shouldered as much of the load as they could carry, left the remainder, and labored up the trail. It rained continuously in torrents. Brown struggled up the muddy track, over tree roots and rocks, up steep embankments, through muddy creeks, wet to the skin. The pack ground down on his shoulders, which ached constantly. The rifle, which he did not dare discard, caught in trees and bushes. Too heavy to use as a walking stick, too large to pack away, and too essential to discard, it became a cursed impediment in a struggle against a hostile trail. After five miles the trail was no longer a track but a venomous, hostile force, alive with seemingly conscious malevolence, yielding reluctant passage, exerting continuous pressure.

Company E had been working for two weeks on the track. They were in better shape than the second detachment that had marched behind them into the tropical rain and heat without much preparation. The troops would not have admitted it, but the training exercises they had undergone in Australia had hardened them. The trail would harden them more. Up steep grades, down into deep defiles, up over slippery rocks, the trail impeded them and met them with a steady resistance.

One mile an hour was the most that could be ground out, and on many days the count would be made in hours per mile when the going became an imperceptible crawl, when each step would be painfully counted out, "one, two, three, four, . . . five, six, seven, eight, nine, . . . ten," with a pause when a man would lean on his rifle to find enough breath to repeat the process for another ten paces.

At 3,000 feet the air became cooler, and so did the rain, but the grades became even steeper, and the march became a crawl—literally a crawl on hands and knees, dragging pack and rifle, grasping at roots and rocks to find leverage, pulling up by sheer force, too breathless and exhausted to curse in defiance.

The rest stops brought no relief and little rest. Fires could not be built in the wet. The food, an unaccustomed diet of crackers and corned beef, became an unpalatable curse. The Australians regularly ate it and fought on it. Exhaustion and fatigue would have caused the digestive process to rebel at any kind of food, even the best. The water, fouled by mud and jungle debris, bred dysentery. The dysentery brought more exhaustion and nausea, and compounded the problems. Then came mosquitoes, and with mosquitoes came malaria. And there were leeches in the night and on the trail.

Finally, at 5,000 feet they reached the village of Laruni. A detachment was counted off to stop there to prepare a site where supplies could be dropped from cargo planes. The rest climbed on up the ridge, past 7,000 feet, one step at a time, gasping for breath and groaning with each step as the tortures became exquisitely cruel and punishing. The grade, still climbing over ridges and then down into precipitous gullies, began to show a noticeable leveling off. Finally, it became apparent that the steep slope down began to run ahead of the uphill climbs. At each turn the height began to rise behind the men, whose ankles and lower legs began to carry the weight against the pull of gravity, causing as much or more agony than the strain on back and upper legs of pushing up slope.

By this time most of the men had suffered the indignities of diarrhea. Trousers became a stinking, fouled mass of mud and ordure that could not be cleaned but only endured. In desperation some used bayonets to cut out the seats of the trousers. It was a sensible solution to the overbearing pressure of an aggrieved nature.

Then, at last, on October 20, Jaure: a nothing spot, a collection of thatched huts, but almost halfway. With Jaure came the knowledge that the worst of the trail had been overcome. Now it was downhill to the kunai grass slopes and finally to the beach. No one realized that in three weeks they would look back to the trail as just an unpleasant memory and would wish they had stayed on the hostile slopes.

Fortunately, the soldiers of the 126th Infantry did not know, as they labored over the long trails, that while they were working so hard to advance, plans were being prepared for a possible retreat. By mid October the navy was in great distress at Guadalcanal. It seemed very likely that Nimitz would have to give up the battle. The Japanese could then move their entire strength against New Guinea. MacArthur fretted that his two divisions could be isolated on the eastern slope of the Owen Stanleys by the Japanese and then cut to pieces.

Early in September, while Eichelberger was marching his battalion over the trail to Jaure, George Kenney was trying to persuade MacArthur to let him fly troops over the mountains. He had found a flat spot at Wanigela and another at Dobodura. The Wanigela strip could be occupied easily. There were no Japanese in that area. Troops flown to Wanigela could move on to Dobodura and hack out a strip there. A thousand men could be flown over every day, saving 30 days of walking.

MacArthur listened eagerly to Kenney and encouraged him. It seemed to Kenney that MacArthur had no doubts that the operation was a feasible one. On September 13 the GHQ staff discussed the proposal. They were doubtful, but MacArthur gave Kenney permission to fly one company from Australia to Port Moresby. Two days later MacArthur went over the heads of Sutherland and the staff and permitted Kenney to fly an entire regiment north.

Kenney saw the staff as "stumbling blocks" who did not share MacArthur's "vision and intelligence."[5] However, his enthusiasm glossed over very real problems. It was very difficult to move the troops over the mountains to Buna, and if events went badly, it would be impossible to get them back. Sutherland reminded Kenney that if the situation in New Guinea crumbled, as it well could, MacArthur would be recalled and relieved in disgrace. Kenney's reaction was that all would go well "if we kept moving."

Sutherland and the staff were infantry soldiers who looked not only to the trail ahead but also to the one behind. They knew that battles can be lost as easily as they can be won. Nothing had happened during 1942 to make them particularly optimistic about the air force. They did not doubt that Kenney could move the infantry forward by air. But could he supply them and, if things went sour, could he evacuate them? Nothing the air force had done in 1942 gave reason to believe Kenney could do either.

While all this was going on, a site was found for an airstrip on the northern side of the mountains at Fasari, high on the slope of a clearing. Tools were dropped at the site, and native workers cleared a primitive strip. The task was completed by October 19. The remainder of the 126th Regiment was then flown to this strip and walked down the slopes to Dobodura.

When the Japanese were forced out of Milne Bay, they left behind several damaged barges. The barges were repaired and put into service to supply the forward area. Three airfields were put into operation at Milne Bay. The small fleet of trawlers chugged up the coast to the Buna area at Pongani, delivering troops and supplies. Various combinations of airlift, sealift, and walking put the 32nd Division into position before Buna.

By the middle of November, the Australians had pulled down from Kokoda, the Americans had assembled before Buna, and all forces were firmly set on three parallel trails leading into the Buna area.

It was a difficult time for Eichelberger, who for reasons not known to him, was shunted to one side. He tried to fit himself into the approaching battle. He wanted his staff members to be in the 32nd Division staff, to give them much-needed combat experience. Sutherland abruptly upset that arrangement, and Eichelberger fretted. For the moment he was to sit on the sidelines and watch the show.

Eichelberger approached MacArthur separately about moving his own head-quarters to New Guinea. MacArthur seemed favorable but suggested that Ei-chelberger talk with Sutherland. Eichelberger saw Sutherland next day to report what he had heard from MacArthur. Sutherland simply cut him off, remarking that the matter of moving I Corps to New Guinea "was off." Eichelberger felt that he was being treated like a lieutenant by Sutherland.

A month later Eichelberger finally got permission from MacArthur and Suth-erland to visit New Guinea. For reasons that were never explained to him, he was ordered by Sutherland to return immediately. Sutherland insisted that Ei-chelberger leave at four the next morning on the scheduled courier plane. Ei-chelberger complained, "I have never been in such a storm nor have I ridden in a more dilapidated plane." The plane was not permitted to drop Eichelberger at Rockhampton, where his headquarters was located, but took him on to Bris-bane. He was forced to find his own way home. Eichelberger told his wife, "A fly may not know when its wings are being pulled off but I did."[6]

It is likely that Sutherland's motives were clear to himself and the GHQ staff. The command structure in New Guinea was very complex. Blamey was touchy about interference in "his" command. The commander of the 32nd Division was responsible to Blamey and the Australian New Guinea Force. He was also responsible to GHQ and wrote letters directly to Sutherland concerning his activities. Little would be gained by injecting Eichelberger's I Corps into this already crowded picture. Moreover, as commanding general, Harding was en-titled to run the 32nd Division without Eichelberger's direct involvement and to have his chance at glory. Finally, if Harding failed, Eichelberger would have to relieve and replace him. It would be easier if Eichelberger was not too involved in the show. Eichelberger did not understand this, and hated Sutherland for what he thought were intentional slights to his dignity.

MacArthur moved to his advance base at Port Moresby on November 6 and enjoyed it in splendid isolation for five days. Then Sutherland arrived with a very small staff to transact business. Port Moresby languished in tropical heat, far from the well-defined, crisply changing seasons of temperate zones. There were two seasons: hot and dry and hot and wet. Hot and dry left a parched gold landscape around Port Moresby. Hot and wet laid green over gold. It was always hot, relatively humid, and uncomfortable, inducing a drowsy laziness that dulled all activity.

Government House sat on a knob on the eastern side of Moresby Bay. I looked directly from my office across the bay into the setting sun. Government House was a ramshackle frame structure of three rectangular units forming a "U." A roof was thrown over the open square and each of the rectangular structures. A veranda, roofed also, surrounded two sides and the front. The open square provided a living and dining area. The two side rectangles were divided into several bedrooms. A special flush toilet and basin were installed at the rear of the veranda; the ancient privies that had served governors-general were relegated to the use of all ranks below MacArthur and Sutherland. A kitchen was loosely attached to the rear of the building. Huge tropical vines and bushes clustered around and festooned over the building. Blazes of red and fuchsia flowers filled the air with fragrance. Palm trees and bushes surrounded the building.

The bay spread wide and blue at the foot of the hill. The beach was hidden by trees, but we could see native huts that stood on pilings above the water. They were deserted because the Papuans had been moved farther inland, away from Japanese air attacks. The men had been called into service as bearers. Directly in front of Government House, far out in the water, an island blocked the entrance to the bay.

A gravel road led from Government House down to a flagpole and then down to the beach. The flagpole was probably some 50 feet high. From it flew the Union Jack which was raised and lowered daily by a squad of Papuan constabulary. Uniformed in khaki kilts with military belts and bandoliers, they were barefoot. Their hair rivaled the shakos of the guards at Buckingham Palace in splendor.

They marched sharply and precisely to their posts. The bugler sounded colors. A detail performed the ritual of raising or lowering the flag. The squad then faced into columns of two and marched away. One day the halyard became tangled in the pulleys. After several unsuccessful attempts to jerk the rope loose, the bugler stood his bugle on the ground, shinnied up the pole, pulled loose the knot, shinnied down, and sounded colors without missing a note.

The native houseboys assigned to GHQ wore special uniforms. White kilts, bordered with red and marked with a blue star set them apart from all others. These civilians, in addition to their colorful uniforms, wore red hibiscus behind their ears, rolls of paper in earlobes or nose, elaborately carved wooden combs, and little else.

They worked, by their standards, at a frightful pace. To mow the lawn, half a dozen men shared a single small bar of iron, sharpened on one side. This mini sickle was used to cut the grass one blade at a time. One man whacked casually away until he became bored, then passed the bar to another. All the others sat on the ground to encourage the single worker and to gossip. It was forced labor with a pittance of a wage, just sufficient to buy tobacco and other luxuries.

The furnishings of the residence were those left by the former tenant. The only additions were desks for MacArthur and Sutherland, the former not used very much and the latter used all day and much of the night. The living room held a table to seat perhaps a dozen persons, several comfortable lounge chairs, and a sofa or two. My desk and that of the junior stenographer were located in a corner of the veranda. It was a cosy arrangement that permitted us to hear a great deal of the conversation and to see what went on. Less obvious to us was the fact that everything we did and said could be seen and heard by MacArthur, Sutherland, and other inhabitants.

By the time I reached the office at 7:30, all of the general officers had break-fasted. The beds were made by their respective orderlies. Filipino soldiers served as housekeeping personnel and cooks. I was at my post until bedtime, and I frequently saw a collection of general officers in pajamas gossiping in the common room before retiring.

Only important visitors used MacArthur's toilet. Other officers used a common latrine behind the cluster of buildings. Various slit latrines were available to ordinary soldiers. I would not have considered using the General's facility, but I did use the other officers' latrine.

The governor-general had left his library, a collection characteristic of a nineteenth-century gentleman, for my sole use, or so it seemed. Books were my delight and passion. Now I had full access to Greek and Latin classics in parallel editions, and proceeded to devour as many as I could. For treats, I had all of Shaw's works. I left books on my desk as I read them. One day while I was away, MacArthur came by and picked up a book of Greek poetry. He asked the other stenographer, "Is Rogers reading this?" The steno answered affirmatively, with the qualification that I read only the English. The General smiled and walked away. One day as I rummaged through the volumes in Government House, Willoughby came by and stopped for a minute to gossip. Looking at the titles with obvious admiration and respect, he said, "Imagine a cultivated, educated gentleman with these tastes wasting away in this wilderness." Willoughby and I had much in common. We might have been better friends were it not for my assignment to Sutherland.

Willoughby later recalled in his memoirs not only the library but also the bougainvillea and the frangipani that cascaded over the house and down over the roof, blazing in the sunlight and filling the night air with fragrance. I remember the sunsets at Port Moresby more than anything else. Every evening I watched from Government House as the sun slipped behind the hills across the bay. At first the clouds turned pink, then red, finally breaking into ribbons of blue, green, purple, red, yellow, orange, in a blaze of brilliance, silhouetting the palm fronds black against the sky. Once Sutherland told me with a soft smile that they could not compare with sunsets in Manila, where they were more brilliant every day of the year.

MacArthur had arrived hoping for a short, quick victory. The field commanders all were sure that it would be over soon. On the day of our arrival MacArthur remarked to Sutherland, "Well, Dick, I won't get a haircut until this is all over and we're back home." I have heard that Mrs. MacArthur cut the General's hair, although I cannot confirm the fact. As it turned out in this case, the services of an army barber would be required. One week after our arrival the offensive against Buna began.

George Kenney, who in August had replaced Brett as a commander of Allied air forces, made his mark at Buna. After preliminary skirmishing with Sutherland to mark the precise boundaries of their respective territories, his place was established and he proceeded to promote himself as intimate companion of MacArthur. I am inclined to say that he served the role of jester, for he made MacArthur laugh and smile. MacArthur smiled often enough, but generally at his own motivation. Kenney dared to be irreverent around the Old Man, and MacArthur enjoyed it. Nevertheless, Kenney was much more than a court jester.

Kenney was an exuberant, uninhibited man, physically small, who gave the appearance of having just climbed out of the cockpit of a World War I SPAD. He spoke with lighthearted disregard of the otherwise restrained dignity of GHQ, brashly exulting to MacArthur of the exploits of his boys. He was rough, unpolished, and very shrewd. Although he seemed to rush blindly into GHQ, bursting with the enthusiasm of a young fighter pilot fresh from a victorious mission, speaking irreverently of both trivial and urgent matters, in reality he was as wary as the proverbial cat on a hot tin roof. I do not know of a time when he lost his step. When backed into a corner he blustered and joked; backed down with obvious anger when forced to; and bounced back with good-hearted glee as his temperature cooled. It was a fine ploy, whether naïve or studied, and it no doubt helped to relieve MacArthur's tension, to soften his anger, but very seldom to moderate his enthusiasm. Around MacArthur, Kenney strutted the part of the fighting airman, hell-bent in hot pursuit of an enemy, flushed with heat of battle.

When the shortage of artillery was a serious deficiency in battle, Kenney set his boys to work to find a remedy. Bouncing into GHQ, he related the progress of the project, saying that his boys down on the field had "that goddamn 105" spread out all over the ground, trying to figure out how to make it fit into an airplane for delivery over the mountains. "By God, I think they'll get the job done." Or "That bastard has worked out a way to mount a 75 in the nose of a B–25 and actually has fired the goddamned thing. It almost tore the plane to pieces but, by God, it will work." Or "My boys will show those Japs over there. We don't need artillery. My boys will blast them out of their damned bunkers and we'll burn them alive."

Chided because "his boys" had just dropped a string of bombs into a U.S. regimental command post and then strafed it as well, red with embarrassment and chagrin, he said, "Well, goddamn it, *you* try flying in over those damned trees at 200 miles an hour. You can't see the damned ground, much less the troops. We can't get it right every time. But, by God, you'd rather have us over there, even with a few misses, than not to have us at all." Everyone had to agree to that.

Or "Those Limeys have figured out a way to drop a bomb at low altitude. The damned thing skips into the side of a ship. My boys are working on it, and in a week or so we'll try it, as soon as we can find a goddamn Nip ship."

MacArthur smiled, for this was what he liked to hear: a fighting general talking about fighting. He could forgive the levity and the language if the message promised a fight.

Like many others, Kenney had his days with Sutherland. He did not always win. He found it useful after the war to set up Sutherland as the bête noire of GHQ and to assert that Sutherland was the wrong man for MacArthur's personality. But at Buna and later he and Sutherland were congenial. Each served MacArthur in his own way. Two Kenneys would have been unbearable. Kenney could not have served in Sutherland's position; the day-to-day detail would soon have dissolved his good humor. He was a combat airman, a fighter, an inspirer of action, and, most of all, a supersalesman for his arm of the service.

Thanksgiving and Christmas came and went. If there was any special arrangement in the way of food and merriment, I do not recall it. I am sure there was no merriment—there never was. Some small attempt might be made to demonstrate that the mess officer, if no one else in GHQ, remembered that these major holidays called for some special observance, if only a token one.

A small radio was set up for the annual Army-Navy game. Reception was not particularly good, but the chief staff officers assembled for the kickoff. For a while they followed the game with perfunctory signs of approval or disapproval. The crackle and sputter of static and interference soon dulled their already diluted enthusiasm, and before the end of the first half they had all wandered away. It was just another day of official business, no different from the others. And with troops pinned down in battle 100 miles over the mountains, official routine was probably more appropriate than anything else would have been.

Food in advanced GHQ mess was the same ration available to troops in the base area—dehydrated, canned, heavily weighted toward mutton and Spam— but served with a modicum of decorum. I always ate with the middle level of field officers, who ranged from major through colonel. I cannot recall why, except that the mess was close to the office and I had unusually well-placed connections. MacArthur had a mess that served him, Sutherland, the other general staff officers, and the aides.

At Port Moresby everything was on an intimate scale. Only a few officers were present, and there was an air of great informality and freedom from military protocol. The work routine, however, did not deviate from the pattern that was followed day in and day out, every day in the year, in rear echelon or at advanced echelon.

The battle at Buna was outside the boundaries of my existence. Like Bataan, it was "an other" world that daily dispatches forced upon my attention. I do not recall feeling a certain uneasiness as I sat in quiet comfort on the veranda of Government House with a splendid library and, when MacArthur and Sutherland were busy out of sight, a bamboo chaise longue to add to the luxury of my existence.

I did what good soldiers always do: take the battle when it comes your way. If you are not called to the action, enjoy your good fortune, for you may be called to tomorrow's battle. I had served my turn, and it was the duty of someone else to serve this one. Moreover, since so many experienced generals were keeping this battle on its prescribed course of action, I did not feel particularly inclined to inject myself into the process. But I was there, and if Sutherland had ordered me into the fight, I would have gone without complaint.

The overlapping of operations and plans was obvious even at Buna. While MacArthur was urging Eichelberger to hasten the capture of Buna because time was running against the Allies, he was urging Blamey to hasten the return of the 9th Division from the Middle East because it would be needed in the Lae-Salamaua operation that was scheduled for September 1943.

About this time the stenos were drawn into a debate over the situation at the front. The junior stenographer had decided, with more enthusiasm then discretion, considering his position and his proximity to the commander in chief, that MacArthur had been wrong in ordering the assault in the first place, and he openly said so. I did not want to argue about it because I felt that young stenographers might easily fall into error in a matter that was being studied and decided by so much experience and rank.

Pushed about the matter, I defended MacArthur, repeating the arguments I had heard him use on one occasion or another, adding that I considered him to be a very great man. I do not recall that we minced words, and I'm sure we did not lower our voices. Consequently our conversations were overheard and served as grist for the General's mess for several days.

A few days later MacArthur's orderly came by to see me. "Rogers," he said, "the General thinks very highly of you. They talk about you a lot while they're eating. He thinks you'll be a college president some day." I was happy for the information and proud of the General's esteem, but I had my own priorities. I wanted to rise even higher—I preferred to be a professor.

I picked up a pair of gloves to wear while flying. I walked onto the veranda, pulling them on my hands, in full pride of possession. MacArthur came out of his bedroom and asked, "Rogers, what have you got there?" I showed him. He took one glove, pulled it on his hand, looked at it admiringly, removed it, and said, "Go get me a pair just like these," which I did. I still have the glove, bronzed by my mother, who had it in her possession for many years.

39

The Battle

By the middle of November the troops had moved down to Dobodura, where they camped in the rain and the mud. Those who had thrown away nonessential items on the trail now had cause to repent their action. Without shelter halves and ponchos they slept unprotected in the open rain, still suffering from malaria and dysentery, and growing malaise.

A battle was in the making. General Edwin Harding, commanding general of the 32nd Division, believed there would be only about 500 outnumbered Japanese, all sick and desperately hungry. A short, sharp battle and then the beach, dry and pleasant, and return to Australia for rest. No one expected much of a fight and no one was prepared for it. Weapons were not cleaned and oiled; ammunition clips were fouled with mud; machine guns and ammunition belts were grimed with muck. Bayonets were not sharpened. Who would need a bayonet?

There was a short delay while Australian troops came up on the flank to permit a coordinated attack. Again there was cursing that Dugout Doug over at Moresby had agreed to hold up the attack to keep the Australians from being excluded from the victory. The "old son of a bitch" had run away from the Philippines, and now he was afraid to fight in New Guinea.

The objective was a strip of beach ten miles long and less than a mile deep. At the western edge of the beach was the village of Gona. About five miles to the east was Sanananda. Perhaps three miles to the east of Sanananda was Buna. Three miles east of Buna was Cape Endaiadere, where two airstrips were located.

All along the front behind the narrow beach was an area of swamps, some of which were covered with trees and underbush, and some with tall kunai grass. The Japanese had constructed an intricate defensive system of fire trenches, earthen breastworks, barbed wire, and fortified bunkers. Fields of fire had been prepared in front of machine-gun emplacements. Bunkers were dug, lined with dirt-filled steel drums, and covered with several layers of coconut logs. The

Map 13
Buna Battle

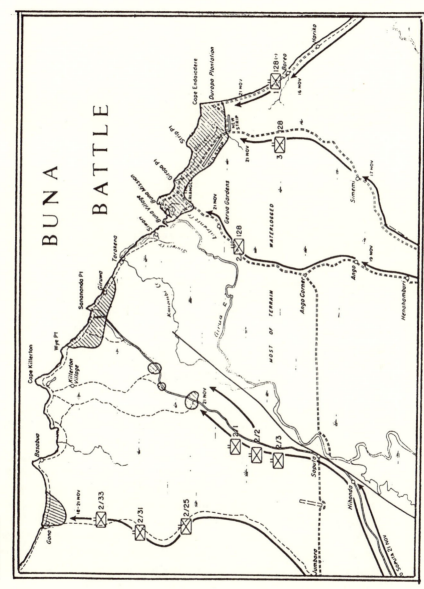

Source: U.S. Army.

entrances were covered with inter-locking steel doors. The vegetation and the terrain provided natural cover.

Every Japanese soldier and sailor in the area had been assigned to combat. When no rifle could be found, bamboo poles were tipped with bayonets to serve as pikes, and those who carried them were told to fight until they could find better weapons. The Japanese were ordered to fight to the death. Reinforcements had come in regularly in spite of Kenney's boys, who had not quite absolute control of the air. If the Japanese could avoid the bombers and fighters of Kenney's Fifth Air Force, they had nothing to fear from naval forces. The U.S. Navy was afraid of an area where there was no room for maneuver and where Japanese aircraft could seek them out. They would be of no help in the operation. The Japanese had not been on the defensive before. Now, solidly entrenched facing the mountains with the sea at their backs, with no expectation of evacuation in the event of defeat, they prepared to obey the orders of the emperor.

With the mountains behind them, Australians and Americans looked down a network of four trails that led to their objectives. Two brigades of the 7th Division held the Australian sector. On the far left the Australian 25th Brigade faced Gona. The Australian 16th Brigade faced Sanananda. The 32nd Division held the eastern sector; the 126th Regiment, the area opposite Buna Village; the 128th Regiment, the coast below Cape Endaiadere.

The 7th Division had seen combat in the Middle East and again on the Kokoda trail. The 32nd Division had never been in action. The Australians could assume the attitude of battle-hardened superiority that was shared by their commander, General Sir Thomas Blamey. What really could be expected of troops who in training quarters slept on mattresses and steel cots and were provided with refrigerators? The 32nd Division, battle-hardened or not, shared an attitude common to Americans in such circumstances: innate superiority, not having much admiration for troops whose standard ration consisted of rice, crackers, "bully beef," and tea, which Americans were forced to share.

The Americans had been prepared for two weeks to wipe out the Japanese and to get back to civilization. They had been held up until the Australians could come into line to permit a concerted attack. The Americans took this delay to be politically motivated, to prevent their outdoing the Aussies. Such remarks were openly made even by officers, and undoubtedly were heard by Australians. Whether the delay was politically oriented or not, it made good tactical sense.

On November 19 the four lines moved down their respective paths to bring the campaign to a rapid close. All field commanders estimated that they were faced by 500 hungry, sick troops who would not be capable of very much defense. Even Charles Willoughby at GHQ, who thought there must be 5,000 had begun to whittle down his estimates in view of the unanimity of the contrary opinion. He should have been more adamant, because he was right.

So they moved forward, the Australians with that serious, businesslike silence which hides the fear and uncertainty of soldiers who have faced fire and who know that the whim of the God of War can have a very personal impact. With all the rest, Company E, dragging Private Sam Brown along, plodded forward down the trail. There was laughing and joking. Dugout Doug had finally "got the lead out" and had ordered the attack. In two hours they would be on the beach, only a quarter of a mile away, bathing in the ocean.

Five minutes later Company E caught the full fury of hell. They walked into the outposts of the entrenched Japanese, behind the shelter of barbed wire, heavily reinforced bunkers, rifle pits and trenches, with machine guns, mortars, and artillery. The defenders were prepared to fight to the death, sick or well, unhurt or wounded, to hold a strip of land ten miles long and a quarter of a mile deep for the glory of the emperor far away in Tokyo. Half an hour later, with men screaming in the grass, clutching rifles in death, Company E came to a halt, unable to advance, not knowing what to do. They would learn the hard way.

At Gona the Australian 25th Brigade took casualties, ran out of ammunition and food, and came to a dead halt. The 16th at Sanananda had the same experience. In spite of some initial success against Japanese outpost positions, the advance came to an abrupt standstill. It had rained that day in torrents. The wet troops had moved forward with one day's supply of ammunition and food, expecting it to be over soon.

At the end of the day, the action had come to a halt. The Australians, who had marched in silence to the front, and the Americans, who had laughed and joked, realized for the first time what lay ahead of them. The dead Japanese on the ground around them were neither sick nor starving. They had been well-fed and healthy when they died, and they had obviously intended to fight.

The next day the Americans would meet even greater difficulty and disgrace. Some men dropped their rifles and machine-gun crews abandoned their weapons in the field, running to the rear. Fouled weapons refused to fire fouled ammunition, and what had seemed an unnecessary chore became the source of disaster. It should be pointed out that the Aussies on the left flank, veterans of the Middle East, who had already fought the Japanese back across the Kokoda Trail, whose weapons were not fouled and did fire, were also brought to a halt, faring no better than the green U.S. troops of the 32nd Division.

Ten days later they were all still bogged down. Some men had crawled in the grass like cowards, while others had run erect with grenades to bunkers, sometimes successful and sometimes dying, and sometimes both successful and dying with their success. Yesterday's cowards became today's heroes, and today's heroes might well be tomorrow's cowards.

They were mired in the swamps, caked with mud and ordure, faint with disease and hunger and fear, not knowing how to fight this battle for which no one had been prepared. No one knew it, but after this day's battle was over, it would be repeated again and again all over the Pacific islands. There was no real solution to the problem except the agony of death for infantry soldiers fighting their way from bunker to bunker, killing an enemy who was determined to die. Planes, tanks, and battleships may make the task easier, but always infantrymen must die. There was no easy substitute.

On November 25th General Blamey came to Port Moresby to visit MacArthur. Sutherland and Kenney were present at the meeting, which was held in the living/ dining room of Government House. My office was at a corner of the veranda that looked into this room. I was at my desk typing, then reading, during the discussion. Blamey found occasion to comment critically on the performance of the U.S. troops at Buna. MacArthur had received his own reports and was smarting under his own doubt. Blamey had already relieved two generals and sat smiling smugly now that the shoe seemed to fit neatly on MacArthur's foot.

MacArthur sent two of his own staff to observe firsthand, and they confirmed what he had heard from Blamey. MacArthur and Sutherland paced the room together for three days, discussing what should be done. On November 30 MacArthur sent Sutherland forward to talk with Harding. Sutherland returned convinced that Harding should be relieved and so reported to MacArthur. he found no pleasure in the recommendation because Harding was a personal friend.

MacArthur said quietly, "Dick, I think you had better bring Bob Eichelberger up here. We are going to need him." Eichelberger was commander of the U.S. I Corps. As corps commander he was Harding's immediate superior. He must do the firing. Eichelberger reported to Government House in the late afternoon to receive his instructions. MacArthur and Kenney were gossiping off to a corner in the living area. Sutherland sat at his desk reading dispatches and reports that had accumulated during his absence. He had just finished dictating and I was seated at my desk. Eichelberger, tall and handsome, passed me, looking concerned and nervous. MacArthur, Sutherland, and Kenney talked with him about the situation in the same room Blamey had occupied a few days before.

MacArthur described the situation remarking with bitterness that U.S. soldiers had dropped their arms and had run away in the face of the enemy. He said that a good leader could still make them fight. He told Eichelberger to relieve Harding, and if he could not do it, he would be fired. His further instructions were "Take Buna or don't come back alive." Even in normal times Eichelberger was a suspicious, nervous, soul, in spite of a firm appearance, and he was sure that MacArthur was angry.

I had heard the same speech for two days. MacArthur was disturbed at the performance of his troops and recalled hard days in France, when in spite of mud, hunger, sickness, and despair, his boys crawled forward at night, dug in at morning, crawled forward again until they were in range of enemy positions, and then took them out with grenades. His voice always had a dramatic quaver, and he paced with eyes flashing, hands rising and falling to punctuate his remarks, voice filled with emotion. Those who did not see him regularly always took this as a sign of agitation or anger. It was simply his habitual manner when concerned with serious matters.

Eichelberger realized that he would have to fill Harding's shoes and would have to relieve a personal friend in the process. I don't think he really wanted to do it, but he did. He left the next morning to carry out the assignment. Two days later Harding came back to Port Moresby to pay his final respects to

MacArthur. He stood by my desk while waiting to see the General, looking at me sadly, with tears in his eyes. "I just couldn't stand to see my boys die." I'm sure Harding meant it, and I felt for him. Since, then, though, I have reconsidered. For the first week or so of the battle, Harding's headquarters at Pongani was 13 miles from the action, and he was forced to walk all day on the round trip to reach his regimental commanders. On one trip, when his signal sergeant became too tired to carry his radio, Harding let him set it by a tree on the trail, and the two continued to walk to the front. He was out of contact with his commanders for some five or six hours.

When I read this fact, it occurred to me that compassion is a fine emotion except for generals in battle. A man who wept over the death of his soldiers might not have been a match for the Japanese, however highly he might be regarded by the saints. Battle is not an exercise in compassionate saintliness. This is an ironic judgment, because I would prefer to live in a world filled with compassionate saintliness where it would not be necessary to send men out to die.

Eichelberger sent Harding packing to the rear. Now he would get things moving. Sam Brown, who had became wise in two weeks of battle, snickered at the thought that both "Butcher Bob" and "Dugout Doug" would soon learn the facts. Two days later Brown helped pick up Eichelberger's aide, who had been seriously wounded at the front, and put him in the jeep on a stretcher. He watched Eichelberger's face twist with suppressed grief and anger at the sudden personal impact of the action.

Eichelberger found conditions at Buna exactly at MacArthur had indicated they would be. There was no discipline at the front. Men exposed themselves and their weapons without apparent concern, although all believed that the Japanese hid in the jungles only a few yards away. They refused to fire because "They won't shoot at us if we don't shoot at them." No protection had been provided for machine-gun positions in spite of the fact that boxes and dirt were available for breastworks and logs for overhead cover. Troops refused to move down trails for fear of hidden Japanese. The bulk of the troops were crowded in the rear area, at aid stations or simply resting, either on order of officers or without it.[1]

Officers, like those on Bataan earlier in the year, had begun to plead the cause of their tired, sick, exhausted troops. The facts obviously were correct, but the excuses indicated that the officers, like the men, did not have much enthusiasm for the fight. This does not constitute a criticism of the feelings of all those involved, for the feelings were based on fact. But it does confirm the existence of an attitude that would never lead to a resolution of the problem. When colonels begin to speak sympathetically of the sufferings of their troops, the troops may be inclined to feel that they are not in condition to carry on a battle. The next step is complete collapse. MacArthur understood the condition at Buna, as well as Eichelberger, perhaps even better. That is why he had sent for Eichelberger. Eichelberger was convinced to the end that the Japanese always had more troops on the line than he did, but acknowledged that he had greater mortar and artillery fire. The problem was to move troops out of rear areas, where they were not needed, to forward areas, where they could be brought to bear against the Japanese.

The forward area was the great swamp that lay along the beach, waist deep or more, almost impassable. Trails led across the swamp on a few stretches of dry land. On one side of the front lay a river; on the other, the ocean. The Japanese had fortified the trails in great depth.

The troops in the forward area had no cigarettes and very little food. The men were eating two tins of C rations per day, cold, when they could get it. There was adequate food and cigarettes in the rear areas but, as on Bataan, neither seemed to reach troops at the front. It had become a war of attrition that the Japanese must certainly win if it continued long enough. They stood on relatively dry ground while Americans and Australians sat in the swamp, wasting away with disease.

Eichelberger replaced two regimental commanders and ordered an attack for December 5. The Australians had sent up five Bren carriers to support the attack in the Cape Endaiadere sector. Air and artillery bombardment preceded the advance of the Bren carriers and infantry. In 20 minutes the Japanese had destroyed all the Bren gun carriers, killing most of the crews. The infantry came to a halt. The Japanese line had not been penetrated.

Eichelberger was present with his staff to observe the action. When the attack bogged down on the Buna front, he insisted that Buna must be taken before nightfall and sent a detachment out to renew the attack. As the detachment started down the trail, Eichelberger and his staff followed. Sniper fire wounded the sector commander. The detachment lost more than half its force and came to a halt, Buna still not taken.

Eichelberger very quickly saw the precise nature of his problem. He lamented that his striking force was built around the 3 rifle companies of each battalion, which had averaged some 65 men each when Eichelberger assumed command. A battalion normally numbers some 700 fighting men. The headquarters company, including communication and pioneer platoons, had a disproportionate share of the battalion force. The heavy weapons company was useless in the terrain. As a result the bulk of the fighting was done by a small proportion of the regiments actually committed, and that small proportion was steadily wasting away in the daily battle of attrition.

MacArthur diagnosed the problem far more accurately and clearly than Eichelberger knew, and wrote on December 13:

Time is fleeting and our dangers increase with its passage. However admirable individual acts of courage may be; however important administrative functions may seem; however splendid and electrical your presence has proven, remember that your mission is to take Buna. All other things are merely subsidiary to this. No alchemy is going to produce this for you; it can only be done in battle and sooner or later this battle must be engaged.

Hasten your preparations and when you are ready—strike, for as I have said, time is working desperately against us.[2]

He also wrote to Blamey on the same day.

With general reference to the infantry reinforcement, the realistic fact is that we already have in the battle area many more troops than are being actively brought to bear against the enemy. The estimate of numbers made from the front gives our strength as three or four to one as compared to the enemy. The study made by General Eichelberger's operations officer three days ago confirms this figure. In addition we have many more automatic weapons, some artillery support which he lacks and air superiority. Our troops in addition are fresher than his. The balance, except in position, is overwhelmingly in our favor. It will do little good to keep massing infantry troops which are not brought to bear upon the enemy and which gradually become worn out by climatic conditions. The remedy for the situation, in my opinion, is a much more active use of the infantry that are present and in much greater proportion of strength in the front than they have been used in the past.[3]

The problem was to commit the entire force then standing before Buna to a concerted effort. The Japanese commander had succeeded in doing just that. Every soldier was expected to fight, sick or well, and further to fight to the death. Outnumbered four to one by Australians and Americans, he held them at bay. With a slight change of luck he might very well destroy them.

Day after day the battle ground on as weary, hungry troops on both sides each morning watched the black sky fill with light and prepared themselves for another round of butchery. For the veterans of Company E a cup of dried crackers, dried milk, and cold dirty water served for breakfast. The bully beef of last night already had made its way through the bowels. The day's dole of sick reported to the aid station, where they were separated into ordinarily sick and very seriously sick and, if they were fortunate enough to be extraordinarily ill, they might be evacuated to hospitals at the rear to join yesterday's battle casualties. The remainder, who were also ill by the standards of civilian life, grasped rifles and automatic weapons reluctantly, with great effort prepared mortars, to begin another day of battle.

On the other side there was no difference. The Japanese soldiers faced the same horrible duty. But for the Japanese there were no aid stations and there was no evacuation to rear areas. Except for a fortunate few, the sick and wounded stood in the trenches to fight as long as weak hands could grasp weapons and as long as unsteady legs could prop them against the muddy, bloody bulwarks where, more often than not, the dead bodies of yesterday's comrades had become a part of the defense.

Allied troops marched forward through grass and trees, watching warily for snipers, who more often got the first sight and the first shots, thereby taking two or three dead or wounded before they fell to earth, riddled with bullets. Then came the rattle of machine guns, which grew to a solid roar of flame and steel in the day's fire fight. Some soldiers fell into the grass, wounded or simply afraid, while others ran forward with grenades to the tops of bunkers, in a cold sweat, leaning over to put a grenade through the firing slot, feeling the explosion of the grenade under the logs that protected the man on top. Another run to another bunker, through a splatter of bullets, with another grenade and another explosion. One soldier took out five bunkers and was killed on top of the sixth.

Then the collapse of the attack as exhausted wills lost the power to drive tired bodies forward. Five or six yards had been gained and would be held while the wounded were carried to the rear. Those who had crouched in the grass joined the others without apology or reproach.

There was a bright spot in the action. One day a soldier who had fought in the Spanish Civil War took his squad away from the main line of attack on Buna and drove directly toward the beach. After knocking out several bunkers he and his men suddenly found themselves on the sand, facing the ocean. They dug in immediately, and there they stayed. It was the first penetration of the Japanese line. The Australians drove into Gona Mission. The Japanese line was beginning to crack, but the end was still a month away.

Why were the tanks so long in arriving? Until the first day's attack had failed, no one had thought about the matter. After the first day Harding asked for tanks, but while everyone might agree that they were needed, getting them into action was another matter. The tanks in Papua were in the hands of Australian troops. To bring tanks into the 32nd Division sector involved going to the Australians with pleas for help.

There was a glint of hope when five Bren gun carriers arrived. They were almost tanks—armored self-propelled gun mounts that should be able to blast out the bunkers. Almost, but not quite! As the five vehicles growled slowly into the line of bunkers and trenches, rolling like ships at sea over rough ground and tree stumps, they were caught by machine-gun fire, grenades, and Molotov cocktails.[4] One by one they were put out of action, their crews dead and dying. In only 20 minutes the glint of hope faded to disappointment. The infantry moved forward again to gain perhaps 3 or 4 of the 500 yards that still stood between them and the beach.

Then came artillery, by air, a 105-millimeter howitzer with 400 rounds of ammunition that could penetrate the reinforced bunkers. Again the glint of hope for an easy solution. The 400 rounds were fired, and some bunkers were hit and destroyed; but when it was over, the infantry was perhaps 10 yards closer than the day before.

MacArthur pleaded with the navy until it finally agreed to provide three corvettes to convoy larger ships from Milne Bay to Oro Bay. At the same time it agreed to send four landing craft that were designed specifically for moving tanks. Four tanks arrived at Buna on December 12. Four more arrived three days later.

Since the bulk of the attacking force on the Cape Endaiadere sector was now manned by Australian tank units, the command was transferred to an Australian commander. So the Australians came in to finish the offensive that Americans had started. It was inevitable and logically necessary—but it smarted! And MacArthur felt the smart.

On December 18 the new Australian command with its tanks was in place, prepared for the attack at Cape Endaiadere. Eight tanks had come ashore and a fresh battalion of Aussies had come into the line, confident and aggressive, not yet soiled by mud and ordure, looking with disdain at the miserable Yanks who had failed to move such a short distance. The first of the tanks rattled into action covered by Australian infantry. Within two hours the tanks sat silent in the heat. The Japanese had turned an antiaircraft gun against them, and with not many more rounds than tanks had brought the action to a halt. Then Australian infantry had to move alone, knocking out bunkers with grenades.

The next day two tanks were mired in the swamp, and one had to be abandoned. On Christmas Eve tanks moved forward again. As three rattled into view, they were knocked out immediately. The Australians refused to use any more tanks until the gun position could be eliminated. Two days later infantry took out the guns, but the entire area was finally cleared without additional use of tanks.

Eichelberger wrote to Sutherland:

... no vehicle can go westward from Cape Endaiadere because as soon as it left the coconut palms it would run into swamp and then Simemi Creek. Therefore an attack on our extreme right, even if we had a hundred General Shermans would still be a limited objective attack.

This morning one of our bombers let go a stick of big bombs on our troops around Buna Creek. Ten casualties have already been reported but the line is out and I cannot get full details yet. Yesterday three friendly planes strafed the front line and set fire to an ammunition dump. Tell George [Kenney] to give us an even break and not treat us worse than he does the Japs. ... Our boys in the front line love the air force like the doughboys liked the artillery in the last war.[5]

By December 15 the Australians on the left had taken Gona and had taken over half of the U.S. sector. Eichelberger was left with Buna Village and Buna Mission. These places were simply two groups of huts separated by several miles of creek, one small point of which was held by Sergeant Boettcher and his squad.

About this time MacArthur sent Sutherland to Buna to talk to Eichelberger. Sutherland listened in obvious discomfort as MacArthur directed him to go over to Buna and get Bob Eichelberger moving. "If Eichelberger won't move, you are to relieve him and to take command yourself. I don't want to see you back here alive until Buna is taken."

After Sutherland had left for Buna, Blamey visited GHQ and sat with a smile while MacArthur paced up and down the room, saying, "I relieved Harding. I sent Sutherland over today to get Eichelberger moving. I told him to relieve Eichelberger if necessary. If I have to, I will relieve Sutherland." I sat in startled surprise, realizing for the first time that such a thing could happen.

Sutherland was away for several days. He returned, leaving Eichelberger in command. Sutherland paced up and down the living room, step for step with MacArthur, and now MacArthur listened while Sutherland talked. They paced and talked for two hours, until the Filipino houseboys came in to set the table for dinner. I was busy typing and did not hear what Sutherland said. I inferred that he was not anxious to become commanding general of I Corps, although later he may have repented his choice.

Eichelberger daily wrote to his wife about "Sarah" (MacArthur) and "Dickey Bird" (Sutherland). He was told by Sutherland that Sutherland would act as his chief of staff for a day or so. Actually, Sutherland had complete authority to relieve Eichelberger. MacArthur told Roger Egeberg in 1944 that he had offered I Corps to Sutherland, who had refused to take it.[6] He knew very well that on his return to Port Moresby he would have to mount a convincing defense of Eichelberger to excuse his own failure to assume the command. Eichelberger believed until the end that Sutherland had tried to take his command but that MacArthur had saved him.

Without tank support Eichelberger's infantry troops had been pushing steadily against Buna Mission, and on January 2 it was taken. Only Sanananda remained. All units were now moved to this area, but three more weeks were required to drive through the Japanese position to the beach. On January 22 the battle for Buna finally came to an end.

What had begun as a quick, "easy" march over a "handful" of Japanese became the most difficult and most costly action in the Southwest Pacific. The United States and Australia committed some 35,000 troops (15,000 US; 20,000 Australian) against some 17,000 Japanese. Allied casualties were 8,500 men, with 3,000 of those dead. The Japanese lost some 12,000 dead. The Allies buried 7,000 of these. It is presumed the Japanese buried the 5,000 that are otherwise not accounted for.[7]

The campaign left a great many "ifs": if there had been more artillery, if tanks had been available, if the Japanese had been permitted to die of starvation, if the attack had not been hurried. Each of these questions was confronted and discussed at Port Moresby, and each was dealt with as circumstances permitted. In all cases the action taken seemed inevitable, given the circumstances.

It had been six weeks. The Japanese defenders had died by the thousands, four Japanese to every Allied soldier. The Japanese were starving and most of them were no longer rational, driven to madness by their ordeal, sustained only by the memory of an order to stand until death because the emperor had ordered it. As they died, the defense weakened and its penetration became easier. But even on the last day of battle, Japanese soldiers killed Allied soldiers who advanced relentlessly to the sea, and some Americans died on the beach that had seemed so close two months before.

There had been 60 days of hell before "Dugout Doug" had his bloody victory. One day after another of advance, the blaze of fire, men screaming with death and wounds; men carried to aid stations with dysentery and malaria; nights in the rain, hungry and exhausted, waiting for the next day's ration of disease, death, and destruction.

And then the beach and quiet and sound sleep; hot rations and time to wash; clean uniforms and razors scraping through hot suds; a march to the airstrip and a cargo plane roaring over the mountains to Port Moresby and then to Australia; hot showers, starched uniforms, warm, inviting girls.

Sergeant Sam Brown had become a veteran and a noncom by sheer attrition. He survived to fight again in the Philippines, where he would laugh at complaints of new recruits and tell them of the really rough days when that son of a bitch MacArthur had put them through a hell compared to which this battle was a picnic.

Twenty years later Brown's son asked, "Who was Dugout Doug?" Brown looked startled, then replied, "You mean MacArthur. I served under General MacArthur out in New Guinea and the Philippines." Only occasionally, after a few beers, sitting alone, looking at the Silver Star and Purple Heart among the medals on the wall, his face would twist with hurt and agony, and he would mutter, "Dugout Doug, you son of a bitch."

Eichelberger and others insisted that they felt MacArthur's lash on their backs, forcing them to drive their troops forward. On MacArthur's side, a battle that dragged on for 60 days was not a hurried affair. Time worked against the Allies more than for them. It is true that Japanese were starving and dying of disease, but so were Americans and Australians. Delay meant additional opportunities for fresh Japanese reinforcements and supplies.

The Japanese had demonstrated the full measure of indomitable force in battle. They died fighting while already dying from starvation and disease, standing on and behind the bodies of their unburied dead. It was an irrational, inhuman display of stubborn courage. In spite of it, they lost the battle! The gods of war are fickle and their favor often seems to be granted on sheer whim, as every soldier knows, without any respect to the sacrifice of the human flesh. Whatever else the Allies lacked, they had air support and supply. If the Australians and Americans complained of their suffering and their misery, it was small compared with that of their less fortunate enemies.

The critical link in the operation was supply. Proper shipping and convoy escort would have been the best answer, but it was not available, whatever the reason. In spite of urgent requests, the navy refused to supply the escort for reasons that seemed irrefutable, at least to the navy, at the time.

40

Shades of Nelson

The battle for Guadalcanal began on August 7. It had been conceived as a joint operation. The direct attack would be controlled by the South Pacific Area (the navy). MacArthur would provide indirect air support and would send his Seventh Fleet to serve as a contingent under South Pacific command. He stripped his command of its entire naval contingent, including as well the cruisers and destroyers of the Royal Australian Navy. When the arrangement was made in July, the Japanese had not yet landed on the Buna coast and it seemed that the Australians would occupy the area without opposition.

The events of July upset that expectation. The landing of the Japanese created an entirely new situation, and their drive over the Owen Stanley Mountains heightened the anxiety. The affair at Milne Bay created even more anxiety. By early November, with Japanese planes still moving freely over the area, the problem was further intensified.

The time had come to send small shipping forward from Milne Bay to set up a supply depot in the Pongani area. It was at this time that Harding had his scrape with death when Japanese bombers strafed and bombed the trawler on which he was a passenger.

Blamey wrote to MacArthur requesting that the navy he called upon to provide destroyers for protection against surface and submarine attack. He anticipated possible objection by pointing out that the destroyers would always be under cover of Kenney's land-based fighters and that air reconnaissance would give adequate warning of any concentration of Japanese naval forces.[1] Sutherland sent the letter to Seventh Fleet for comment. The reply was abrupt: "I am not in favor of sending destroyers north of Milne Bay . . . and I strongly recommend against their being so employed."[2] He then passed the buck to Kenney, asserting: "A surface attack in the Buna area can best be stopped by aircraft . . . air cover by day should protect this shipping from enemy attack."

By November 19 the situation at Buna had become deadly serious, and Blamey renewed his request:

> I would like to point out that the bulk of the land forces in New Guinea have had to move into positions where it is impossible to support them, and extremely difficult to give them the necessary ammunition and supplies to maintain them. They are facing the ordeal of battle where defeat may mean destruction. The attitude of the Navy in regard to the destroyers appears to be to avoid risk at a time when all services should give a maximum of cooperation to defeat the enemy. I regret that it does not impress me as a valid reason for not giving support which the necessarily dangerous position of the Army properly requires.[3]

MacArthur passed this message, over his own signature, to Seventh Fleet.[4] Carpender, the commander, replied that a destroyer had been sent to Milne Bay, but he refused to permit its use beyond Cape Nelson because the waters there were not navigable for destroyers.[5]

MacArthur radioed an immediate reply directing Carpender to make a study of the navigability for destroyers to the Buna area. Blamey was informed of the action being taken. Carpender repeated his previous conclusion that destroyers should not proceed to Buna but advised that PT boats had been requested from Halsey.

Blamey injected the only creative concept that came out of the Buna operation. He outlined the difficulties faced on the Buna front, then proposed:

> If, however, one or two destroyers can be made available it would be possible to take the enemy in the rear by surprise. . . . Such a landing in cooperation with a night attack by 32nd U.S. Division would allow a junction of two forces south of Girua River near the Buna Mission, and the position would soon be dealt with.[6]

MacArthur accepted the idea enthusiastically, agreeing that the advantages of such a move were obvious. The navy, however, would not provide destroyers and no landing craft were available. Two antisubmarine vessels might be employed for this operation. The plan projected by Blamey would have to be reworked to fit this unpromising reality.[7]

Blamey pounced on the navy with scorn, emphasizing that Japanese naval units moved in and out of the area without hesitation. The troops were beginning to comment on the obvious inactivity of naval forces in their support: " . . . the enemy is bringing in both supplies and a limited number of reinforcements in this way and he is able to withdraw sick and wounded."[8] He asked again for naval cooperation in an amphibious landing. He enclosed a report from the Royal Australian Navy that seemed to support his position that naval escort could be provided from Milne Bay to Buna.

MacArthur replied to Blamey. He supported the navy's position because he could not force the Seventh Fleet to act, but he promised that PT boats eventually would be available. He pointed out that the Royal Australian Navy report had recommended that the area would have to be charted before destroyers could be committed to action there.[9]

On December 8, with the situation still in stalemate at Buna, Blamey returned to the attack, proposing the movement of a battalion of tanks from Milne Bay: "This requires at least two destroyers and two corvettes. I understand that the Navy is reluctant to risk its vessels. I desire to point out that the Navy is only being asked to go where the Japanese have gone frequently."[10] He ended his letter with unconcealed sarcasm. It should be inscribed in stone over the graves of the troops who died at Buna: "It is somewhat difficult to understand the Navy attitude of non-cooperation because of risk. 'Safety First' as a Naval motto— Shades of Nelson!"[11]

One cannot say whether MacArthur remembered a statement he had made only ten months before. On Corregidor he had urged on attack on the Japanese navy: "Councils of timidity based upon theories of safety first will not win against such an aggressive and audacious adversary as Japan. . . . The only way to beat him is to fight him incessantly."[12]

Supply was left to the air force. Kenney's boys wiped out the memories of past records. The entire operation rested from the beginning on the C–47s that moved troops, supplies, and heavy equipment to the front. They found ways to move objects that had never been moved by air with the planes available in those days. When necessary, combat planes substituted for cargo aircraft. It was a tight squeeze, since demand for matériel always ran ahead of the airlift capacity. Priorities had to be set, bringing inevitable complaints that one man's "essential" item of supply was not nearly as "essential" as the need of someone else. But the planes kept the action going.

Artillery and tanks were not available because the navy could not move them to the front. The only piece of heavy artillery at Buna was a 105-millimeter howitzer that had been dismantled and moved forward by air, a task held to be impossible until Kenney's boys figured out how to do it.

When tanks and artillery became available at the front, they did not make a decisive difference. As the record shows, they made it only momentarily easier and less costly for the infantry; in the end the infantry still fought in the mud to take out the guns that stopped the tanks. This is not meant to belittle tank and artillery support but to emphasize that in that kind of terrain, only infantry could perform the task that was required.

The air force contribution at the Coral Sea and Midway had been negligible; the navy had delivered the telling blows. At Buna, however, the tale was reversed. The navy was having difficulties of its own across the Solomon Sea at Guadalcanal. Nothing was left for gallant efforts in Papua. Moreover, Papua was MacArthur's territory. Guadalcanal was referred to as "Operation Shoestring," yet compared with Buna, the forces assigned to Guadalcanal were immense: the carriers *Saratoga*, *Enterprise*, and *Wasp*; the battleship *North Carolina*; the cruisers *Minneapolis*, *New Orleans*, *Portland*, *Atlanta*, *San Fran-*

cisco, *Salt Lake City*, *Australia*, *Canberra*, *Hobart*, and *Chicago*; numerous destroyers; and 21 large transports.

At Papua not even one landing craft was available to move tanks until the campaign was half over, and no transports, even very small ones, were available until the campaign was ending. The few small corvettes assigned to convoy for the landing craft that were used to move tanks pulled away at the first threat of air attack. In the final stages torpedo boats came into action. This is not particularly a denunciation of the navy, but one wonders now why destroyers that could maneuver in the confines of Guadalcanal, Tulagi, and Gavutu could not have done so on the Papuan coast.

Toward the end of the campaign at Buna, four small freighters with a cargo capacity of some 400 tons each made nine trips from Milne Bay to Buna and delivered some 4,000 tons of cargo. During the entire campaign, stretching transport planes to the limit, Kenney's boys had flown in some 2,500 tons.

Adequate cargo shipping would have moved artillery, tanks, and enough supplies to change the structure of the entire campaign. The line that separated SWPA from the navy was about as deep as the line that separated the 32nd and 7th Divisions from the Japanese.

The air transport command supplied the troops. The fighter and bomber commands ripped up enemy supply lines. The Japanese advance over the Owen Stanleys had been brought to a halt by the fighters and bombers that swept the trail daily, strafing and bombing everything they could find.

As the Japanese settled into the defensive position at Buna, Kenney's fighters and bombers covered the sea approaches and broke up convoy after convoy. Although several Japanese convoys were able to get through under cover of bad weather, they could not maintain the flow of supplies and reinforcements. And it was this, more than anything else, that brought them to destruction.

Buna was taken on January 22, 1943. Guadalcanal was secured on February 7. MacArthur had finished first, and in the one-upmanship of affairs he had reason to smile softly. The matter of finishing first was not a frivolous one. The stakes had been quite high, however one measured the outcome. The command of future operations swung precariously in the balance. Had Blamey's forces been swept back in defeat, to perish on the mountain trails of the Owen Stanley's, MacArthur's career would have ended. He would have gone back to the States in disgrace. But the navy had been checked in this gambit. MacArthur was still in the game.

MacArthur returned to Brisbane on January 8, glad to be with his family after an absence that had extended far beyond the two weeks he had envisioned on his departure. The barber had made his way to Government House four times. MacArthur and Sutherland in turn sat on the veranda, draped in a white towel, while the barber clipped and trimmed. MacArthur sat patiently. Sutherland carried papers with him and, while the barber clipped, read with a concentration that surpasses my understanding.

As MacArthur climbed down from his staff plane in Brisbane with Kenney behind him, he must have felt that a great burden had been lifted from his shoulders. It had been a wearing time, an unpleasant time, a time of great stress. He knew what the troops were feeling and saying. He was prepared for their anger and hatred and revulsion. Bataan had taught him to endure these emotions. He could remember other days in other battles when his soldiers undoubtedly cursed him, but with affection.

But now he carried laurels of victory. His troops had given him and themselves a victory. It had been touch and go, a forlorn "poor man's" war, stretched, pulled, tied together; but it had produced a victory. The navy had the ships and the marines; but his infantry, U.S. and Australian, with Kenney's boys, had crossed the line first.

The Japanese had taken a decisive defeat. Standing for the first time on the defensive, they had been boxed into a corner, with their air and navy blocked out of the game by the fighters and bombers of the Fifth Air Force. They had fought with the ferocity of demons of hell and most of them had died. The rotting corpses at Buna notwithstanding, some 3,000 of those who were able to walk had crept away through the Allied lines at Sanananda and moved north to continue the fight. At Rabaul plans were already being made for another thrust at Port Moresby. But MacArthur would never give his troops another Buna.

Buna did not fall. It simply suffocated under the weight of time, heat, humidity, diarrhea, hunger, and general discomfort. There was no exultation in victory. There was no glory in the defeat. Those of the enemy who had not been killed in battle finally starved or turned to cannibalism. One Japanese soldier wrote in his diary: "This is the first time I have ever tasted human flesh and it is very tasty."[13]

Eichelberger toured the field after the battle, shaking his head in wonder, unable to understand how the defenses had been broken. For every Australian and U.S. soldier killed or wounded, two had been struck down by some form of debilitating disease. Perhaps MacArthur had been right in the beginning. A concerted assault in force, whatever the short-run casualty rate, might have been more merciful and far less costly in the long run.

The MacArthur Files

The MacArthur Files include the documents that MacArthur viewed as his own files. They are to be distinguished from the general files of his headquarters and of its various staff sections. Many of the documents are the joint work of MacArthur and Sutherland and in some cases are the work of Sutherland alone, especially after 1943, when MacArthur began to speak with Sutherland's voice and to write with Sutherland's hand. Sutherland's signature, under the rubric "For the Commander in Chief," was sufficient to move armies and would stand undisputed until MacArthur chose to disaffirm the act. To my knowledge MacArthur did so just once or twice.

The MacArthur Files involve three commands: Army Forces in the Far East, Southwest Pacific Area, and Army Forces in the Pacific. The changes in command organization did not alter the structure of the headquarters or the ordinary routine of business.

1. *The Personal File* (July 26, 1941–March 11, 1942), MacArthur Memorial RG–2, Boxes 1 and 2.

This file began with the assumption of command of USAFFE by MacArthur. It was intended to be a record of his new command, to contain the most significant documents that passed through his headquarters. One of the assistant adjutants general made a daily check of each day's business and identified what he considered to be the most important items. These were passed on to Major LeGrande Diller, MacArthur's aide, who made a second cut of the materials.

Those items which survived the process were filed chronologically with an index for each folder. Seals had physical control of the file. MacArthur had an uncanny ability to recall specific items and referred to some of them as late as 1943. The file contained letters dictated by MacArthur to Turner or to Rogers, or even to Sutherland for redictation to Rogers.

After December 8, 1941, Sutherland's role in the Personal File was augmented. MacArthur did not dictate to stenographers after that date but wrote longhand drafts, which went to Sutherland for dictation. In those days Sutherland did not presume to make changes in the material but simply read it off to Rogers who then typed it. See the first item in the folder for 12/25/41–1/22/42 as an example. Many of the items are marked for "aide," some for "RKS." One radio in October carries the identification RKS:PR; it was probably one of the first documents I typed for Sutherland.

The Personal File continued to be processed until the evacuation. I was simply a stenographer in those days. I typed many of the items, as either original or second copies. I did not know that the file existed until I began this book in 1979. It was stored somewhere in GHQ in Australia.

2. *The Secret File* (December 8, 1941–March 11, 1942),
MacArthur Memorial, RG–2, 3 folders.

With the outbreak of war three new activities required special attention: high-level strategic radios, daily operations reports, and the diary of Sutherland's daily activities. These were seen only by MacArthur, Sutherland, and the very few people who were required for preparation and transmission: Rogers, Seals, Spencer Akin, and Joseph Sherr, who was the cryptographer for such materials.

In those days MacArthur wrote the daily operations report on small note paper and handed it to Sutherland, who then dictated it to me. No one else saw this report except Akin and the code clerks.

Wilson conferred with Sutherland at intervals to record Sutherland's activities. Sutherland kept a record on a yellow pad on his desk and dictated it to Wilson. Wilson recopied the dictation and gave it to me to be typed. Wilson assumed that we would all be captured and the documents would be destroyed.

MacArthur instructed Sutherland to segregate these items into a special "Secret" file. Wilson was in charge of it. I did not know of the file although, of course, I typed most of its contents.

3. *The Sutherland Files* (December 8, 1941–March 11, 1942),
Sutherland Papers, RG 200, The National Archives, Personal
Records, Box 1, Folder 3.

The Personal File and the Secret File were kept in one copy only for MacArthur. Nothing was kept for Sutherland even though he was a major participant in the drafting of the papers contained especially in the Secret File.

Sutherland began to set up his own file of the most important documents. He copied them out laboriously all during the Corregidor period. They left Corregidor with him and were kept in a file folder in my office.

Sutherland kept the copy of Executive Order No. 1, which he wrote and I typed. It also was filed in my office in Australia. I remember showing it to

Bothne in early 1944. The document remained in the Sutherland papers until 1980, when it was discovered and a copy was made for MacArthur Memorial. In the Sutherland Papers it is Item 27, Box 4, Folder 2.

After the move to Australia, all the USAFFE records described above were filed away and I was not aware of them. Wilson was given the task of continuing the accumulation of records.

The old Personal File disappeared. The flow of documents was too great to maintain any record for MacArthur except the most important materials. Thus the Secret File replaced the Personal File during the SWPA period. Wilson simply filed the materials by addressee in loose folders that were stored in a safe in Sutherland's office. By late 1943 the safe could no longer accommodate the mass of loose material, and Sutherland could not find documents when he needed them. He asked me to make a proposal for reorganization.

My efforts produced the MacArthur/Sutherland Secret File. It was now kept in duplicate, one copy for MacArthur and the other for Sutherland. Operations reports were written by Stephen Chamberlin as G–3 and filed in his office.

4. *The MacArthur/Sutherland Secret File (MSSF)* (March 16, 1942–August 31, 1945)

This was a joint file maintained in filing cabinets in my office, under my direct control, for the benefit of MacArthur and Sutherland. It contained duplicate sets of the following official correspondence:

War Department (WD)

Navy (SOPAC)

Australian Government (AUST)

Philippine Government (QUEZON)

Netherlands East Indies Government (NEI)

Allied Air Forces (AAF)

Allied Land Forces (ALF)

Allied Naval Forces (ANF)

Eichelberger

Sixth Army

Southeast Asia Command

U.S. Army Forces in the Far East (USAFFE)

U.S. Forces in the Philippines (USFIP)

Commanding General Pacific Ocean Area (COMGENPOA)

Moscow Mission

Miscellaneous (four of these)

These are located in the Sutherland Papers, Items 1–9, 14, and 20. In the MacArthur Memorial they are in RG–4, Boxes 6–11, 14–17. The miscellaneous folders somehow did not find their way into the MacArthur Memorial Archives but were picked up in Sutherland's collection.

MSSF was a continuation of the folder "Secret Radios." The notation "Personal File" or "Secret File" is on many of the documents in this collection. Some of the documents came out of Corregidor at the time of the evacuation. MSSF was designed to be a working office file and was not conceived of as a historical record. Outgoing dispatches are not always matched by the incoming dispatches to which they refer. Sutherland or MacArthur frequently indicated that an item should be filed, but in many cases I made the judgment on my own authority to include or exclude an item. When Bonner Fellers became military secretary, he remarked to me that he would have included every scrap of paper. MacArthur himself had ordered that only completed documents should be retained and that the preliminary drafts were to be destroyed.

Outgoing documents destined for MSSF were typed with two extra copies, which were sent with the original to the adjutant general or to the signal office for certification that they had been dispatched. They were then returned to my office. At first the duplicates were marked "Return to W/O Rogers." Later the notation was changed to show two copies to the Office of the Chief of Staff. At Tacloban, while Sutherland was at rear echelon, items were marked for return to the Office of the Commander in Chief.

We frequently received only one copy of incoming dispatches, and a second copy had to be typed for the duplicate file. This became a burden for me, so I asked Jim Larkin if he could type. He could, and he became custodian of the files.

The GHQ historical officer, Colonel Niederpruem, regularly came to my office in 1943–1944 seeking documents that he had identified but could not locate. I interceded for him with Sutherland but was regularly refused permission to let him see MSSF.

The office symbol identifies the person who dictated the item, followed by the typist's initials. The system was finally regularized in June 1942 (WD 103). CC indicates that the item came directly from MacArthur as a handwritten draft. WD 203 and WD 295 are MacArthur's work. CS indicates that Sutherland dictated the item (it may have been a joint product, worked out by MacArthur and Sutherland). An example of the process is WD 902. In the absence of the drafts it is impossible to know the extent of each person's contribution. DCS indicates that Richard Marshall, who filled in at Sutherland's desk when Sutherland was away, dictated the item. In several cases Chamberlin either dictated or authenticated the item. WD 225 was written by MacArthur, typed by Curtis, and authenticated by Chamberlin.

The documents in MSSF carry typist's initials PPR, HBC, EEB, FH, JDL, or VHL. Because we decided one day to let Kozlowski have a place in history, we gave him a dispatch to type and JRK appears just once.

PPR	Paul P. Rogers	1941–1945
HBC	Harry B. Curtis	1942–1943
EEB	Edwin E. Bothne	1943–1945
FH	Fred Harrison	1944–1945
JDL	James D. Larkin	1942–1945
VHL	Vernon H. Lewis	1945
JRK	Joseph R. Kozlowski	1942–1944

WD 902 is a rare item. The corrections in the upper 18 lines are made by Sutherland, and the changes in lines 21–22 are MacArthur's.

WD 364 came directly to the file from MacArthur, with the notation "For Secret File. MacA." It does not carry Sutherland's initials.

WD 252 is an example of a dispatch authenticated personally by Sutherland to prevent its passing through the hands of adjutant general personnel. I carried this directly to the Signal Office for dispatch. WD 132 is another example.

WD 169 is marked for CinC File.

WD 182 is marked for C/S File.

WD 183 is ambiguous, having been marked C/C File and changed to C/S File (or vice versa).

Quezon 135 has Sutherland's notation "Mr. Rogers File. RKS."

SOPAC 530 carries my note "File."

AAF 50, page 2, is a draft of a letter to the prime minister of Australia from MacArthur. The corrections are by MacArthur. The draft was prepared by Kenney's chief of staff.

WD 663 carries my note "To be filed in W/D File. PPR."

WD 491 and WD 483 have directions to return copy to W/O Rogers.

Very few documents were approved exclusively by MacArthur. One such is WD 467. Sutherland was in Port Moresby when this item was written.

MacArthur usually referred to MSSF as the "Secret File." Sutherland was not always consistent. WD 150 refers to "Personal File"; WD 259 refers to "Strategic File"; WD 258 refers to "Sp. File." I do not know if Sutherland had in mind any particular distinction but I filed the documents in the same location.

MSSF, of course, does not include all of the materials that passed over the desks of Sutherland and MacArthur, nor does it include all of the radios, letters, and memoranda written by them. I kept a log of the documents that passed over Sutherland's desk and regularly recorded more than 500 items per day.

MSSF is complicated by the following facts:

Sutherland accumulated a file of personal items in my office filing cabinets and in his desk. They were never well organized but simply placed in loose folders. The Sutherland Papers, Items 10, 13, 15, 20 (Box 1), 26, 27, and Personal Records fall in this category.

GHQ SWPA/AFPAC began to disband in August 1945. The files of various staff sections were made available to MacArthur, Sutherland, and others as the supply permitted. These materials were boxed and delivered to their new owners. They had never been a part of my regular office files. These items are shown in the Sutherland Papers as Items 15–19 and 21–25. All of the materials in the MacArthur Memorial, RG–3, Boxes 15–179, fall in this category.

Item 27 of the Sutherland Papers, Box 1, contains three folders of navy radio messages for 1942; Box 2 contains three folders of navy radios for 1943. These probably overlap and supplement the navy section of MSSF.

Item 27, Box 6, contains a very large envelope of original copies of dispatches between Wainwright on Corregidor and MacArthur in Melbourne from March 11 through May 6, 1942. These were given to Sutherland by Spencer Akin on August 22, 1945. They probably overlap and supplement the items in the USFIP section of MSSF.

Item 27, Box 7, contains a folder of original copies of dispatches for 1942. These probably overlap and supplement MSSF.

The files of the adjutant general contain the mass of material that flowed through GHQ. Most of it was never seen by Sutherland or MacArthur. A card index for this file, probably not complete, is in the MacArthur Memorial Archives. The G–3 journals are not in the MacArthur files. These journals contain memos written by Sutherland concerning planning matters.

There is no systematic file of the limited correspondence that passed between MacArthur and Sutherland. In Item 20 of the Sutherland Papers, Miscellaneous Folder 4, last section, is an exchange concerning the division or authority between them in late 1944. Correspondence between the two men during Sutherland's various missions to Washington is in Item 9 of the Sutherland Papers.

MSSF was kept in duplicate. The copies were referred to as Number One and Number Two. Undoubtedly the Number One file was presumed to be Mac-Arthur's set. Generally I ignored the distinction and made them identical, even when I received instructions to the contrary, symmetry of the files seeming to be a more reasonable guide than apparent pride of exclusive possession.

Item 10 of the Sutherland inventory identifies a group of dispatches that were withheld by Sutherland in a "Strategic File." I have checked the items in this group against MSSF. In most cases the item in the Sutherland "Strategic File" is also in MSSF. Sutherland probably retained the originals of these because he had authenticated them personally rather than sending them through the adjutant general for routine processing. Extra copies were made for MSSF.

There are about 20 other items between May 2, 1942, and July 31, 1945, that do not appear in MSSF. Most of these items would not normally belong there. Some are intercepts of dispatches from other commands. Some are communications between Sutherland and MacArthur. They are neither more nor less important than the items that routinely entered MSSF. There is no pattern. They represent sporadic ad hoc decisions by Sutherland to withhold the item.

By the middle of July 1945, GHQ was beginning to disintegrate with the anticipation of the move to Japan. By the end of the month MSSF had been closed as an official record. During early August, Sutherland was in the United States on leave. Chamberlin filled in as acting chief of staff and authenticated important dispatches that were held for Sutherland's information and disposition. There is no evidence of irregularity or breach of established procedure. It was a matter of internal security.

In the literature there are references to papers kept by Sutherland in "a vault in his office." I do not recall anything in his office except an ordinary safe about three by three by four feet. I had a key for it. Sutherland had a small portable safe in his quarters, the key for which was kept in his office safe. I regularly opened the safe and do not recall any papers except the day-to-day flow of "IN" basket accumulations. In 1944 I broke open the portable safe when the key was lost. It contained an envelope of money that belonged to Sergeant Abug, Sutherland's orderly, and one document that is now the first unnumbered item in the Australian Government folders.

5. The Personal Correspondence File

The daily flow of "fan mail" from the meek and the mighty was answered over MacArthur's signature. Where the mighty were involved, MacArthur usually made a handwritten draft. The meek received letters composed by the aides. All were signed personally by MacArthur, who read all the letters. Occasionally he would make corrections on a letter that had been submitted by aides and it would be retyped.

6. The Communiqué File

Two copies of the daily communiqué and special press releases were kept in the office file. Both the communiqués and the press releases were the personal work of MacArthur. The communiqués were based on drafts prepared by Charles Willoughby, corrected by Sutherland until late 1942, and always given final shape by MacArthur, who frequently made substantial revisions of the draft until he found a style that pleased him. These are in the Sutherland Papers, Item 11, and in the MacArthur Memorial, RG–4, Boxes 47–49 (Folders 1–4) and RG–2, Box 3. A sample communiqué packet that demonstrates the manner in which the communiqué was developed is in the Sutherland Papers, Item 27, Box 1, Folder 1.

7. *The Diaries.*

The MacArthur Diary. The section of the diary that covers the period July 26, 1941 through January 11, 1942, is carefully written with obvious attention to style and detail. After January 11 there are only sketchy entries on five scattered dates. It is as if MacArthur had lost interest in recording details of what he felt would be the bloody end of his command. His birthday is recorded on January 26. The first artillery bombardment of Corregidor is recorded on February 7. The departures of Quezon, of Clark Lee and the two Jacobys, and of Sayre are recorded on February 20, 22, and 23, respectively. The Corregidor section of the diary ends almost with a whimper. In Manila the diary was typed by Turner and by me. I typed it on Corregidor. I do not know who wrote the diary. It may have been Major LeGrande Diller or even Jean MacArthur, but this is purely conjecture. I doubt that MacArthur was the author.

After the move to Australia, the diary was kept by Charles Morhouse and Lloyd Lehrbas, and its quality deteriorated. It is not a complete record of various people seen by MacArthur. I suspect that it registers only those people who called for appointments that were duly noted on the calendar. It was dictated by the aides or, more likely, it was typed by Curtis, Bothne, or Lewis directly from the calendar. I doubt that MacArthur ever bothered to look at it. The MacArthur Diary is in the MacArthur Memorial Archives, RG–2.

The Sutherland Diary. Sutherland kept an hour-by-hour record of his daily activities on a yellow ruled pad. On Corregidor, Wilson was responsible for the diary. I typed it, and proofread it and initialed the typed pages. In Australia, I typed the diary for several months, then the duty passed to Larkin. Sutherland was conscientious and meticulous. His diary may be presumed to be a true record. The section for December 8, 1941, through March 11, 1942, is in the MacArthur Memorial Archives, RG–2; for succeeding years see the Sutherland Papers, Item 18.

8. *The Missing Report.*

I have not been able to locate a document that may be the most significant record of the relationship between MacArthur and Sutherland. Sometime in the summer of 1945, Fred Harrison told me that Sutherland had sent him to tell me that Sutherland had just written a special secret report to the War Department. The report, which he said was long, dealt with Sutherland's activities as MacArthur's chief of staff. I did not see the document, nor did Harrison describe its contents. I did not want to see it at the time. I wish now that I had been more curious.

Notes

References to Various MacArthur Files

Personal File: MacArthur Memorial, RG–2, Box 1.

Secret File: MacArthur Memorial, RG–2, Box 2. This includes radios and letters dealing with plans and policies; operations radios; and the office diary for Sutherland covering December 8, 1941–February 22, 1942.

Sutherland Diary: The section for December 8, 1941–February 22, 1942, is filed with the Secret File. The section for the remainder of the war is in the Sutherland Papers, Personal Records, Box 1, Folder 3, located at both the National Archives and the MacArthur Memorial.

MacArthur Diary: The section for July 1941–February 1942 is in MacArthur Memorial, RG–2; the section for the remainder of the war is in RG–5.

Rogers Diary: A copy of the shorthand diary with transcription and notes is at MacArthur Memorial.

MacArthur-Sutherland Secret Files: Citations that refer to WD 10, ALF 4, etc., without any further information, are in this file. It is a continuation of the Secret File. Sixteen groups of documents, filed by addressee, are included. They are in the MacArthur Memorial and in the Sutherland Papers at The National Archives. At the MacArthur Memorial the collection is in RG–4, Boxes 6–11, 14–17. In the Sutherland Papers the collection is Items 1–9, and 20.

Sutherland Manuscript File: Sutherland Papers, Personal Records, Box 1, Folder 3, at both MacArthur Memorial and National Archives. During the Corregidor period Sutherland decided to keep his own personal file of the important radios that he drafted. He laboriously copied them in his own hand. Sutherland continued this file during SWPA days, but instead of making manuscript copies, he kept the original messages as they were returned from the Signal Office. This latter file is Item 10 of the Sutherland Papers inventory.

Chapter 3

1. This section is based on Churchill, Davis, Mahajani, Quezon, Romulo (*Mother America*), Sawyer, and Wolff.
2. Davis, 352.
3. Wolff, 217.
4. Sawyer, 128.

Chapter 4

1. This section is based on Churchill, Friend, James, MacArthur, Quezon, Romulo (*Mother America*), Watson, and Wolff.
2. Friend, 64.
3. Ibid., 35.
4. Ibid., 56–67
5. Ibid., 254.
6. Watson, 16.
7. Ibid., 22.
8. MacArthur, 110–111.
9. James, I, 430.

Chapter 5

1. This section is based on Friend, Hunt, James, MacArthur, and Military Mission File.
2. The concept was not an unusual one. It had been argued by reputable authority early in the century that "a moderate military force at one or two important centers, a naval force of gunboats able to move freely among the islands and ascend the many rivers and inlets of the sea" could defend the Philippines. Sawyer, 117.
3. MacArthur, 117.

Chapter 6

1. Natalie Carney, Sutherland's daughter, conversations and letters; Army Register 1946; *New York Times*, June 27, 1946; *Time* December 7, 1942. 66–67; *The West Virginia Heritage Encyclopedia*, XXI (courtesy of Professor Boyd D. Holtan); Sutherland's personal letters in the Sutherland Papers; various conversations with Sutherland.
2. Diller is the source of this information. In the U.S. Army Military History Institute there are other recollections, but those who related the incidents were far removed from the events. Diller has given a realistic, first-hand account. See also comments by McMicking in Beck, 270–271, fn. 8; Luvaas, 99, fn. 9; Sayre, 209; James, I, 526; Clay, Oral History #1, 29–30.

Chapter 7

1. This chapter is based on Brereton, Friend, Kirby, Leutze, Matloff and Snell, and Watson.

2. Watson, 415.

3. Ibid., 425.

4. Ibid., 438–439.

5. Ibid., 424.

6. Personal File, 10/30/41; Brereton, 67; Friend, 205; Sayre, 221; Kirby, 121.

7. MacArthur, 112.

Chapter 8

1. The above incident is a collage based on mannerisms and patterns of behavior that are authenticated. The literal truth of the collage as a whole is not documented.

2. Various letters in MacArthur Memorial, RG 1, Box 2.

3. Personal File, 7–28–41.

4. Ibid., 8–30–41.

5. Ibid., 9–13–41.

6. Ibid., 9–23–41.

7. All of the orders are in the Personal File. Diller, conversation.

8. Rogers Diary.

9. Personal File, 1–1–42; also Morton, 49.

10. Letters from Akin to Sutherland, Sutherland Papers, Personal Records, Box 2.

Chapter 9

1. Personal File, 7–28–41, 7–30–41.

2. Ibid., 7–30–41.

3. Ibid., 8–1–41.

4. Ibid., 8–5–41.

5. Ibid., 8–19–41.

6. Ibid., 8–31–41.

7. Ibid., 9–7–41.

8. Ibid., 1–30–42.

9. Friend, 167–168; Brougher, 6–8; Morton, 25–30; various documents in Morton's OCMH (Office of the Chief of Military History) file at the Military History Institute, including letters from Collier and Houser and Sutherland letter 5–29–51; Sawyer, 222.

Chapter 10

1. Personal File for July and August.

2. Ibid., 9–11–41.

3. Ibid., 9–9–41.

4. Ibid., undated, unnumbered item, paraphrase of a War Department radio written before October 1.

5. Secret File, 1–4–42.

6. Brereton, 18–25.

7. Ibid.

8. Personal File, 10–28–41.

9. Ibid., 11–29–41.

10. Brereton, 20.
11. Ibid., 25.
12. Personal File, 11–29–41.

Chapter 11

1. Leutze, 218ff.
2. Personal File, September and October 1941; Leutze, 217–219.
3. Personal File, 10–11–41.
4. Ibid., 10–19–41; shortly thereafter Ernest J. King replaced Stark.
5. Ibid., 10–23–41.
6. Ibid., 11–7–41.
7. Ibid.
8. Ibid., 11–12–41.
9. Ibid., 11–14–41.
10. Ibid., 11–29–41.
11. Ibid., 12–1–41.
12. Ibid., 12–5–41.
13. Leutze, 228–231.

Chapter 12

1. Personal File, 10–18–41.
2. Ibid.
3. Sayre, 216–217.
4. Ibid., 209, 216.
5. Ibid., 218–219.
6. Personal File, 10–10–41.
7. Ibid.
8. Ibid.
9. Ibid., 10–18–41.
10. Ibid.
11. Ibid., 11–13–41.
12. Ibid., 11–15–41.
13. Ibid.
14. Sayre, 207–208.
15. MacArthur War Memorial.

Chapter 13

This section is based on Bergamini, Matloff and Snell, Morton (*Strategy and Command*), and *Reports of General MacArthur*.

1. U.S. Army investigation into the handling of certain communications prior to the attack on Pearl Harbor, 1944–1945, SRH 115 #1066, Nomura to Tokyo, November 10, 1941, located in the National Archives.

Chapter 14

1. Rogers, letter 10–29–41.

2. Ibid., 11–22–41.

3. Secret File contains the message of 11–24–41. The message of 11–27–41 is cited in Beck, 9, and Brereton, 33. I remember seeing the message.

4. Secret File, 11–28–41. I remember typing these.

5. Morton (*Fall*), 72–73.

6. Brereton, 38.

7. This collage is based on typical behavior but is not documented.

8. Brereton, 38; Beck, 11, gives details; also Wainwright *Report*, 25, in the files of the Military History Institute, Carlisle Barracks, Pa.

9. Rogers Diary.

10. Sutherland Diary.

11. Morton (*Fall*), 79ff.

12. Bergamini, 856ff., gives details.

13. Morton (*Fall*), 79ff.

14. Sutherland Diary.

15. Brereton, 40–50.

16. Secret File, 12–8–41.

17. Brereton, 46–47.

18. Ibid., 50.

19. Ibid., 55.

20. Craven and Cate, V, 581–582.

21. Author's recollection.

22. MSSF, USAFFE 1. There were radios on December 8 and December 9. I saw both. The second report gave details of losses at Pearl Harbor. I cannot find it in the file.

Chapter 15

1. Sutherland Diary.

2. Morton (*Fall*), 113.

3. Davao Force Records, Sutherland Papers, Item 14. All subsequent quotes by Mays are from this item.

4. Sutherland Diary.

5. Secret File, operations radio 12–21–41.

6. Ibid.

7. Morton (*Fall*), Ch. 8.

8. Sutherland Diary, 12–22–41.

9. Sutherland Diary; Secret File, operations radio 12–22–41.

10. Secret File, 12–22–41.

11. Ibid.

12. MacArthur Diary.

13. Sutherland Diary.

14. Secret File, operations radio 12–23–41.

Chapter 16

1. Morton (*Fall*), 230.
2. Personal File, 8–14–41.
3. Quezon, 194.
4. Friend, photograph #12; Beck, 24–25.
5. Sutherland Diary.
6. Secret File, 12–22–41; Sutherland Manuscript File.
7. Secret File, 12–24–41.
8. Beck, 37; Secret File, 12–24–41.
9. Personal File, 12–25–41.

Chapter 18

1. Egeberg notes in this respect: "You say you were a loner and I suppose you were. I remember I thought you were self-contained, knew your business and were efficient. I wondered if you weren't also shy." Egeberg was correct about the shyness.
2. I was not alone in theft and sense of guilt. Romulo reports that he stole cookies from a colleague. *Fall*, 168.
3. USAFFE 43.

Chapter 19

1. Brougher, 32.
2. Personal File, 1–13–42; Secret File, 12–22–41, 1–4–42, 1–30–42.
3. Secret File, 2–10–42.
4. Beck, 193, cites McNarney.
5. Barbey, 143.
6. Personal File, 1–16–42.
7. Beck, 119.
8. Sayre, 239.

Chapter 20

1. Personal File, 12–5–41.
2. Secret File, 1–7–42.
3. Ibid., 1–8–42.
4. Ibid., 1–12–42.
5. Despatch, 3.
6. Ibid., 4.
7. Secret File, 1–28–42.
8. Kirby, 255.
9. Ibid., 182.
10. Owen, 135.
11. Ibid., 136.
12. Ibid., 138.

13. Rogers Diary.
14. Secret File, 2–16–42.

Chapter 21

1. Personal File, 10–18–41
2. Friend, 212.
3. Beck, 40; author's recollection; Quezon, 196ff.
4. Beck, 48–50; MacArthur Diary; Quezon, 241.
5. Quezon, 237–240.
6. Ibid.
7. Secret File, 1–2–42.
8. Ibid., 2–11–42.
9. Sutherland Manuscript File, 1–30–42.
10. Secret File, 1–28–42.
11. Ibid., 1–30–42.
12. Ibid., 2–3–42.
13. Beck, 93–94.
14. Rogers Diary, 2–7; Secret File, 2–8–42.
15. Beck, 94–107.
16. Secret File, 2–8–42.
17. Ibid.
18. Ibid.
19. Ibid.
20. Ibid., 2–10–42.
21. Ibid., 1–2–42.
22. Ibid., 2–11–42.
23. USAFFE 30; Secret File, 2–11–42.
24. Secret File, 2–12–42.
25. Paul P. Rogers, "MacArthur, Quezon, and Executive Order Number One—Another View," *Pacific Historical Review* 52, no. 1 (February 1983): 93–102.
26. Personal File, Box Z, RG-Z, MacArthur Memorial.
27. Quezon, 221.
28. MacArthur, 101.
29. Secret File, 2–16–42.
30. Rogers Diary.
31. Secret File, 2–19–42; Quezon, 282–292.

Chapter 22

1. Rogers Diary.
2. Personal File, 1–3–42.
3. Enemy Publication no. 151, "Combat in the Mt. Natib Area, Bataan." Sutherland Papers, Item 27, Box 5, Folder 4.
4. Personal File, 1–15–42.
5. Morton (*Fall*), 268, fn.9.
6. Rogers Diary; USAFFE 7.

7. Sutherland Diary.

8. Ibid.

9. USAFFE 10; Secret File, 1–28–42.

10. USAFFE 43.

11. USAFFE 21.

12. USAFFE 30.

13. USAFFE 46.

14. Beck, 120.

Chapter 23

1. USAFFE 4.

2. Beck, 89–90; Secret File, 2–3–42.

3. Secret File, 2–10–42; Beck, 111ff.

4. Secret File, 2–11–42; Personal File 2–14–42; Beck, 117.

5. Sutherland Diary 2–16 and 17–42; also Beck, 120–121. Beck cites various materials (263, fn 22). The information he cites was drawn from memory. The citation from Richard Marshall's letter indicates that Marshall was not involved in the discussion of February 21–23. That from Willoughby contains only a restatement of Willoughby's reading of MacArthur's *Reminiscences*. Willoughby's statement about a staff meeting is merely an expansion of what MacArthur wrote. When challenged about details of the meeting, Willoughby could not provide substantiation. MacArthur does not specify that a staff meeting was held. He says only that the "entire staff would have none of it."

6. Beck, 117; MacArthur, 152, refers to a message of 2–21–41. A handwritten transcript is in Sutherland Manuscript File.

7. USAFFE 45; Personal File, 2–23–42.

8. USAFFE 46.

9. USAFFE 54 and 56.

10. USAFFE 59; Personal File, 2–25–42; Rogers Diary.

11. Rogers Diary.

12. After great search I finally found a map reference to Beri (Biri) Island, which is at the entrance to San Bernardino Strait at the northern tip of Samar Island. This dominates the strategic entrance from the east to the Visayan waterways. The north-south line drawn through this point runs through Del Monte to Australia. The shorthand symbol reads Beri (Biri) precisely. The spoken word would sound as bee-ree in either spelling. I am convinced that the sentence refers to evacuation, although I cannot locate a document that contains it.

13. USAFFE 56.

14. MacArthur, 152.

15. Hunt, 234.

16. MacArthur had resigned in 1937 to serve as military adviser.

17. USAFFE 65.

18. LeGrande Diller made the same offer to his close friends.

19. Diller conversation.

20. Beck, 265, fn. 5.

21. Henry Godman, conversation and letter.

22. Beck, 154.

23. Ibid., 152–158.

Chapter 24

1. Barbey, 9, 183.
2. AUST 31.
3. AUST 36.

Chapter 25

1. Rogers letter, 6–30–42.
2. Godman, letter to the author.

Chapter 26

1. Sutherland Manuscript File, 2–4–42.
2. Beck, 175ff; author's recollection of events.
3. Beck, 184.
4. USFIP 3.
5. Edwin P. Ramsey, "The East Central Luzon Guerrilla Area," paper read at the History Seminar of the National History Institute, Manila, September 15–16, 1983.
6. Beck, 193ff.; USFIP 15.
7. Beck, 195. I recall the incident.
8. USAFFE 86.
9. MacArthur Correspondence File.
10. WD 172.
11. Brougher, 32.

Chapter 27

1. A letter from Brett to Curtin, 3–19–42, Chamberlin Papers, Military History Institute, denies that Curtin made such a request. Brett asserts that the statement had been made by the War Department to counteract any enemy propaganda concerning the evacuation. Brett may have misunderstood the matter. In view of messages cited elsewhere in this book concerning MacArthur's future role in the "far South," there can be no doubt that Washington was committed to MacArthur's appointment to the command. Curtin would have understood this reality even if no explicit statement had been made to him. It is quite certain that he was not informed about the details of the evacuation, and it is possible that MacArthur's arrival came as a surprise.
2. AUST 635.
3. MacArthur Correspondence File.
4. Luvaas, 28–30.
5. ALF 10.
6. WD 836.
7. WD 462.

Chapter 28

1. James, II, 844, fn 23; MacArthur Correspondence File.
2. WD 813.

3. MacArthur to Curtin, 12–28–42, MacArthur Correspondence File.

4. ALF 85.

5. Egeberg, *The General*, 56–57, and conversations.

Chapter 29

1. Barbey, 24.

2. WD 896. I typed this message, which was dictated by Sutherland, probably from Kenney's draft.

3. ALF 53.

4. Egeberg, *The General*, 52.

5. Barbey, 232.

6. AUST 32.

Chapter 31

1. Chamberlin Papers; see also Chapter 27 n. 1 (this volume).

2. WD 1.

3. WD 48A.

4. WD 49.

5. WD 54.

6. WD 61.

7. WD 62.

8. AUST 20.

9. WD 76.

10. AUST 151.

11. AUST 1A.

12. AUST 10.

13. WD 50.

14. WD 48.

15. WD 51.

16. Ibid.

17. WD 54.

18. AUST 32.

Chapter 32

1. AUST 73.

2. AUST 81.

3. Letter to Curtin, 8–20–42, MacArthur Correspondence File, MacArthur Memorial, RG–3.

4. Secret File, 1–2–42, operations radio.

5. Secret File, 1–19–42.

6. Sutherland Papers, Item 27, Box 1, Folder 1.

7. MacArthur Correspondence File.

8. Ibid.

Chapter 33

1. WD 210.
2. WD 248.
3. WD 62.
4. WD 201.
5. SOPAC 1. This and other references to King, or Ernie King, do not reflect personal antagonism or disrespect. This is how MacArthur and Sutherland referred to him, frequently with the expression of one who has bitten into a lemon. With MacArthur it was generally just "King." Sutherland more often referred to "Ernie King." Neither man referred to him as "Ernie." The office staff almost universally used "Ernie King," and still do. A letter written by MacArthur in 1944 carries the formal salutation "Dear Admiral King."
6. Barbey, 24.
7. WD 118, WD 135.
8. SOPAC 16.
9. WD 123.
10. WD 124.
11. SOPAC 31.
12. WD 228.
13. WD 229.

Chapter 34

1. AAF 10. Sutherland Papers has the only copy of this item.
2. AAF 6, AAF 7.
3. AAF 9.
4. AAF 11.
5. AAF 13.
6. AAF 15.
7. AAF 17.
8. AAF 18.
9. AAF 19, AAF 22.
10. AAF 23.
11. WD 120.
12. WD 128, WD 132.
13. AAF 30; Kenney, 78–79.
14. AAF 34.
15. AAF 35, WD 223, WD 220.
16. Kenney, 26.
17. Ibid., 29.
18. Ibid., 30.
19. Ibid., 33.
20. Ibid., 47.
21. Ibid., 79.
22. AAF 40.
23. WD 233. The reference is to General Harold George.

Chapter 35

1. Mayo, 12–14.

Chapter 36

1. SOPAC 3.
2. SOPAC 4, SOPAC 5, SOPAC 7.
3. WD 35.
4. WD 37.
5. WD 40.
6. WD 41.
7. ALF 1.
8. WD 56.
9. WD 68.
10. WD 75.
11. In April 1942 a U.S. carrier penetrated the Japanese defenses to permit a flight of B–25 bombers over Tokyo. The flight was led by General James Doolittle.
12. WD 84.
13. WD 83.
14. WD 86.
15. WD 94.
16. WD 97.
17. WD 96.
18. WD 101.
19. WD 105.
20. WD 106.
21. WD 116.
22. WD 118.
23. WD 121.
24. WD 126, WD 127.
25. WD 135.
26. WD 137, WD 140.
27. WD 145.

Chapter 37

Morison is the basic source for the Guadalcanal action.
1. Morison, 178, 185, 224.
2. ALF 8.
3. WD 211.
4. WD 215.
5. Luvaas, 31.
6. ALF 17.
7. ALF 9.
8. WD 216.
9. WD 218.

10. WD 225.
11. Ibid.
12. WD 226.
13. WD 227, WD 234, WD 237.
14. WD 244, WD 245.
15. WD 254.
16. WD 255.

Chapter 38

1. WD 225.
2. ALF 15, ALF 16.
3. Kenney, 90ff.
4. Memorandum 9–29–42, Eichelberger Papers.
5. Kenney, 102.
6. Luvaas, 29.

Chapter 39

1. Luvaas, 38–39.
2. ALF 45.
3. Ibid.
4. A Molotov cocktail is a glass bottle filled with gasoline and corked with a twisted rag that serves as a fuse. The fuse is ignited, and the bottle is thrown to shatter and explode.
5. Letter 12–11–42, Eichelberger to Sutherland, Eichelberger Papers.
6. Egeberg, conversation; WD 483. Sutherland went to Buna on December 25–27 and December 29–30.
7. Milner, 370–373.

Chapter 40

1. ANF 4.
2. ANF 5.
3. ANF 12.
4. Ibid.
5. ANF 13, ALF 31A.
6. ALF 32.
7. ALF 33.
8. ALF 35.
9. ALF 36.
10. ALF 41.
11. Ibid.
12. USAFFE 16.
13. Barbey, 27.

Sources

This book is a documented memoir, not a researched history. The primary source is my own memory. I have used documentary primary sources to provide verification and elaboration, and I have drawn on authoritative secondary sources as the occasion required. My first major documentary search involved the resurrection of my old office files at the MacArthur Memorial and the National Archives, which provided basic documentation for much of the study.

My use of other sources was selective and limited. In most cases I had identified a problem that required a solution. In other cases I sought the recorded opinion of another person with respect to some personal judgment of my own. In the very early period of my labor I wanted most of all to validate my memory.

Even this restricted methodology provided far more material than could be incorporated in the present book. I could have written another volume without much difficulty.

A visit to the U.S. Army Military History Institute at Carlisle Barracks, Pa. made as the manuscript was drawing to a close, in a vain attempt to find one document, opened a treasure chest of materials in the form of debriefing interviews of officers who had served in the subordinate commands. They could be used only sparingly or not at all.

The judgments made in the book are my own, based on my direct contact with the personalities and the events. I am happy to say that they have been more often confirmed than refuted.

Archives

Franklin D. Roosevelt Library, Hyde Park, New York.
George C. Marshall Research Foundation, Lexington, Virginia.
Harry S. Truman Library, Independence, Missouri.
Herbert Hoover Library, West Plains, Iowa.
Library of Congress, Washington, D.C.
MacArthur Memorial Archives, Norfolk, Virginia.
National Archives, Modern Military Division, Washington, D.C.
National Archives, Military Archives Division, Washington, D.C.

National Historical Institute of the Republic of the Philippines, Manila.
National Personnel Records Center, St. Louis, Missouri.
Naval Historical Center, Washington, D.C.
U.S. Army Military History Institute, Carlisle Barracks, Pa.
William R. Perkins Library, Duke University, Durham, N.C.

Archival Collections

Almond, Edward M. U.S. Army Military History Institute.
Belote Papers, U.S. Army Military History Institute.
Chamberlin, Stephen J. U.S. Army Military History Institute.
Clay, Lucius D. U.S. Army Military History Institute.
Decker, George H. U.S. Army Military History Institute.
Eddleman, Clyde D. U.S. Army Military History Institute.
Eichelberger, Robert. Duke University.
Luvaas, Jay. U.S. Army Military History Institute.
MacArthur, Douglas. MacArthur Memorial.
Marshall, Richard J. U.S. Army Military History Institute.
Morton, Louis. Office of the Chief of Military History, File, U.S. Army Military History
       Institute.
Sutherland, Richard. National Archives and MacArthur Memorial.

Bibliography

Barbey, Daniel E. *MacArthur's Amphibious Navy*. Annapolis, Md.: U.S. Naval Institute, 1969.

Beck, John J. *MacArthur and Wainwright*. Albuquerque: University of New Mexico Press, 1974.

Bergamini, David. *Japan's Imperial Conspiracy*. New York: William Morrow, 1971.

Brereton, Lewis H. *The Brereton Diaries*. New York: William Morrow, 1946.

Brougher, W. E. *South to Bataan, North to Mukden*, edited by D. Clayton James. Athens: University of Georgia Press, 1971.

Churchill, Bernardita Reyes. *The Philippine Independence Missions to the United States*. Manila: National Historical Institute, 1983.

Craven, Wesley Frank, and James Lea Cate. *The Army Air Forces in World War II*. 5 vols. Chicago: University of Chicago Press, 1953.

Davis, Oscar King. *Our Conquests in the Pacific*. New York: Frederick A. Stokes, 1898.

Egeberg, Roger Olaf. *The General*. New York: Hippocrene Books, 1983.

Friend, Theodore. *Between Two Empires*. New Haven: Yale University Press, 1965.

Hunt, Frazier. *The Untold Story of Douglas MacArthur*. New York: New American Library, 1954.

James, D. Clayton. *The Years of MacArthur* volumes I and II. Boston: Houghton Mifflin, 1970.

Kenney, George C. *General Kenney Reports*. New York: Duell, Sloan & Pearce, 1949.

Kirby, S. Woodburn. *Singapore: The Chain of Disaster*. New York: Macmillan, 1971.

Leutze, James. *A Different Kind of Victory*. Annapolis, Md.: U.S. Naval Institute, 1981.

Luvaas, Jay, ed. *Dear Miss Em: General Eichelberger's War in the Pacific 1942–1945*. Westport, Conn.: Greenwood Press, 1972.

MacArthur, Douglas. *Reminiscences*. New York: Fawcett, 1965.

Mahajani, Usha. *Philippine Nationalism*. St. Lucia, Australia: University of Queensland Press, 1971.

Matloff, Maurice, and Edwin M. Snell. *Strategic Planning for Coalition Warfare: 1941–1942*. Washington, D.C.: Department of the Army, 1953.

Mayo, Lida. *Bloody Buna*. Garden City, N.Y.: Doubleday, 1974.

Milner, Samuel. *Victory in Papua*. Washington, D.C.: Department of the Army, 1957.

Morison, Samuel Eliot. *The Struggle for Guadalcanal*. Boston: Little, Brown, 1950.

Morton, Louis. *The Fall of the Philippines*. Washington, D.C.: Department of the Army, 1953.

————. *Strategy and Command: The First Two Years*. Washington, D.C.: Department of the Army, 1962.

Owen, Frank. *The Fall of Singapore*. London: Michael Joseph, 1960.

Quezon, Manuel Luis. *The Good Fight*. New York: Appleton-Century, 1946.

Renato, Constantino. *A History of the Philippines*. New York: Monthly Review Press, 1975.

Rhoades, Weldon E. *Flying MacArthur to Victory*. College Station, Texas: Texas A&M University Press, 1987.

Romulo, Carlos P. *I saw the Fall of the Philippines*. Garden City, N.Y.: Doubleday, Doran, 1942.

————. *Mother America*. Garden City, N.Y.: Doubleday, Doran, 1943.

Sawyer, Frederic H. *The Inhabitants of the Philippines*. New York: Scribner's, 1900.

Sayre, Francis B. *Glad Adventure*. New York: Macmillan, 1957.

"Studies in the History of General Douglas MacArthur's Command in the Pacific," edited by Charles A. Willoughby, Washington, D.C., 1966. Manuscript in MacArthur Memorial, RG–4, Box 24.

Wainwright, Jonathan. *General Wainwright's Story*. Westport, Conn.: Greenwood Press, 1945.

Watson, Mark Skinner. *Chief of Staff: Pre-War Plans and Preparations*. Washington, D.C.: Department of the Army, 1950.

Wavell, General Sir Archibald. "ABDACOM." An Official Account of Events in South-West Pacific Command, January–February 1942. Copy at MacArthur Memorial.

————. Despatch on Operations in Southwest Pacific January 15th–February 25th, 1942. Copy at MacArthur Memorial.

Wolff, Leon. *Little Brown Brother*. Garden City, N.Y.: Doubleday, 1961.

Index

About the Author

PAUL P. ROGERS, retired professor of economics and insurance, served as secretary and office manager for General Douglas MacArthur and his chief of staff, Lieutenant General Richard Sutherland, for the entire period of World War II. Rogers was the only enlisted man to be evacuated from Corregidor with the MacArthur party. He had intimate daily contact with the men, the events they dominated, and the documents they created. Rogers was an objective, perceptive observer and has brought to this memoir the mature judgment of critical scholarship. Rogers has published numerous articles and two books about the Soviet insurance system, which has held his scholarly interest for more than 40 years.